# BROOKINGS PAPERS ON EDUCATION POLICY

## 2001

# ₿ THE BROOKINGS INSTITUTION

The Brookings Institution is an independent organization devoted to nonpartisan research, education, and publication in economics, government, foreign policy, and the social sciences generally. Its principal purposes are to aid in the development of sound public policies and to promote public understanding of issues of national importance.

The Institution was founded on December 8, 1927, to merge the activities of the Institute for Government Research, founded in 1916, the Institute of Economics, founded in 1922, and the Robert Brookings Graduate School of Economics and Government, founded in 1924.

The general administration of the Institution is the responsibility of a Board of Trustees charged with safeguarding the independence of the staff and fostering the most favorable conditions for scientific research and publication. The immediate direction of the policies, program, and staff of the Institution is vested in the president, assisted by an advisory committee of the officers and staff.

In publishing a study, the Institution presents it as a competent treatment of a subject worthy of public consideration. The interpretations and conclusions in such publications are those of the author or authors and do not necessarily reflect the views of the other staff members, officers, or trustees of the Brookings Institution.

BROOKINGS PAPERS ON EDUCATION POLICY contains the edited versions of the papers and comments that were presented at the third annual Brookings conference on education policy, held on May 15–16, 2000. The conference gives federal, state, and local policymakers an independent, nonpartisan forum to analyze policies intended to improve student performance. Each year Brookings convenes some of the best-informed analysts from various disciplines to review the current situation in education and to consider proposals for reform. This year's discussion focused on the status of standards-based reforms. The conference and journal were funded by the Herman and George R. Brown Chair in Educational Studies at Brookings. Additional support from the Miriam K. Carliner Endowment for Economic Studies and from the John M. Olin Foundation is gratefully acknowledged.

The papers in this volume have been modified to reflect some of the insights contributed by the discussions at the conference. In all cases the papers are the result of the authors' thinking and do not imply agreement by those attending the conference. Nor do the materials presented here necessarily represent the views of the staff members, officers, or trustees of the Brookings Institution.

---

**2001 Subscription Rates**

Individuals $19.95
Institutions $34.95

For information on subscriptions, standing orders, and individual copies, contact Brookings Institution Press, 1775 Massachusetts Avenue, N.W., Washington, DC 20036. Call 202/797-6258 or toll free 800/275-1447. Email bibooks@brook.edu. Visit Brookings online at www.brookings.edu.

Brookings periodicals are available online through Online Computer Library Center (contact OCLC subscriptions department at 800/848-5878, ext. 6251) and Project Muse (http://muse.jhu.edu).

**Conference Participants**

John Barth, *National Education Goals Panel*
Tiffany Danitz, *Pew Center on the States*
Denis P. Doyle, *Denis Doyle and Associates*
Lynda Edwards,*U.S. Department of Education*
Laurence Feinberg, *National Assessment Governing Board*
William Galston, *University of Maryland*
Mathew Gandal, *ACHIEVE*
Jennifer Garrett, *The Heritage Foundation*
Janet Hansen, *Committee for Economic Development*
John Hoven, *Gifted and Talented Association*
Gerunda Hughes, *Howard University*
Sylvia Johnson, *Howard University*
Richard Kahlenberg, *The Century Foundation*
Sally Kilgore, *Modern Red Schoolhouse Institute*
Kevin Kosar, *New York University*
Casey Lartique Jr., *The Cato Institute*
Thomas Loveless, *Brookings Institution*
Christine Lynd, *Center for Education Reform*
Laura McGiffert, *ACHIEVE*
Bruce MacLaury, *Brookings Institution*
Lynn Olson, *Education Week*
Jake Phillips, *Empower America*
Michael Ross, *National Center for Education Statistics*
John Sanderson, *University of Virginia*
Thomas Toch, *Brookings Institution*
Roy Truby, *National Assessment Governing Board*
Maris Vinovskis, *University of Michigan*
Ben Wildavsky, *U.S. News and World Report*
Emily Wurtz, *National Education Goals Panel*

# Introduction

## DIANE RAVITCH

The 2000 conference of the Brown Center on Education Policy of the Brookings Institution was devoted to discussion of academic standards in the United States. Participants represented a wide variety of views, some strongly supportive of standard setting, others very critical, and many at different points on the spectrum in between. Nonetheless, all recognized that the United States has embarked on a historically unprecedented path of public policy during approximately the last two decades of the twentieth century. The nation, so long entrenched in patterns of localism and so long averse to external education standards, was in the midst of multiple efforts to establish academic standards and the means for assessing whether students had met them. Almost every aspect of education—including teacher education, testing of students and teachers, professional development, textbooks, preschool instruction, and financing of schools—seemed likely to be affected by the new emphasis on standards.

How did the search for academic standards became a national goal, carried out in almost all fifty states at the same time? One important impetus was the famous report *A Nation at Risk*, published in 1983 by the U.S. Department of Education's National Commission on Excellence in Education. The commission warned in fiery rhetoric that the nation's future well-being was threatened by a "rising tide of mediocrity." Among the evidence offered for this judgment was the relatively poor performance of American students on various international assessments. After *A Nation at Risk*, the public and elected officials of both major political parties agreed that expectations were far too low and that American students were not learning nearly enough to prepare for college or for the demands of work in a rapidly advancing economy. In 1989 President George Bush convened the nation's governors in an education summit, where they agreed to set national goals for the year 2000. Two of the six goals pledged higher performance in the key academic subjects taught in

1

school. In 1991 and 1992 the Bush administration commissioned the development of voluntary national standards, an ambitious and unprecedented undertaking that was fraught with peril because of a lack of planning, time, and experience.

The Clinton administration relied not on voluntary national standards, which had quickly become mired in controversy, but on state action. Its signature education legislation, called Goals 2000, provided funds for states to draft their own standards and tests. By 1996, nearly every state was engaged in this exercise and was trying to figure out how to align tests to standards, whether to produce test results for schools or students or both, how to use test scores, and how to add resources to the system wisely.

Three other factors contributed to the nation's seemingly sudden turn to academic standards. First and perhaps of primary importance, concern about academic achievement was truly bipartisan, thus a great deal of partisan wrangling was avoided. Second, periodic opinion surveys found that the public enthusiastically supported standards and testing. Parents, citizens, teachers, and even students agreed by overwhelming margins that the public schools should put greater emphasis on basic academic subjects. The public wanted higher academic standards and greater specificity about what children were expected to learn. It also wanted students to pass tests to show that they had reached standards. In survey after survey, public opinion concurred that students should not graduate from high school until they had demonstrated their mastery of writing and speaking English.

Third, the push for higher standards was advanced by regular reporting on student performance by the National Assessment of Educational Progress (NAEP). NAEP is the federal testing program of various academic subjects, based on national samples of students. It has been in operation since 1969 and has been supervised since 1990 by the bipartisan National Assessment Governing Board (NAGB). Until 1991, NAEP reports described what students knew and could do on a scale that was not easily comprehended by the public. After 1991, the NAGB adopted achievement levels, which were standards describing what students should know and be able to do. It established three levels, called Advanced, Proficient, and Basic. In most reports, a large minority of students scored Below Basic, which communicated quickly to the public that academic performance was inadequate according to an external standard. NAEP reports were acknowledged by most researchers to be the only reliable indicators of American student performance over time.

Critics of academic standards derided the *Nation at Risk* report, saying it expressed undue pessimism about the nation's economic prospects vis-à-vis its global competition. They also said that the nation's schools were doing better than expected or as well as might be expected in light of demographic changes and the social stresses of modern life. According to opinion research, however, the public was unmoved by such arguments and continued to support state and local efforts to raise academic standards and to test whether students were ready for promotion or graduation.

To understand how far removed the education profession was from such concerns, one must turn to the nonpartisan Public Agenda's survey of education professors. While the public insisted with near unanimity on the importance of safety, order, and the basics, education professors had a different set of priorities. The qualities most admired in prospective teachers by their professors were "being life-long learners" and teaching children to be active learners. The qualities that the professoriate considered least essential were "maintaining discipline and order in the classroom," "stressing correct spelling, grammar, and punctuation," and "expecting students to be neat, on time, and polite." A striking 92 percent thought that teachers should see themselves as "facilitators of learning," while only 7 percent wanted teachers to see themselves as "conveyors of knowledge who enlighten their students with what they know." The authors of the Public Agenda report noted that the views of education professors differed markedly from those of most parents, taxpayers, and classroom teachers.[1]

The controversy over academic standards has placed in bold relief the contrasting views of the education research community, which has been negative, and of the public, business leaders, and elected officials, who see academic standards as a commonsense proposition. Supporters of standards see them as a definition of expectations for students and their teachers, as explicit aims for education that should guide instruction, testing, teacher preparation, and other facets of education. People from other fields, as well as parents, do not understand why the aims of education should be obscure and implicit, instead of clear and comprehensible.

One way to gain insight into pedagogical thinking is to consider one of its canonical sources, the writings of John Dewey. In 1916 Dewey wrote about "aims in education" and said definitively that "education as such has no aims." He compared the educator with the farmer who "has certain things to do, certain resources with which to do [sic], and certain obstacles with which to contend." The farmer, he wrote, must deal with these conditions "independently of any purpose of his. Seeds sprout, rain falls, the sun shines, insects devour, blight comes, the seasons change. His aim is simply to utilize these various conditions." Dewey chose a poor metaphor. While the farmer must consider the conditions of soil and climate, presumably he would decide in advance which crop to grow; he would pay close attention to whether his methods produced a good yield; he would compare the yield produced by different seeds and different treatments; and he would vary his seeds, crops, and treatments by what he had learned in previous years. But for the generations of educators who studied Dewey's work as if it were a revealed gospel, the practice of establishing standards—that is, laying out one's aims in advance—was bad pedagogy that might in Dewey's words "do more harm than good."[2]

In the year 2000, the subject of standards remained controversial, and the reasons were many. To begin with, most states were new to the task of describing what students should know and be able to do. In addition, a certain redundancy existed in the idea that fifty states (and various territories) should each establish its own standards for subjects such as reading and mathematics. Because these subjects do not inherently vary from state to state, the effort to set state standards was always fraught with a peculiar parochialism, a need to assert that teaching mathematics was somehow different in New York than in Alaska or Oregon. Nonetheless, given the politics of the age and the impossibility of reaching political consensus around national standards, the states were the logical level of government that would set academic standards.

Even though public opinion embraced standards and assessments, the opinion among education elites was far from enthusiastic. As states began to deploy their standards and assessments, complaints against them increased. In 2000, with more and more states beginning to implement standards-based reform, now seemed a good time to assess the state of standards in the United States.

Seven papers were delivered at the Brown Center annual conference on May 15-16, 2000. Each considered a different aspect of the drive for standard setting, and each paper was rigorously analyzed by two independent discussants. In some cases, the discussants disagreed strongly with the papers, and readers should be sure to read the discussants' remarks to capture the sense of animated debate that typified this two-day session.

"Incentives and Equity under Standards-Based Reform" by Julian R. Betts of the University of California and Robert M. Costrell of the University of Massachusetts provides a comprehensive analysis of the rationale and functioning of standards-based reform. It begins by explaining the economic theory of this strategy, describes its incentive effects, weighs the difference between centralized and decentralized standards, and considers the current state of education standards in different jurisdictions. Betts and Costrell offer a careful review of the evidence for the effects of education standards on student achievement, with particular attention to how different groups of students are affected by them.

One of the most vigorous supporters of standards-based reform has been the business community at national, state, and local levels. In their paper, "Why Business Backs Education Standards," Milton Goldberg of the National Alliance for Business and Susan L. Traiman of The Business Roundtable explain that standards-based reform is key to the nation's future economic performance. Both Goldberg and Traiman were deeply involved in the writing of *A Nation at Risk*. They argue, on behalf of American business, that employers want not only a well-trained work force but also a highly educated work force. They see standards as the starting point toward higher achievement for nearly all children.

Because the shaping of standards has become a primary responsibility of states, Chester E. Finn Jr. and Marci Kanstoroom of the Thomas B. Fordham Foundation, in "State Academic Standards," assess how well the states have performed this function. Based in part on the periodic surveys conducted by the Thomas B. Fordham Foundation, the authors find that few states have been able to promulgate clear and useful standards. They do note, however, that the number of good state standards has been increasing over time and that some state standards might serve as models for others.

But is standards-based reform making any difference when it is implemented? This question is answered by analysis of state NAEP data in "Searching for Indirect Evidence for the Effects of Statewide Reforms" by David Grissmer and Ann Flanagan of RAND. Grissmer and Flanagan search for evidence of changes in achievement during the period from 1990 to 1996. They find that only three states (North Carolina, Texas, and Michigan) show statistically significant increases in math achievement during this period, unrelated to changes in resources. Although tentative in their conclusions, they suggest that these improvements were likely the result of statewide education reforms.

In virtually any analysis of the progress of American education, scholars and policymakers rely heavily on the results from national and state NAEP, the only continuing source of national test scores for samples of students in different grades and different subjects. Whenever a new NAEP is released, the press promptly reports whether student performance is up, down, or flat in fourth, eighth, and twelfth grades. Yet even NAEP, which has been reporting on student performance for three decades, has been controversial. Within the psychometric world, NAEP has been criticized on technical grounds, especially after its governing board—the National Assessment Governing Board—agreed to establish achievement levels, or standards. Some critics have complained that students do poorly on NAEP because they have no incentive to do well on a no-stakes test where they never even learn their scores. Mark D. Reckase of Michigan State University, who has been a technical adviser to NAGB, describes "The Controversy over the National Assessment Governing Board Standards." NAEP has been since its inception a work in progress, with continual technical improvements. There are two distinct versions of NAEP, one that reflects the current state of curriculum (what is taught) and another that captures long-term trends—that is, questions in basic subjects that have been asked continuously since the early 1970s. No single aspect of NAEP has been more valuable to the public than its standards, which clarify public reporting, nor has any single aspect of NAEP been more controversial, as Reckase's paper demonstrates.

As states put their standards into place, the standards are supposed to serve as guidelines for assessment. In "The Role of End-of-Course and Minimum Competency Exams in Standards-Based Reforms," John H. Bishop, Ferran Mane, Michael Bishop, and Joan Moriarty explain that different types of examinations have varying effects on dropout rates, graduation rates, academic achievement, college attendance rates, and early labor market experiences of students. Policymakers at the state and local level need to understand how different groups of students are influenced by the particular examination system employed and in what ways their behavior changes in response to the exams they take.

Ronald F. Ferguson of Harvard University presents "A Diagnostic Analysis of Black-White GPA Disparities in Shaker Heights, Ohio." Ferguson analyzes racial and gender differences among students in Shaker Heights, an affluent and well-integrated suburb of Cleveland. Ferguson finds a black-white achievement gap in Shaker Heights, and his close examination of the social determinants of student behavior and attitudes offers an intriguing insight into the possible sources of the racial gap.

Taken together, these essays and the commentaries upon them present a portrait of a nation in the midst of redefining its educational system. The quest for academic standards and accountability is occurring within a context of large-scale organizational change in American education, most notably efforts to devise new forms of educational management, such as charter schools, magnet schools, schools-within-schools, and, on a limited basis, voucher programs that allow public funds to follow students to nonpublic schools (in Milwaukee and Cleveland and possibly in Florida as well). None of these initiatives would likely have much traction if the American public were content with the level of achievement in the schools today. That is why so much interest has been generated in academic standards and accountability—not because theorists demand it, but because every large and successful enterprise somehow figures out how to establish its goals and to determine whether or not it is advancing toward those goals.

From the discussion at Brookings in May 2000, it seemed clear that the nation's education system was seriously attempting to transform its quality, even as debates raged about the appropriate course of action. Most people agreed on the importance of improving education and raising expectations for all students. On ends, the American people seemed to concur; on means, the dust had not yet settled and the path ahead remained obscure. The public education system is large, diverse, and administratively cumbersome. Change will come slowly, almost imperceptibly. What will be decided in the next decade is whether change will come at all or will be stalemated by interminable dissension.

## Notes

1. Steve Farkas and Jean Johnson, *Different Drummers: How Teachers of Teachers View Public Education* (New York: Public Agenda, 1997), pp. 9–11.
2. John Dewey, *Democracy and Education* (New York: Macmillan, 1916), pp. 124–25.

# Incentives and Equity under Standards-Based Reform

JULIAN R. BETTS *and*
ROBERT M. COSTRELL

S tandards-based reform is a strategy that includes specifying what
is to be learned, devising tests to measure learning, and establishing
consequences of performance for students and schools (for example, setting
cut scores for grade promotion and high school graduation). The goal of this
strategy is to raise student performance across the spectrum, especially for students from those schools, often heavily minority, where expectations are
chronically low. The point is to alter incentives and change the behavior of students, teachers, administrators, and parents in a way that improves learning.

Popular support remains strong for standards-based reform, according to
national polling data as well as local data in the states implementing this strategy.[1] For example, a recent poll in Massachusetts, which is implementing one
of the more rigorous sets of exams (effective for the class of 2003), indicates
that 70 percent of the general population favors graduation exams. Support is
slightly more emphatic from urban than suburban respondents, and somewhat
broader (75 percent) from those with income under $25,000. When respon-
dents are asked if they would still support the exams should 25 percent of
students in their communities fail on the first try, support remains unchanged
overall at 70 percent and rises to 81 percent among those with income under
$25,000.[2]

Nonetheless, vocal, if not yet necessarily wide, opposition has emerged in
several states, in the run-up to full implementation of standards-based reforms.
Objections fall into different categories. One source of discord concerns the
content of what should be learned. The battles of the mid-1990s over national

9

content standards in history and English, and more recently in science and mathematics, have had their counterparts in the states.[3] Despite continuing conflicts, certain broad (if not universal) agreement can be obtained in basic content areas (at least mathematics and English). The focus here will not be on content disagreements, but on disputes over testing and cutoff scores. However, at least some of the more vocal opposition to testing is based (if not always explicitly so) on unresolved disagreements over content standards, because tests give force to the content standards.

Opposition to testing-with-consequences is based on a simple, fundamental fact of life: Almost any change creates winners and losers. For example, technological progress has always had its losers, from the hand-loom weavers to the buggy-makers to current-day bricks-and-mortar retailers, computer illiterates, and those of low cognitive skills. The technologically caused losses of those with low cognitive skills over the last two decades have driven much of the standards-based reform movement. So, too, may standards-based reform create losers (at least in the short run) in the attempt to create more winners from technological progress. The fact that there are losers, along with winners, is not, in itself, a compelling reason to roll back the standards any more than it would be a reason to try to halt technical progress (by, say, shutting down the U.S. Patent Office). Instead, the nature of the losses must be examined and an appropriate set of policies must be crafted to minimize them.

The most obvious potential losers are those who may not meet the standard, and who may not earn a high school diploma as a result. But this is only the beginning of the analysis. For example, whether the failure rate rises as a result of sorting or whether it also reflects adverse incentive effects makes a great deal of difference. The distinction is important both for evaluating the costs of increased standards and for focusing policies to mitigate costs. Similarly, distinguishing sorting and incentive effects among the winners from various points on the educational spectrum is important.

Standards generate a mix of sorting and incentive effects. How are incentives altered by standards-based reform, for better or for worse, to encourage or discourage achievement? What are the trade-offs between some students' losses and others' gains, in learning or income? Do these trade-offs adversely affect equity, as opponents to standards-based reform often claim? Or is equity enhanced by raising standards in schools attended by disadvantaged students? Why does some of the most vocal opposition often come from the most advantaged districts? Finally, and most important, what steps can and should be taken to minimize the losses and spread the gains most broadly from standards-based reform?

## The Economic Theory of Educational Standards

The economic theory of educational standards attempts to elucidate the likely effects on learning incentives and economic outcomes by means of a simplified model. Economic theory is applied to the subject of standards because economics offers a well-developed framework for the study of incentives, which lie at the heart of standards-based reform. It also offers a systematic method for identifying likely winners and losers, and, more important, the reasons behind and nature of the gains and losses. Finally, economic theory helps point to policy measures that might ameliorate trade-offs (a familiar phenomenon in economics). However, the economic analysis of standards also has limitations.

The analysis largely focuses on the passing score required for an educational credential, for a given test, covering a given set of content standards. Consider the effect of a rise in the cutoff in a simple pass-fail situation, with a single undifferentiated diploma. All the theoretical models that we are familiar with predict a rise in the failure rate, along with other, more salutary, effects. This literature is silent on the magnitude of the rise in the failure rate (which is critical in comparison with the beneficial effects), but it does help distinguish between more and less compelling reasons for concern.[4]

### *Sorting Effects of Graduation Cutoffs*

Consider first a simple sorting model, in which behavior and thus learning are held constant, independent of the standard. A rise in the cutoff merely relabels some students as failers who would otherwise be considered passers. There is, by assumption, no effect on learning or productivity. The aggregate income generated by the students is unchanged, but the distribution of it does change. The students who pass are now a more elite group, so their average productivity is higher. To the extent that graduates are pooled together in the eyes of employers (who may make only limited use of individual information, as economist John Bishop has long argued), their wages tend to rise. This point is well understood: Higher standards raise the value of a high school diploma.

Less widely understood, however, is that higher standards also raise the average quality of the pool of nongraduates, insofar as some students who would previously have passed now fail. Because nongraduates (like graduates) are evaluated by employers in part on the average quality of their pool, their wages also tend to rise. This is not a minor point. The reason nongraduates typically fare so poorly under the existing system is that the ease of social promotion exacerbates the stigma attached to nongraduation.[5] Thus, it is a logical fallacy to argue, as many do, that higher standards will reduce more students to the current economic level of nongraduates; the stigma on nongraduates depends on their average quality, and that depends critically on the standard itself.

A rise in standards thus leads to gains for two of the three groups—those at the top, who graduate, and those at the bottom, who would not have graduated anyway. The losers are those in the middle, who would have graduated under a less stringent standard, but who now fail. Those individuals suffer from being pooled with a group that includes those less skilled than themselves (those without the diploma) instead of with those more skilled than themselves. No efficiency loss has occurred in this pure sorting model, only a distributional effect stemming from the individuals' relabeling. Do these losses constitute a compelling case against higher standards? The answer is no, for two reasons.

First, in terms of the narrow choice between high and low cutoffs, a high cutoff does not necessarily lead to less egalitarian outcomes. The redistribution is from the losers in the middle to the winners at both the top and the bottom. Those with the most egalitarian preferences (so-called Rawlsians, after the philosopher John Rawls) place the highest priority on raising incomes at the bottom, so they should favor a rise in standards.[6] The equity implications of higher standards are not limited to those who are at increased risk of failing but include those who would fail in any case, and whose stigma stands to be reduced.

Second, the standards themselves are not at the heart of the losses from adverse pooling. The crux of the matter is the imperfect information that underlies such pooling. How disturbing is it if someone loses from no longer being confused with those of greater skill? While those able students who are now pooled with those of lesser talent should be of concern, the answer is not necessarily to reverse the rise in standards and reclassify them with those of greater talent. Perhaps, instead, information flows should be improved, if possible, such that individual talents are more accurately conveyed than with a simple binary pass-fail credential, as Bishop argued.

*Incentive Effects of Graduation Cutoffs*

The losses incurred from sorting may not be of first-order policy importance, but neither are the gains from sorting the reason for implementing standards. The rationale for standards is to alter incentives of students, parents, teachers, and administrators to change behavior in a way that advances learning. Microeconomic analysis, the study of how rational actors respond to incentives, may offer some insights.

Economic theory predicts that the effect of raising the graduation cutoff depends on where students lie in the distribution of ability and attitudes toward study.[7] Suppose the cutoff is raised from a level at which 10 percent fail to one at which 20 percent would fail under existing behavior. Under a pure sorting model, in which behavior is held constant, this rise in standards would lead to a doubling of the failure rate. Under a more realistic model, students (and their parents) respond to higher standards by reevaluating the costs and benefits of student effort.[8]

How are the incentives for student effort affected at different parts of the distribution? Consider first those students at or near the twentieth percentile under the original distribution of achievement. In this example, these are students who passed under the old standard by a margin of ten percentiles, but who are now just on the margin of passing under the new standard. It would take only a small increase in their effort for a number of them to pass. The cost in doing so would be less than the substantial benefit of passing instead of failing, and so the higher standard will have a positive incentive effect on utility-maximizing individuals in this part of the distribution. As a result, one can predict with some confidence that the failure rate will not rise as much as would be naively predicted under the preexisting distribution of student achievement, because students in this part of the distribution will rise to the challenge.[9]

These students, the ones for whom the most positive response is predicted and who have the most to gain from higher standards, are not the elite (they are near the twentieth percentile in this example). Unlike the elite, who will easily pass the higher standard with unchanged effort, these students are stimulated to higher effort because otherwise they will fail. These students are typically non-college-bound or marginally college-bound. For those non-college-bound students who rise to the challenge, the benefit is a high school diploma of enhanced value—a matter of great importance for those who will not have a college degree with which to distinguish themselves. For the marginally college-bound, the benefit of being prodded to meet a higher standard is better preparation for college, which, in turn, raises the probability of successful college completion.[10]

However, the incentives are different farther down the distribution. Specifically, consider those students who are on the margin of failing under the old

**Figure 1. Incentive Effects of a Rise in Standards, across Productivity Levels**

Density of student distribution

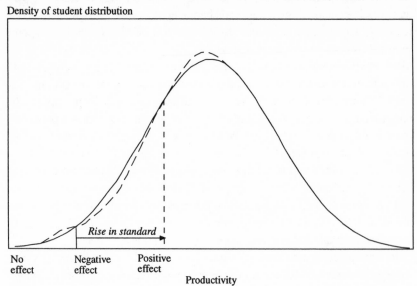

No          Negative      Positive
effect      effect        effect
                                Productivity

standard (students at or slightly above the tenth percentile in this example). The effort they are exerting yields expected benefits that barely exceed the costs of the effort. A rise in the standard reduces the probability of passing with that level of effort and thereby reduces the expected benefit below the cost. For these students, the rise in standards has a negative incentive effect, leading them to reduce their effort, discouraged by the low prospects of success. They may drop out of school, as critics of standards-based reform warn. This effect is more troubling than the sorting effect, because it reduces the amount of learning in this portion of the distribution.[11]

Thus, standards have different effects on students in different parts of the distribution, even among those of lesser achievement.[12] Four groups of students are at risk of failing under the higher standard (see figure 1):[13]

1. Some students who met previously low expectations will be stimulated to greater effort by a rise in standards, with the help of teachers and parents. (In figure 1, the dashed distribution of productivity depicts a rightward shift from just left of the new standard.) These are the most important gains from high standards.

2. Other students who would have passed under low standards will not change their behavior and will now fail. (In figure 1, these students remain

between the old and new standards, on the dashed distribution.) These students lose, but only by virtue of being relabeled.

3. Other students, farther down the distribution, will be discouraged and reduce effort or drop out. (In figure 1, the dashed distribution of productivity depicts a leftward shift from just right of the old standard.) These are the most important potential losses from high standards, toward which mitigating policies should be aimed.

4. For those students at the very bottom (the left-most portion of figure 1), who would not pass anyway, behavior is unaffected, but they may passively gain from the sorting effect.

Policymakers and others may differ on how to weigh the fortunes of these groups in arriving at the optimal set of standards. The way out of this dilemma is not necessarily to forgo the benefits of higher standards, but, if at all possible, to craft accompanying policies for those students whose efforts may flag, especially those who might drop out.

Much of the most vocal opposition to standards-based reform, however, comes from a completely different segment of the population—that of generally high achievers. For example, according to recent reports, "Wisconsin scuttled plans for a high school exit exam after a protest lodged mainly by more-affluent parents."[14] Similarly, efforts in Massachusetts to boycott the statewide exams have been concentrated in affluent and high-achieving suburbs, as well as high-spending communities such as Cambridge, rather than such urban areas as Boston. State representative Ruth Balser told a group of Brookline test critics that most of her legislative colleagues support the exams. "It's just those of us from districts that were already doing really well, like Lincoln-Sudbury, Brookline, and Newton, who feel that our systems are at risk of being dragged down by ed reform," she said.[15]

Perhaps the most plausible claim that suburban critics have to offer is that higher-order skills may be deemphasized by teachers of high-achieving students, students who are at relatively low risk of failing. It is not entirely clear why this would be so at the high school level, if students are sorted among basic and honors classes.[16] The more elite students, aiming for selective college admissions, are more likely focused on the Scholastic Assessment Test (SAT), Advanced Placement (AP) exams, and a high school transcript enhanced with high grades in honors courses than on high school exit exams. However, if the school reallocates resources, or changes its teaching methods to bring up those at risk of failing, these equity-enhancing efforts could adversely affect those of high achievement.[17] If so, these objections to standards-based reform are not based on equity concerns, but the opposite.[18]

The policy implication is not necessarily to forgo the benefits of higher standards, just because they may be concentrated among those for whom expectations are low, relative to the high-achieving critics. The challenge is to meet these objections by accompanying the standards with policies addressed toward the high achievers as well. This is an easier and less pressing challenge than the one concerning lower achievers, who might be discouraged from continuing academic effort.

### Centralized versus Decentralized Standards

What is the proper locus of standard-setting—federal, state, or local? The movement toward standard-setting began with the states in the late 1970s (minimum competency testing), shifted toward the federal level from the late 1980s to the early 1990s, and has shifted back to the states since the mid-1990s, where it has made its greatest strides.[19] Leaving aside the question of where content standards should be set, economic theory does have something to say about whether graduation cutoffs should be set locally or centrally.

In the simplest case, where all districts are alike, decentralization probably would lead to inefficiently low standards.[20] Suppose each district's non-college-bound graduates are pooled to some extent with graduates of other districts in the labor market. That is, employers do not fully distinguish graduates of any district that chooses a different standard.[21] The reward to raising standards in any given district is thus attenuated. The district's graduates would be of higher quality, but would not be fully identified as such, and so would only reap some of the benefits; the rest of the gains would spill over to graduates of other districts, with whom they are pooled in the labor market. As a result of this externality, local standard-setters have an incentive to free ride on the standards of other districts, establishing cutoffs that are too low to maximize their collective welfare.[22] A centralized standard-setter would avoid this problem.

Even in this simple case, with identical districts, there are winners and losers in the choice between decentralized and centralized standards. Given that centralization raises standards, the winners are those who rise to the challenge, and the losers are those who become discouraged from exerting effort. But each district would, on the whole, be better off with a centralized standard-setter choosing the same cutoff for all districts.[23] This logic is independent of the weights attached to winners and losers. Even the most egalitarian collection of standard-setters would prefer standards set centrally, rather than each of them riding free in a standard-cutting race to the bottom.[24]

Heterogeneity across districts makes things more complicated but is also an important factor in understanding current controversies.[25] For example, centralization typically raises standards in low-achieving districts but may lower them in high-achieving ones. To the extent that diplomas reflect some degree of district reputation (that is, pooling is not total), this means low-achieving districts' graduates benefit from the rise in their standard while those from high-achieving districts lose from the drop in theirs.[26] Thus, a conflict of interest may arise between those high-striving urban black students whose diploma is enhanced in value and those suburban students whose diploma could be depreciated from that obtained under decentralized standards.

With heterogeneity across districts, centralization need not always outperform decentralization.[27] However, suppose the centralized standard serves as a minimum requirement for graduation, with the localities retaining the option of setting a higher standard. This arrangement outperforms decentralized standard-setting and is at least as good as central standard-setting without the local option. The result is the best of both worlds, with the centralized minimum standard putting a floor on free-riding by districts, while the high-achieving districts retain the option of exceeding that standard, if enough of the benefits accrue to their own graduates.[28]

The model considered here helps frame questions that arise from current controversies. For example, in Massachusetts (among other states), the demand for local control of graduation requirements is strongest in the suburbs, while urban superintendents are generally the biggest supporters of rigorous state standards (even though their students are most at risk of failing). The urban districts suffer from a poor reputation but have still found it difficult to unilaterally raise it. One possible explanation that goes beyond the simple model but is consistent with its spirit is that a district's reputation adjusts only slowly to its own actions. A long period of low standards will result in a low reputation, but a unilateral rise in standards may only raise the reputation over time, increasing dropouts in the short run with no reward. On this view, the imprimatur of state standards promises to be a more informationally powerful signal, more readily recognized, than the urban districts could establish on their own. Political considerations beyond the model probably are also important. The state mandate provides valuable cover to superintendents who would like to raise standards but who face local political and union obstacles to doing so and to taking steps necessary to meet them.

The model assumes some pooling, or blurring of credentials across districts even in the long run. If there is no such blurring of credentials—if each district's diploma is fully understood by employers to represent that district's own graduation cutoff—then the model's case for decentralized standard-setting is stronger. But even then, high-striving students in low-achieving districts suffer from having their accomplishments depreciated by the low standards that local authorities tend to set in those districts. If policymakers are able to reduce the degree of cross-district pooling to lessen the need for centralization, then why not reduce intradistrict pooling as well, so that high achievers in any district can be evaluated by their individual accomplishments?

### Binary Credentials versus Fuller Information

John Bishop has long argued that credentials such as a high school diploma, which convey only a binary signal to employers, are far inferior to richer and more finely graded information flows, such as those conveyed in high school transcripts. Economic theory speaks to the incentive and equity implications of improved information flows and largely bears out Bishop's argument. A difficult question, however, is why employers often choose not to use the fuller information flows that are available. This question, to which no satisfactory answer has been found, is important in designing policies to ameliorate the trade-offs carried by a system of binary credentials.

In understanding the effects of improving information flows over that of binary credentials, sorting effects must be distinguished from incentive effects. Consider the simplest case, in which a single measure of productivity (such as a test score) is available, but a credential truncates that measure into a pass-fail signal. In a simple sorting model, in which behavior is assumed constant, the truncation of full information redistributes income by pooling. Among those who fall below the cutoff, the average income is unchanged, but it is redistributed from those just below the cutoff toward those at the very bottom, with whom they are pooled. Similarly, among those above the cutoff, the truncation of full information redistributes from those at the very top downward to those just above the cutoff. Thus, in the simplest sorting model, binary credentials generate outcomes that are more egalitarian than full information. However, even within the confines of these assumptions, the case for redistribution by blurring of differences is not compelling, unlike a case based on improved incentives.

Even before considering incentive effects, however, another aspect of sorting bears examination—the issue of job matching. Better sorting improves the match between workers and jobs. Truncating information with a binary credential reduces the efficiency of the match and reduces output. Who bears the brunt of the lost efficiency: those at the top or those at the bottom? In one recent model the answer depends on where in the job ladder accurate sorting is most important.[29] Suppose it is most important at the top; that is, getting the very best people into the very top jobs is more important than getting the least productive people into the very bottom jobs. Then the burden of the efficiency loss from truncating information will tend to fall on the least skilled, and this can outweigh any beneficial pooling effect they may enjoy. The wage earned by the least skilled depends on the ability of those higher up the job ladder who can only do those top jobs with the support of those lower down. If those who will fill the top jobs are not as well identified, because of truncated information, then the reward to the least skilled for supporting those in the top jobs will fall. In this case, the use of full information enhances both efficiency and equity.

Now consider the incentive effects of full information.[30] If employers have and use individual information, diplomas and standards become irrelevant, because they add nothing to it. Each student chooses his or her own preferred level of achievement and is rewarded accordingly. More realistically, information flows can be improved by generating a discrete number of differentiated credentials. Either way, fuller information affects incentives in different ways across the spectrum of students.

Compared with a coarse pass-fail signal, better information about high achievement is a stimulus to those at the top of the distribution, who would otherwise find no payoff in exceeding the cutoff. This provides much of the answer to the criticism that high-achieving districts are dragged down by standards-based reform. High-achieving students are already motivated to excel by an array of credentials over and above high school graduation exams (for example, SAT and AP exams). If these are insufficient, differentiating diplomas based on the level of performance on the graduation exams, as a number of states do, is a relatively simple matter.

Moreover, differentiated consequences for differentiated credentials seem particularly straightforward to arrange for college-bound students. Admission to public higher education can be made contingent on higher performance levels than are required for graduation; scholarships can be based on higher levels yet. These credentials may be multidimensional, for those who find traditional graduation requirements overly narrow. For example, students can place many credentials based on artistic and musical talent on their college applications. There are literary contests, outlets such as the *Concord Review* (for historical essays), and science fairs , to name just a few more credentials that high-achieving students can aim for, with confidence that they will be recognized.

Schools might arguably be under pressure to divert attention from these types of credentials toward the graduation exam, even for those students who are at no risk of failing. There could be some truth to this, insofar as districts reap rewards based on mean exam scores, instead of pass rates only (for example, the real estate market may tend to do this). However, this effect should not be exaggerated, because districts will continue to be attuned to how well their students do in college admissions, which still rests on these other types of credentials. That is why some high-achieving districts choose not to teach to the graduation exams any more than is necessary to achieve passing performance. In short, the introduction of graduation exams only adds information to the existing array of high-end credentials and should not pose any serious incentive problems for high-achieving students.

At the bottom of the distribution, the incentive effect from fuller information should also be positive. Those students who have no other way to convey their skills short of a graduation standard that is beyond their will or ability to meet would certainly gain from finer signals. As John D. Owen points out, fuller information at this end of the distribution advances egalitarian goals by giving students less extreme alternatives to dropping out.[31]

This rationale is behind the proposal that students who repeatedly fail the state graduation exam might receive instead a local diploma or a local certificate of completion. Such a credential could convey the achievement of noncognitive skills such as persistence, punctuality, and discipline that are also important and rewarded in the labor market.[32] The general equivalency diploma (GED) already exists as an alternative credential and should continue to signal a certain level of cognitive skills. But its payoff in the market is considerably less than a high school diploma, probably because it does not convey the same level of noncognitive skills as even a diploma based on seat time alone.[33] So room remains for a credential to certify such noncognitive skills (which may be particularly important for some special education children).

The challenge is to make sure that such a noncognitive credential is properly differentiated from a standards-based credential that signifies both cognitive and noncognitive skills, and that it is treated as such by end-users (employers or colleges). This is at the heart of the dispute between those who would grant a local diploma option and those who would allow only a local certificate of completion. For reasons perhaps better understood by psychol-

ogists than economists, such terminological distinctions seem to be empirically important.

The concern is that a local diploma would not be treated with sufficient differentiation from a state diploma and would thereby undermine incentives for
those students who would otherwise meet the state standard. (This seems to
have been the rationale for New York's decision to phase out the local diploma
option, leaving only the Regents diploma.) A certificate of completion could
and perhaps should convey the same information that a high school diploma
currently conveys in those states where the requirements are almost entirely
local (such as Massachusetts, until the state standards bind in 2003). Once
employers recognize that a certificate of completion is equivalent to the old
local diploma, there should be no basis for objecting that students are denied
a diploma by the higher state standard. *Diploma* is only a word. If it takes a
different word—*certificate* versus *diploma*—to differentiate those who have
met the old local standards from those who meet the new state standards, then
this would provide the finer information flows that are called for. Remaining
will be those who object to such differentiation, as to all differentiation, on
the grounds (perhaps unstated) that it will deny certificate-holders the benefits of being pooled with those who hold diplomas. But such sorting arguments
are not persuasive.

Finally, consider students between those near the top and those near the bottom, those who would meet the state standard, but not by much. These are
students for whom the incentive effects of full information are negative. They
are students who rise to the challenge of the standard only because the alternatives are so much worse. If information flows are improved, these students
would choose to meet a lesser level of achievement that has a lesser payoff, but
not as dramatically as dropping out. The problem here is that too many students evaluate the payoffs to higher achievement differently from adults, such
as their parents or state standard-setters or from the adults that they will become
themselves. The labor market signals to students are somewhat remote, and
many students are notoriously present-oriented.[34] Furthermore, schools likely
have a greater incentive to bring students up to a given standard when the alternative is dramatically worse than simply meeting a lesser standard. In short,
while the coarse instrument of pass-fail blunts incentives for those at the bottom and the top, it does elicit greater effort from those near the passing margin.

A key policy dilemma thus emerges from our theoretical analysis: How
much differentiation should exist between the state-certified standards-based

diploma and any lesser credentials? If the differentiation is too large, then students near the bottom will have no incentive to achieve beyond the low level certified by the lesser credentials. If, alternatively, the gap between the lesser credentials and the state diploma is too small (as with continuous measures, such as the test score itself, affixed to the diploma or the transcript), then too many students who might meet the state standard would be willing to settle for less, especially if employers ignore the differentiation.

Our theoretical analysis shows that some problems alleged by critics of standards-based reform are not particularly compelling, notably those based implicitly on the logic of pooling and those concerning incentives for high-achieving students. But it also points to a trade-off between incentives for those lesser achieving students who will be stimulated to meet high standards and those low-achieving students who will be discouraged. The analysis clearly indicates that the key to ameliorating this trade-off is not so much one of setting the standard high or low as it is one of filling in the information spectrum with credentials that allow lesser achieving students to demonstrate their cognitive and noncognitive skills. The optimal degree of differentiation among these credentials can probably be worked out only in practice over time, by trial and error, because it depends much on the way employers will treat different credentials, which is not something that is easily foretold.

## A Description of Current State Educational Standards

Effective educational standards require the following three components:

1. Content or curriculum standards that clearly delineate what students should learn in each grade.

2. An assessment system that measures student progress toward mastery of the content standards.

3. An accountability system that stipulates a set of rewards and interventions based on student progress. Such a system should hold accountable not only students but also teachers, principals, and entire school systems for the rate of learning of students.

How close are the states to implementing educational standards that fit these criteria, and how do states vary in that regard? Complicating the analysis is that, even though standards in practice typically resemble the binary pass-fail model, these standards have taken many forms. Some states have implemented high school exit exams. Other states have left the task of assessment to individual schools but have set minimum sets of courses that students must complete before graduating from high school. Some states also use achievement scores to make decisions about whether to promote students from one grade to another, or to assign students to remedial or other courses.

Throughout the 1990s states' graduation requirements varied radically. For instance, according to the Department of Education, in 1993 the number of courses states required students to complete before graduating with a standard diploma varied from thirteen in California and Wisconsin to twenty-four in Florida and Utah. By 1996, California still required only thirteen courses to graduate, but Wisconsin had increased its graduation requirements from thirteen to twenty-one and a half. At the top end, three states—Alabama, South Carolina, and Texas—either had joined or were about to join Florida and Utah in requiring twenty-four courses for high school graduation.[35]

These variations in course requirements become stronger once the specific courses required to graduate are examined across states. For instance, in 1996, over half of the states required that high school students take at least two math courses to graduate. Another fifteen states required three courses, and two states (Alabama and South Carolina) required four. A number of states' requirements defy a simple categorization. Colorado, Iowa, Massachusetts, Michigan, Minnesota, and Nebraska rely mainly on local boards to set graduation requirements.[36] In other states, including perhaps most notably California, districts are free to impose their own additional requirements.

Several states have more than one class of diploma, to recognize advanced achievement. The American Federation of Teachers (AFT) reported in 1999 that twenty states offered advanced diplomas, up from only eight in 1996.[37] Perhaps most famously, New York for over a century has offered the Regents examinations and the Regents diploma as an advanced diploma to supplement local diplomas. The creation of multiple credentials can increase the efficiency with which schools transmit information on students' strengths and weaknesses to the labor market, provided the credentials are sufficiently differentiated from one another.

In the late 1990s, New York decided to begin phasing out local diplomas in favor of requiring all students to acquire a Regents diploma. This transition process had not yet finished by 2000. By moving to eliminate the lower tier of high school diplomas, the state of New York will in a sense be restricting the flow of information between schools and the labor market. Most other states have been moving in the opposite direction, providing additional credentials or recognition to students who surpass the minimum achievement levels required for graduation. New York deserves to be closely studied over the next few years. The abolition of local diplomas may make it more difficult for employers to evaluate the skills of the middle group of students—high school graduates who currently do not qualify for Regents diplomas. Alternatively (although authorities have given no indication of this), New York may yet decide in the future to award certificates of completion to students who would previously have received a local diploma. If so, they will merely be relabeled. But it will be important to ascertain how employers and institutions of higher education respond to such relabeling, for that will govern the incentives generated for students. Clearly policymakers in New York are working on the assumption that eliminating the local diploma option will generate positive incentive effects for most students to work harder.

Educational standards will in practice include far more than stipulations about the number of courses required. For instance, standards must also include descriptions of the content that schools expect students to master. The AFT has published an annual review of each state's content standards, assessment, and accountability systems. Recent trends in the number of states "with clear and specific standards," "with assessments aligned with the standards," and "with promotion policies based on achievement toward the standards" are represented in table 1. For a state to qualify as having clear and specific standards, AFT researchers had to determine that the state had clearly worded and specific content descriptions in English, math, science, and social studies at the elementary, middle school, and high school levels. The second AFT variable measures the quality of states' assessment systems, while the third partially describes the states' student accountability system. (Unfortunately, the AFT report does not include as detailed information on the ways, if any, in which teachers, principals, and district administrators are accountable for the performance of their students.)

The data in table 1 reveal that by all three measures—content standards, assessments, and student accountability—the national trend is toward more stringent requirements. The data also indicate large variation across states in these three components of educational standards and accountability.

Equally important, the AFT study shows a disturbing pattern: All states but Iowa, Montana, and North Dakota have implemented or plan to implement tests or other assessments that are aligned with their standards, yet only twenty-two states have implemented content standards that the AFT deems clear and specific. Lack of clarity in standards will create difficulties for teachers. In

Table 1. Number of States with Various Components of Standards in Place, by Year

| Year | Clear specific standards | Assessments aligned with standards | Promotion policies based on standards |
|------|------|------|------|
| 1995 | 13 | 33 | n.a. |
| 1996 | 15 | 42 | 3 |
| 1997 | 17 | 46 | 7 |
| 1998 | 19 | 47 | 7 |
| 1999 | 22 | 49 | 13 |

Source: American Federation of Teachers, *Making Standards Matter 1999* (Washington, 1999).
Note: The counts include the District of Columbia and Puerto Rico. n. a. = Not available.

many cases, states have purchased off-the-shelf standardized tests that do not necessarily link well to the content standards.

For example, beginning in spring 1998, California required that all students take the Stanford 9 tests. In the first year, the test items were not altered to reflect the state's newly developed content standards. In spring 1999, the state added a battery of questions that more closely reflect content standards but is not yet using results from this add-on to the Stanford 9 tests to evaluate schools.

In 1996 almost no states based decisions to promote students to the next grade on standards, but, by 1999, thirteen states had such policies in place. This number underestimates the extent to which schools base promotion decisions on objective assessment measures such as achievement tests. Many school districts have gone beyond existing state promotion policies and implemented their own criteria, and interventions, for student promotion. Particularly well known is the ambitious program implemented by the Chicago public schools in 1996–97. Other districts have followed suit. For instance, the San Diego Unified School District, one of the ten largest in the country, in 2000 implemented its own radical program for assessment, additional spending on students lagging behind in reading, and, if necessary, summer school and grade retention.

Promotion policies represent only one of the many ways in which policymakers can link standards and assessment to overall accountability. Another incentive for students that a large number of states have adopted is high school exit exams. According to the AFT, twenty-eight states currently have or plan to implement graduation exams that are aligned with the state's curriculum standards.

The most difficult aspect of implementing a graduation or exit exam apparently is to design the exam so that it links well to curriculum standards. It can be done, but it cannot be done quickly. For instance, California published science and history-social science content standards in 1999, on the heels of adoption of language and math standards the year before. The state plans to require that all students pass a high school exit exam before leaving school, beginning in the year 2003–04. California's efforts to implement a school-leaving exam that is well articulated with its content standards have led to delays in the program. Not a single commercial test-preparation firm submitted a bid in response to the state's tender in fall 1999, apparently because of concerns that it was not possible to prepare a specifically tailored test for a trial run in spring 2000.

A third aspect of accountability is whether states complement the stick of grade retention with the carrot of incentives for students to excel. The AFT reports that twenty states offer advanced diplomas to recognize exceptional achievement. Eight states also grant preferential college admissions or college financial aid to top-performing students. Others, such as California, are in the process of implementing such policies. A probable weakness of the carrot-and-stick system of educational incentives for students is that the students who vie for the carrots are a different group from those who face grade retention. By the start of high school, some students are likely to view college attendance as a somewhat dim prospect. What positive incentives can be created for such students remains to be seen, especially given the possibility open to high school students to drop out of school altogether.

A state educational policy that focuses on only one or two of the three pillars of educational standards—content, assessment, and accountability—is likely to achieve little. How many states have passed muster, at least according to the AFT, in all three of these categories? Because student accountability can take many forms, we list a state as having implemented student accountability if it has implemented or has plans to implement either promotion policies based on content standards, high school exit exams, or differentiated graduation diplomas to recognize students achieving beyond the requirements for a basic high school diploma. We categorize a state as having succeeded if the given accountability measure was implemented in either elementary, middle, or high school. (For this reason, the numbers in our state-by-state calculation differ somewhat from the aggregate results reported by the AFT and shown in table 1.) Our calculations of the number of states that fit into each of eight possible categories are presented in table 2. The results are revealing: Only a

**Table 2. Number of States Meeting Three Criteria in at Least One of Elementary, Middle, and High School Grades, 1999**

| Number of states | Clear standards in all core subjects | Assessments aligned with standards in all core subjects | Promotion or exit policies |
|---|---|---|---|
| 5 | Yes | Yes | Yes |
| 12 | No | Yes | Yes |
| 1 | Yes | No | Yes |
| 9 | Yes | Yes | No |
| 4 | No | No | Yes |
| 3 | Yes | No | No |
| 11 | No | Yes | No |
| 7 | No | No | No |

Source: American Federation of Teachers, *Making Standards Matter 1999* (Washington, 1999).
Note: The counts include the District of Columbia and Puerto Rico.

handful of states—California, Georgia, North Carolina, South Carolina, and Virginia—have succeeded in all three categories so far.[38] Moreover, seven states had not implemented any of these three types of educational standards to the satisfaction of the AFT researchers. These states were Connecticut, Iowa, Montana, North Dakota, Pennsylvania, Rhode Island, and Wyoming.

### What Explains Variations in State Standards?

Given the considerable variations in standards across states, knowing what causes these variations becomes important. Proponents of national standards may worry that as states set their own standards, states in which student performance lags the most will have an incentive to do the least to implement educational standards. After all, not many incumbent politicians will want to create an assessment system that might show that most of the state's children are failing to meet expectations. However, the existing federally mandated National Assessment of Educational Progress (NAEP) data, which beginning in the 1990s released results by state, may have induced legislators in states that fared poorly to implement content standards, state testing, and student accountability.

State population represents a second factor that might influence the extent to which states have implemented standards. Smaller states will have less incentive to set standards high, because of free riding. Larger states are also likely to have progressed further simply because in such states the fixed cost of developing content standards, tests, and accountability mechanisms can be spread over a greater number of taxpayers.

The degree of socioeconomic homogeneity, and the overall socioeconomic status (SES) of the state population, may also influence standards. On the one hand, states with fewer disadvantaged families may set higher standards in the belief that most students will be able to fulfill them. On the other hand, those states with greater socioeconomic heterogeneity, and lower socioeconomic status more generally, might do more to implement standards in the conviction that such policies can improve the life outcomes for the most disadvantaged students.

To test these three propositions informally, we first calculated an overall measure of the quality of standards based on the three measures listed in table 2. Each state (but not the District of Columbia or Puerto Rico) was allocated from 0 to 1 point for each of the three components of standards. For content standards, we calculated the proportion of the four core subject areas that according to the AFT have clear and specific content standards in at least one grade-span. Thus this measure can equal 0, 0.25, 0.5, 0.75, or 1. Second, each state earned either 0 or 1 point depending on the AFT judgment on whether it had implemented student assessment sufficiently well linked to the content standards. Third, to capture the extent to which states have established student accountability, each state earned either 0, 0.5, or 1 point based on whether it had implemented promotion criteria based on the standards or exit exams aimed at grade-ten standards or a higher level. These three measures were then added together. A state that had failed by 1999 to satisfy any of the AFT criteria would receive a score of 0; a state that had satisfied all the criteria would receive a perfect 3.

We then calculated the relation between this overall measure of the quality of state standards and measures of student achievement in the mid-1990s when most states were just beginning to implement rigorous standards. We used three different measures: the percentage of public students scoring at the basic or higher levels in the 1994 fourth-grade reading assessment on the National Assessment of Educational Progress, the analogous percentage in the 1996 fourth-grade math assessment, and the average of these two achievement measures. We also calculated the correlation between our overall measure of standards and the natural log of population in the state in July 1995, and three measures of socioeconomic status.[39]

In figure 2, the states' scores on our measure of overall quality of standards are plotted against the average of the percentage of public school students at or above basic levels on the reading and math assessments. A negative relation emerges strongly. States that in the mid-1990s had weaker student

**Figure 2. Quality of State Standards in 1999 versus Average Percent of Fourth-Grade Students at or above Basic Level, 1996 Math NAEP and 1994 Reading NAEP**

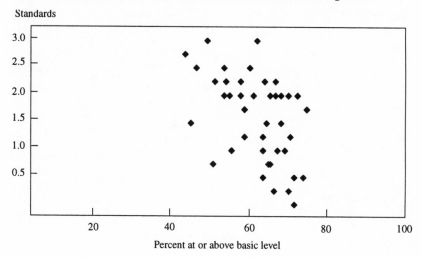

Standards

Percent at or above basic level

Note: NAEP = National Assessment of Educational Progress.

performance tend to have implemented more fully articulated systems of content standards, assessment, and accountability by 1999. Thus the large variations in state standards to some extent reflect greater efforts by states with lagging test scores to use standards to reform the existing educational system. This is likely to engender greater equality in student outcomes across states.

In figure 3, the extent to which each state had implemented standards by 1999 is plotted against the natural log of population in 1995. Here a strong positive relation is apparent. As predicted, larger states have gone further in implementing content standards, assessment, and accountability.

The correlation coefficients for the relationships depicted in figures 2 and 3 and for more disaggregated relationships are presented in table 3. The table gives the correlations between the three components of our overall measure of standards, as well as their composite, versus the individual measures of student achievement in reading and math, the average of these measures of achievement used in figure 2, and the natural log of population. In all cases, the standards measures are related to achievement and population in the same direction as indicated above, although the strength of the relation varies. Initial student achievement and population in the state do not determine all of

**Figure 3. Quality of State Standards in 1999 versus Natural Log of Total State Population, July 1995**

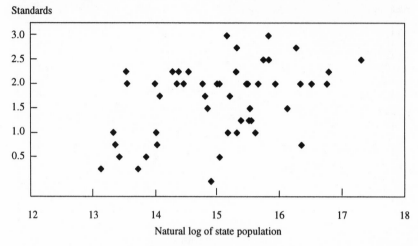

Standards

Natural log of state population

the variation across states in the standards that they have set, but these variables do seem to matter in important ways.

The data in table 3 also depict the correlation between the individual and overall measure of standards with three measures of socioeconomic status: the percentage of the population that is white (non-Hispanic), the percentage of adults age twenty-five and higher who hold at least a high school diploma, and the percentage of the population living above the poverty line.[40] These measures of socioeconomic status are weakly negatively related to the quality of the states' educational standards. That is, states with a greater proportion of disadvantaged residents have set slightly higher standards on average. This finding should come as good news. It suggests that decentralized (state-level) standard-setting (versus nationally mandated standards) might over time lower inequality in educational outcomes across the country. The level of standards is more strongly related to initial student achievement than to the three measures of socioeconomic status. Low student achievement rather than socioeconomic disadvantage seems to have been the more important factor driving the move to higher standards.

We have documented a rise in courses required for graduation in many states in the 1990s, a rapid expansion of state content standards, assessments linked to these standards, and student accountability and incentives in the form of exit exams and grade promotion and retention policies. A trend toward tougher

**Table 3. Correlation Coefficients between Measures of Quality of State Standards in 1999, and Measures of Student Achievement in 1994 and 1996 and State Population**

| | Content standards | Assessments | Accountability | Overall standards |
|---|---|---|---|---|
| Math percent at basic level, 1996 | -0.31 | -0.22 | -0.49 | -0.46 |
| Reading percent at basic level, 1994 | -0.32 | -0.19 | -0.55 | -0.47 |
| Average percent at basic level | -0.32 | -0.19 | -0.54 | -0.47 |
| Natural log population | 0.28 | 0.27 | 0.31 | 0.42 |
| Percent population white non-Hispanic, 1997 | -0.16 | -0.04 | -0.49 | -0.31 |
| Percent with high school diploma or higher, age 25 and above | -0.19 | -0.32 | -0.22 | -0.37 |
| Percent of population above poverty level | -0.20 | -0.12 | -0.21 | -0.25 |

Source: Authors' calculations based on American Federation of Teachers data on standards, National Assessment of Educational Progress test scores, and Bureau of the Census demographic estimates.

Note: In a small number of cases, only one test score was available, so the average percent of students at or above basic levels was set using the one available test score.

educational standards and accountability is sweeping the country, even though some states lag behind. States in which student performance on the NAEP was relatively low in the middle of the 1990s tend to have done more to implement content standards, testing, and accountability since that time. Similarly, larger states and states with relatively disadvantaged populations tend to have made more progress.

## The Evidence on Effects of Educational Standards

How will the new educational standards affect student achievement? The literature on what happens to student outcomes under different sets of academic standards is small but growing.

### Graduation Requirements

Given that all the published theoretical models agree that a rise in educational standards must, other things being equal, cause fewer students to meet the standard, it makes sense to begin by examining how many students lose from higher standards in this way. Dean R. Lillard and Philip P. DeCicca compare high school dropout rates and attrition rates among states in 1980 and 1990, and individual-level data from about the same times.[41] Overall, the authors conclude, a one standard deviation increase in graduation standards, which corresponds to an additional 2.5 courses, is correlated with a 0.3 to 1.6 percent rise in the share of high school students who drop out. The basic finding that past increases in graduation requirements have led graduation rates to be lower than they otherwise would be meshes with theoretical predictions and needs to be taken seriously. Policymakers will require much more detailed information on what measures, if any, were targeted toward students who were at risk of dropping out as a result of the move to more rigorous standards. Policymakers will also want to know why some students appear to have been induced to drop out, as well as what alternative credentials and career paths might reasonably be made available to those students who will drop out in any event. (The companion paper in this volume by John H. Bishop, Ferran Mane, Michael Bishop, and Joan Moriarty provides a more detailed summary of existing work as well as extensive new findings on this important issue.)

## Homework and Grading Standards

A number of papers that do not explicitly address the impact of changing standards over time nonetheless provide relevant insights. These papers consider the impact of variations in homework and grading standards.

Some papers examine the correlation between homework and test scores. Harris Cooper provides a detailed review of earlier research on the link between homework and student achievement.[42] He cites numerous experiments, some but not all of which suggest a positive link. However, the sample sizes in these studies are very small (thirty-nine to four hundred students) and the studies examined only one to eight schools each. A larger literature examines the correlation between achievement and time spent on homework in a nonexperimental, cross-sectional framework. For instance, Cooper reports the results of eleven studies that model student achievement as a function of homework while controlling for background variables. Most of the eleven studies indicate a positive link between homework and achievement. But in some cases the research used small samples that are not nationally representative. In other cases, researchers used national samples but did not control well for prior achievement, thus increasing the risk of omitted variable bias. However, two notable exceptions are research done by Timothy Z. Keith and others and by

Herbert J. Walberg, Barry J. Fraser, and Wayne W. Welch, who use High School and Beyond and the National Assessment in Science, respectively, to establish a correlation between student test scores and the amount of homework that the student reported doing per time period, while controlling well for prior achievement and characteristics of the school environment.[43]

Unfortunately, these studies, like the vast majority of the literature, use a student report on hours of homework done per week. This is not a policy variable that a school administrator or teacher can directly control. In particular, much of the variation in homework performed by students might reflect unmeasured differences in student ability or attitudes. Another typical problem in the literature is that achievement in a given subject is regressed on homework performed in all subjects. The ideal measure of homework would be the amount of homework assigned by the student's teacher in the given subject.

Julian R. Betts attempts to get around these problems by analyzing a nationally representative sample of students attending grades seven through twelve.[44] Because teachers indicate the amount of homework they assign per week, chances are reduced that the analysis merely picks up more highly achieving and more highly motivated students choosing to do more homework. The results, for models of math test scores, are very strong, indicating that math homework is a more important determinant of gains in achievement than any of the standard measures of school quality, such as teacher education and experience or class size. The results are robust to the addition of a dummy variable for each student to control for omitted ability or motivation among students.

Betts also addresses the questions of how much homework is too much and whether only the best students respond to additional homework. Homework assignments ranged from zero to roughly eight hours per week. Within this range, no trailing off of the effectiveness of math homework emerged. (This study, focused on math homework, cannot indicate the optimal amount of homework that schools should assign across all subjects.) Betts also concludes that additional math homework appears to be equally effective in increasing the rate of learning across all students, regardless of their initial level of achievement. This is an important finding, given that one of the chief criticisms of higher standards and higher expectations has been that some students will respond by simply giving up.

Another Betts study examines variations across schools in math and science grading standards.[45] It estimates the stringency of grading standards in each school by comparing test scores in these two subjects with grades in math and science courses, while controlling for the type of course taken, student demographics, and school resources such as class size and teacher preparation. In the second stage, the analysis tests whether students learn more quickly if they attend schools with more stringent grading standards. The answer appears to be yes. However, in this case, unlike the case of homework, a policy of higher grading standards might help all students, but it seems to help most those near the top, increasing inequality in the distribution of student achievement.

### Grade Retention and Summer School

Our theoretical analysis focused on a pass-fail standard in which there are repercussions for students who do not fulfill the academic requirements established by the educational standards. An increasingly common implementation of this idea calls for students to repeat a grade if they lag too far behind established standards for the students' grade level. Grade retention differs from the theoretical analysis in that students receive a second chance to meet the standard. Another variant requires students who do poorly on achievement tests to attend classes after school, on weekends, or in summer school. These approaches provide additional resources to the students most in need.

The impact of grade retention has received considerable attention. In a review of the literature, Thomas Holmes reports that grade retention is typically associated with poorer student performance after the student is held back a year.[46] Only nine of sixty-three studies found that retention improved the students' performance. Holmes indicates that in most of these nine studies, the treatment of students was not simply retention but retention accompanied by intensive remediation. Additional attention to the students who lag furthest behind is likely to be necessary in a system that sets strict content standards.

Summer school for students who have fallen well behind grade level seems to offer an alternative, and perhaps less stigmatizing, option.[47] The Chicago public school system has received national attention for a bold program called Summer Bridge. As reported by Betts, beginning in the 1996–97 school year, students in grades three, six, eight, and nine whose performance lagged behind national norms on either the reading or mathematics portion of the tests were required to attend summer school. The cutoff points below which students were required to attend summer school were 2.8 for grade three, 5.2 for grade six, 6.8 for grade eight, and 7.9 for grade nine. (The tests were given in spring, so that a student progressing at the normal rate should have attained a grade equivalent of about 3.8 by May of the third-grade school year.) At the end of summer school, students were tested again and were promoted to the next grade if they then met the standard. Betts calculates that, in the initial testing, 27.1–62.2 percent of students failed at least one of the two tests, depending on the grade level. Unfortunately, not all students who should have attended summer school did so. But when calculated as a percentage of those who took the summer tests, the success rate at the end of summer ranged from 38.4 percent to 49.6 percent, with the highest success rate among eighth-grade students.

The first-year evidence suggests that the summer school program provided an extremely cost-effective way of improving student performance. The mean increase in students' grade equivalent during summer school varied by grade from about one half to a full year. These increases hint at large incentive effects on the students and their teachers. But important questions remain. If the Summer Bridge program merely drilled students on testing techniques, then much of the gains over the summer should disappear during the following school year. Further, improvement over the summer might in part represent regression to the mean after some students on the spring test had an off day. A longitudinal analysis should be able to provide direct information on some of these issues, including whether the creation of high-stakes tests increased student effort.

Melissa Roderick and others present the results of a two-year study of Chicago students.[48] Among the important findings:

—Students who attended Summer Bridge in the summer of 1997 retained most of their large achievement gains. However, their rate of improvement during the 1997–98 school year was much smaller than for other students, so that part of the achievement gap reemerged during the 1997–98 school year.

—To test for the incentive effects, the authors compared scores for students in spring and summer 1997, during the first year of the program, with scores of students in spring 1995, before the new summer school and grade retention policy was in place. Gains in grade three were fairly muted. However, the percentage of students making the grade cutoffs during spring testing increased considerably between 1995 and 1997 in grades six and eight. The largest gains accrued to students who were particularly far behind at the start of the school year.

This latter finding suggests that the imposition of new standards and accountability led to significant increases in student effort, teacher effort, or both, at least in grades six and eight. Results for the reading test in grade six—the percentage of students in various categories who met the reading cutoff at stated times—are listed in table 4. Students were divided into groups based on how

**Table 4. Percentage of Sixth-Grade Students Meeting Reading Test Score Cutoff in 1995 and 1997 in Chicago Public Schools by Number of Grade Equivalents Behind in Previous Year**

| Initial number of grade equivalents behind | May 1995 | May 1997 | After summer bridge, August 1997 |
|---|---|---|---|
| > 1.5 | 20 | 31 | 52 |
| 1.5 to 1 | 36 | 43 | 65 |
| 1 to 0.5 | 50 | 57 | 79 |
| 0 to 0.5 | 65 | 71 | 88 |

Source: Melissa Roderick and others, *Ending Social Promotion: Results from the First Two Years* (Chicago, Ill.: Consortium on Chicago School Research, 1999).

many grade equivalents they would need to gain during grade six to reach the stipulated cutoff. The table has the results for students who needed to gain at least some positive fraction of a grade equivalent by May of their year in grade six to be promoted to grade seven. The first column of numbers shows the percentage of students making the cutoff in spring 1995. These students provide a benchmark case because the Summer Bridge and promotion policy were not yet in place. The second column shows the percentage of students making the cutoff in May 1997, the first year of the new policy. The third column combines this percentage of students who met the cutoff in May 1997 with those who failed in May but met the cutoff during a second test after participating in Summer Bridge.

The data in the table show a marked increase in the percentage of students making the cutoff in May 1997 relative to May 1995, with the largest gains among the students who were initially furthest behind. For example, among students who needed to improve their test scores by more than 1.5 grade equivalents, only 20 percent met the cutoff by May of the following year in 1995, compared with 31 percent in 1997. Because these two groups of students had similar initial achievement, the 11 percent gain suggests that the replacement of social promotion with strict grade promotion policy in the 1996–97 school year induced strong incentive effects. Weaker incentive effects are apparent among students whose initial grade equivalents were higher, as shown in the table.

The data in table 4 also make clear that summer school for at-risk students led to major gains in achievement. Roderick and others report that these impressive gains persisted in the second year, but Summer Bridge did not lead to greater rates of learning for these children during the subsequent school year, so that part of the achievement gap reemerged over time.

Whether the apparent incentive effects derive from greater effort among students, teachers, or parents of at-risk children, or all three, is not certain. In addition, as Roderick and others note, the simple comparison they make across two cohorts cannot establish whether the new grade promotion policy or some other unobserved change in the Chicago schools was the main cause.

Still, the results provide indirect evidence in favor of strong incentive effects related to the raising of standards, as posited in our theoretical analysis. Four groups of students who are at risk of failing should be considered. In order of increasing achievement, these groups are: those at the very bottom who exerted no effort with or without the new standard, slightly more highly achieving students who reduce their effort after the standard is raised because they believe that they cannot meet the new cutoff, students who do not change their effort and fail under the new system, and students who work harder after the standard is raised. (At the very top are top-achieving students who can easily meet the new cutoff without increasing effort.) Our main concern is the size of the bottom three groups compared with the fourth group, which increases its achievement. The Chicago results summarized by Roderick and others yield no trace of the bottom three groups of students who either do not change their effort or reduce it.[49] Students who had to improve by more than 1.5 grade equivalents showed the strongest improvement relative to similarly weak achievers who entered grade six before the standard was raised.

Caution must be exercised in inferring the cause of the large achievement gains observed in Chicago. But the finding that higher standards help the lowest achieving students the most is potentially of great importance. It also squares well with the finding by Betts that additional math homework has strong positive effects on the achievement of all students, regardless of their initial level of achievement.

## The Case of Massachusetts

The 1993 Massachusetts Education Reform Act (MERA) established two prongs in a seven- to ten-year plan. The first prong, in response to a state court ruling in a district finance adequacy case, established a seven-year schedule for a massive rise in state aid to bring all localities up to a newly formulated foundation budget by 2000.[50] Real state aid more than doubled over this period.[51] The annual growth rate of state aid in current dollars averaged 12.4 percent, exceeding inflation plus enrollment growth by 7.7 percent.

As a result, all districts were successfully brought up to foundation budget, and the gaps in spending were markedly narrowed. Low-income districts (bottom quartile) now spend more per pupil than middle-income districts (middle two quartiles).[52] At the same time, even the higher spending communities received some increase in state aid, over and above inflation. Per pupil spending in districts at the tenth percentile (that is, low spending districts) rose $862 (in 1999 dollars) from 1993 to 1998, and by $449 at the ninetieth percentile, because of a combination of local and state funding.[53] This achievement of raising all districts to foundation budget is widely viewed as remarkable, thanks to the surprisingly robust growth of the economy and the bipartisan commitment to education reform.

The other prong of MERA was standards-based reform. The law stipulated the development of state curriculum frameworks, to be followed by aligned assessments, which would be administered for a few years before triggering consequences. Accountability would first apply to school officials, through a school accountability program, and finally to students. MERA stipulated that a Massachusetts diploma would become contingent on demonstrating tenth-grade proficiency in the core subjects.

Both prongs of MERA were essential to the broad, bipartisan consensus among the Democratic legislature, Republican governor, the press, and the public, in an otherwise politicized state. Of note is that the money came first, while the accountability measures were being developed, and the consequences of the standards were scheduled to be the last step. The wisdom of this approach (facilitated by good economic times) is that it not only provided the wherewithal to localities, but also strengthened the backbone of public officials for phase two: They are now committed to follow through on accountability measures to justify the massive increase in funding that has taken place over the previous seven years.

### The MCAS Exams

The curriculum frameworks took longer to develop than originally scheduled, in part because of changes in leadership of the Massachusetts Board of Education. Some of the more contentious frameworks, notably history and social science, went through many twists and turns before being adopted.[54] This delayed the development of some of the exams in the Massachusetts Comprehensive Assessment System (MCAS), given that they are specifically aligned with the state frameworks. Unlike some states, which have purchased off-the-shelf tests, Massachusetts spent the time and money to develop its own exams.

The first exams were administered in the spring of 1998 to students in grades four, eight, and ten, without high stakes attached to them. In the fall of 1999, the Massachusetts Board of Education voted to go ahead with the scheduled graduation requirement for the class of 2003, ten years after the enactment of MERA, but on a temporarily more limited basis than was originally envisioned. Instead of requiring students to pass exams in all the core subjects, only math and English language arts (ELA) would initially be required. The board also voted to set the initial cutoff for graduation on these exams at the bottom of the Needs Improvement category, instead of the originally intended cutoff at Proficient, because the initial tenth-grade failure rates exceeded 50 percent.[55] Students will have at least four opportunities to retake the tests before the end of twelfth grade.

Both math and ELA exams include sizable open-response and essay sections, in addition to multiple-choice questions. Specifically, the ELA exams for each of the three grades include two sessions for a long composition (one for drafting and one for revising, as well as extra time granted upon request), four open-response questions, and thirty-two multiple choice. The spring 1999 fourth- and tenth-grade compositions were as follows:

> "Some days are more fun than others. Describe a day that was great for you and tell WHY it was great. Include details so the reader can enjoy the day as much as you did."

> "In literature, as in life, things are not always as they appear to be. Identify a work of literature that you have read in or out of class in which this is true. Select one event, scene, or episode from this work of literature and explain in an essay what the situation appears to be and what the situation really is."

The grading standards for passing performance on such essay questions are not overly demanding, to judge by the examples of student essays released by the Department of Education (DOE).[56] Essay exams are graded by teachers in a summer program that converts many initial skeptics into true believers, according to the DOE.

Each year all of the questions that student scores are based on are publicly released, and they are not used again. This greatly reduces the problem of artificial test-inflation compared with exams in which the questions on existing forms become more widely known over time.[57] This raises the cost of testing, but at about $15 a head, it is still cheaper than AP and SAT exams.

*Early Test Results*

The 1998 and 1999 failure rates were high on math in grade eight (over 40 percent) and grade ten (over 50 percent), as well as on ELA in grade ten (about 30 percent). The failure rates are much higher in most of the urban districts (over 75 percent in Boston and over 80 percent in Springfield). Moreover, the tenth-grade scores did not improve in the second year of the test. Two math examples illustrate some of the range in level of performance.

From the 1998 eighth-grade test:

According to the 1990 census, the population of Massachusetts was 6,016,425. Approximately what percent of those people lived in Boston?

Population of Cities in Massachusetts

| City | Population |
|------|-----------|
| Boston | 574,283 |
| Cambridge | 95,802 |
| Fall River | 92,703 |

A. 10%
B. 20%
C. 30%
D. 40%

Only 28 percent of Massachusetts's eighth-graders answered correctly, barely more than the 24 percent that would obtain if those who answered the question guessed randomly.[58] This was a particularly low scoring question, but performance on the following question was slightly better than most.

From the 1999 tenth-grade test:

Which of the following functions will yield the largest value for $x = 50$?
A. $f(x) = 5 + x$
B. $f(x) = 5x$
C. $f(x) = x^2$
D. $f(x) = 5^x$

Students were allowed to use calculators during this part of the exam, but still only 52 percent got it right. Other questions were harder, primarily because they demand that students know how to apply mathematical concepts, including multistep problems.

Some factors contributing to the high failure rates have been identified in a study for Mass Insight Education, which examined records of a sample of urban and nonurban students who failed one or both tenth-grade exams.[59]

Approximately one-fourth of these students were absent more than five weeks of the school year. Many of these students, clearly disengaged, are likely to become dropouts independent of the MCAS. It seems unlikely that MCAS would have negative incentive effects on such students once it starts to count and may have positive incentive effects for some, once students realize they will have to attend school to pass.

A number of students left entire sections of the exam blank, including 13–19 percent of the failing urban students in this sample who answered no multiple-choice questions at all, and 20–23 percent who left all the open-response questions blank. It seems reasonable to predict that a significant number of these students, and others as well, would behave differently once the test starts to count for graduation.[60]

Other factors that give some reason to believe the failure rates will drop once the exam starts to count include the fact that about 10 percent of the failing students in math came close to passing on the first try and will likely do so with multiple retake opportunities in grades eleven and twelve.[61] Also, about 20 percent of the students who failed the math exam are special education students, some of whom will be eligible for test-taking accommodations or alternative examinations starting in 2001.

A quarter or more of these failing students were also failing the math or English course they were taking at the time. For the majority who were passing these courses, a big part of the problem is the level of the math course. Well over half of students failing the tenth-grade math exam were enrolled in remedial or basic math or algebra 1, so they have not been taught much of the tenth-grade material expected from them on this exam. The math exam is a much greater hurdle than the ELA exam, and a huge part of the challenge will be to get students completing algebra 1 by ninth grade at the latest.

In short, good reason exists to believe that the failure rates will be substantially lower once the exam starts to count, but they still threaten to be high on the math portion. Consequently, a full array of remedial measures is currently being implemented in a number of districts. As in other states, these include after-school, summer school, and in-school programs, to provide short-term help for students who have fallen behind.[62]

But deeper changes are also called for, reaching farther back in the curriculum, so that students will be ready in the normal course of study for the exams they will face. This is definitely happening, at an accelerated pace because of MCAS, according to many superintendents across the state. Widely noted changes include greater emphasis on writing and on open-ended math problems. Scores on the fourth-grade MCAS exams have already shown improvement in the second year of testing.

### An Econometric Analysis of ELA-4 and ITBS-3 Scores

In 1999, the second year of the MCAS, the mean score on ELA-4 rose approximately 4.0 percentiles, and the median score rose 4.5 percentiles over the scores of the previous cohort.[63] The question arises as to how much of this improvement stemmed from a change in the quality of the cohort (a better group of students), as opposed to more fundamental change, in the amount of learning in grade four. Fortunately, the Massachusetts DOE has assembled a useful micro data set that allows one to answer this question for the ELA-4. The state required all school districts to administer the third-grade Iowa Test of Basic Skills (ITBS) reading test for the years 1997–99. The ITBS scores are far and away the best predictor of the following year's MCAS scores. But the third graders in 1998 scored worse on the ITBS than their predecessors in 1997 and then, the next year, scored better than their predecessors on the MCAS. This suggests that the MCAS improvement was not the by-product of a higher quality cohort. The cohort effect worked in the opposite direction, masking an even larger MCAS improvement, apparently reflecting more fundamental change in fourth-grade learning.

More rigorous statistical analysis bears this out. The DOE has linked the third-grade reading scores with the fourth-grade MCAS ELA scores for over two-thirds of the state's seventy-five thousand fourth graders, to validate the MCAS exam. The ITBS score accounts for 56 percent of the variance in individual MCAS scores a year later. We ran regressions with additional controls for race and gender, plus indicators for the nearly one thousand schools in the sample, for MCAS scores from 1998 and also from 1999. This allows us to decompose the mean gain in MCAS scores into that part which comes from changes in the explanatory variables (especially ITBS scores) and that part which reflects changes in the effects of those variables, the regression coefficients (especially the school effects). This decomposition (known as an Oaxaca decomposition) suggests that the adverse cohort effect (from lower ITBS scores) masked an underlying improvement in mean MCAS scores of over 5 percentiles (versus 4.0 in the raw data).

We take the analysis a few steps further, to shed some light on whether the improvement in MCAS scores represented a superficial test-specific improvement or whether broader skill improvements were set in motion. We begin with a decomposition of changes in the ITBS scores, analogous to that of the MCAS. Controlling for race, gender, special education, limited-English proficient (LEP), and free-lunch status (but without a prior test score to control), we find that ITBS scores improved dramatically from 1998 to 1999, despite an adverse cohort effect. The underlying improvement in mean ITBS scores was more than eight percentiles, after correcting for the cohort effect.[64]

Was it a coincidence that third-grade ITBS scores rose dramatically the same year that fourth-grade MCAS scores rose by 5 percentiles? If both events reflect improved practices or curriculum, stimulated by the introduction of MCAS the year before, this would be a finding of great interest. It is impossible to test this hypothesis directly, but some suggestive circumstantial econometric evidence is available. Roughly speaking, schools that added more to 1999 student performance on their third-grade ITBS scores than would have been predicted based on how much the school added in previous years also tended to add more to their 1999 fourth-grade students' MCAS scores than would have been predicted.[65] This is consistent with, though it does not prove, the hypothesis that those schools that were stimulated most to action by the introduction of MCAS were likely to have made improvements in third-grade reading instruction as well as fourth-grade reading and writing. If so, this would indicate the positive effects of MCAS go beyond superficial test coaching to more pervasive improvements. These improvements seem to go back to earlier grades, providing the foundation on which to build.

## Controversy over MCAS

In the third year of MCAS, controversy has escalated. Media attention has focused on student and teacher boycotts, even though the number of boycotters is small (about two hundred to three hundred students). Students are by tradition averse to exams, so the more important question is why some adults are encouraging them.[66]

Objections fall into several categories. The protestors (and groups such as FairTest and the American Civil Liberties Union) claim the test is unfair to disadvantaged students in low-income, poorly funded districts. But funding gaps have narrowed markedly, and the largest urban districts spend above the state average per pupil. The opposition is "mostly in the affluent suburbs west of Boston and in pockets of progressivism like Cambridge."[67] With a few exceptions (such as the local chapter of the National Association for the Advancement of Colored People), representatives of the minority communities have largely targeted their anger at the failure of the school system to bring up the skills of their children, rather than at the MCAS. They already knew the general message MCAS was bearing.

A disproportionate number of the teacher opponents to MCAS comes from the history and social studies departments. They object to the MCAS history exam. It will not yet be required for graduation for 2003 but is being administered because MERA includes history in the core competencies. These teachers believe it narrows the scope of what they teach. One prominent and vocal group of opponents is employed by Facing History and Ourselves, a company that sells history curriculum to the schools (built around the Holocaust) and argues that its curriculum will be squeezed out by MCAS.

Some of the opposition in the higher achieving localities is based on the concern that the exam is too long and takes too much time from other activities. The state is responding to this concern by spreading out the testing over more grades, such that no student in grades one through seven will spend more than seven hours a year in MCAS testing, from 2001 on.

Another objection, common elsewhere as well, is to the idea that a student may be denied a diploma on the basis of a single test. However, MCAS is an extensive set of examinations, so that students who write strong essays or excel in open-response questions can offset poor performance on multiple-choice sections (or vice versa). The objection seems not so much directed to a single test, but to a set of external common assessments versus a set of local and possibly idiosyncratic criteria.

The Massachusetts Teachers Association (MTA), the state affiliate of the National Education Association (NEA), has also joined in opposition to the MCAS. The MTA recently announced its intention to file legislation to eliminate the MCAS graduation requirement.[68] The MTA also began a $700,000 TV ad campaign explicitly designed to counter the perceived attack on public education by those who point to low MCAS scores.[69]

What seems to be at issue here is that the MCAS is the key component in the accountability phase of Massachusetts's education reform. The MTA is understandably threatened. Thus far, however, with few exceptions, the legislature and administration stand firm behind MCAS. Too much money has been spent over the last seven years to lightly abandon the insistence on results.

Meanwhile, in the school districts that face the highest failure rates, the most important story is unfolding:

Little of this [anti-MCAS] grumbling . . . is coming from the urban districts and poor communities that are the true targets—and primary beneficiaries—of education reform. In places filled with the neediest, low-income, immigrant and transient student populations, school leaders have, by and large, embraced the state's regimen of standards and accountability. For districts that, prior to 1993, hadn't been pushed to serve all students well or didn't have the resources to do so, the $5.6 billion spent statewide has been a godsend. From Boston to Springfield, city school chiefs have latched on to standards-based reform not only as a quid-pro-quo for the new dough, but as their preferred vehicle for improving instruction.[70]

The ways in which school chiefs are using MCAS to improve instruction go beyond changes in curriculum and remedial programs to more general leverage (the term commonly used by superintendents) over those teachers and administrators who resist changes such as the reorganization of the school day, revamped professional development, and so on.[71]

One of the most striking instances of this leverage arises in the hard bargaining stance taken in the spring and summer of 2000 by the Boston School Department over the issue of seniority. As is commonly the case, the union contract (of the AFT affiliate) grants senior teachers first refusal of new jobs and the right to apply for jobs held by new teachers. In an unusual development, a broad coalition of about thirty parent and community groups, such as the Urban League and the Black Ministerial Alliance, joined together to side with school officials in limiting seniority rules. As the *Boston Globe* reports, "Parents say the drumbeat of reform—from stiffer curriculum standards to a standardized test as a graduation requirement—underscores the importance of this year's negotiation."[72] One cannot help but note the contrast between the Boston parent groups whose response to standards-based reforms is to challenge problematic union rules, while efforts to derail the standards are largely confined to the more affluent and progressive districts, along with the state NEA affiliate.

## Obstacles to Strengthening Educational Standards

Based on our knowledge of reform efforts in California, Massachusetts, and other states, and the theoretical and empirical research on standards, we identify four key obstacles that can stand in the way of higher educational standards: opposition arising from concerns about the distribution of student achievement, problems in defining standards and assessing students' progress toward those standards, the need to align the incentives of all participants in public education, and equity concerns created by the large gap in school resources that currently exists among students from various socioeconomic groups in some states.

### Opposition to Standards Based on Distribution of Student Achievement

Opposition to higher educational standards can arise for many reasons, but in our judgment the source of opposition that resonates most strongly (if not always most convincingly) derives from concerns about equity. According to our theoretical analysis, any change in standards typically leaves some students worse off. This makes the politics of higher standards inherently divisive. Legislators in most states have determined that a movement toward higher educational standards is worth the effort. However, as parents become more fully aware of the gap between published standards and the performance of their children, opposition could swell.

Many parents and legislators might be surprised to learn just how much variation there is in student performance at present. The twenty-fifth through seventy-fifth percentiles and the minimum and maximum in student performance on a standardized math test by grade level, in the Longitudinal Study of American Youth (LSAY), are depicted in figure 4. The LSAY sampled a representative population of American school students between 1987 and 1992. Particularly striking is how large the variation in achievement is within grades, compared with the average rate of improvement between grades. Betts uses these data to calculate the percentage of students who would be held back a year if the school's policy were to retain students whose test scores were below the national average for students one or two grade levels below the student's current grade.[73] In other words, what percentage of ninth-grade students would be held back if their math scores were below the national average for students in grade eight or even grade seven? The predicted percentage of students who would be held back if their achievement lagged by a year ranged from 37 to 46 percent, depending on grade, in grades eight to twelve. If, instead, students were retained only if their scores lagged national norms by two years, then 26–40 percent of students would have been retained. These are very large shares of the student population.

The estimates are an upper bound in the sense that if strict grade promotion policies based on test scores were implemented, it would provide an incentive for students to study harder and for schools to reform curriculum

**Figure 4. The Distribution of Test Scores by Grade, 1987–92**

Math scores

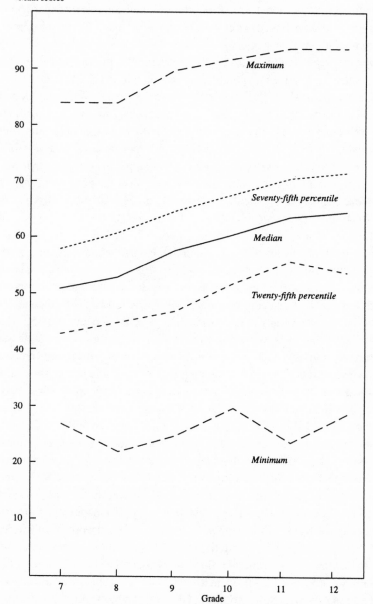

Source: Julian R. Betts, "The Two-Legged Stool: The Neglected Role of Educational Standards in Improving America's Public Schools," *Economic Policy Review*, vol. 4 (1998), pp. 97–116. Data are from the Longitudinal Study of American Youth.

and teaching practices. Evidence from the Chicago public schools suggests that the development of standards, testing, and accountability can spur much greater effort among students at risk of failing. Nonetheless, early experiments with grade promotion linked to test scores suggest that these discouraging numbers are not outlandish.[74]

Given the large variations in student achievement at present, what policies might reduce the chance that political opposition will overturn recent moves to institute standards? One solution might be to devote additional attention to marginal students including those who are most likely to give up after standards are raised, in a bid to ensure that no student's achievement falls after standards are raised. The Summer Bridge program in the Chicago public schools represents one example of an effort to supplement higher standards with programs aimed specifically at the students most in need.

However, opposition to standards appears to come not typically from families whose students are most likely to fail when the standards are raised, but from families in areas served by good schools. (In Massachusetts and Wisconsin, at least, the most vocal opposition to tighter standards has come from affluent communities.) Parents in more successful schools may fear that districts will shift resources from their schools to underperforming schools in the district. Parents' fear that administrators will reduce funding at top schools is a legitimate one, especially in systems with large heterogeneous districts. The only evident solution is to expand total funding so that no school suffers a reduction in programs, while at the same time the schools most in need receive additional resources. Thus, implementing higher standards makes sense at a time when state budgets make higher funding a real possibility. Massachusetts appears to have followed this policy prescription closely.

Some affluent parents might worry that higher standards will make standing out from the crowd more difficult when their children apply to university. Such concerns become potentially relevant when a state imposes a single standard, but the existence of other high-end credentials (AP exams, SATs, and so on) renders this concern less compelling. Further, if the existing array of credentials is insufficient to differentiate high-end performance, the state can create a range of high-end standards, which in turn create incentives for a wider range of students to excel. If a multitiered set of standards induces almost all students to work at least as hard as they had without the standards, and if the minimum standard is set to ensure that even the weakest students leave school with a good set of basic skills, a multitiered set of standards makes good sense. It provides incentives for a wider range of students than the group of students near the margin under a simple pass-fail standard, while providing top students with a means to signal their high effort levels to universities and employers. Many states have taken this lesson to heart, creating differentiated advanced diplomas for students who meet strict standards.

*Problems in Defining Content Standards and*
*Assessing Student Achievement*

Implementation of content standards and assessment of student progress have often proven difficult. The design of content standards has been contentious in many states. Perhaps this is best seen in the history of the movement for national content standards in public schools. In brief, the National Council of Teachers of Mathematics (NCTM) developed national math standards during the 1990s. These standards have provided an influential framework for individual states as they have striven to develop their own standards in math. However, certain elements of these standards have elicited objections from parents and many prominent mathematicians.[75] Similarly, when California first attempted to develop science standards, two rival groups, one led by Nobel Prize–winning scientist Glenn Seaborg, and a second led by educators from state schools of education, clashed. In the end, the state urged the two sides to come together, with some success.[76]

The care and attention to detail that are required to develop a set of content standards suggests that for reasons of cost, it probably makes no sense for individual schools or smaller districts to write their own set of standards. But given the limited success of the movement to create nationally adopted standards, the states will continue to play a paramount role in standard-setting.

Similarly, several problems arise in the creation of tests. First, most commercially available tests may be related only weakly to the given state's curriculum standards. It will take time for all states to develop more suitable test instruments. For example, California adopted the Stanford 9 test for use in spring 1998 and is now moving this off-the-shelf test toward the new state content standards by adding several components.

Second, preparing tests that provide both in-depth and sufficiently wide coverage of a subject creates challenges.[77] The solution would appear to be to lengthen existing test instruments so that they provide an in-depth coverage of a wide area within a subject. Essay and open-response questions, of the sort used in the MCAS test in Massachusetts, represent a step in the right direction in that they gauge students' level of mastery of written expression and problem solving that no pure multiple-choice exam could approach. However, broadening the test then evokes the complaint that it is too long, diverting student time from other learning activities. Often the same critics who object to a single test being used for high stakes also object to the length of a multi-faceted set of exams, indicating that the objections are not being accurately framed. The external nature of the assessments is really at issue.

A third problem can arise from the natural tendency of teachers to teach to the test. This is compounded by the fact that, in many cases, the same form of the test instrument is given several years in a row, so that teachers, and perhaps students, become familiar with the specific questions over time. This can lead to inflation of test scores without accompanying gains in true student achievement. Daniel Koretz summarizes earlier work he conducted with coauthors in which a school district had introduced a new test form in 1987, only to find a significant drop in the average grade equivalent of students on the test.[78] Over the next three years, however, successive cohorts of students improved in this test, to the point where students were performing at about the same level as students had the year before the switch to the current form. Two questions arise: First, did the large drop in test scores in 1987, the year that the new form was introduced, represent a true drop in achievement? Second, did the steady improvement over the next three years that the same form was used represent true gains in performance of students, or merely teaching to the test as teachers became better acquainted with the new questions? To test the latter hypothesis, Koretz and coauthors arranged to test students in the district during 1990 using the same test form that had last been used four years earlier, in 1986. Their findings suggest that the large drop in achievement in 1987 and the subsequent gains reflect the switch to a new test form and then teaching to the test on the new form. Little change in true achievement occurred.

There seem to be two solutions to this problem. First, annual changes in the test form should reduce gains in test scores that result from teaching to the test. This may raise the cost of testing but seems worth the price if policymakers and parents want a reliable indicator of trends in student achievement. Second, it seems inevitable that teachers will teach to the test, especially if schools and teachers are held accountable for student performance. This tendency can be transformed from a vice into a virtue as good tests that accurately and fairly test the students' knowledge of the given content standards are developed. With the creation of excellent tests, teaching to the test should eventually become a good thing.

*Creating Incentives for Students, Teachers, and Administrators*

Many states now hold students accountable for performance, through policies of grade retention, summer school, and exit exams. However, most states
lag behind considerably in creating incentives for teachers and school administrators to work toward student success in mastering content standards.

California's Public School Accountability Act of 1999 provides one example of the limited incentives that states have put in place to date. California
schools that lag furthest behind in the Academic Performance Index (a non-
linear average of student achievement) are eligible to participate in the
Immediate Intervention/Underperforming Schools Program (II/USP).[79] Initially, schools in this program receive money to speed improvement in student
achievement. However, any school that does not meet its growth target must
hold a public hearing and is subject to intervention by the local district board.
If, after two years, the school still shows few signs of improvement, then the
state superintendent can take over the school. The principal can be reassigned.
In addition, the state superintendent can take a number of other actions, including allowing parents to send their children to other schools or to create a charter
school, reassigning certified administrators or teachers, or even closing the
school. The threat that a principal could be removed from a school creates
incentives for the principal to improve student achievement quickly.As the
legislation behind these accountability measures was passed only in 1999, it
will take some time to observe how often and how effectively the measures
come into play in California.

The II/USP program and similar programs in other states create incentives
for teachers and principals, but they seem weak compared with the incentives
already facing students, such as the threat of grade retention. For instance,
outright firing of teachers or principals seems unlikely given the collective
bargaining agreements that typically apply. Similarly, large merit bonuses for
teachers, in groups or individually, to reflect gains in student achievement are
by no means a widespread phenomenon. Merit pay for teachers has been
attempted many times in the past. But as Richard J. Murnane and others show,
such programs have typically collapsed because of legitimate teacher concerns
that principals were setting merit pay based on unverifiable information, opening up the possibility of cronyism.[80] One reason for hope in this regard is that
current attempts to improve student assessment might provide mutually agree-
able and objective ways of gauging the overall performance of teachers in a
school or the performance of individual teachers. A number of states, and per-

haps most notably the city of Denver, are beginning to experiment with rewards for teachers based on the rate of progress of their students.[81]

Much remains to be done to increase the incentives of all participants in public education, especially teachers, principals, and administrators, to work toward fulfillment of content standards by all students.

### Gaps in School Spending and Opportunity-to-Learn Standards

Inequities in school spending among districts can threaten to derail the movement to impose uniform educational standards. During the 1990s, a movement for what became known as opportunity-to-learn standards argued forcefully for equalization of school spending before implementing student accountability.[82]

The call to partly or fully level the playing field in terms of school spending before holding all schools equally accountable makes sense and is sometimes required to meet a state constitutional provision for adequacy or equity.[83] But the public should not overestimate the achievement disparities that are attributable to existing inequalities in school finance per se. The reason is simple: Existing research suggests that school resources such as class size, and to a lesser extent teacher education and experience, have fairly limited effects on student achievement.[84] Similarly, the link between school resources and longer-term measures of student outcomes, such as educational attainment and wages, is modest.[85]

Consider, for example, Julian R. Betts, Kim Rueben, and Anne Danenberg, who analyze the distribution of school resources and test scores on a school-by-school basis in California.[86] The authors find strong inequalities in teacher preparation among schools (even within the same district), with lower socioeconomic status students receiving teachers who are considerably less well prepared, whether measured by teacher certification, experience, or education. (SES is measured by the percentage of students receiving full or partial lunch assistance.) For example, in elementary schools in California, in the lowest SES quintile of schools, on average 32.6 percent of teachers hold no more education than a bachelor's degree, compared with only 8.8 percent in the highest SES quintile of schools. Low SES schools also have much lower test scores, raising the question of whether low achievement in these schools is caused by a lack of resources or by the direct effects of poverty.

Regression analysis suggests that school resources do affect achievement, but the effects are small. The predicted effects on the percentage of students

**Figure 5. Predicted Effect of Changing School Characteristics on the Percentage of California Fifth-Grade Students Scoring at or above National Median in Reading Test, Spring 1998**

Percent

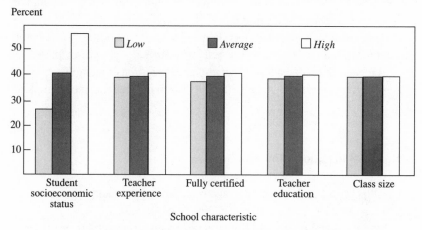

Source: Julian R. Betts, Kim Rueben, and Anne Danenberg, *Equal Resources, Equal Outcome? The Distribution of School Resources and Student Achievement in California* (San Francisco, Calif.: Public Policy Institute of California, 2000).

scoring at or above national norms in reading when a school moves from the twenty-fifth to the fiftieth and then the seventy-fifth percentile in a number of school resources are represented in figure 5. All variables in the figure except for class size have a statistically significant impact on student achievement. But the figure demonstrates that variations in poverty can account for a far higher share of variations in student performance than can variations in school resources, in spite of the large variations in teacher resources that currently exist in California.

Thus, equalization of resources among all schools might reduce inequalities in student outcomes, but only modestly. Looking at the data another way, existing inequalities in resources bear only a small part of the blame for variations in achievement in California. The creation of uniform educational standards might provide the incentive to improve student performance in a way that spending hikes alone cannot. The results on the Summer Bridge program in Chicago imply that reasonably small interventions such as several weeks of summer school can bring impressive and lasting improvements in student performance. The lesson from Chicago seems to be that higher standards, accompanied by judicious new expenditures aimed at the truly needy students, can produce meaningful gains in achievement.

A similar finding emerges from analysis of the effects of grade retention. Grade retention appears to work only when schools try to do something different, possibly with additional resources, for students as they attempt to complete a grade for a second time.

States that reduce historical inequalities in school spending before creating content standards reduce the risk of political opposition based on opportunity-to-learn lines. States that implement rigorous standards while targeting programs of demonstrated effectiveness to the students most at risk do even better.

### Conclusions and Policy Implications

Our theoretical and empirical analysis and review of standards in practice suggests a number of conclusions and policy implications:

—Standards and accountability systems do affect incentives of students, parents, and schools. Limited, but growing, empirical evidence establishes that significant numbers of students rise to greater levels of achievement than when little was expected of them and their schools.

—Assessments should be aligned to standards; they should include open-ended questions and essays worth teaching to; and new forms should be introduced annually to avoid artificial inflation of test scores.

—Localities should retain the option to set higher standards than those set by the state.

—School financing systems should meet state constitutional requirements for adequacy or equity across districts before high-stakes standards take hold (as in Massachusetts).

—Judicious additional spending targeted at students who are likely to fail to reach standards without help makes sense. For example, programs of demonstrated effectiveness, such as Chicago's mandatory summer school at early grade levels for those who fail to meet standards, should be replicated.

—Incentives should be strengthened for schools, especially school leaders, to ensure that students meet standards. Examples include reconstituting failing schools, reassigning teachers and administrators in these schools, and providing sanctuary for students from these schools in other schools or in new charter schools.

—Potentially harsh trade-offs can be minimized by multiple credentials, signaling different levels of achievement. Such signals already exist for high levels of achievement. At the other end, for those students who cannot be remediated to reach stipulated levels of cognitive skills, credentials need to be developed to signal important noncognitive skills. These credentials, such as certificates of completion, should be sufficiently differentiated from cognitive credentials to maintain the incentive to acquire cognitive skills.

No such list of recommendations can fully anticipate what will work and what will not work as full-blown standards-based reform takes effect. Not everyone will meet the new standards, just as not everyone met old standards in the past, before social promotion became the norm. New answers will evolve to the question of what shall be done for those who fail to meet the new standards. In the past, the GED arose to meet the needs of those who wished to convey some level of cognitive achievement without attending school through grade twelve. For others, alternative settings will be developed, such as the ninth-grade remedial schools in Chicago. Proposals have been made in Massachusetts for the community colleges to admit students into special nondegree remedial programs, for those who fail the MCAS but receive a certificate of school completion. After-school programs analogous to the Japanese jukus will also arise, whether by public or private initiative.

Although the optimal configuration of credentials is not yet known, one thing is certain: It would be a disservice to all too many high school graduates to continue granting diplomas that provide no guarantee of minimal literacy and numeracy skills. Amid all the rising controversy, it is a remarkable fact that not even the most vocal critics of standards-based reform claim that a diploma currently guarantees these skills. The only logical conclusion is that those who would go back to the old system believe students should receive a diploma even if they have not been taught basic cognitive skills, so that they may continue to be pooled with those who have. This may seem to be a convenient arrangement for those schools that graduate mostly high achievers, while waving through their lagging students with a wink and a nod. But it is no longer a credible option for those schools in disadvantaged districts whose graduates are known to often lack basic skills and whose communities have been notably absent from the protests against standards-based reform.

# Comment by Herbert J. Walberg

Julian R. Betts and Robert M. Costrell have contributed a splendid paper with useful policy implications. Two of their major arguments are the focus of my comments: (1) multiple cut points are better than single cut points for standards, and (2) standards appear to be working.

## Multiple Cut Points

When I chaired the Design and Analysis Committee of the National Assessment Governing Board (NAGB), the committee considered the possibility of a dichotomous criterion of proficient versus nonproficient. But the committee members and I felt more information would be useful. In the end, we proposed three levels—Basic, Proficient, and Advanced. NAGB maintained these distinctions, and other groups have since found them useful. (In fact, there is a fourth level; that is, Below Basic.)

A disadvantage of several cut points, however, stems from the technical limitation of psychometric tests, particularly non-multiple-choice varieties. Conventional tests are optimized for discriminating best at a single cut point, often near an average. Other things being equal, they cannot discriminate equally well at other cut points. Computer-adaptive testing and longer tests can overcome this problem. However, these solutions may be innovative, costly, and difficult to implement.

Betts and Costrell emphasize that multiple cut points and differential standards give individual students across the ability spectrum reasonable targets to aim for. I would add that such differentiated standards can serve as goals for schools, local school districts, and states. If a dichotomous criterion of proficiency were employed, schools, for example, might concentrate all their energies on proficiency and neglect students near NAGB's Basic and Advanced levels. Still, it is not clear how many levels are needed, and several precedents may be useful in planning the best choice, given several variations in education policy.

The most long-lasting professional precedents for standards are the M.D. and the J.D.—both dichotomies. The medieval craft distinction was apprentice and journeyman, another dichotomy, which still reigns in many apprentice and other induction systems. The value to consumers of such dichotomous distinctions may be their simplicity; they economize on mental effort, a surprisingly precious resource. People want a proficient plumber or physician.

Nonproficient practitioners such as apprentice plumbers and medical students may require extra negotiation, supervision, and uncertainty. Nonetheless, advanced specializations signaled by board certification and extensive experience may be useful indicators when nonroutine decisions are in order, as in the case of choosing a surgeon. Michael de Bakey, for example, as a consequence of carrying out thousands of heart operations, has dealt with rare complications that naturally arose in his specialized practice.

Occupational and professional practices and education systems in other countries may suggest tying standards to examination performance, years of schooling, or both. Many countries, for example, employ a trichotomous system of education—six years of primary school and three years of lower secondary school, both of which are compulsory. Three years of upper secondary education are elective. This third level may require matriculation examinations, and it may provide a terminal technical diploma or stepping-stone to managerial and professional careers requiring a university education.[87]

Americans would like all of their students to be excellent and equal, too. But the country has not been successful at either of these contradictory criteria. U.S. test scores, especially valued-added test scores, compare unfavorably with those in other countries. At the same time, the United States has fallen behind other countries in the egalitarian ideal of providing a secondary education for all students.[88]

For these reasons, it may be useful to consider standards-based school-leaving examinations required for a diploma. These might even be dichotomous standards required for diplomas, say, after nine and the ususal twelve years of schooling. The lower secondary diploma might guarantee general or basic proficiency for many nontechnical, nonmanagerial, and nonprofessional jobs. Several kinds of upper secondary diplomas could be created, one of which would be college preparatory; others might qualify students for specialized technical occupations such as computer programming.

Some may want to avoid combining standards with the length of schooling. If so, I would still maintain as a psychologist that students will vary in their learning rates and their knowledge and skills at age eighteen (and even when they start school). At the end of twelve years of schooling, some high school students can exceed the performance of college graduates; others score at primary school achievement levels. For this reason, the possibility should be considered of granting diplomas for achieving standards instead of spending time in school. Such a possibility would allow some students to graduate from high school with as little as nine instead of twelve years of schooling.

Betts and Costrell have reasonably argued for more finely graded information on standards attainment. The next step is to formulate precisely how such information, however finely divided, may be employed in specific policies, especially those that would boost achievement and save costs—including the often forgotten costs of student time. A fascinating menu of possibilities is on offer, and the most promising should be tried and evaluated.

*Standards Work*

The theory and evidence presented by Betts and Costrell and others suggest that standards elicit academic effort and improve achievement. This conclusion accords well with common experience. The assumption, for example, which economists share, is that people usually arrange their affairs to accomplish what they value while minimizing their time, costs, and risks. Most managers in the workplace take pains to specify performance standards and related incentives. Not only might standards improve students' performance in school but they would also better prepare them for the real accountability that is customary in workplaces.

Even though some evidence suggests that standards would improve achievement, Betts and Costrell are cautious about reaching this conclusion. In addition to their concerns, other worries are teaching to tests, possibly higher dropout rates, intense disciplinary battles over content such as in history, and so on. There may be further problems that have not been emphasized, such as breaches of test security engendered by high stakes. These problems can be overcome as policymakers and administrators gain more experience.

Chester E. Finn Jr. and Marci Kanstoroom show that states are only slowly and fitfully enacting standards, and few have powerful carrots and sticks. Because theory, evidence in hand, and experience in other fields support the causal efficacy of standards, faster and more forceful implementation and experience in remedying obstacles could produce substantial results. This would seem especially likely if such efforts included desirable implementation features.

*Incentives*

Although it seems their implicit assumption, Betts, Costrell, and others deal less directly with the added effect that incentives bring to standards. Evidence suggests that the assumption is reasonable, and greater incentives are needed given that they appear to have substantial large effects. A 1997 Public Agenda national survey of high school students showed that three-fourths believe stiffer examinations and graduation requirements would make students pay more attention to their studies.[89] Three-fourths also said students should not graduate who have not mastered English, and a similar percentage said schools should promote only students who master the material. Almost two-thirds reported they could do much better in school if they tried. Nearly 80 percent said students would learn more if schools made sure they were on time and did their homework. More than 70 percent said schools should require after-school classes for those earning D's and F's.

In these respects, however, teacher educators differ sharply from students and the public. A 1997 Public Agenda survey of education professors showed that 64 percent think schools should avoid competition. More favored giving grades for team efforts than did those who favored grading individual accomplishments.[90]

Teacher educators also differ from employers and other professions on measuring standards or even employing them at all. Employers use standardized multiple-choice examinations for hiring. And selective colleges and graduate and professional schools use them for admission decisions. Such examinations are required in law, medicine, and other fields for licensing because they are objective and reliable. Yet 78 percent of teacher educators wanted less reliance on them.

Nearly two-thirds of teacher educators admitted that education programs often fail to prepare candidates for teaching in the real world, and only 4 percent reported that their programs typically dismiss students found unsuitable for teaching. Thus, even starting with their undergraduate education, many prospective educators are laden with anticompetitive ideas against standards and incentives.

Seventy-nine percent of the teacher educators agreed that "the general public has outmoded and mistaken beliefs about what good teaching means." They apparently have forgotten that citizens, who pay for schools, constitute their ultimate clients. Perhaps the public and students are right. It seems a good time to raise the question of whether standards associated with incentives and disincentives can work in schools as they do in much of the rest of society.

Educators hope that long-range and somewhat vague incentives will motivate students, but graduating from high school, going to a good college, and making money may seem hopelessly distant. Instructional psychologists like clear and immediate feedback, preferably within seconds. This is a potential aspect of the new computer and Internet technologies.

I recently evaluated an Advanced Placement (AP) incentive program for the O'Donnell Foundation in Dallas, Texas. This program is to my knowledge the first clear-cut, large-scale trial of monetary incentives for public school students. The program made use of the Advanced Placement examinations, the only national tests that provide external, objective, and rigorous standards for high school students. More than half a million high school students take AP exams on the content of more than twenty-five college-level courses. More than twenty-five hundred colleges grant course credits for passing grades, allowing students to graduate early or take more advanced college courses.

Beginning with the 1990–91 school year, the incentive program paid students $100 for each passing AP examination score in English, calculus, statistics, computer science, biology, chemistry, and physics plus a reimbursement for the cost of taking the exam. The program also provided a $2,500 stipend to each teacher undergoing training to teach advanced courses in these subjects. The teachers also received $100 for each passing AP examination score of their students.

In the nine participating Dallas schools, sharply increasing numbers of boys and girls of all major ethnic groups took and passed the AP exams. The number rose more than twelvefold from 41 the year before the program began to 521 when it ended in 1994–95. After terminating, the program continued to have carry-over effects: In the 1996–97 school year, two years after the program ended, 442 students passed, about eleven times more than the number in the year before the program began.

Though these numbers speak for themselves, interviews with students, teachers, and college admission officers revealed high regard for the incentive program. They felt that even students who failed AP exams learned better study habits and the importance of hard work to meet high standards.

In addition, the program had other benefits: Students could take courses that are more advanced in college. Those who passed a sufficient number of AP courses could graduate from college early, which saves their families the cost of tuition and saves taxpayers the cost of subsidies. Those who passed AP courses also had a better chance for merit scholarships and entry into selective colleges.

### Conclusion

The Advanced Placement incentive program shows that standards with incentives work in schools as they do in many spheres of life. The lack of school incentives may be the reason that students find academics so boring and sports so exciting. Social promotion and graduating students for mere attendance are insufficient. Nor can paying teachers for their degrees and years of experience bring out their best. Though not all incentives are monetary, rational people require reasons to work hard.

---

## Comment by Meredith Phillips and Tiffani Chin

Julian R. Betts and Robert M. Costrell make several contributions to policymakers' understanding of standards-based reform. First, Betts and Costrell's economic analysis helps identify the likely costs and benefits of policies that require higher standards for high school graduation. Their analysis reveals where policymakers should target resources to mitigate the probable costs of raising standards. They point out, for instance, that policymakers should focus their energies on the group of students who may reduce their effort or drop out of school because they do not expect to be able to meet the higher standard.

Second, the authors try to determine how higher standards will affect the achievement of high school students. Because accountability policies are so new, direct evidence of their effectiveness is thin. Therefore, the authors review data about the effects of more homework, harder grading standards, and summer school on student achievement. Although more research is needed on these topics, Betts and Costrell's review of this literature suggests that asking more of students generally raises their achievement. This conclusion is consistent with claims from the Effective Schools movement of the 1980s about the importance of "academic press" for student achievement.[91] And although Betts and Costrell correctly worry about possible negative effects of raising standards for lower-achieving students, most of the evidence they review points to the benefits of high standards for all students. Only time will tell whether this conclusion continues to hold after states implement higher standards for retention and high school graduation.

Because microeconomics is the study of how rational actors respond to incentives, microeconomic theory provides a good starting place for an analysis of the likely costs and benefits of standards-based reform. However, Betts and Costrell's economic perspective ignores some insights from sociology and psychology that may be useful for constructing policies that maximize the benefits (and minimize the costs) of standards-based reform. Moreover, much of Betts and Costrell's analysis focuses too narrowly on how high school students will respond to high-stakes assessment. The effects of standards-based reform on younger students and parents, as well as the people and institutions implementing the reform such as teachers, schools, and districts, deserve as much, if not greater, attention.

Much of Betts and Costrell's discussion, and much political rhetoric, assumes that high-stakes testing will improve student achievement by encouraging students to work harder. This assumption has several flaws. To begin with, it relies on a reinforcement theory of motivation. Scholars of motivation have identified a number of problems with trying to improve student achievement by using extrinsic rewards and sanctions.[92] First, several studies have shown that external rewards may make students less willing to take on challenging tasks. When students expect to be rewarded for some discrete accomplishment, such as reading a certain number of books or earning straight A's, they typically choose the path of least resistance so as not to jeopardize their chances of receiving the reward. Second, if students are encouraged to engage in a behavior, such as learning, simply to receive a reward, such as a high school diploma, this may convey the message that learning is not worth doing for its own sake. Emphasizing external incentives for learning may not be an optimal long-term strategy for encouraging students to become life-long learners. Third, worries about punishment and failure can cause excessive anxiety, which may hinder learning.[93] In our study of fourth graders, we found that some students whose report cards were marked "may be retained" because of their low performance on Stanford 9 exams would raise their hands in the middle of lessons and go up to teachers and aides in the middle of activities to ask, often for the third or fourth time that week, "Am I going to pass?" Clearly, for these students, the possibility of failure interfered with the learning process.

Finally, and most relevant to the testing-with-consequences debate, if punishment is inappropriately applied, it can have disastrous consequences for students' future effort and learning. Consider, for example, children who study hard and pay attention in class but fail a test (perhaps because they know little English because they recently immigrated to the United States, or because they often miss important lessons because their parents consistently bring them late to school). If these children are punished (for example, retained) because they did not meet a particular academic standard, they are effectively being punished rather than rewarded for their effort. As the behaviorists would predict, if punishment follows effort, these children will exert less effort the next time around. While teachers' grades typically try to reward effort, even when a child does not perform as well as other children, high-stakes tests are less subjective and thus cannot distinguish poor performance because of low effort from poor performance despite high effort. Any system that punishes students when they have done their best will, in effect, encourage such students to decrease their effort in the future. Policymakers want to avoid this unintended negative consequence, especially among young children. If these children become discouraged and their efforts flag, they will have many years to disrupt not only their own learning, but also that of their classmates.

A second problem with Betts and Costrell's assumption that high-stakes testing will improve student achievement by encouraging students to work harder is that it ignores differences between elementary school-age children and adolescents. While adolescents may be expected to rise to challenges by exerting more effort, younger children usually try their best from the outset. And, although higher standards may push adolescents to direct more time and energy into academic rather than social endeavors, when younger children divert their energy from school-related tasks, they tend to do so for irrational reasons (for example, they are unintentionally distracted by peers or emotional issues). Thus, for younger children, even the strongest incentives may not be enough to improve academic performance, a conclusion that the study by Melissa Roderick and her colleagues seems to support.[94] Roderick and her colleagues found strong incentive effects of the threat of retention for sixth and eighth graders, but little effect for third graders. Although this may just be an anomaly of the data, it may also signal developmental differences in how children of different ages respond to the same incentives.

A third problem with assuming that high-stakes testing will boost students' effort and thus improve their academic achievement is that many factors beyond student effort affect how much math students can do and how well they can read and write. Although a certain level of student effort may be necessary for passing high-stakes assessments, it is unlikely to be sufficient. For students to meet high standards, parents and teachers also have to exert more effort. But, ultimately, effort alone cannot improve students' skills. Suppose policymakers created the ideal package of incentives that encouraged students to pay attention and complete their schoolwork, parents to help with their children's homework, and teachers to spend extra time preparing lessons and helping students. All this effort would probably not raise students' math scores much unless the students also had high-quality textbooks that they could take home, parents who had learned and still remembered some geometry and algebra, and teachers who both knew and could teach math. In other words, imposing consequences on students is unlikely to pay off in higher achievement unless it comes packaged with other standards-based reforms that encourage parents,

teachers, schools, school districts, states, and the federal government to provide both the effort and the resources needed to raise achievement.

Providing sufficient resources for students to meet standards will also help
make standards-based reform fairer for the students it impacts the most. When
schools raise the bar for promotion to the next grade or for high school graduation, the consequences (both positive and negative) will be greater for
disadvantaged children than for advantaged children. Under higher standards,
African American, Latino, and poor children will probably work harder, be
taught more, and thus learn more. Because standards-based reform is targeted
at the bottom of the achievement distribution, it has the potential to reduce the
achievement gap, which would be an important accomplishment.[95] However,
raising standards will also mean that a greater percentage of African American, Latino, and poor children will be retained or denied a high school diploma.

Although Betts and Costrell downplay the negative effects of this relabeling of some students as nongraduates, the persistent salience of race in the
United States may make these sorting effects more negative than the authors
assume. Retained students or the nongraduates will, at least in the short run,
be disproportionately African American and Latino. This pooling of ethni-
cally identifiable students into the category of "failures" will perpetuate the
already prevalent stereotype that non-Asian minorities are intellectually inferior to whites and Asians.

The continuing salience of race may also make the negative incentive
effects of high-stakes testing more egregious for some groups than for others.
For example, if students suspect that tests are culturally biased and thus do
not measure useful and important skills, students may decrease instead of
increase their effort in the face of higher standards. Moreover, Claude M. Steele
and Joshua Aronson have shown in randomized experiments that African
American students tend to underperform relative to whites in settings where
they risk confirming stereotypes about their group.[96] This "stereotype threat"
may not only negatively influence African American students' scores on high-
stakes exams, but it may also interfere with their assessments of their likelihood
of passing high-stakes tests. If African American students routinely underestimate their probability of passing the test, they may become more discouraged
(and possibly drop out earlier) than students from other ethnic groups with
the same level of academic skills.

These race-related, negative effects should not discourage policymakers
and educators from raising academic standards for all students. They should,
however, highlight the importance of making standards-based reform fair.[97]

This can be done by developing a general consensus about the skills and knowledge that high-stakes tests should measure and by making prototypical test items available for public scrutiny. Giving students a number of opportunities to take and retake high-stakes tests will also improve fairness. And because grades are better measures of students' effort and enthusiasm than tests are, consequential decisions should incorporate both tests and teachers' evaluations.[98]

Perhaps most important, standards-based reforms can improve fairness by ensuring that disadvantaged students have sufficient access to high-quality extra instruction (in summers, in pullout programs, and after school) so that they can boost their test performance. Parents also need accurate information about how they can help prevent their child's failure. In one community we have been studying, when affluent parents learn that their child may be retained, they pull out all the stops. They buy educational computer software and hire private tutors at fifty dollars per session to teach the child how to take a test apart, avoid the "tricks," and navigate the easiest parts of the test to gain confidence.

But the lower class children are relegated to district-run Saturday school where teachers who were never trained in test preparation ineffectively coach the students for the high-stakes test. Not only do the teachers repeatedly drill the children with tests that are too difficult for them (making the actual test seem only more daunting) but the children are also taught poor test-taking strategies. In one instance, a teacher explained to the children that the best way to find the "main idea" in a reading comprehension passage is to look at the first sentence. She then required the children to repeat this technique over and over again. While this technique generally works on the fourth-grade tests, a quick glance at fifth grade (and higher) tests shows that passages often start with an anecdote and the first sentence quickly becomes the standardized test's favorite "trick" answer. Thus, even though these lower-class children commit to spending their Saturdays in a classroom, they leave feeling more discouraged, with their heads drilled full of incorrect techniques.

While disadvantaged children are the most likely to fail under higher standards, Betts and Costrell note that most of the emerging opposition to standards-based reform comes from affluent communities. Highly educated and affluent parents (and, in fact, any parent of a high-achieving child) should worry that teaching to a test that is targeted at the bottom of the achievement distribution will short-change their high-achieving child. This is a big concern in heterogeneous classrooms (such as most elementary classrooms) because high-stakes tests give teachers incentives (and often a moral imperative) to focus time and effort on lower-achieving students. In the fourth-grade class-room that we have been studying, the teacher devoted almost a month to preparing her students for a performance assessment of the concepts of area and perimeter. The high-achieving students learned the new skills eagerly but mastered them within the first couple of lessons. They then spent the next four weeks repeating the skill over and over again while the rest of the class caught on. That same year, these children found themselves stuck with a science cur-riculum that never covered anything but volcanoes, largely because so much class time was devoted to test preparation. Even in districts where high-achiev-ing and low-achieving students attend different schools, high-achieving students may still be shortchanged if administrators are forced to take resources away from high-performing schools to help low-performing schools meet the new standards.

Although we support the general principles of raising academic standards and creating a high school diploma that "means something," we are less opti-mistic than Betts and Costrell about the positive consequences of standards-based reform. Assuming that children and teens will respond strongly to the positive incentives of higher standards glosses over motivational dif-ferences among children and teens who are moving through a range of developmental stages and come from a variety of ethnic and social class back-grounds, home and community support structures, and past experiences with academic success and failure. Further, placing the burden of meeting high-stakes standards on these students, without providing generous institutional support, will doom too many of them to failure. Finally, dismissing middle-class parents' concerns as purely self-serving seems shortsighted. To maximize every child's academic potential and maintain sufficient political support for standards-based reform, policymakers should avoid reforms that impede the academic progress of bright students from any background. In the end, stan-dards-based reform cannot be a quick fix to the problem of low academic performance. But if policymakers consider all these complexities, it may turn out to be a step in the right direction.

## Notes

1. See Public Agenda polls in recent years.
2. Mass Insight Education poll, November 1999.
3. See Sandra Stotsky, ed., *What's at Stake in the K-12 Standards Wars: A Primer for Edu-cational Policy-Makers* (New York: Peter Lang Publishers, 2000). Authors such as Stephen

Arons have argued that such battles over content are a permanent feature of the public (or common) school system and can only be fully resolved by a thoroughgoing system of school choice and vouchers. Stephen Arons, *Short Road to Chaos* (Amherst: University of Massachusetts Press, 1997).

However, with or without vouchers, the demand for educational accountability in the use of public funds seems likely to rise, particularly in states where the share of funding is shifting from the localities toward the state. The specification of content standards and measurable outcomes is central to these accountability efforts.

4. Robert M. Costrell, "A Simple Model of Educational Standards," *American Economic Review,* vol. 84, no. 4 (1994), pp. 956–71; and Julian R. Betts, "The Impact of Educational Standards on the Level and Distribution of Earnings," *American Economic Review,* vol. 88, no. 1 (1998), pp. 266–75. These papers, and others cited below, provide the formal models underlying the summaries given in the text.

5. A century ago, when a high school diploma was held by a small minority of the population, far less stigma was attached, economically or otherwise, to being a nongraduate. Similarly, under the traditional British system that prevailed until recently, many students left school at age sixteen. Far more students left school at this age than occurs in the United States, and the stigma was presumably much less, because their numbers included more capable workers.

6. Under this model, they should favor standards that are so high that everyone fails, so that the lowest achievers are pooled with the very best. This may seem indistinguishable from the opposite extreme, where the standard is set so low that everyone passes and is similarly pooled together. However, unless the results are perfect, with a 100 percent pass rate, the strategy of a very low standard will lead to the least egalitarian outcome, by the Rawlsian standard, because the rare failure is most highly stigmatized. In short, the wage of failers rises monotonically with the standard in this simple model. See Betts, "The Impact of Educational Standards on the Level and Distribution of Earnings."

Robert M. Costrell relaxes a key technological assumption of this model—that the productivity of any individual is independent of other individuals (perfect substitutability, to use the technical term from economics).Suppose, instead, workers operate in teams, providing complementary services in the production of output, as in the job assignment model of Robert M. Costrell and Glenn C. Loury. Then it can be shown that another effect of raising standards works in the opposite direction from the pooling effect. High standards reduce the number of workers supported by those of lesser skill, which tends to reduce the wage of failers. Taken together with the pooling effect, raising standards need not have a monotonic effect on the wage of failers. Costrell finds that, in a benchmark case, the relationship between the wage of failers and the standard is U-shaped, and, moreover, the standard that minimizes the failers' wage maximizes output. Costrell also analyzes the effect on this relationship of varying technology, cost of acquiring skill, and test accuracy. An important finding, however, is that those cases in which a rise in the standard reduces the wage of failers are also the cases in which equity is most likely advanced by moving away from pass-fail systems altogether, toward fuller information.Robert M. Costrell, "Are High Standards Good or Bad for Those Who Fail?" University of Massachusetts at Amherst, Department of Economics, 1999; and Robert M. Costrell and Glenn C. Loury, "Distribution of Ability and Earnings in a Job Assignment Model," University of Massachusetts at Amherst and Boston University, 2000.

7. See Costrell, "A Simple Model of Educational Standards," and other literature cited there.

8. In addition, schools facing the prospect of higher failure rates would also respond with interventions to assist at-risk students.

9. It is an empirical matter of some importance how much less the rise would be, whether it would be closer to the full ten-point rise or closer to zero.

10. See Robert M. Costrell, "An Economic Analysis of College Admission Standards," *Education Economics*, vol. 1, no. 3 (1993), pp. 227–41, for a formal analysis of the effect of standards in the context of college attendance, where students are uncertain how difficult college will be until they get there. A rise in admission standards forces applicants to be better prepared and can raise the resulting number of graduates, even though the number of attendees declines.

11. The analysis here excludes consideration of possible externalities created by peer effects. If there are adverse peer effects generated by some of those who are unwilling or unable to exert extra effort to pass, and if the potential benefit for some of staying in school is low, then the optimal dropout rate may not be zero. Disruptive students provide an obvious example that is unfortunately not as rare as one might hope. The best solution in such cases is not necessarily to encourage dropouts, but to create alternative educational settings for such students, such as those under creation by systems in Boston and Chicago, as long advocated by the American Federation of Teachers, among others.

12. Evidence consistent with the bifurcation in this part of the distribution is found in the contribution to this volume by John H. Bishop, Ferran Mane, Michael Bishop, and Joan Moriarty. They find that among C/C- students, minimum competency exams raise both the number of noncompleters and the number of college attendees.

13. Although the general points discussed here and depicted in figure 1 derive from the theoretical literature cited, figure 1's continuous distribution is not strictly consistent with that literature's simplest theoretical models. Those models generate distributions with discrete segments and a discontinuity in the vicinity of the standard.

14. Anjetta McQueen, "Lawmakers Seek to Limit Standard Tests," *Boston Globe*, April 5, 2000, p. A16.

15. Andreae Downs, "Parents, Educators Debate MCAS," *Boston Globe*, February 13, 2000, City Weekly, p. 5.

16. It seems more likely that there could be some redistributive effect on learning in the lower grades, where heterogeneous grouping prevails.

17. J. E. Jacobsen, in "Mandatory Testing Requirements and Pupil Achievement," mimeo, Massachusetts Institute of Technology, 1992, found some evidence of this as a result of state minimum competency tests in the late 1970s and early 1980s. For classroom-based evidence that teachers devote more attention to the lowest achieving students in class, see B. W. Brown and D. H. Saks, "The Microeconomics of the Allocation of Teachers' Time and Student Learning," *Economics of Education Review*, vol. 6 (1987), pp. 319–32; and Julian R. Betts and Jamie L. Shkolnik, "The Behavioral Effects of Variations in Class Size: The Case of Math Teachers," *Educational Evaluation and Policy Analysis*, vol. 20, no. 2 (Summer 1999), pp. 193–213, who show that reductions in class size lead teachers to spend more time on review and individual instruction, ostensibly directed toward the lowest achieving students.

18. This does not prevent some of the critics in these communities (both parents and educators) from couching their objections in egalitarian terms, as the defenders of those children in less-advantaged areas whose parents have chosen not to object.

19. For a contemporary account of the national standard-setting movement, see Diane Ravitch, *National Standards in American Education: A Citizen's Guide* (Brookings, 1995), chapters 2 and 5; and for more of a retrospective, see Robert B. Schwartz and Marian A. Robinson, "Goals 2000 and the Standards Movement," *Brookings Papers on Education Policy 2000* (Brookings, 2000), pp. 173–206.

20. See Costrell, "A Simple Model of Educational Standards," section IV.

21. John Bishop has provided evidence in a number of papers over the years that is consistent with this behavior of employers. See, for instance, John Bishop, "Incentives for Learning: Why American High School Students Compare So Poorly to Their Counterparts Overseas," *Research in Labor Economics*, vol. 11 (1990), pp. 17–52.

22. The extent of this problem is inversely related to the strength of local reputation, which in turn depends on the size of the entities in question.

23. This assumes that no systematic difference exists between local and central authorities regarding the weights attached to winners and losers (that is, they hold the same social welfare function).

24. With cross-district heterogeneity, it can be the case that egalitarian societies—those that assign greatest weight to preventing dropouts—should prefer centralization even more than nonegalitarians. The problem of free-riding under decentralization is more pronounced for egalitarians because they tend to cut standards further below the optimal level. That is, egalitarians may like low standards in their own district, but they face particularly high losses from the free-riding of their fellow egalitarians in other districts choosing particularly low standards. Both egalitarians and nonegalitarians favor centralization if all districts are alike, but under cross-district heterogeneity, egalitarians may favor centralization in some cases that nonegalitarians do not.

25. Robert M. Costrell, "Can Centralized Educational Standards Raise Welfare?" *Journal of Public Economics,* vol. 65 (September 1997), pp. 271–93.

26. Different patterns can emerge, depending on the degree of pooling. But the general point remains: There are winners and losers in any system of standard-setting, compared with any alternative.

27. It is not even certain that a centralized standard-setter would choose a higher standard than any of the localities. If the optimal central standard is tailored to the weakest districts (as it will be under some circumstances), then the central standard could end up even lower than those weak districts would choose on their own. The reason is that under decentralization, the stronger districts would choose high standards, raising the wage of non-college-bound graduates everywhere, including those in the weaker districts, to the extent they are pooled together. This would enhance the incentive for students in the weaker districts to graduate, which, in turn, allows those districts to set higher standards than otherwise without deterring too many students from graduating. In this way, it is possible that under cross-district heterogeneity central standards could be lower than under decentralization. Even if standards rise for some or all districts under centralization, the constraint that all districts face the same standard may still lead to lower social welfare than under decentralization.

28. This is the law in Massachusetts: No district will be able to award a diploma to students who fail the Massachusetts Comprehensive Assessment System (MCAS), but districts can impose additional graduation requirements, including a higher MCAS score.

29. Costrell and Loury, "Distribution of Ability and Earnings in a Job Assignment Model," applied to the issue of standards by Costrell, "Are High Standards Good or Bad for Those Who Fail?"

30. For a formal analysis, see Costrell, "A Simple Model of Educational Standards," section VI.

31. John D. Owen, *Why Our Kids Don't Study: An Economist's Perspective* (Johns Hopkins University Press, 1995).

32. See James Heckman, "Doing It Right: Job Training and Education," *Public Interest,* vol. 135 (Spring 1999), pp. 86–107.

33. A considerable econometric literature exists on this point, beginning with Stephen V. Cameron and James J. Heckman, "The Nonequivalence of High School Equivalents," *Journal of Labor Economics,* vol. 11, no. 1 (1993), pp. 1–47.

34. Economists have documented that they have a generally high rate of time preference.

35. Department of Education, *Digest of Education Statistics 1996* (National Center for Education Statistics, 1996); and Department of Education, *Digest of Education Statistics 1998* (National Center for Education Statistics, 1999).

36. For Massachusetts, this will change dramatically, beginning with the class of 2003.

37. The American Federation of Teachers (AFT) has published an annual review of the educational standards in each state, Puerto Rico, and the District of Columbia. These publications provide a succinct overview of progress, and because the AFT gives each state an opportunity to respond to the annual synopses, the synopses gain credibility. The summary draws heavily from these AFT analyses. Data for 1999 and 1996, respectively, are from American Federation of Teachers, *Making Standards Matter 1999* (Washington, 1999), and American Federation of Teachers, *Making Standards Matter 1996* (Washington, 1996).

38. Massachusetts meets the criteria for clear standards and aligned assessments, but its exit exams for the class of 2003, which were established by law in 1993, were not formally voted upon by the Board of Education until the fall of 1999 (and only for math and English), too late for inclusion in the AFT tables.

39. Our sources for the math, reading, and population data are, respectively, Clyde M. Reese and others, *NAEP 1996 Mathematics Report Card for the Nation and the States: Findings from the National Assessment of Educational Progress* (National Center for Education Statistics, 1997); Jay R. Campbell and others, *NAEP 1994 Reading Report Card for the Nation and the States: Findings from the National Assessment of Educational Progress and Trial State Assessment* (National Center for Education Statistics, 1996); and *State Population Estimates: Annual Time Series, July 1, 1980 to July 1, 1999,* ST-99-3(Bureau of the Census, 1999).

40. These three variables were obtained from Bureau of the Census, *Statistical Abstract of the United States: 1998* (Government Printing Office, 1998), pp. 34, 169, 479.

41. Dean R. Lillard and Philip P. DeCicca, "Higher Standards, More Dropouts? Evidence within and across Time," *Economics of Education Review* (forthcoming).

42. Harris Cooper, *Homework* (New York: Longman, 1989).

43. See Timothy Z. Keith and others, "Parental Involvement, Homework, and TV Time: Direct and Indirect Effects on High School Achievement." *Journal of Educational Psychology*, vol. 78 (October 1986), pp. 373–80; and Herbert J. Walberg, Barry J. Fraser, and Wayne W. Welch, "A Test of a Model of Educational Productivity among Senior High School Students," *Journal of Educational Research*, vol. 79 (January/February 1986), pp. 133–39.

44. Julian R. Betts, "The Role of Homework in Improving School Quality," University of California, San Diego, Department of Economics, 1997.

45. Julian R. Betts, "Do Grading Standards Affect the Incentive to Learn?" University of California, San Diego, Department of Economics, 1997.

46. C. Thomas Holmes, "Grade Level Retention Effects: A Meta-Analysis of Research Studies," in Lorrie A. Shepard and Mary Lee Smith, eds., *Flunking Grades: Research and Policies on Retention* (London: The Falmer Press, 1989), pp. 16–33.

47. For a review of national trends toward increased use of summer school, see Catherine Gewertz, "More Districts Add Summer Coursework," *Education Week*, June 7, 2000. The analysis in this paragraph is based on Julian R. Betts, "The Two-Legged Stool: The Neglected Role of Educational Standards in Improving America's Public Schools," *Economic Policy Review*, vol. 4 (1998), pp. 97–116.

48. Melissa Roderick and others, *Ending Social Promotion: Results from the First Two Years* (Chicago, Ill.: Consortium on Chicago School Research, 1999).

49. We do not know what is happening among the individuals within any grade equivalent (G.E.) category. There may be individuals in the lower G.E. categories whose effort is at the same low level that it would have been without the standards, among those who still fail to pass the test after summer school. However, we are struck by the fact that the strongest average response is in the lowest G.E. category.

50. The other important piece of background, aside from the court case, was a large drop in state aid that occurred in Massachusetts's deep recession of 1989–92, which followed the

unsustainably rapid growth in spending in the latter part of the 1980s.During that recession the income tax rate was temporarily raised to balance the budget, but it remained high after the recession ended and has not yet been returned to its 1989 rate.

51. Compared with the prerecession figure, real state aid grew by about one-half.

52. Calculations by the Executive Office for Administration and Finance.

53. Thomas J. Kane, "An Update on School Reform in Massachusetts," John F. Kennedy School of Government, Harvard University, 2000. Compared with the prerecession year of 1989, the corresponding rise by 1998 was $513 at the tenth percentile and $165 at the ninetieth.

54. See Robert M. Costrell, "Discipline-Based Economics Standards: Opportunity and Obstacles," in Sandra Stotsky, ed., *What's at Stake in the K-12 Standards Wars: A Primer for Educational Policy-Makers* (New York: Peter Lang Publishers, 2000), pp. 169–209, for an account of the tortuous development of the economics strand in the history and social sciences framework.

55. John Silber, who was chairman of the Massachusetts Board of Education until early 1999, was a vociferous opponent of this weakening of the standard. Exams in the Needs Improvement category were judged by standard-setting panels to meet the description that "Students at this level demonstrate a partial understanding of subject matter, and solve some simple problems." Neil M. Kingston, "The Body of Work (BoW) Standard Setting Method: Massachusetts Comprehensive Assessment System," presented at the annual meeting of the National Council on Measurement in Education, New Orleans, La., 2000. For the tenth-grade math exam, this required twenty-four out of sixty possible points.

56. See Massachusetts Department of Education, "1999 MCAS Sample Student Work and Scoring Guides" (www.doe.mass.edu/mcas/student/1999 [October 10, 2000]).

57. Students also take a few matrix-sampled questions each year, which do not count toward their scores, but from which future core questions are drawn. That means that each year core questions have been seen by a few students the previous year but have not been made public. The English language arts essay questions, however, are not matrix-sampled the previous year.

58. Less than 4 percent left this question blank.

59. *Up and Over the Bar* (Mass Insight Education, April 2000). The factors isolated in this study are not mutually exclusive, so percentages sum to more than one hundred.

60. Twenty-five of twenty-eight superintendents interviewed for the Mass Insight Education study report that "motivation on the test" was one of the primary factors.Many of them report a significant difference in attitude toward the test between current tenth graders, for whom it does not count, and those in ninth grade, for whom it will.

61. In Indiana, 54 percent of tenth graders passed the math and English exit exams on the first try that counted, in fall of 1997, but by time that class was to graduate, in 2000, 86 percent had passed both exams. The exam is pitched at a ninth-grade level. Students also have two alternative routes to a diploma. Lynn Olson, "Indiana Out in Front on Giving Students Extra Help," *Education Week*, May 31, 2000.

62. Boston superintendent Thomas Payzant, an advocate for MCAS, uses the MCAS and other exams to identify students most at risk.Over 30 percent of students in grades two through nine (except four) now face mandatory summer school, to avoid grade retention. Ed Hayward, "12,000 Hub Kids Face Summer School," *Boston Herald*, June 7, 2000, p. 1. During the regular school year many of these students will receive doubled instruction in literacy and math, and customized lessons. A *Boston Globe* editorial (April 24, 2000) opined, "This is the kind of urgent remedial attention that many students need and should have been getting for years. They are getting it now because the state Education Reform Act of 1993 is supplying money and MCAS is applying pressure." Payzant observed, "We wouldn't be as far along with our reform efforts if there weren't high stakes along the way."

63. This section draws on Robert M. Costrell and Kenneth Ardon, *MCAS and the Rise of Literacy Skills in the Early Grades, 1998–99*, Massachusetts Executive Office for Administration and Finance, Policy Report Series No. 6, October 2000 (www.state.ma.us/eoaf/PolicyReports/mcas/index.htm).

64. These are Massachusetts percentiles, not U.S. percentiles. Because Massachusetts performs above the national average, at a thinner portion of the U.S. distribution, the shift in U.S. percentiles would be smaller. It should also be noted that the improvement in Iowa Test of Basic Skills (ITBS) scores bypassed the lower third of the Massachusetts distribution. One possible interpretation is that efforts of third-grade teachers to prepare students with skills useful for fourth-grade MCAS paid off only for those third graders who were academically more prepared for the challenge. Another possible factor was a 1999 change in the Massachusetts regulations, which expanded the number of limited-English proficient (LEP) students required to take the test. The ITBS scores considered here are reading total, which is an average of reading comprehension and vocabulary. The rise in reading comprehension was larger than that of vocabulary and reading total.

65. Specifically, we analyze the ITBS school effects for 1997, 1998, and 1999, and the MCAS school effects for 1998 and 1999. The 1998 ITBS school effect is fitted to an equation with the 1997 ITBS school effect. Using that equation to predict the 1999 ITBS school effect, we calculate, school-by-school, how much better the ITBS school effects turned out than predicted. These second-year-effects for ITBS are then added to MCAS 1998 school effects in a regression for MCAS 1999 school effects and found to be highly statistically significant.

66. Not all students are averse to the exams. The Massachusetts Student Advisory Council defends the MCAS. "No one would argue that passing the MCAS is all education is about," said the student representative to the Massachusetts Board of Education. "But the idea of sending someone out without ascertaining that they can write a coherent paragraph or do algebra or geometry is unthinkable." Jules Crittenden, " Some Students Call MCAS Boycott Counterproductive," *Boston Herald*, April 14, 2000.

67. Millicent Lawton, "The Acid Test," *Commonwealth Magazine*, Spring 2000, p. 46. Cambridge spends about $12,000 per pupil, among the highest in the state, but nonetheless scores below the state average on MCAS.

68. Stephen E. Gorrie, "Just Raising the Bar Won't Help Kids Jump Over It," *MTA Today*, June 2000, p. 4.

69. The ads feature students cheering their Scholastic Assessment Test (SAT) scores, which have risen of late in Massachusetts. The Massachusetts Teachers Association (MTA) had not previously been known to advocate for the SAT, but its spokesman now says, "The SAT scores are one of the most reliable indicators in the public's mind about how the schools are doing. On the MCAS, the jury is still out." Steve Leblanc, "Teachers Union Touts SAT Scores in Television Ads," Associated Press, April 18, 2000. More recently, a $600,000 MTA ad campaign against MCAS portrayed students suffering from anxiety during that exam.

70. Lawton, "The Acid Test," p. 46. See also Ed Hayward, "Urban Parents Support MCAS Tests," *Boston Herald*, April 16, 2000.

71. *Up and Over the Bar*, pp. 14–15.

72. Anand Vaishnav, "Coalition Targets Teacher Seniority," *Boston Globe*, May 2, 2000; see also Anand Vaishnav, "Seniority at Issue in Boston Teacher Contract Talks," *Boston Globe*, May 3, 2000, p. B2, which specifically mentions MCAS in this regard.

73. Betts, "The Two-Legged Stool."

74. A comparable percentage of Boston students in grades two through nine is now being held back, contingent on successful summer school remediation.

75. See, for instance, Anemona Hartocollis, "The New, Flexible Math Meets Parental Rebellion," *New York Times*, April 27, 2000, p. A1. There was also a heated dispute in Massachusetts over these issues.

76. See Tanya Schevitz, "State Panel Drafts Set of Tough Educational Standards," *San Francisco Chronicle*, April 3, 1998.

77. Koretz, Daniel, "Using Student Assessments for Educational Accountability," in Eric A. Hanushek and Dale W. Jorgenson, eds., *Improving America's Schools: The Role of Incentives* (Washington: National Academy Press, 1996).

78. Koretz, "Using Student Assessments for Educational Accountability."

79. For a summary of this program, see Julian R. Betts, Kim Rueben, and Anne Danenberg, *Equal Resources, Equal Outcomes? The Distribution of School Resources and Student Achievement in California* (San Francisco: Public Policy Institute of California, 2000), chapter 1.

80. Richard J. Murnane and others, *Who Will Teach? Policies That Matter* (Harvard University Press, 1991).

81. See "Pay-for-Performance: An Issue Brief for Business Leaders," The Business Roundtable, 2000.

82. See chapter 5 of Ravitch, *National Standards in American Education*, for a summary and critique of this movement.

83. But see Caroline Minter Hoxby, "Are Efficiency and Equity in School Finance Substitutes or Complements?" *Journal of Economic Perspectives*, vol. 10, no. 4 (Fall 1996), pp. 51–72, for an analysis of the pitfalls in moving too far toward state finance of local education, as a result of equalization suits.

84. See Eric A. Hanushek, "School Resources and Student Performance," in Gary Burtless, ed., *Does Money Matter? The Effect of School Resources on Student Achievement and Adult Success* (Brookings, 1996); and Gary Burtless, "Introduction and Summary," in Gary Burtless, ed., *Does Money Matter? The Effect of School Resources on Student Achievement and Adult Success* (Brookings, 1996).

85. See Julian R. Betts, "Does School Quality Matter? Evidence from the National Longitudinal Survey of Youth," *Review of Economics and Statistics*, vol. 77 (1995), pp. 231–50; and for a review of the literature, see Julian R. Betts, "Is There a Link between School Inputs and Earnings? Fresh Scrutiny of an Old Literature," in Gary Burtless, ed., *Does Money Matter? The Effect of School Resources on Student Achievement and Adult Success* (Brookings, 1996).

86. Betts, Rueben, and Danenberg, *Equal Resources, Equal Outcomes?*

87. See the descriptions of the education systems of more than one hundred countries in Torsten Husen and T. Neville Postlethwaite, eds., *The International Encyclopedia of Education* (Oxford, England: Pergamon Press, 1994).

88. See, for example, Organization for Economic Cooperation and Development, *Education at a Glance* (Paris, France, 1998), pp. 172–173, 315.

89. Jean Johnson and Steve Farkas, *Getting By: What American Teenagers Really Think About Their Schools* (New York: Public Agenda, 1997).

90. Steve Farkas and Jean Johnson, *Different Drummers: How Teachers of Teachers View Public Education* (New York: Public Agenda, 1997).

91. Meredith Phillips, "What Makes Schools Effective? A Comparison of the Relationships of Communitarian Climate and Academic Climate to Mathematics Achievement and Attendance during Middle School," *American Educational Research Journal*, vol. 34 (1997), pp. 633–62.

92. The following discussion is drawn from Deborah J. Stipek, *Motivation to Learn: From Theory to Practice*, 2d ed.(Boston: Allyn and Bacon, 1993).

93. Tiffani Chin, "Sixth-Grade Madness: Parental Emotion Work in the Private High School Application Process," *Journal of Contemporary Ethnography,* vol. 29 (2000), pp. 124–63.

94. Melissa Roderick and others, *Ending Social Promotion: Results from the First Two Years* (Chicago, Ill.: Consortium on Chicago School Research, 1999).

95. Christopher Jencks and Meredith Phillips, "The Black-White Test Score Gap: An Introduction," in Christopher Jencks and Meredith Phillips, eds., *The Black-White Test Score Gap* (Brookings, 1998), pp. 1–51.

96. Claude M. Steele and Joshua Aronson, "Stereotype Threat and the Test Performance of Academically Successful African Americans," in Christopher Jencks and Meredith Phillips, eds., *The Black-White Test Score Gap* (Brookings, 1998), pp. 401–27.

97. Jay P. Heubert and Robert M. Hauser, *High Stakes: Testing for Tracking, Promotion, and Graduation* (Washington: National Academy Press, 1999).

98. Meredith Phillips, "Grades vs. Standardized Tests: Which Is a Better Measure of Student Achievement?" paper presented at the annual meeting of the American Sociological Association, Washington, 2000.

# Why Business Backs Education Standards

MILTON GOLDBERG *and*
SUSAN L. TRAIMAN

B usiness cares about education standards because the well-being of their companies and every American is at stake. In the international marketplace, says former Lockheed-Martin chief executive officer (CEO) Norman Augustine, the United States is involved in a "battle of the classrooms." As a result, business leaders believe that standards are a sine qua non for addressing education problems and moving ahead.

If the United States is to compete effectively in the demanding international economy, and if each person is to contribute to and benefit from the nation's economic success, the most potent weapons in its competitive arsenal are skill and intelligence. The country cannot rely on history or good luck to provide these tools to the work force. They must be developed, nourished, and honed by the education system. Students need to know what the modern world expects them to know and be able to do, in clear, unequivocal statements. The nation's schools must use standards to enhance learning.

Standards express a clear mission for schools or unmask schools that are ineffective. They shape curriculum. They challenge students to achieve and teachers to perform at their best. They guide assessment. Accountability and professional development for teachers also depend on clear standards for authentic assessment and excellence in teaching. Standards are compass and rudder, pole star and map, for schools.

Higher standards are a necessity, lest low ones become self-fulfilling prophecies—prescriptions for personal failure, not only in the classroom but also in life. The standards movement allows the ultimate equity issue to be addressed; that is, aiming for the best for every student regardless of race or economic status. Standards mean that students grow as they learn; without them, they learn to settle. If U.S. companies are to succeed in the global marketplace and individuals are to become self-supporting contributing citizens, American students must be expected—not simply cheered on—to master difficult material in core academic subjects. That, after all, is what is routinely expected of students in the classrooms of America's fiercest competitor nations. A high school diploma or college degree must bear testimony to a high level of achievement, not just to having filled required hours of seat time.

Today's business leaders expect that a person looking for a skilled job has mastered basic and advanced knowledge and skills in the arts and sciences, the processes of oral and written communication, and the use of computers and electronic databases. Most important, this person should know how to learn. New hires should also bring to the job the competencies outlined in the Secretary's Commission on Achieving Necessary Skills (SCANS) requirements (see box opposite). If this basic repertoire is not mastered in schools, business leaders reasonably believe that "people who lack such skills will be isolated—at risk, socially, politically, and economically—posing dire consequences for the nation as well as the individual."[1]

## The New Economy

In *The Lexus and the Olive Tree*, journalist Thomas L. Friedman tells a story about Secretary of the Treasury Lawrence H. Summers that shows how the twin forces of globalization and communications technology have combined to change daily life.

In 1988, while working in Chicago on the presidential campaign of Democrat Michael S. Dukakis, Summers reports that he was temporarily assigned to a car equipped with a telephone. Summers thought this was "sufficiently neat" to call his wife, solely for the purpose of telling her he was riding in a car that had a phone in it. In 1997 Summers was on Treasury Department business in the Ivory Coast, visiting a village accessible only by canoe. Just as he was stepping into the canoe to make the trip back to the capital, a government official in his party handed him a cell phone and said, "Washington has a question for you." In less than a decade he had gone from thinking it was "neat" to have a phone in his car in Chicago to total equanimity about talking to his office from a phone-equipped canoe a few miles upstream from Abidjan.[2]

The two most powerful forces redrawing the map of business today are globalization and technology. The two together have created demand for a

---

### Secretary's Commission on Achieving Necessary Skills Requirements

*Five Competencies*

—The ability to identify, plan, and allocate such *resources* as time, money, materials, facilities, and human resources;

—The ability to *work with others* as a team member, teacher, leader, negotiator; to negotiate agreements; to work with others from diverse backgrounds;

—The ability to acquire, evaluate, organize, maintain, interpret, and use *information*, and to use computers to process information;

—The ability to understand, monitor and correct, and improve *systems* and other complex inter-relationships; and

—The ability to select, apply, and maintain a variety of *technologies*.

*The Three-Part Foundation*

—*Basic skills*, such as reading, performing arithmetic and mathematical operations, listening, and speaking;

—*Thinking skills*, such as thinking creatively, making decisions, solving problems, visualizing, reasoning, and knowing how to learn; and

—*Personal qualities*, such as taking responsibility, self-esteem, sociability, self-management, and integrity/honesty.

Source: *What Work Requires of Schools: A SCANS Report for America 2000*, Report of the Secretary's Commission on Achieving Necessary Skills (Department of Labor, 1991), p. xv.

---

new kind of worker, one whose personal well-being and ability to participate in the new economy are rooted in quality education.

GLOBALIZATION. Loosely defined, *globalization* means the relentless, worldwide expansion and integration of commerce and finance, the growing scale—and importance—of exchanges of people, products, services, capital, and ideas across international borders. When most Americans hear the word *globalization*, they tend to visualize logos of multinational corporations such as AT&T,

General Electric, General Motors, IBM, Disney, Microsoft as well as the ubiquitous Coca-Cola and McDonald's. Today, all thirty corporations that make
up the Dow-Jones Industrial Average do business on a worldwide scale, with
globally scattered capabilities in research and development, manufacturing,
marketing, sales, and distribution, not to mention wholly owned subsidiaries
and in-country partners. It is not just these large familiar companies that have
global reach. For example, ten-year-old PSI Net in Herndon, Virginia, is now
a major Internet player in the twenty largest telecommunications markets
worldwide.

Globalization, however, is not primarily a phenomenon of overseas American economic expansion. Globalization is now deeply embedded in the world
economy. One index of the change is that the U.S. worldwide share of production for both goods and services has been cut in half since the end of World
War II (from 40 percent to 21 percent), while the share of worldwide gross
domestic product (GDP) accounted for by trade has quadrupled since the late
1950s (from 7 percent to nearly 30 percent).[3] The globalization of finance,
capital, technology, and labor means that a product can be designed in one
country, manufactured in an another, and distributed anywhere in the world
within twenty-four hours or sooner. More than 70 percent of American manufactured products have competitors abroad.[4] Today, everyone has a market
stall in the global souk.

How central are global companies to the U.S. economy as a whole? Imports
and exports of goods and services are the two components of U.S. GDP that
have gained most in importance in the past two decades, with exports growing at a 7.8 percent annual rate between 1988 and 1998.[5] According to one
recent study, the parent companies of U.S. multinationals had a GDP of $1.5
trillion in 1997, making up a little over a quarter of the private U.S. economy
(excluding banks) in that year. Adding in the output of foreign-affiliated firms,
the total exceeded $2.0 trillion.[6] The wave of internationalization in U.S. busi-
nesses peaked around 1980. By then, strong industrial and technological
growth in other countries (for example, Germany, Italy, Japan, and Sweden)
had leveled the U.S. share of international markets, so that it is today about
what it was in 1977.[7] The moral of the tale is a simple one: The world economy is now knit together as a relatively stable, integrated, organic whole. As
free-market democracy further transforms societies, governments, and
economies, the world is increasingly one.

TECHNOLOGY. Since the invention of the plow, which kicked off the agrar-
ian revolution about ten thousand years ago, technology has been a primary

driver of change, whether social, cultural, or economic. Technological innovation alters the nature of work itself. In the 1970s, a popular scientific magazine published the first plans for an unusual hobbyist's project—a personal computer. Over the past quarter century, operating according to Moore's Law, the computing power of microchips doubles every eighteen months, while costs decline by 25 percent per year.[8] Nor is the end in sight. Noted computer scientist Raymond Kurzweil has predicted that, by 2019, a $1,000 computer will be able to perform 20 million billion calculations per second and will be equivalent in sophistication to the human brain.[9]

The rate of change in the new economy escalates as the life cycles of products and services are compressed. The result is that competitive advantage becomes more deeply rooted in agility and a commitment to continuous improvement. Success in the United States is now measured against international standards, as knowledge and skills become the core resources of every economy worldwide. In the process, *work* has been redefined.

From ancient times until well into the 1970s, *work* basically meant the process of producing goods from raw materials and providing skills and services for those who needed them; new ideas, tools, efficiencies, and economies of scale all induced change. While that basic definition of *work* still holds, the application of information-based technologies to every form of enterprise, combined with the ability to assemble and transmit information to any point on the globe, has created a new way of thinking. For all practical purposes, *work* has been redefined as the process of recasting the world, and much of what people want to do in it, in the form of information and know-how.

The transformation of work has spawned the need for a new kind of worker: intellectually supple, multiskilled, multidimensional, flexible. In the process, businesses the world over have created, as Peter Drucker argues, a new form of wealth besides the classical forms of land, labor, and capital—knowledge itself. In 1979 the Bureau of Labor Statistics reported that the largest occupational category in America was, for the first time, "clerk"; that is, people in jobs in which the work revolved largely around generating and redirecting information, increasingly on desktop computers. As information and the technologies derived from it have expanded at warp speed, businesses find more and more that what creates value and spawns change is the ability to add knowledge to work. The need for knowledge and knowledge-manipulating skills is so great that companies are now adding CKOs—chief knowledge officers—to the upper echelons of their corporate staffs, paying them premium salaries to help companies maintain a competitive edge.

The convergence of these two forces—globalization and technology—has generated a need for a new kind of worker and has created a demand for new ways to prepare workers for productive lives. The cutting-edge worker in the Information Age economy is now the "knowledge worker" (the term is Drucker's), a continuous and highly adaptable learner who possesses a wide range of skills and abilities, for example, the ability to pose problems and solve problems, the ability to think both analytically and synthetically, the ability to work collaboratively, and the ability to convert observations into judgments and decisions.

CHANGING SKILLS, KNOWLEDGE, AND EDUCATIONAL REQUIREMENTS. The economies of the United States and its global rivals have recast the configuration of skill, knowledge, and educational demands to which today's workers must respond. Knowledge and skill needs are changing and escalating so rapidly that the demand for educated workers now exceeds the supply. Knowledge consumers (employers) and knowledge suppliers (educators and trainers) increasingly are working together to coordinate the effort to keep the work force vital. By managing the knowledge supply chain (that is, K-12 schools, postsecondary institutions, and both traditional and alternative providers of education and training), employers, educators, and trainers are aligning work-force preparation to a market-based, competency-driven system.

A telling example of the changes in the skills package required of new hires in America's global, technology-driven economy comes from the machine tool industry. Operators of lathes and drilling machines used to be considered blue-collar workers. They had to know how to operate machinery and to read gauges and other measuring devices. They had to possess a high degree of manual dexterity, acquired over long apprenticeships. Most likely, they came out of a local vocational-technical high school's machine shop course. But today's preprogrammed CNC (computer numerically controlled) machine tools have almost entirely replaced the industry's need for manual dexterity with a need for strong computer skills—often including programming. Not uncommonly, a basic knowledge of calculus is a job requirement as well. Today's machinists often have at least an associate's degree from a local community college; many are graduates of four-year colleges or technical institutes. In addition, many firms expect their master machinists and floor supervisors to exercise considerable discretion over production processes, making decisions that show up on the company's income statement.[10]

The change in the kind of workers businesses need arises from anticipated changes in various sectors of the economy. For the 1996–2006 period, for example, the Bureau of Labor Statistics has projected that the need for workers in the professions will increase by 26.4 percent; the need for technicians and related support personnel will increase by 20.4 percent; the need for administrators, executives, and managers will increase by 17.2 percent. By contrast, the nation will need only 6.9 percent more workers in precision production and repairs; 7.5 percent more operators, fabricators, and repair workers; and 1 percent more workers in farming, forestry, and fishing altogether.[11] The information technology industry, which did not exist a generation ago and now employs 10 million workers, is contributing heavily to the change in the American job mix. The Information Technology Association of America estimates that information technology companies will create roughly 1.6 million jobs in 2000, at least half of which will go begging for want of enough skilled people.[12]

In this changing business climate, the high school diploma is no longer a passport to a good job. Companies are demanding better educated workers to meet more stringent competitive demands. The escalation of business's expectations begins with various degrees of literacy. (*Literacy* here refers not merely to the ability to read and write but also to the ability to process written information at various levels of skill, from extracting basic information from a news article to being able to convert a data table into a graph.) In assessing the expected changes in five task-defined levels of literacy that arise from the changing distribution of jobs in the information economy, researchers at Educational Testing Service found that the highest increases in literacy levels correlated with the twenty-five fastest growing occupational categories. In other words, the more likely you are to be in a growing job category, the more likely that job is to be demanding in terms of verbal skills. In these fastest growing quarters of job categories, researchers found, the literacy skills levels anticipated for 2006 were higher than for all categories of occupations in 1996.[13]

Not surprisingly, the highest literacy levels—and the highest weekly wages—were achieved by those with the most years of education. Moreover, a growing earnings gap between low and high earners paralleled the rise in literacy levels; persons with four years of college earn 30 percent more per week than those with only a high school diploma.[14]

But changes in the skills and knowledge needed for the job market are not limited to literacy, or numeracy, for that matter. Broad-based studies of the labor market strongly confirm that the demand shift in employment is directly traceable to information technology and its application across the board to virtually every category of job. The effect of information technology thus involves far more than simple automation and substitution. It goes to fundamental changes in the nature of work itself and in how corporations are reorganizing to improve service, increase efficiencies, and hone their competitive edge.[15] Relative job demand is shifting in the direction of both cognitive and personal interaction skills.[16]

These shifts in the kinds of jobs being created relate directly to the issue of work-force preparation. Philip R. Day Jr. and Robert H. McCabe point to a tectonic shift in the needs of the work force: In 1950, 80 percent of all jobs were classified as "unskilled labor," but by 2000, 85 percent of all jobs were classified as "skilled labor."[17] In 1991 the Department of Labor's SCANS found that more than half of America's youth leave school without the new range of skills they need to succeed in the workplace, dictated by an economy that has moved into a new era. Without such skills, the commission concluded, "young people will pay a very high price. They face the bleak prospects of dead-end work interrupted only by periods of unemployment."[18]

Workplace preparation and know-how, the SCANS report said, must rely on the development of five basic competencies built on a three-part foundation of basic skills. These requirements, SCANS insisted, were essential preparation for all students, whether they are planning on higher education or immediate entry into the work force. SCANS warned that the nation's schools were not preparing students adequately for the future.

The nation's higher education system has been supplying better-educated workers. Twenty-five years ago, just over a third of the work force had at least a high school diploma; in 1997 less than 11 percent of the work force had earned less than a high school diploma.[19] Since 1975, the proportion of all adults with four years of high school education or more has risen from 63 percent to more than 80 percent, and the number of associate degrees has risen fivefold.[20] More high school students are choosing to go to college; two-thirds did so in 1997 compared with just under half in 1979.[21] The number of bachelor's degrees awarded has doubled since 1965 and has risen by almost 25 percent since 1975. These better-educated workers are making up a larger part of the work force. In 1996, for example, only six in ten high school dropouts were in the labor force, compared with eight in ten high school graduates. For college graduates, the number was almost nine in ten.[22] The Department of Labor estimates that the occupations requiring an associate's degree, which accounted for a quarter of all jobs in 1998, will account for 40 percent of all job growth between 1998 and 2008.[23] Thus, the economy has not only absorbed these educational gains, but it also continues to cry out for more, especially in technical fields.

A clear trend has been visible since at least 1964. More and more, college graduates are occupying positions that were formerly occupied by high school graduates, while high school graduates are occupying positions formerly occupied by workers with no diploma.[24] In addition, continuing education and life-long learning are becoming increasingly important as workers seek additional training to keep up with the skill demands of their jobs. In 1995 more than a fifth of students in sub-baccalaureate programs had already attained degrees–2.2 percent, a BA or higher degree, and 18.3 percent, an associate's degree.[25]

Most of the fastest growing occupations are, not surprisingly, in technical fields where the law of supply and demand rewards well-prepared workers with higher earnings. Bureau of Labor Statistics projections for 1998–2000 revealed that more than two-thirds of the thirty occupational categories expected to have the fastest growth already had median hourly earnings above the median for the nation.[26] For example, eleven of those occupations were in the top quartile of earnings ($16.25 an hour and over). The four occupations expected to experience the fastest earnings growth were computer engineers, computer support specialists, systems analysts, and database administrators; all were in the top earnings quartile for 1997. Among the 20 million jobs created in the U.S. economy since 1993, more than four out of five (81 percent) have been in job categories above the median wage and 65 percent of them were in the highest paying third.[27]

GROWTH OF HIGH-SKILLED JOBS. But it is not just that the character of jobs and job requirements are changing, or that the paycheck rewards follow better work-force preparation. In today's globally competitive economy, the number of high-skilled jobs is growing daily. Across all industries, the Labor Department reports, professional and managerial employment are the most rapidly expanding job categories. These two categories together account for more than 60 percent of all new jobs, attracting more than 70 percent of all college graduates.[28] In other words, the rising employment opportunities in these newer job categories reflect the rising premium the economy places on skill acquisition. The quality of these jobs, and the skills they demand, are further underscored by the slight but steady decline in part-time employment, which has fallen 2 percent since 1994. Employer data show that average hours worked for all jobs remains roughly constant. Thus, with fewer part-time jobs available, employer selectivity in hiring is reinforced.

HIGH-SKILL JOBS: LOOKING AHEAD. Business's need for high-skilled workers shows no sign of abating. But doubters remain. Many critics of the job-creating power of the new economy like to point out that the need is over-stated, that much of the employment being created by high-tech firms is in the form of low-level, low-skill jobs—a revisiting of the so-called McDonald's effect. They note that the new jobs in many high-tech firms are the equivalent of the warehouse workers at Amazon.com, who are hired to fetch books and fulfill orders, but that comparatively fewer workers are hired to fill jobs demanding higher skills.

Labor Department figures show that lower skill jobs in lower pay ranges increased by 9.7 percent between 1989–97, while jobs in the mid-range of compensation grew by only 0.7 percent. What critical observers fail to mention, however, is that three-quarters of all job growth between 1989 and 1995 (6.7 million new jobs) occurred in the ranks of relatively high-paying positions in managing, marketing, and professional occupations (that is, essentially information workers), with the remainder in service occupations and among factory workers. Also neglected is the fact that jobs in the very highest pay ranges have increased by 20 percent over the same period; that is, at almost twice the rate for lower- and mid-range paying jobs.[29] In addition, demand for skilled workers is increasing within occupations.[30]

New jobs will doubtless require more education. While one in five jobs required a B.A. in 1996, the Department of Labor has estimated that nearly one in three would require a B.A. or more by 2001.[31] Richard W. Judy of the Hudson Institute, citing both Labor Department projections for 1996–2006 and the research done on "key work-skill levels" by the American College Testing Board, estimates that "60 percent of new jobs in the early 21st century will require skills possessed by only 20 percent of the present work force."[32] The competitive disadvantage latent in these numbers offers a sobering outlook for American businesses and individuals.

Congress has taken action to meet the national demand for skilled professionals in high-tech computer fields. The so-called H1B Visa Bills (S 1723 and HR 3736) were designed to sustain the flow of high-skilled workers to American businesses that need them. Passed in 1998, the legislation raised the annual ceiling of 65,000 on worker visas by 20,000; for 1999 the cap was set at 95,000, for 2000 at 105,000, and for 2001 and 2002 at 115,000. Legislation passed by both houses in October 2000 raised this cap to 195,000. The message here is stark. American firms need certain kinds of high-skilled workers, and this need is simply not being met by the U.S. education and work-force preparation systems. Nor, apparently, can businesses train workers fast enough to maintain competitiveness. They must import these people in ever-growing numbers.[33]

The skills gap—a bona fide competitiveness issue—is widening. A further contributing factor is that educational attainment is projected to increase rapidly between now and 2020, especially in developing economies. According to a 1995 World Bank study, the attainment of a secondary school education and beyond is projected to increase in China from between 30 and 35 percent in 1995 to between 45 and 50 percent in 2020; in East Asia the percentage will climb from between 30 and 35 percent to about 55 percent; in the Middle East and North Africa, the rate will climb from between 15 and 20 percent to just over 50 percent.[34] These workers, many of whom are out-performing American youth on international comparisons of educational achievement, have begun fueling the economies of America's competitors.

Those who monitor America's employment needs agree that globalization and technology have transformed the way America does business; that the skills and knowledge requirements of today's and tomorrow's jobs are changing; and that the nation needs workers who are increasingly better educated and possess an entire battery of different kinds of skills, more of them, and at higher levels. Meanwhile, competitors are catching up to the United States.

## Education and Earnings

Perhaps the most widely cited correlation in work-force economics in the United States (and the world over) is the one that links educational attainment with earnings (see table 1).

INDIVIDUAL EARNING POWER. Across all age groups, a college graduate can expect to earn almost three times more in a year than a high school dropout.

At the other end of the income scale, a professional person at the top of his or her earning power averages almost $146,000 per year, more than 5.5 times the average earned by a high school graduate. Over just ten years, the difference amounts to almost $1.2 million. This earnings gap compounds over the earners' lifetimes. At age twenty-five, a high school graduate is out-earned by a college graduate by $15,619 a year; by retirement age, the college graduate is out-earning the high school graduate by $32,212 annually, a 123 percent difference.

Not surprisingly, this earnings growth shows up in the economy as a whole. Between 1980 and 1996, a typical high school graduate started out earning 20 percent more than a high school dropout, but by 1996, the gap between these two groups had doubled to 40 percent.[35] The earnings gap between high

**Table 1. Earnings and Educational Attainment, 1997**
Dollars

| Age | High school dropout | High school graduate | Four-year college graduate | Professional degree |
|---|---|---|---|---|
| All ages | 16,355 | 22,895 | 47,678 | 95,148 |
| 23–34 | 17,287 | 21,637 | 37,256 | 58,079 |
| 35–44 | 19,142 | 26,235 | 51,977 | 103,418 |
| 45–54 | 23,116 | 27,354 | 56,497 | 99,956 |
| 55–65 | 22,196 | 26,202 | 58,414 | 145,699 |

Source: "Hard Work Pays," booklet (Washington: American Federation of Teachers, n.d.), p. 2. Data are from the U.S. Census Bureau.

school graduates and college graduates is also widening. The earnings of high school dropouts and graduates have fallen in real terms since 1979. So while a college degree is more valuable than ever, a high school degree provides workers with lower real earnings than their parents twenty years earlier and fewer opportunities.[36] More than ever, graduation at any level must denote achievement based on high standards.

A parallel gap shows up in the nation's unemployment figures, which show, broadly, that the higher an individual's level of educational attainment, the less likely that person is to be out of work. Among persons twenty-five years of age and over in 1997, the unemployment rate among those with no high school diploma was 8.1 percent; among high school graduates it was almost half that (4.3 percent); and among college graduates, it was 2.7 percent—a third of the rate among those with the least educational attainment.[37]

FREQUENT JOB CHANGES. The era when a person left school, entered a job, worked in it for forty years, and retired with a slap on the back and a gold watch came to an end sometime during the last generation. A person graduating from college in the 1980s could expect to hold eight to nine jobs in a lifetime and could expect to be involved in three to four different careers. The sheer fact of frequent job and career changes creates a strong argument for an educational and employment preparation system that delivers transferable skills; that is, the kind of cognitive skills and basic competencies that cut across a broad spectrum of job categories.

The question is: Are the schools doing the job? Are they equipping graduates with the transferable skills required to get and keep the higher paying jobs the economy is producing and to contribute to the civic health of their communities? The answer seems to be an equivocal one: only sometimes.

## Are Schools Delivering?

Since the National Commission on Excellence in Education in 1983 delivered a national wake-up call in its landmark document *A Nation at Risk*, report after report has decried the state of American education, the declining performance of young people on standardized tests, their disappointing showing in international comparisons of academic achievement, the lack of competence among their teachers, and a host of other ills.[38]

The commission focused almost entirely on the education of older adolescents, with thirteen bulleted "indicators of the risk." Among them were a 13 percent functional illiteracy rate among seventeen-year-olds, consistent declines in performance on the Scholastic Aptitude Tests, a twenty-five-year decline in student performance on standardized achievement tests, and a fourteen-year decline in science achievement on the National Assessment of Educational Progress (NAEP). Over the next seventeen years, these figures saw some improvements, but not nearly enough.

The commission concluded that the blame lay with too little time for learning, a "homogenized, diluted, and diffused . . . cafeteria-style" curriculum, impoverished preparation, poor quality among the teacher corps (especially in mathematics and science), and minimal expectations for student performance. The report intoned a litany that would be heard time and again in subsequent analyses: that standards for high school seniors had decreased, that far too little time was spent on rigorous subjects, that foreign languages were not required (a serious lack in today's globalizing economy), that graduation requirements were cheapened by superfluous electives, that admission standards for higher education had been lowered in private colleges and sometimes eliminated in public higher education, and that expenditures for educational materials had declined precipitously.[39]

*Legacy of Learning,* a fresh look at the nation's schools by former Xerox CEO David Kearns and education writer James Harvey that was published in 2000, provides little encouragement.[40] Mincing no words, the authors report that three of the major problems characterizing American education today are "misplaced smugness" about the quality of suburban schools, the financial headaches of rural schools, and the "national disgrace" of education in urban America.[41]

Kearns and Harvey noted that the percentage of students who embarked on a recommended course in what *A Nation at Risk* called "the new basics" (four years of English; three of science, social studies, and mathematics) had risen from 13 percent in 1982 to 55 percent in 1998. The number of students taking Advanced Placement courses had also increased dramatically. Fewer students were taking remedial math in high schools, and the dropout rate had decreased by 5 percent.

But a closer examination provides a good deal less encouragement. NAEP, which assesses the performance of nine-, thirteen-, and seventeen-year-olds, has revealed the deep trouble American schools are having in translating the gains achieved in the early years of schooling into a successful secondary school career. "What begins to emerge," Kearns and Harvey say, is "a pattern of stability, sometimes even modest improvement, for elementary and middle school students in all areas, accompanied by stagnation and decline for senior high school students. Looked at overall and evaluated without excuses, the NAEP assessments reveal a dreadful possibility: the longer today's American students remain in the school system, the poorer their performance in comparison with their predecessors."[42]

Viewed from an international perspective, this depressing domestic pattern is confirmed by two major assessments. The 1996 International Educational Assessment of reading literacy (fourth graders in twenty-seven countries and ninth graders in thirty-one) and the Third International Mathematics and Science Study (more than 500,000 students in five grades in forty-six countries) both showed that "the longer American students are in school, the poorer their performance in comparison with their peers abroad. . . . Even the most advanced American students do not measure up. . . . They are not world class."[43]

The disparity is evident most forebodingly in those areas where work-force quality issues hit home—where the future increasingly requires high-skilled workers for the high-tech, global economy. It is disquieting to learn that the small proportion of America's top high school seniors who take classes in advanced mathematics and physics perform much more poorly than their counterparts in other countries. In the aggregate, "out of twenty nations, none scored significantly lower than the United States in advanced mathematics and only one (Austria) did so in physics."[44]

This poor showing, unfortunately, also has an equity component. Minority students are less well served by the U.S. educational system than are others. The 1994 NAEP testing of fourth-grade reading shows, for example, that 57 percent of inner-city youngsters were unable to score at even a basic level, a proportion that rose to 77 percent in schools where half or more of the students were poor. Similarly, in 1996 testing of mathematics and sciences among eighth graders, these proportions were 58 and 67 percent, respectively.[45] These are the same students who have the fewest teachers with majors in the disciplines they teach. In short, minority and poor students are not well prepared for the competitive global economy.

Defenders of America's educational system often argue that it educates all American children, while those of most other nations deliberately winnow out less able students and bring only the best to—and through—higher education. But, as Kearns and Harvey show, the success of the United States in achieving high school graduation rates is a myth. For one thing, the U.S. school system graduates only about three-fourths to four-fifths of its students (depending on the time frame for which the calculation is made). According to the Organization for Economic Cooperation and Development (OECD), the United States, once a world leader in the proportion and number of its students who graduated from secondary school, now trails twenty-two other industrial countries in this vital statistic.[46] Nor is it that the United States is doing so abjectly in this area; the real problem is that others have caught up and surpassed America.

## Remediation: The Costs to Business

The inadequacies of the American education system and its failure to meet the escalating demand for higher skilled workers create significant costs for both higher education and business in the United States. Especially significant here is the remediation needed to help poorly prepared high school graduates cope with the demands of a college education (now required by more and more jobs), as well as to help new hires just out of high school to become productive workers. However, the better the education the workers get before they enter the work force, the more likely they are to enjoy accelerated professional, technical, and communications training.

Although many major American corporations report that a growing number of their new hires are college graduates, this good news is not unalloyed.[47] According to the American Association of Community Colleges, four out of ten students matriculating at community colleges are inadequately prepared in basic reading, writing, and mathematics.[48] Similarly, 78 percent of the nation's institutions of higher learning, which turn out the potential new hires, are offering remedial courses in these same core subjects because too many first-year students are not ready for college work. Almost three of every ten first-year students (29 percent) enroll in a remedial course each fall.[49]

Workers who are poorly prepared for the workplace cost employers money. A joint report of the Departments of Labor and Education, *The Bottom Line: Basic Skills in the Workplace*, illustrates the point:

> In a major manufacturing company, one employee who didn't know how to read a ruler mismeasured yards of sheet steel, wasting almost $700 worth of material in one morning. This same company had just invested heavily in equipment to regulate inventories and production schedules. Unfortunately, the workers were unable to enter numbers accurately, which literally destroyed inventory records and resulted in production orders for the wrong products. Correcting the errors cost the company millions of dollars and wiped out any savings projected as a result of the new automation.[50]

Mistakes cost. Remediating the lack of skills that produces those mistakes can be expensive as well. The American Society for Training and Development (ASTD) reports that approximately $55 billion (1.8 percent of payroll) was spent by businesses to provide employee training in 1995, at an average cost of $250 per trainee per day.[51] What proportion of that figure is spent on remediation is uncertain. Whatever the total, it is estimated that almost half of American companies were offering some form of make-up training.[52] The Department of Labor has estimated the economic impact of illiteracy on eight southern states and found it to be huge: $31 billion in lost productivity, unrealized taxes, and social problems; plus $24.8 billion in lost time and substandard work; plus another $1.8 billion in unemployment claims—a total of $57.6 billion. Even if these numbers on remediation costs are overstated by a factor of two or three, the national total for the cost of illiteracy alone is staggering, let alone the costs to make up for what workers are not bringing to the job on the first day of work.

These kinds of costs are not new to business. *A Nation at Risk* reported that:

> Business and military leaders complain that they are required to spend millions of dollars on costly remedial education and training programs in such basic skills as reading, writing, spelling, and computation. The Department of the Navy, for example, reported to the Commission that one-quarter of its recent recruits cannot read at the ninth grade level, the minimum needed simply to understand written safety instructions. Without remedial work, they cannot even begin, much less complete, the sophisticated training essential in much of the modern military.[53]

Beyond the direct costs of remediation and mistakes resulting from poorly trained employees, lower levels of educational attainment also translate into higher poverty rates, which all Americans pay for in the taxes that support the welfare system, job-training programs and youth training initiatives, higher crime and incarceration rates, as well as in the billions of dollars in lost tax revenue attributable to unemployment and underemployment. According to the U.S. Census Bureau, 24.1 percent of dropouts were living below the poverty level in 1995. But among college graduates, the poverty rate was one-tenth that, at 2.4 percent. Because dropouts are twice as likely to be on public assistance as high school graduates, social costs pile atop educational and economic ones. Indirectly, these costs also show up in the social price paid by communities, where the vibrancy of family life and the vitality of neighborhoods are eroded by the undertow of undereducation, dragging down would-be workers and residents. In the end, these people themselves suffer most from inadequate education.

All of this is by way of stating a basic fact of the early twenty-first century: Business productivity increases directly with the educational level of the work force. But that productivity is diminished, often dramatically, by what the schools are not doing. As a result, America is paying twice, and sometimes three times, to develop fundamental skills in its work force—once in public school, where students lose ground over the K-12 sequence; once in higher education, where almost a third of all entering students have to take remedial courses; and once when students are hired and found unfit to write a coherent letter or report, follow any but the simplest instructions, compute a cost ratio, or formulate a problem coherently.

In reckoning the cost of all this, one is reminded of the tag-line of the old TV commercial about changing the oil filter in your car: "You can pay me now—or pay me later." The point of the commercial was that preventive maintenance pays off. Researchers have likewise learned that a 10 percent increase in the educational level of a company's work force (approximately one year of additional education) increases productivity by 8.6 percent in the manufacturing sector and by 12.9 percent in the nonmanufacturing sector.[54] These are competitive gains the nation's businesses cannot afford to forgo, and must expand, to compete successfully.

## Why Business Backs Standards and Standards-Based Reform

THE BASIS FOR STANDARDS. Poll after poll reveals the same result: Americans across the board believe strongly that schools should expect more from children—that they should work harder, tackle more demanding material, perform at higher levels, learn more skills, and become more accomplished. In a world of work increasingly defined by all sorts of new technologies, from robotics to artificial intelligence, such requirements make sense. Business people understand that "an American strategy of global competitiveness built on the sand of educational mediocrity will crumble just as surely as one built on second-rate manufacturing and services."[55] They want educators to understand this same point.

At a time and in a world when and where the ability to compete effectively is critical to both personal performance and the nation's economic future, the one factor that correlates overwhelmingly with achieving success is a sound education. But what makes an education sound? The only way to make the term meaningful is through criteria, which, at bottom, is what standards are. Standards state what students should know and be able to do in relation to particular subject matter; they specify the level of performance expected when students undertake specific tasks—in other words, competency. Put differently, the argument is not about whether standards are appropriate to education, but about what specific knowledge and skills to expect, at what points, in the education process.

Several (school-leaving) standards crucial to employment in today's competitive economy are offered in the SCANS requirements. National and state groups have also developed and advanced content standards for core academic subjects including English, mathematics, history, science, and the arts. These standards are necessary to ensure that the education offered in these core areas is internationally competitive, to ensure that the education offered in the nation's schools reflects the best available knowledge about teaching and learning, and to ensure that a broad consensus on learning stands behind state and local education policies.

The education standards developed in the various academic disciplines, while remaining a matter of some debate, nevertheless translate into basic capabilities. Significantly for employers, those capabilities compose the academic infrastructure that undergirds most basic business tasks, whether being able to write a cogent paragraph, use an instruction manual, acquire a new skill, do mathematical calculations, understand basic scientific concepts, or work productively as a member of a team. Children who do not learn under such a regimen, and businesses whose employees are not educated to be responsive to such standards, will be, in Norman Augustine's prophetic phrase, "more than economically disadvantaged; they will be economically irrelevant."[56]

The business leaders we work with as part of the National Alliance of Business and The Business Roundtable are unanimous in their agreement that standards lie at the heart of the continuous process of reform that is required in America's schools. These men and women understand, from their own experience, that every aspect of business life—from making a microchip to manufacturing a turbine, from deciding who gets a promotion to redesigning a production line—depends on knowing first what you want to accomplish. That is, knowing where the bar is set and what is required to clear it. The reason for a standard, any standard, is that you cannot tell how far you have come or have to go unless you have one. You cannot assess what you cannot measure.

But standards can never be ends in themselves. The most carefully wrought education standards in the world are to no avail if they do not result in higher student achievement. Assessment and accountability make standards more than idle wish-statements.

ASSESSMENT REINFORCES PERFORMANCE. Business supports education standards because a fundamental precondition to success in the marketplace states that trying hard is simply not enough. It takes more; it takes achieving. Standards are therefore a bottom-line issue. Parents, educators, policymakers, and employers all need to be able to compare student performance to some stated level of achievement or competence, whether in the international arena or in the classrooms of the local school. And the entire taxpaying public is entitled to receive regular information on all performance indicators, including dropout rates, how well students are doing on standard-based assessments, and the performance of high school graduates both at work and in higher education.

STANDARDS YIELD ACCOUNTABILITY. Intrinsic to standards are the consequences tied to performance. Some schools and school districts will, by themselves, own up to how well their students and employees are doing by making needed changes. Others may require support, or even compulsion, in making those changes. Parents and education officials need to keep in mind, however, that any time students and schools are not meeting standards, the direst consequence is not a sanction that might be brought, but the denial of both quality and equity in education.

No reasons exist, then, that that same denial of equity and quality should be tolerated by default. If that denial were to be imposed on children as a condition of schooling, Americans would not tolerate it.[57] When schools are permitted to operate whose students consistently fail to meet standards or make progress toward meeting them, they should be called to account.[58] Steps should be taken to remedy the lack, and the reasons for lack of performance should be made the basis for both sanction and a plan for improvement. Conversely, when schools are meeting standards and students are living up to their learning potential as expressed in meaningful standards, both should be rewarded commensurately. And the standards should be raised to encourage even better performance.

THE OBLIGATIONS OF BUSINESS. If teachers and trainers in K-12 schools, school-to-work programs, two- and four-year colleges, and work-force training programs are to understand the expectations that the workplace has of young people, these expectations must be spelled out. Employers thus have an obligation to articulate clearly the standards they adhere to, whether the expectation is for specific levels of knowledge or for particular academic, technical, and people skills.

In this light, perhaps one of the most important shifts schools must make is the change from looking at the inputs to the education system (for example, money spent, degrees held by teachers, computers bought, courses taken, texts mandated, new schools built) to measuring educational outputs (for example, subject matter learned, skills acquired, performance tracked) at clearly stated levels of competence. No business in the world measures its success by what it expends, but by what it creates. Schools should be doing no less.

Reading skill is one such output. Reading for simple comprehension (Walk/Don't Walk) or for acquiring information (Take one pill every four hours), for example, are relatively low-level skills, something that every American should acquire in elementary school. But reading for comprehension is part of another realm entirely. Doing that requires thinking skills related to the crucial faculties of analysis, synthesis, and evaluation. Thus, a person who can read a writer's words as well as weigh their meaning is far better educated—and a more valuable employee—than a reader who cannot.

Business leaders are solidly behind the move to replace minimum competency tests with measures of what students should know and be able to do by the time they graduate from high school.[59] The business community, in an effort coordinated by the National Alliance of Business, launched a national campaign, Making Academics Count, that encourages employers to ask for high school transcripts or other school records as part of the hiring process. To date, more than ten thousand employers have signed on to the campaign.[60]

For workers, as well as for businesses, time is money. More and more, learning certifications are playing a key role in informing learners about the importance of marketable skills. For employers, such certificates accelerate the action of the market by clarifying the signals sent out by the supply and demand system.[61] Not surprisingly, certification programs offered by businesses and education institutions are proliferating. These certificates, however, like diplomas, are no more valuable than the paper they are printed on unless they reflect inputs from employers who expect to benefit from the skills the certificates represent, they are the product of a competency-based curriculum, and they certify specific levels of competency.

## The Lure of Lifelong Learning

Learning in the global economy no longer means merely going to school and acquiring what one needs to know for a lifetime. Learning now reflects society's relentless commitment to affording all citizens opportunities to stretch their minds to full capacity, from early childhood through adulthood. Education is no longer a matter of career goals but of quality of life. Formal education may provide the foundation, but lifelong learning is necessary to keep knowledge from becoming obsolete and skills from becoming rapidly dated (engineering schools report, for example, that half of what they teach undergraduates is obsolete in five years). These facts are widely recognized by working Americans, three-quarters of whom reported in 1995 that they had received job-related training in the past three years.[62]

But a caveat is also in order about academic preparation for the workplace. Diane Ravitch warns that, since the days of John Dewey, a reversal of thinking has occurred in America about the basic function of schooling. The emphasis has shifted, she says, from using the school as a lever of social reform to viewing the school's prime function as helping the individual student adjust to society.[63] As school curricula have focused more and more on the social and emotional development of children, the upshot for standards has been to put less and less energy into intellectual development and the mastery of subject matter. As one education professor cited by Ravitch notes, demanding standards were supplanted by a diversified curriculum, the better to meet the needs of "children of mediocre or inferior ability who lack interest in abstract and academic materials."[64] As a result, standards had been leveled.

Leveling of this kind is not acceptable. Business people who support standards need to reach for the wisdom that sees not merely their instrumental value vis-à-vis specific business tasks and goals, but also their connection to creating the kind of human being who is valuable as an employee and citizen.

Finally, standards are needed no matter what the education delivery system is. Today, a continuing need exists for standards in public schools, whether the schools are supported by tax dollars or the education they provide is under-written by vouchers or some alternative financing system. Standards are also needed to assure quality education among the sizable number of young people whose parents are educating them at home (estimated at more than two million), as well as among the many who are being educated in telecommunications-based, distance-learning settings.

## Standards Work

Of all the arguments that can be advanced in favor of education standards, none is more powerful than the simple fact that they work. When they are in place and supported by local policy, by teachers and parents, and by a consistent program of assessment tied to a sensible accountability structure, student performance goes up and student achievement improves. To the question "Do standards generate better results?" the answer is "Yes."

Although forty-nine states have adopted academic standards, the adoption process has been uneven and a national picture has been slow to form. That being said, some strong gains are already apparent. Maryland's new emphasis on standards, for example, has resulted in 44 percent of the state's students testing at the "satisfactory" level in 1999, up fourteen points from the 1993 average; in 77 of 1,357 schools in Maryland, seven of every ten students scored at the "satisfactory" level, up from only 11 schools in 1993.[65] Similarly, ten years after a complete overhaul of the state's education system, Kentucky has climbed from the bottom rungs of the NAEP into the middle ranks.

Both North Carolina and Texas, in particular, have been praised in their use of standards to improve student achievement. David Grissmer and Ann Flanagan of the RAND Corporation analyzed key factors in the progress of these two states. Specifically, the states made the largest average gains in their NAEP scores between 1990 and 1996, and evidence exists that disadvantaged students are progressing much more rapidly than before. Grissmer and Flanagan found that the rapid achievement gains were not related to traditional policies such as increased spending, smaller classes, or more qualified teachers. The results derived, instead, from the comprehensive and sustained approach each of these states has taken to improving its schools, relying heavily on the reform triumvirate of standards, assessments, and accountability as the foundation for other reforms.[66]

What specific reforms have North Carolina and Texas undertaken that seem to be making the difference?

—Grade-by-grade standards, with textbooks and curricula aligned to the standards;

—Expectations that all students will meet the same standards;

—Statewide assessments closely linked to the standards;

—Accountability linked to assessment results, with rewards and sanctions for performance;

—Deregulation and increased local flexibility granted for meeting standards;

—Computerized feedback systems and achievement data used for continuous improvement; and

—Reallocation of resources to schools with more disadvantaged students.[67]

Other states have implemented similar policies, but not all have seen similar results. What sets North Carolina and Texas apart is the comprehensiveness of their approaches. Just as important has been the longevity of their commitment. Even as political administrations have changed, new governors and committed business leaders in both states have stayed the course.[68]

In a local example, teachers at Bessemer Elementary School in Pueblo, Colorado, were devastated in November 1997 when the first year's scores on the state's Student Assessment Program were announced. Only 12 percent of fourth graders met the reading standard, and just 2 percent met the writing standard. Teachers declared war on illiteracy and, within weeks, greatly increased the length of the school days and the amount of time spent on these key areas. When students took the second year's test, 64 percent passed, and the numbers have kept going up since.[69] Similarly, in one of the toughest environments for education in the country, central Harlem, the Frederick Douglass Academy holds out the high standard of beginning college preparatory courses in the seventh grade. Members of the class of 2000 have been accepted to Yale, Princeton, Cornell, Dartmouth, Duke, Tufts, Amherst, and at top historically black colleges, including Morehouse, Lincoln, Morris Brown, and Xavier. Within a few years of its founding in 1991, Frederick Douglass's Regents scores in English, U.S. history, and precalculus were among the best in New York City. Even after a slight decline last year, test scores ranked twelfth out of 235 middle schools in New York City, 32 percentage points higher than the city average in reading and 26 percentage points higher in math.[70]

What is particularly heartening amid the return to standards is the realistic and open-minded attitudes students have shown to higher performance criteria. In 1997 half of public high school students said their schools did not challenge them to do their best and let them get away with too little work. Almost three quarters said they should be promoted only when they have learned what is expected of them, and that they would study harder if they were given tougher tests.[71]

### Addressing the Backlash

State requirements that students pass a minimum competency test to qualify for high school graduation date to the late 1970s. But in recent years, concern has grown in many communities that a high school diploma had become little more than a certificate for seat occupancy. Dissatisfaction with minimum competency tests thus led many states to develop more rigorous assessments to measure what students should know and be able to do by the time they graduate.[72]

Not surprisingly, these new assessments have generated opposition. A backlash resulted, fueled in part by legitimate concerns about educational equity, by questions about the degree to which particular tests are well aligned to specific standards, and by the way periodic major assessments can turn into life-altering events for youngsters ill prepared for tests with consequences.

For many parents, it came as a shock that their children were not doing as well in schools as they had been led to believe by their grades. They had been lulled into complacency as promotions, diplomas, and admissions to postsecondary institutions continued without incident. Parents understandably got angry when new tests told them their children did not deserve to advance. In states such as Michigan, where performance assessments were voluntary, parents of students in a few affluent communities opted initially to keep their children home on test day, lest their admission to highly selective colleges and universities be jeopardized.[73] For their part, elected officials knew enough to fear the political consequences if large numbers of their constituents' children were prevented from graduating. Standards began losing friends in the legislatures.

But testing such as the NAEP, the Third International Mathematics and Science Study (TIMSS), and new state-developed assessments was telling the truth. According to the University of California at Los Angeles's annual survey of college freshmen, released in January 2000, even though students continued to receive higher school grades than their peers in earlier generations, between 1966 and 1998 no parallel improvement was evident on these broader measures. Unfortunately, too many American parents have remained blissfully unaware of how their own children's achievement compares with children in the same state, across the country, or internationally.[74]

Edward B. Rust Jr., CEO of State Farm Insurance Companies and chairman of the National Alliance of Business and The Business Roundtable Education Task Force, in correspondence to other CEOs stated: "It is wiser and more humane to identify academic weaknesses early. That way, teachers and parents can intervene and help students, too many of whom find out after they've graduated that what they've learned in school doesn't cut it in college or at work."[75]

A prominent court case has heaped fuel on the backlash bonfire. On January 7, 2000, in a case filed by the Mexican American Legal Defense and Educational Fund (MALDEF), a U.S. District Court in San Antonio ruled in favor of the Texas Education Agency (TEA). MALDEF had argued that the use of the Texas Assessment of Academic Skills (TAAS) as a requirement for high school graduation unfairly discriminated against Texas minority students. The court determined that TAAS did not violate the right of Texas students to due process. The court also found that while the TAAS test does adversely affect a significant number of minority students, the TEA had demonstrated an educational necessity for the test and had ensured that the exam was strongly correlated to material taught in the classroom. The *MALDEF* v. *TEA* decision served to reaffirm a 1979 Florida decision, *Debra P.* v. *Turlington*, which had established two major requirements for denying students a high school diploma based on statewide test results: adequate notice and curricular validity. States that adopt high-stakes testing must now demonstrate that students have received sufficient notice before the test sanctions being implemented and that the schools are teaching what is being tested.

In *MALDEF*, both criteria were met, but opponents launched a blistering attack on the decision, arguing, in the words of U.S. senator Paul Wellstone (D-Minn.) that "high-stakes testing" represented a "full-scale retreat from educational equity."[76] We believe the opposite to be true. For years, large groups of American children have been demeaned by imagining that less should be expected of them because they were poor or minority. It is time to expect more and invest what is needed to help all children achieve more. As state testing reforms began to be implemented in the 1990s, particularly those with consequences for schools and students, reality began to sink in. By 1999, parents, educators, and policymakers were beginning to see the same kinds of disquieting results from state testing programs as had already shown up on the NAEP and the TIMSS. In the most recent NAEP results on reading, for example, 31 percent of fourth graders, 34 percent of eighth graders, and 40 percent of twelfth graders scored at the Proficient or Above level.[77] In mathematics the results for the most recent testing year (1996) were even lower. Only 20 percent of fourth graders, 23 percent of eighth graders, and 15 percent of twelfth graders scored at Proficient or Above.[78]

Banner headlines in influential newspapers such as the *Boston Globe,* the *New York Times,* the *Washington Post,* and the *New Orleans Times-Picayune* reported large numbers of students and schools failing to meet state-developed standards on the first rounds of new state tests, quoting statements of consternation from policymakers and parents. But while newspapers and TV stations covered the test boycotts and demonstrations against standards in Massachusetts, for example, the fact that 70 percent of the public in that state support the Massachusetts Comprehensive Assessment System got little play. Similarly, polling by Public Agenda and The Business Roundtable shows strong support for higher standards and graduation requirements, and strong opposition to social promotion among all groups, including minority parents and students.[79] Meanwhile, state policymakers continue to struggle with where to set the bar for tests. Some states, such as Texas, have set standards that they seek to raise over time; others, such as Virginia, are setting high standards and giving schools and students a timetable for catching up.

Business-led groups have learned from the backlash that strong public communication is essential to the standards message. The Maryland Business Roundtable for Education, the Partnership for Kentucky Schools, and the Washington Partnership for Learning have all conducted particularly effective efforts to help teachers, parents, and the press understand and support higher standards and new tests. Take-the-Test days for parents, elected officials, and other policymakers, together with extensive media coverage, have been especially useful in helping build support for new assessments. The business community in many states has also strongly supported releasing test items on the Internet and in newspaper supplements so people can learn what is expected from students today.

Business leaders are therefore making a public case for sticking with standards-based reform through the pain they may cause in the short run. In a recent article, Louis V. Gerstner, CEO of IBM, told a story that makes the point well. "British royal archers of the [nineteenth] century would wait until the queen had shot an arrow at a target, then run to draw a bull's-eye around where it struck. That dramatically improved the queen's archery score, but not the quality of the queen's archery. Unfortunately, a number of people today believe it's possible to apply the same slippery strategy to the issue of academic standards in our schools."[80]

Business leaders recognize that standards and assessments are far from perfect and that an obligation exists to align assessments with standards and curriculum, and to give students sufficient time and resources to prepare to take them. Business leaders know that investments may need to be increased. They understand, as well, that students and teachers will need help to meet the higher expectations for performance. But after continually pointing out the emptiness of the high school credential, business leaders are committed to moving forward. Delaying indefinitely, dumbing down the tests, or abandoning testing, as some critics suggest, will perpetuate current inequities, not correct them. Jerry Weist, superintendent of Montgomery County public schools in Maryland, says the challenge is to "raise the bar and close the gap."

Business leaders believe that higher academic standards can be used to drive other improvements, such as accountability and professional development. But to do that, standards must be transparent—well understood by teachers, parents, students, and the public. In some states, assessments are not measuring what they purport to, or standards are still too vague to be useful. In other states, students are wasting time taking an array of local and state tests because none has been eliminated as others have been added. And clearly, children learn many important and useful things in school that cannot be assessed on state tests.

The point that arises time and again relates to the bitter pill. Those who plead the need for more time before installing standards delay only at the expense of the children already in school who are being underprepared and even miseducated for a lifetime of learning, productive employment, and responsible citizenship. The fact that standards cause some dislocation is not an argument for indefinitely delaying the consequences that must accompany them. The purpose is not to punish children, but to do everything possible to help them succeed, even when there is a price. The union leader Albert Shanker often recalled that students would ask him about a quiz or assignment, "Mr. Shanker, does it count?" The students would determine how much effort to invest based on whether it counted or not.

So long as consequences are postponed, failure is obscured. Even as the public raises legitimate concerns about testing that policymakers need to address, according to the National Education Summit, "every recent public opinion survey shows overwhelming support for higher standards for all students, coupled with stronger accountability for results. . . . We must build on this strong public support and not waver as states and districts phase in challenging assessments and tougher promotion and graduation requirements. . . . We must help [the public] understand the consequences for both young people and society if we lower our standards in the face of public pressure."[81]

For its part, the business community's commitment to standards is long-term and, for many reasons, a good deal less self-serving than simply beefing up the future work force.[82] Businesses do not expect schools to simply churn out productive worker bees. Employers and employees are parents, too. They want to live and work in communities with good schools because they know that good schools and healthy communities go together. They know, too, that education is important in helping young people become mature adults, caring family members, and effective citizens. They know that as partners in shaping communities, they have to work for the kind of change in schools that will make a difference—both to students and to the country. Precisely because setting and supporting high learning standards can make that kind of difference, the business community welcomes an active role in strengthening standards as a means to improving education.

---

## Comment by Alex Molnar

Milton Goldberg and Susan L. Traiman's analysis harks back to the 1980s and is largely consistent with the line of reasoning advanced in *A Nation at Risk*.[83] Essentially, *A Nation at Risk* explained the American economic woes of the 1970s and 1980s as the outgrowth of the failure of public schools to adequately educate children for the emerging global economy. Time has not been kind to this point of view. I find, for example, the critique offered by David C. Berliner and Bruce J. Biddle in *The Manufactured Crisis* persuasive.[84] On an everyday level, the surging economy of the 1990s suggests either that American public education improved dramatically during the 1990s or that the link between schooling and the economy described in *A Nation at Risk* is spurious.

In the face of the economic successes of the 1990s, the almost two-decade-old argument favored by Goldberg and Traiman has about it the musty quality of ideas not refreshed by better information or guided by a healthy skepticism. One wonders why they cling to a view of the relationship among education, business, and the needs of the work force so divorced from real-world experience. Can they have studied very closely where the greatest number of new jobs are being created, what skills those jobs call for, and what pay they command? The esoteric charts, graphs, and erudite incantations of the new econometric clergy perhaps befog them. Whatever their reasons, Goldberg and Traiman have pledged allegiance to a movement that is, in my view, more about public relations and political ideology than substantive education reform. This movement is reinforced by publications such as the transparently political scorecard of state efforts to implement academic standards issued by the Thomas B. Fordham Foundation every year.[85]

### A Glib View of Standards

In considering the public relations aspects of the standards debate, I have been instructed by the work of Edward Bernays, considered the father of American public relations. Bernays, for example, organized the Light's Golden Jubilee to promote the sale of light bulbs (his client was General Electric). The jubilee, ostensibly celebrating the fiftieth anniversary of Thomas Edison's invention, became an international media event. In an interview with Bill Moyers decades later, Bernays recounted his public relations triumph: "Light"—who could be against light and in favor of darkness?; "Golden"—who would be in favor of lead?; and "Jubilee"—who could be in favor of an unhappy gathering? The title, Light's Golden Jubilee, thus provided what Bernays described as "rhetorical hegemony."[86]

The current standards movement has similarly succeeded in establishing rhetorical hegemony. The basic principles underlying the idea of standards are unassailable. Without a doubt, most people would agree that adults should think seriously about what children are to be taught. Adults should figure out whether or not children have learned it. And adults should help children learn those things if they do not do well. Diane Ravitch, in *National Standards in American Education: A Citizen's Guide*, expressed each of these adult responsibilities as a different type of educational standard.[87] According to Ravitch, content standards refer to what is to be taught and learned. Performance standards establish the degree of attainment expected (that is, answering the question, "How good is good enough?"). Opportunity-to-learn standards govern the resources made available to students to allow them to accomplish what is expected of them. As Ravitch accurately notes, the three types of standards are interrelated. While the impulse to have standards appears commonsensical, nearly every aspect of the implementation of standards (from content development to who enforces them) remains controversial.

The battle over content standards has been going on for a long time in the United States. Much of the argument today over content standards seems to revisit the cultural struggles of the sixties, positioning advocates of fact-filled standards against proponents of concept-based standards. The result of the struggle between the two sides is often unwieldy. Some states have produced standards that amount to lists of facts spiced with comically overblown descriptions of what children must learn. Consider, for example, this tenth-grade social studies objective from the Virginia Standards of Learning program: "The student will analyze the regional development of Asia, Africa, the Middle East, Latin America and the Caribbean in terms of physical, economic, and cultural characteristics and historical evolution from 1000 AD to present."[88]

When it comes to measuring performance, the emphasis is increasingly on tests, often so-called high-stakes tests, to assess the quality of public schools and determine if students can advance from grade to grade or graduate. This approach is enormously profitable for the testing industry. However, grave questions remain about whether such tests adequately measure performance or promote increased student learning. Moreover, a high-stakes testing regime may cost more in social and economic terms than it is worth. What is the cost imposed if, for example, the tests push students who do poorly—or who fear they will do poorly—out of school? Evidence already suggests this is happening.[89] Thus the cost of the standards movement may be the loss of the positive behavioral outcome associated with continued school attendance.

Opportunity-to-learn standards are given the least attention in the current standards debate. These are the much criticized inputs that many argue do not increase educational performance. The work of Eric A. Hanushek, who finds no systematic relationship between expenditure and student academic outcomes, is widely quoted in support of this view.[90] Hanushek's work has been well and convincingly critiqued by Larry V. Hedges, Richard D. Laine, and Rob Greenwald, among others.[91] Nevertheless, the devotion that some people have for Hanushek's argument is such that I sometimes wonder if they would not prefer to cut off inputs altogether and rationalize it as a way of maximizing outcomes.

The current drive for academic standards and accountability creates the public impression of doing something consequential to improve education. However, it may not be of much benefit to most American schoolchildren, their parents, or their communities.

## A Distorted Perspective on the Work Force

The standards discussion as outlined by Goldberg and Traiman is not, for example, likely to produce much of educational value. When I look at the structure of the American job market, I simply do not see, in large measure, the crying need for so-called knowledge workers. Perhaps this is because I do not define clerks as knowledge workers. In Goldberg and Traiman's formulation, a fast-food restaurant cashier who pushes a register button with a hamburger icon on it is a knowledge worker, and the grocery store clerk who scans the Universal Product Code is a knowledge worker.

In contrast to Goldberg and Traiman, I would argue that the transformations occurring in the economy are creating a relatively small number of highly technical occupations that are well paid. At the same time, these transformations create large numbers of low-skilled occupations that do interact, to a considerable extent, with high-tech equipment, but not necessarily to the benefit of workers. In short, I see a different structure of the American economy than Goldberg and Traiman see. When the assumptions that underlie their argument are examined, something fundamentally perverse is revealed.

First, Goldberg and Traiman put forth the idea of a world in which every student should be held accountable to high standards. The reason that every student should be held accountable to high standards is that high standards are necessary to find a good job in the evolving high-tech world of the twenty-first century. The data deployed by Goldberg and Traiman to make this argument deal with the correlation between educational attainment and income. While the credentialing of the American work force has proceeded apace over the last twenty or thirty years, credentials do not necessarily have anything to do with the skills necessary to do the jobs credentialed employees do. Credentials often have little connection to occupational performance standards.

Second, the standards argument, as characterized by Goldberg and Traiman, rests on the brutal assumption that it is reasonable to withhold a life with dignity—adequate housing, adequate health care, and so on—from a person unable to scramble to the top of the information elite in the new economy. This is a socially irresponsible point of view. With or without standards, the majority of Americans are going to be engaged in occupations such as garbage

collector or maintenance worker, which would be sorely missed if they dis-
appeared tomorrow. These jobs are necessary, and an outcry would be heard
if they were not done.

*Lack of Context*

Society will always need people to occupy low-skill positions, and talent
is not distributed by social class. The daughter of a cleaning woman might be
a genius and the son of a newspaper magnate a dolt. Most people, including
Goldberg and Traiman, I suspect, would agree with these propositions. And
most would recognize that choking off opportunities for any child to contribute
to the fullest of his or her abilities would be socially destructive.

Whether workers in low-skill occupations lead lives of desperation that
effectively foreclose opportunities to their children is, therefore, of prime
importance. The wretched housing, inadequate health care, and nutritional deficiencies that the poor and working poor in the United States live with every
day should be part of the standards debate. In other words, the standards discussion must be much more complex than is allowed within the framework
provided by Goldberg and Traiman.

Businesses may need more educated workers in a variety of different occupations. But the discussion of the performance of schools and the asserted
desirability of developing standards has been skewed all out of proportion relative to that need. Goldberg and Traiman, for example, argue that low-income
workers compete with each other and thus keep each other's wages down. If
only, they say, more low-income workers could be propelled into the ranks of
high-skilled workers, then the remaining low-income workers would have more
power to bargain wages up. My reading of the labor market hydraulics embedded in this analysis, however, indicates that it would be at least as likely that
an increase in the number of highly skilled workers would mean a general
reduction in the wages of high-skill workers. Moreover, evidence exists that
corporate America is prepared to lay off highly skilled workers and relocate
to India, to Mexico, and so on, where it can get cheaper labor. I doubt Goldberg and Traiman would suggest that the reason American corporations set
up shop in the third world is that third-world countries have higher educational standards than America does. Moreover, even if businesspeople believe
their own rhetoric with regard to standards and do want to help create a highly
trained, educated work force, the discussion is necessarily an incomplete one
when it is limited to economic considerations and driven by self-interest.

To its detriment, the standards debate today is largely governed by mech-anistic nineteenth-century ideas. You can almost hear the machine clanking. You can almost see the arrows being drawn to the rectangles and the squares. The U.S. economic and social systems are, however, more complex and chaotic than the Goldberg and Traiman essay allows.

No one, especially critics of the current standards movement, could be against striving to create a population of well-educated, highly skilled peo-ple. When standards are debated, however, the conception of work embedded in them must be examined. How society and its work are related to educators, educational institutions, and their roles must be considered. Education is much more than preparation for work. And Goldberg and Traiman acknowledge as much.

Nevertheless, in the political push for standards with high-stakes testing and for what is called consequences, or accountability, it is easy to lose sight of the flesh and blood reality of schools and of the children who attend them. Where are the children to be found in this discussion?

## *Simplistic Pedagogical Ideas*

In his essay "The Rhythmic Claims of Freedom and Discipline," Alfred North Whitehead talks about learning going through three stages, which he calls romance, precision, and generalization.[92]

Whitehead said that of the three, only romance provides the motivation, the desire, and the impulse to be disciplined, to become precise, to focus, to develop, to find one's life work, and to stick with it. And out of the discipline built on romance, one ultimately makes contributions to knowledge and to the general welfare, via the process he called generalization. Yet standards, as they are currently being expressed and when they are attached to high-stakes test-ing, undermine the possibility for children to do what Whitehead described as being romantic with ideas. No opportunity exists for children to play around with ideas, to be fascinated—to be all of the things that enlightened business leaders say they would like their workers to be. Sadly, the standards move-ment that Goldberg and Traiman embrace works against and subverts those qualities.

The digital age, for whatever else it has done, has radically decontextual-ized experience for students. A proper role for schools is not to decontextu-alize it further by relying on standardized tests, but to build on the human relationships that inhere in schools and to use those human relationship as a basis for recontextualizing the experience of students.[93] Thus the currently popular view of standards with its lists of facts, top-down assessments, and state-imposed punishments operates against sound pedagogy.

### Alternatives to the Standards Movement

It would be fair for Goldberg and Traiman to ask what alternatives business has outside of supporting current standards movement. At least two examples come quickly to mind. The business community, which, according to Goldberg and Traiman, wants and needs students to perform to a higher academic standard, could stop marketing to children in schools. That dramatic act on the part of businesses would increase standards immediately.

The quality of the American school curriculum is under assault by the same corporations that Goldberg and Traiman claim want to improve student academic performance. Virtually every corporation with a product or service to sell or a point of view to promote is busy figuring out ever more ingenious ways to bend the school curriculum to its short-term purposes—at the expense of defensible academic standards. My research suggests that commercializing activities in the schools increased dramatically during the nineties.[94] Commercial activities now shape the structure of the school day, influence the content of the school curriculum, and may determine whether children will have access to a variety of instructional technologies. A business community that took its standards rhetoric seriously would not have any part of the cheesy, sleazy, marketing mayhem that corporate money has unleashed on America's schools and their students.

A second, and much more costly, step would be to dismantle secondary education, as it is currently constituted.[95] In my view, high school might best be replaced by creating educative environments dispersed throughout America's social, political, cultural, and economic institutions. This would mean a long-term commitment to transform those institutions to make room for young learners. No insurance office, state legislature, dance company, charity, or other organization would be untouched by a reformation of this magnitude. However, this is a real alternative to the youth ghettos called high schools, populated by adolescents who are too disconnected from too many meaningful opportunities to learn how to come of age.

Few executives likely will rush to take up either suggestion. Eliminating marketing to children in schools means the loss of a potential market. Dismantling high schools would cost a considerable amount of money and require a fundamental redefinition of the way business is conducted. In the absence of any interest in these or similarly uncomfortable proposals, earnest conversations with the business community probably will continue about less consequential, less expensive, and thus more palatable reforms; that is, reforms such as standards.

In the final analysis, the issue is not how well what seventeen-year-olds should know is specified but what kind of world society wishes to create. On that issue, Goldberg and Traiman offer little useful guidance.

---

# Comment by John H. Stevens

Since the publication of *A Nation at Risk* in 1983, the business community has been one of the most persistent and effective participants in the effort to improve America's public schools. Business has stayed the course with education reform because knowledge and skills are even more important to the nation's economy and individual success now than they were two decades ago. The title of Milton Goldberg and Susan L. Traiman's paper, "Why Business Backs Education Standards," indicates that two of America's most knowledgeable and influential business organizations—the National Alliance of Business and The Business Roundtable—have concluded that education standards must be the centerpiece of education reform. Goldberg and Traiman do not argue that standards-based reforms are more effective than others, but they present from a business perspective a well-reasoned and powerful explanation of why that is the only approach that will prepare America's young people to compete economically now and into the future.

## *The New Economy*

Goldberg and Traiman's description of the new economy provides the broad context necessary to understand the business perspective regarding education standards. Arguing over whether or not one likes recent economic developments and their educational and social consequences is of little value. The combined forces of globalization and technology that have been unleashed in the world are both inevitable and irreversible. Those who fight them will lose; and those who work with them to the greatest advantage will win. These combined forces are not only contributing to increased economic productivity but are also improving the quality of life for people around the world.

Critics are rightly concerned that some people are being left behind by these changes. Throughout the course of history, significant technological advances have always favored those who create and learn to use new tools most effectively. The emergence of the new economy as described by Goldberg and Traiman places a greater premium on education than ever before. The challenge to America is to educate as many of its people as possible to levels that will enable them to contribute to and participate more fully in the new, internationally integrated, highly technological world.

The United States will never again dominate the world economy to the extent that it did for decades after the Second World War. Strong industrial, technological, and educational developments in other nations have caused America's share of world markets to remain about the same as it was two decades ago. Despite what critics may say, the proliferation of free-market democracies, free-trade zones, and other such open structures are positive developments. The resulting emergence of an integrated economy with the constant interaction and flow of people, ideas, products, and services across international boundaries has opened up exciting opportunities for people to participate in worldwide business activities, if they have the attributes necessary to do so.

The chancellor of the Texas A&M System, Barry Thompson, commissioned a study about the work-force needs of Texas businesses and the extent to which graduates from A&M institutions met those requirements. The report, *Changing Employment Demands and Requirements for College Graduates: Focus Group Interviews with Industry, Agency, and School District Representatives in Texas,* by Mary Zey, Alvin Luedka, and Steven Murdoch, was released in January 1999. Its findings associated with globalization and technology apply just as well to public school students as to university graduates.

In the several focus groups conducted, human resource professionals reported that graduates from Texas A&M institutions possess some desirable qualities and lack others. Texas A&M graduates were valued for their technical expertise, personal work habits, and organizational loyalty. But they were found lacking in cultural sophistication, human relations, and other soft skills that are needed in business today. One participant remarked, "To be more competitive, they need more life experiences, out of cow towns, so they can interact in Fortune 500 companies." Another noted that graduates of A&M universities were less sophisticated than graduates from other institutions. He said, "We can't send them to New York, much less Japan." Yet another remarked that production facilities were being moved to Mexico and that finding people who could work and live there was difficult. Participants agreed that, in the future, employees would be required to move from one location to another and integrate into various teams in global corporations and a variety of cultural settings. The study found that businesses are willing to sacrifice a measure of technical expertise if a prospective employee could function effectively in another language and culture.[96] The report concluded that people who have both technical competence and the ability to function in multilanguage and multicultural settings have an enormous advantage over others who lack those proficiencies.

This reality is not easy for Americans to accept. Relatively few U.S. citizens are bilingual, much less multilingual. Cultural awareness is not only lacking, it is often frowned upon, and Americans have a well-earned reputation for not being particularly adept in international settings. Perhaps only business can bring this message to America's people and its schools.

The profound educational and social consequences of the emerging technologies similarly are not well understood by the American people and the educational establishment. After years of unprecedented economic growth and expansion, unemployment in the U.S. is today at an all-time low and businesses find it particularly difficult to hire the scientists, engineers, and technicians they need to operate competitively. Companies compete for qualified people in the communities where they are located and recruit employees from other states and countries around the world. American business executives, and even higher education leaders, have demanded that Congress increase the number of H1B visas so they can employ even for a limited time highly qualified professionals and technicians from other countries.

Other developments in the business world have similar effects. Economic globalization has brought on a constant stream of business mergers and acquisitions, many of which are international in scope. These consolidations usually result in major reductions in the overall work force of the companies involved. The merged enterprise eliminates redundant positions and flattens the organization by reducing the number of managerial and supervisory personnel. It also releases production workers who lack the knowledge and skills to operate the advanced technologies being employed by the business. At the same time, new employees are brought in who can use emerging technology effectively, work independently without extensive supervision, and help develop new processes to increase the productivity and competitiveness of the enterprise.

The new international (globalized) enterprises locate business activities and functions wherever they can be carried out most cost-effectively. Business must employ the skilled personnel required to operate competitively, and decisions about where to locate are affected by work-force quality and availability. Other factors, including transportation, availability and cost of energy, and tax policy, also are involved in business decisions to expand, relocate, or start up. But even if skilled workers can be secured from elsewhere, Goldberg and Traiman point out that it is difficult to move executives, managers, scientists, engineers, and other professionals, as well as skilled technicians, to a community with a substandard public school system.

*Education and Earnings*

Most Americans understand generally that people with more education have greater earning power, but Goldberg and Traiman refute some common misunderstandings about what is happening in the workplace and the job market:

—Technology has not eliminated or even reduced the demand for skilled workers as some experts had expected only a decade or so ago. Instead, it has devalued the contributions of unskilled workers while increasing the value of skilled workers. As a result, the spread in compensation between skilled (educated) and unskilled (uneducated) workers has increased dramatically in recent years and continues to grow.

—Contrary to what many people believe, the new economy is creating large numbers of very good jobs. Three-quarters of the job growth between 1989 and 1995 occurred in the ranks of relatively high-paying occupations. An increasing demand has been evident for people in the professions, at executive and managerial levels, and with high levels of technical competency.

—Relatively few jobs are classified now as "unskilled labor," and a high school diploma no longer represents adequate preparation to succeed in the job market.

—The pervasive use of advanced technology has created a whole new job category, the knowledge worker, which places an unprecedented premium on education beyond high school.

The good news is that more and more American students are completing a four-year or two-year college degree, and these better-educated young people are making up an increasingly larger part of the work force. However, too many Americans still do not complete high school and many who do finish still lack the academic foundation to succeed in postsecondary education. As Goldberg and Traiman quoted from the Secretary's Commission on Achieving Necessary Skills report, without the necessary knowledge and skills, young people "face the bleak prospects of dead end work interrupted only by periods of unemployment."

Too many Americans and too many American communities find themselves on the low side of the educational divide. Those who lack the knowledge and skills to fill the new jobs that are being created cannot participate in and benefit from the economic development that occurs in their own communities. Entire communities and many individuals are left out completely. If the present trends continue, the inability of many Americans to participate in the new economy will have serious social consequences for the nation.

## *Are Schools Delivering?*

Goldberg and Traiman do not ask, "Are schools improving?" but instead, "Are schools producing students with the knowledge and skill levels sufficient for them to succeed in this internationally competitive economic situation?" I agree with the authors' conclusion that the answer is no, particularly when considering the achievement levels of American high school students. Goldberg and Traiman refer extensively to *A Nation at Risk.* The fact that the report is still relevant after seventeen years of reform activities gives cause for alarm. Although data can tell different stories depending upon how they are used, there is no evidence that students and schools have improved their performance sufficiently to secure the economic future of the country. Consider the following:

—With only a few exceptions, National Assessment of Educational Progress results are flat over the last decade, with ethnic minority and disadvantaged students continuing to show significantly lower performance in all subjects and at all grade levels tested.

—Little improvement, if any, has been seen in college entrance test scores. Many experts argue that these scores are not a valid measure because the samples are not representative or consistent over time. Furthermore, the growing proportion of students taking college entrance tests means that the average results include increasing numbers of lower ranked students. However, this is another indicator of the failure of American schools to meet the present-day challenge. Students who aspire to attend college deserve an education that will prepare them to succeed there.

—The performance of U.S. students on international assessments is generally disappointing, but the news is not entirely bad. American elementary students generally compare well with the best-performing students in the world. American middle school students score about average. But American high school students regularly perform poorly, and Goldberg and Traiman point out another harsh reality that contradicts conventional wisdom. Although some progress has been made in the coursetaking patterns of high school students, the best-prepared American students still do not perform as well as students taking similar courses in other countries. The quality of the courses and instruction in American high schools as well as the efforts of its students do not compare well with most of the countries with which the United States must compete.

The message outlined by Goldberg and Traiman has not gotten through to many segments of the population, including far too many students, parents, and educators. Educators still advise students in ways that suggest they do not understand what is going on in the world today. For instance, American educators have not made a commitment to teach math and science to all students. Math proficiency is used to sort students at an early age, and schools make little effort to inform students and their parents about the academic preparation necessary to succeed in education, training, and employment after high school.

American students expect to make a good living during their lifetime, but they are not particularly interested in taking math, science, and other rigorous courses that will prepare them for the jobs that are most in demand today and that command the highest levels of compensation. Evidence shows that many students are making choices that constitute an avoidance of a rigorous high school education.

ACT research based on the company's tenth-grade PLAN assessment program confirms that some students' high school coursetaking patterns do not correspond to their aspirations. Of more than half a million PLAN-tested sophomores, 74 percent expected to attend a two-year or four-year college or university, but only 68 percent of these college-bound students had taken or were taking the courses needed to complete a college-prep curriculum by the time they finished high school. Yet many of those students self-reported that they needed extra help, particularly in math and science. Their self-perceptions were confirmed by performance on ACT's PLAN assessments. Only 36 percent scored twenty or above in math, meaning that only one-third of them could do higher level mathematics involving algebra, geometry, or trigonometry. Only one-third scored twenty or above in science, indicating that they understood and could analyze more complex scientific problems and procedures.[97]

Furthermore, the message about the career possibilities available for those with a sound technical preparation is not getting through. Parents, students, and educators do not understand that completing a rigorous certificate or two-year technical program leads to employment that commands beginning salaries far exceeding those of many jobs requiring baccalaureate degrees. They do not know that companies will invest in the continuing education of these employees and help them to build their careers to virtually any level they might choose.

Goldberg and Traiman also refute the old argument that American schools seek to educate all young people while school systems in other countries track many students into low level programs or force them to drop out entirely. The academic achievement of American students, particularly at the end of secondary school, does not measure up to that of students in the nations with which America competes, and many other industrialized nations graduate larger proportions of their student populations from secondary school. Given that reality, no reasonably informed person could argue that American young people are currently being well served by the public school system.

### *Remediation: The Costs to Business*

Goldberg and Traiman note that getting a handle on the remediation costs to business is difficult. The extent to which employers invest in developing the basic academic skills of their workers has not been documented and may be overstated. Employees with higher levels of education clearly produce fewer mistakes, increase productivity, and contribute more to any enterprise. Businesspeople are concerned about the high recruitment costs associated with hiring such employees. They must go to great lengths to find workers who have the desired proficiencies, and they often choose to leave positions vacant rather than fill them with unqualified people.

Remediation costs at the college level have been documented, and they are high. Presuming that almost everyone will need some formal education or training after high school to participate in the work force, such remediation costs are an important and useful measure of public school performance. Goldberg and Traiman point out that a lack of job-related proficiency leads to persistent underemployment and unemployment with unavoidable social costs and consequences.

### *Why Business Backs Standards and Standards-Based Reform*

A broad cross section of Americans agrees with business that more should be expected of students. People know that education provides the foundation necessary for success today and into the future.

No debate should arise about whether education standards are needed. Improvement can be measured against a baseline, but performance must also be measured against a stated goal or standard to know if it meets expectations. Businesspeople understand that defining clearly what one seeks to achieve is a necessary precondition for any purposeful action. In a similar way, education standards define what students are expected to know and be able to do at the end of each grade as they progress through the system to high school graduation. Standards provide the necessary centerpiece around which the rest of the educational system—curriculum, materials, instruction, pre- and in-service professional development, assessments, accountability, and resource allocations—must be organized.

Goldberg and Traiman are correct when they state that standards alone are not sufficient to drive school improvement. Standards establish performance expectations, but assessment and accountability cause purposeful action. Accountability requires that meaningful consequences be associated with performance. Thus, real sanctions are imposed for persistent low performance; recognition and possibly rewards are provided for success. For accountability purposes, student achievement should be measured by criterion-referenced tests aligned with the standards. Educators should not have to choose whether to aim instruction toward the standards or the tests.

The Texas public school accountability system is acknowledged widely as one of the most effective in the nation. It requires the Texas Education Agency to assign annually one of four ratings to each district and school campus— Exemplary, Recognized, Acceptable, or Low Performing—based mostly on the percentage of students who pass the state's standardized Texas Assessment of Academic Skills (TAAS) tests. The commissioner of education has the authority and is required to apply a progressive series of sanctions to entire school districts or individual school campuses that are rated Low Performing. School campuses that receive the highest ratings are recognized and receive financial awards through the Texas Successful Schools program. Although many Texas reforms date back to the 1980s, significant measurable school improvement began only after the legislature established the accountability system in 1993 at the urging of the business community.

Although it sounds simple enough, defining education standards—what students should know and be able to do—is a difficult, and often contentious, process. States have taken different approaches. Some have adopted rigorous standards that might be considered world-class in nature. In those states, most students have not met expectations and public school performance has been labeled an overall failure. Other states, such as Texas, have taken an incremental approach to standards-based reform and raised performance expectations for students and schools gradually over a period of years. Even though Texas had an education commissioner named Mike Moses, it did not carve its new student learning standards in stone when they were adopted by the state Board of Education in 1997. At the same meeting in which the standards were adopted, the board also adopted a schedule through 2020 for reviewing and revising those standards. This reexamination will not only allow Texas to raise its performance expectations for students and schools, but it will also enable the state to revise the standards in a way that reflects recent changes in expectations of postsecondary education and the workplace. Finally, setting standards should not be an abstract academic exercise, but an effort to focus the school system on levels of achievement that will prepare students for success in the real world.

To facilitate this, Goldberg and Traiman emphasize that "employers . . . have an obligation to articulate clearly the standards they adhere to, whether the expectation is for specific levels of knowledge or for particular academic, technical, and people skills." Higher education must similarly clarify the knowledge and skills that are necessary for students to succeed in college programs. Evidence is available that this has not yet been done.

The ACT Successful Transition to College series compares the learning priorities of high school teachers and college professors within various academic disciplines. A significant and disturbing lack of agreement exists regarding what they believe is most important for students to learn. The ACT research confirms that the American curriculum generally has too much material at every grade level in every discipline. Professors identified the relatively few learning objectives that were most important to succeed in college. High school teachers generally thought that all objectives were of nearly equal importance and frequently ranked objectives very highly that professors believed were insignificant. If educators within the same discipline do not agree, why should anyone believe that business has communicated its needs with sufficient clarity so that educators and students understand them and can work toward achieving them?

## The Lure of Lifelong Learning

Lifelong learning is not just a lure; it is a necessity. No point in education can ever represent all the knowledge and skill an individual will need to meet the challenges of a lifetime. People must acquire in elementary and secondary school the basic functional abilities—reading, writing, speaking, problem-solving, and technological competence; the academic foundation in the core subjects; and the intellectual capacity to learn continuously in formal and informal settings. Unfortunately, most students do not come out of high school ready to succeed in postsecondary education, much less engage independently in lifelong learning.

In this regard, high school graduation requirements, another form of education standards, are significant. Goldberg and Traiman mention Diane Ravitch's observations regarding the changed function of schooling. Ravitch correctly argues that the system seems to have succumbed to a "whatever mentality." Especially at the high school level, the school experience has been adjusted to cater to the multiple interests of young people or has been watered down so they can succeed without much effort. I was advocating the rigorous core course requirements of the Texas Recommended High School Program in a discussion in spring 2000 with a counselor in a leading Texas high school. She responded that I must keep in mind that our discussion was about high school, where students should be encouraged to choose from a wide variety of curriculum offerings in a way that best serves their individual needs and interests. In my view, encouraging students to select from a wide variety of courses in this way is not responsible if it distracts them from acquiring a solid academic foundation.

Goldberg and Traiman made an important point when they said, because a sound education is so necessary for success in life, standards are needed regardless of whether students attend public schools, are supported in private schools by vouchers, or are home-schooled. That position is not held generally by school choice advocates.

*Standards Work*

Standards do work. When students, educators, and the public understand clearly what is expected and there is accountability for results, improvement occurs. The experiences in North Carolina, Texas, and elsewhere are well documented. A comprehensive standards-based approach to public school improvement brings positive results.

Since the Texas legislature established the public school accountability system in 1993, student performance on statewide tests has improved steadily and significantly. The percentage of students passing all TAAS tests from 1994 through 2000 is presented in table 1. Reading and math tests are administered at grades three through eight and grade ten; writing tests are administered at grades four, eight, and ten.[98]

**Table 1. Test Takers Passing All Texas Assessment of Academic Skills Tests**
Percent

| Grade | 1994 | 1995 | 1996 | 1997 | 1998 | 1999 | 2000 | Change |
|-------|------|------|------|------|------|------|------|--------|
| Three | 56 | 65 | 67 | 70 | 73 | 78 | 76 | +20 |
| Four | 52 | 61 | 63 | 67 | 74 | 78 | 80 | +28 |
| Five | 56 | 63 | 69 | 74 | 79 | 82 | 85 | +29 |
| Six | 53 | 58 | 65 | 72 | 75 | 79 | 81 | +28 |
| Seven | 53 | 56 | 63 | 70 | 74 | 77 | 79 | +26 |
| Eight | 47 | 48 | 55 | 62 | 68 | 76 | 77 | +30 |
| Ten | 50 | 52 | 57 | 64 | 69 | 75 | 80 | +30 |

Source: "Texas TAAS Passing Rates Hit Seven-Year High; Four Out of Every Five Students Pass Exam," news release, Texas Education Agency, May 17, 2000.

Texas has made a firm commitment to close the historic performance gaps that have existed among various student groups. Schools are rated on how well each student group (African American, Hispanic, white, and economically disadvantaged students) performs in each subject (reading, math, and writing) separately. This disaggregation has had its desired effect. For example, the passing rates of all student groups have improved in fifth-grade reading, eighth-grade math, and all the tenth-grade tests (reading, math, and writing) that students must pass as a minimum high school graduation requirement, but African American, Hispanic, and economically disadvantaged students have made greater gains than white students (see figures 1–3).[99] Similar growth patterns exist in every grade level and for every subject.

Perhaps the most significant result of disaggregation is that Texas educators no longer believe that "those kids can't learn." By and large, they believe that effective teaching will allow virtually all students to perform up to statewide standards and expectations.

Initiatives to end social promotion are often another important, and controversial, element of a standards-based approach to education reform. Although agreement is not universal, these efforts have support from both business and education. Businesses have long abandoned the practice of checking for quality only at the end of the production line. They know that continual monitoring is the best way to assure that a quality result is achieved. Teachers, too, know that promoting students into learning situations for which they are not prepared is not good practice. Students who cannot participate successfully in class activities become disinterested, fall farther behind, and eventually drop out. But initiatives to provide extra help to these students have often been misreported by the media and misrepresented by critics. In 1999 Texas governor George W. Bush made a pledge that no child would be left

**Figure 1. Fifth-Grade Passing Rates in Reading**

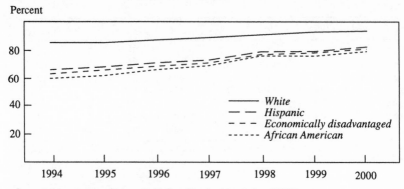

Source: Author presentation of data provided in Texas Education Agency's *Annual AEIS Reports.*

**Figure 2. Eighth-Grade Passing Rates in Mathematics**

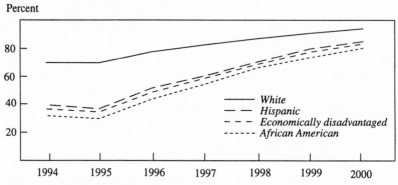

Source: Author presentation of data provided in Texas Education Agency's *Annual AEIS Reports.*

**Figure 3. Tenth-Grade Passing Rates for All Tests (Reading, Mathematics, and Writing)**

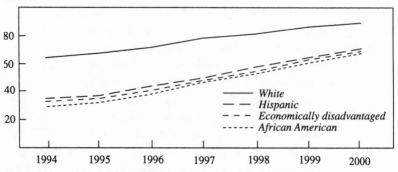

Source: Author presentation of data provided in Texas Education Agency's *Annual AEIS Reports.*

**Table 2. Texas Assessment of Academic Skills Performance at Student Success Initiative Checkpoints, 1994 and 1999**

| | 1994 | | | 1999 | | | |
|---|---|---|---|---|---|---|---|
| | Tested | Passing | Percent | Tested | Passing | Percent | Difference |
| Third-grade reading | 237,415 | 180,694 | 76 | 248,113 | 217,171 | 88 | +36,477 |
| Fifth-grade reading | 240,256 | 180,956 | 75 | 251,388 | 216,144 | 86 | +35,188 |
| Fifth-grade math | 241,963 | 144,556 | 60 | 254,344 | 228,016 | 90 | +83,460 |
| Eighth-grade reading | 235,638 | 174,578 | 74 | 263,578 | 230,903 | 88 | +56,325 |
| Eighth-grade math | 236,016 | 130,287 | 55 | 263,165 | 224,886 | 85 | +94,599 |

Source: Author analysis and presentation of data provided by the Texas Education Agency, Department of Curriculum, Assessment, and Technology, February 4, 2000.

behind and outlined a series of actions to help all students succeed. Initial media coverage projected the increasing numbers of students who would repeat a grade because they could not pass the state's standardized tests and failed to report on the rest of the governor's proposal. The legislature established the governor's Student Success Initiative, which requires students to be promoted at certain checkpoints on the basis of their academic achievement. The legislation also provided extensive resources for teacher training and extra help for students who need it as had been initially proposed.

Over the past few years, the standards-based reforms in Texas helped thousands of students reach the performance levels set out in the plan. The increasing numbers of student passing the TAAS tests at the checkpoints of the Student Success Initiative—third-grade reading, fifth-grade reading and math, and eighth-grade reading and math—are indicated in table 2.[100] Tens of thousands of Texas students at each grade level are meeting standards in reading, math, and writing that many of their counterparts could not reach only five years ago. Although ending social promotion for all students is an ambitious undertaking, the Student Success Initiative will help thousands more students learn the basic functional skills that are necessary for further schooling and in the real world.

Goldberg and Traiman document similar success with standards-based reforms in other states and school districts. I know of no other approach through which such impressive gains have been achieved. But no matter how well these reforms have worked, considerable resistance is still evident to standards, assessment, and accountability.

## Addressing the Backlash

The use of standardized tests in education has long been debated and is especially questioned when the stakes are high for students. For example, Goldberg and Traiman point out that the exit-level (tenth-grade) test used as a high school graduation standard in Texas recently withstood a challenge in federal district court from the Mexican American Legal Defense and Education Fund (MALDEF). This ruling was important because the graduation test is the ultimate standard toward which the whole statewide student assessment program is pointed. Ironically, at the same time the concept of an exit-level test was being challenged in the courts, the staff of the Texas Education Agency was developing specifications for a new exit-level test to be administered in the eleventh grade. Texas students completing the seventh grade in the spring of 2000 will have to pass the new, more rigorous eleventh-grade tests as a minimum high school graduation requirement. This change from testing students at the tenth grade to the eleventh grade was advocated by the Texas Business and Education Coalition (TBEC), whose supporters sought to establish a high school graduation standard that more closely matched the knowledge and skills required for success in postsecondary education and the workplace.[101] The author of the legislation, Senator Teel Bivins, was adamant that the new tests have predictive value in terms of the students' readiness for college.

Assessments must not measure only the extent to which students have achieved the described standards; they should have meaning in terms of some real accomplishment in the students' lives. For instance, concern exists across the country about the thousands of students who do not finish high school. Testing critics allege that standardized tests are obstacles that prevent students from succeeding in school and ultimately graduating. However, the tests at lower grades are fairly reliable indicators of student readiness to succeed in high school. Two years ago, fifty-three thousand Texas high school students were retained in the ninth grade because they did not pass a sufficient number of high school level courses to be promoted to the tenth grade. Research by Texas Education Agency staff at my request showed that students who failed any one of the assessments at the eighth-grade level were four times as likely to be retained in the ninth grade as students who passed all the tests. Students who passed all tests were retained in the ninth grade at a 7 to 8 percent rate while those who failed any one test—reading, math, writing, or social studies—were retained as a 30 to 32 percent rate.[102] The relatively large number of ninth-grade retentions was not caused by the challenges represented by the eighth-grade or tenth-grade tests, but by the fact that many students lack the knowledge and skills necessary to succeed in high school course work. The testing program helps schools identify students who are falling behind and get them the extra help they need to succeed in subsequent grades. The same principle applies to the knowledge and skills required for success in higher education or on the job. Unfortunately, these and other positive uses of standardized test results do not receive the wide publicity that critics have been able to generate.

The critics of high-stakes testing for students frequently say that focusing on improving opportunities for students to learn would be a better strategy. They have a point, but it should not be an either/or proposition. Standards, tests, and accountability mechanisms are not sufficient to get the job done. They are powerful drivers of change, but school capacity issues must also be addressed. Student achievement and school performance have not improved anywhere without considerable attention and investment focused on improving curriculum, materials, and, especially, teaching.

In several states, the failure of many students to perform up to expectations on new statewide tests has caused a backlash against standards-based school reforms. People do not accept that students and schools that had been performing adequately are suddenly labeled "low performing." When public support is thus jeopardized, state policymakers have felt it necessary to extend the time period for implementing new performance standards or delay the application of any consequences.

Goldberg and Traiman state that such delays are not good policy because they allow students and schools to continue performing at inadequately low levels. I believe that such actions may be necessary to sustain public support for reform and that delay is preferable to lowering the standards. By keeping the standards high, the desired effect of driving improved student achievement and school performance is preserved, and educators know they must still seek to achieve them. Being forced to abandon a standards-based approach altogether would be much more destructive than extending its implementation.

In any event, opposition to standards-based reforms will continue from certain critics, especially when they are associated with real stakes for individual students. But those who see standards, tests, and consequences as the enemy—even for students—are simply wrong. In a *Minneapolis Star Tribune* article about exit-level testing, I responded to an accusation by U.S. senator Paul Wellstone (D-Minn.) that high-stakes testing for students is cowardly by saying, "Let me tell you what I think is really cowardly, and it's the worst thing you can say to kids. Because of the circumstances of your birth, we don't believe that you can learn this stuff; we don't think you can pass these tests because you're poor, because you're African-American, because you're Hispanic, because you came from another country. . . . So we're not going to ask you to perform to these standards; we're just going to have you go through school, and if it feels good, we'll give you a diploma."[103]

Better communications about the standards and the whole reform package are needed in most states to build understanding, acceptance, and support among educators, students, parents, and the general public. The message is straightforward common sense. The state should define clearly what students should know and be able to do at the end of high school and at each grade level. Teachers should know the material their students are to learn (and more), and they should know how to teach it effectively to students who have different learning needs. The system must provide textbooks and other instructional materials that address the standards. Reliable and valid ways (tests) must be established to measure the extent to which students have learned what is expected of them. Consequences must be associated with the extent to which schools succeed in teaching their students. And finally, policymakers, educators, students, parents, and the general public must do their part if young people are to be adequately prepared to contribute to and participate fully in all aspects of life, now and in the years to come.

Just as business has played a crucial role in building the political will to engage in a serious, standards-based approach to school improvement, it must protect and sustain the reforms. America's future will be determined largely by how well this is done.

## Notes

1. *Continuing Commitment: Essential Components of an Educational System* (Washington: The Business Roundtable, 1995), pp. 6–7.

2. Thomas L. Friedman, *The Lexus and the Olive Tree* (New York: Farrar, Straus, Giroux, 1999), p. 41.

3. *1999 World Development Indicators* (Washington: World Bank, March 1999).

4. *Learning a Living: A SCANS Report for America 2000,* report of the Secretary's Commission on Achieving Necessary Skills (Department of Labor, 1992).

5. Norman C. Saunders and Betty W. Su, "The U.S. Economy to 2008: A Decade of Continued Growth," *Monthly Labor Review* (November 1999), p. 11.

6. Herbert Stein and Murray Foss, *The Illustrated Guide to the American Economy*, 3d ed. (Washington: AEI Press, 1999), p. 160.

7. Stein and Foss, *The Illustrated Guide to the American Economy*.

8. Robert D. Atkinson and Randolph H. Court, *The New Economic Index: Understanding America's Economic Transformation* (Washington: Progressive Policy Institute, 1998), p. 19.

9. Raymond Kurzweil, *The Age of Spiritual Machines: When Computers Exceed Human Intelligence* (New York: Viking, 1999).

10. The machine tool industry provides an excellent illustration of globalization as well. According to John Logan, chairman of the Association for Manufacturing Technology, U.S. machine tool builders are losing market share to offshore competitors at a worrisome rate. "Not long ago, 80 percent of all Ford and GM orders went to U.S. builders; now it's 50 percent." John Logan, address before the fourth annual meeting of Association for Manufacturing Technology, Lake Buena Vista, Fla., April 14, 1999.

11. *Futurework: Trends and Challenges for Work in the 21st Century* (Department of Labor, 1999), pp. 96–98.

12. *Bridging the Gap: Information Technology Skills for a New Millennium*, Executive Summary, a study conducted by the Information Technology Association of America, April 2000 (www.itaa.org/workforce/studies/hw00execsum.html).

13. *What Jobs Require: Literacy, Education, and Training, 1940–2006* (Princeton, N.J.: ETS Policy Information Center, 1999), p. 14.

14. *What Jobs Require*, p. 21, figure 5.

15. Timothy S. Bresnahan, Erik Brynjolfsson, and Lorin M. Hitt, "Technology, Organization, and the Demand for Skilled Labor," in Margaret M. Blair and Thomas A. Kochan, eds., *The New Relationship: Human Capital in the American Corporation* (Brookings, 2000), pp. 145–46.

16. See, for example, David R. Howell and Edward N. Wolff, "Trends in the Growth and Distribution of Skills in the U.S. Workplace, 1960–1985," *Industrial and Labor Relations Review*, 44 (April 1991), pp. 486–502.

17. Philip R. Day Jr. and Robert H. McCabe, "Remedial Education: A Social and Economic Imperative," Issue Paper (Washington: American Association of Community Colleges, October 1997).

18. *What Work Requires of Schools: A SCANS Report for America 2000*, Report of the Secretary's Commission on Achieving Necessary Skills (Department of Labor, 1991), p. xv.

19. National Alliance of Business, *Workforce Economic Trends* (September 1998), p. 3.

20. *What Jobs Require*, pp. 32–33.

21. National Alliance of Business, *Workforce Economic Trends* (February 2000), p. 2.

22. National Alliance of Business, *Workforce Economic Trends* (June 1998), p. 2.

23. Douglas Braddock, "Occupational Employment Projections to 2008," *Monthly Labor Review* (November 1999), p. 51.

24. John K. Folger and Charles B. Nam, "Trends in Education in Relation to Occupational Structure," *Sociology of Education* (Fall 1964), pp. 19–33.

25. National Alliance of Business, *Workforce Economic Trends* (February 2000), p. 7.

26. "The Editor's Desk," *Monthly Labor Review* (www.bls.gov/opub/ted/tedhome.htm [December 9, 1999]). See also Douglas Braddock, "Occupational Employment Projections to 2008," *Monthly Labor Review* (November 1999), pp. 51–77.

27. Department of Labor, *20 Million Jobs: January 1993–November 1999*, report by the Council of Economic Advisors and the chief economist, Department of Labor (December 3, 1999) (www.dol.gov/_sec/public/media/reports/20mill/main.htm [March 13, 2000]).

28. Department of Labor, *20 Million Jobs.*

29. *Jobs: Preparing a Workforce for the 21st Century,* a National Issues Forums Book, prepared by Public Agenda (Dubuque, Iowa: Kendall/Hunt Publishing, 1998), pp. 3–4.

30. Memorandum from Anthony Carnevale, vice president for public leadership, and Donna Desrochers, research scientist, Education Testing Service, May 2000.

31. National Alliance of Business, *Workforce Economic Trends* (June 1998), p. 12.

32. Telephone interview with Richard W. Judy, director, Center for Workforce Development, and president, Hudson Institute, Indianapolis, Ind., April 19, 2000.

33. Provisions are written into the legislation to protect American workers from losing their jobs to professionals from abroad who qualify as H1B workers.

34. National Alliance of Business, *Workforce Economics Trends* (Summer 1999), p. 7.

35. National Alliance of Business, *Workforce Economic Trends* (June 1998).

36. Memorandum from Carnevale and Desrochers.

37. *Employment Status of School Age Youth, High School Graduates and Dropouts, 1997* (Department of Labor, Bureau of Labor Statistics, 1997).

38. National Commission on Excellence in Education, *A Nation at Risk: The Imperative for Educational Reform* (Government Printing Office, 1983).

39. National Commission on Excellence in Education, *A Nation at Risk*, pp. 18–21.

40. David Kearns and James Harvey, *A Legacy of Learning* (Brookings, 2000).

41. Kearns and Harvey, *A Legacy of Learning*, pp. 4–5.

42. Kearns and Harvey, *A Legacy of Learning*, pp. 26–28.

43. Kearns and Harvey, *A Legacy of Learning*, pp. 28–29.

44. Kearns and Harvey, *A Legacy of Learning*, p. 30.

45. Kearns and Harvey, *A Legacy of Learning*, p. 34.

46. Organization for Economic Cooperation and Development, *Education at a Glance: OECD Indicators, 1998* (Paris, France, 1998), table C23, as cited in Kearns and Harvey, *A Legacy of Learning*, p. 33.

47. Arthur Andersen reports, for example, that 81 percent of its new hires are college graduates; at Hallmark, the number is 68 percent; at Chase Manhattan and Xerox, it is 48 percent. See Kearns and Harvey, *A Legacy of Learning*, p. 15, table 1-1.

48. American Association of Community Colleges, "Remedial Education: A Social and Economic Imperative," Issue Paper (October 1997).

49. See David W. Breneman, "Remediation in Higher Education: Its Extent and Cost," in Diane Ravitch, ed., *Brookings Papers on Education Policy 1998* (Brookings, 1998), as cited in Kearns and Harvey, *A Legacy of Learning*, p. 14.

50. *The Bottom Line: Basic Skills in the Workplace* (Departments of Labor and Education, 1988), p. 12.

51. "Frequently Asked Questions," American Society for Training and Development (www.astd.org [April 21, 2000]).

52. In 1995, for example, MCI spent about 10 percent of its $75 million training budget on remediation; Polaroid spent $700,000 in the late 1980s at its Cambridge, Massachusetts, operations to teach basic English and math to about one thousand both new and veteran employees; Motorola spent an average of $1,350 per worker per year for six basic skills courses; and in 1994 the American Management Association estimated that its members spent an average of $244 on remediation per employee. See Nelson Smith, "Standards Mean Business," a study paper prepared for the National Alliance of Business, 1996, p. 2.

53. National Commission on Excellence in Education, *A Nation at Risk*, p. 9.

54. National Alliance of Business, *Workforce Economic Trends* (June 1998), p. 11.

55. Bruce O. Boston, *The Cutting Edge of Common Sense* (Washington: National Alliance of Business, 1993), p. 1.

56. Norman R. Augustine, "Foreword," *A Business Leader's Guide to Setting Academic Standards* (Washington: The Business Roundtable, 1996), p. 2.

57. As *A Nation at Risk* stated the point (p. 5): "If an unfriendly foreign power had attempted to impose on America the mediocre educational performance that exists today, we might well have viewed it as an act of war."

58. *Continuing Commitment,* pp. 6–8.

59. "A Common Agenda for Improving American Education," joint statement by The Business Roundtable, U.S. Chamber of Commerce, and National Alliance of Business, Washington, 1996.

60. *Hiring Smart: An Employer's Guide to Using School Records* (Washington: National Alliance of Business, The Business Roundtable, and U.S. Chamber of Commerce, 1977).

61. National Alliance of Business, *Work America* (March 2000), p. 2.

62. *What the Public Wants from Higher Education* (Washington State University, Social and Economics Sciences Research Center, 1995).

63. Diane Ravitch, *The Troubled Crusade: American Education, 1945–1980* (Basic Books, 1983), p. 48.

64. Ravitch, *The Troubled Crusade*, p. 55, as cited in Kearns and Harvey, *A Legacy of Learning*, p. 41.

65. *The Progress of Education Reform, 1999–2001* (Denver: Education Commission of the States, 1999).

66. David Grissmer and Ann Flanagan, *Exploring Rapid Achievement Gains in North Carolina and Texas* (Washington: National Education Goals Panel, 1998), pp. 9–10, 12ff.

67. Grissmer and Flanagan, *Exploring Rapid Achievement Gains in North Carolina and Texas,* passim.

68. Matt Gandal, "Are We Seeing Better Results?" National Education Summit Briefing Book (Washington: Achieve, 1999).

69. *Denver Post*, February 29, 2000.

70. Frederick Douglass Middle School (www.noexcuses.org/report/hodge.html [April 25, 2000]).

71. Jean Johnson and Steve Farkas, *Getting By: What American Teenagers Really Think of Their Schools* (New York: Public Agenda, 1997).

72. See, for example, "A Common Agenda for Improving American Education."

73. *Building Support for Tests That Count* (Washington: The Business Roundtable, 1998).

74. "Public Agenda Reality Check 2000 Special Report," *Education Week* (February 16, 2000).

75. The Business Roundtable, "Holding the Line on Higher Standards and Tougher Tests," *CEO Education Update* (March 2000), p. 1.

76. Paul Wellstone, "High Stakes Tests Fail Our Children," *USA Today*, January 13, 2000.

77. P. S. Donahue and others, *The NAEP 1998 Reading Report Card for the Nation and the States* (Department of Education, National Center for Education Statistics, 1999).

78. C. M. Reese and others, *The NAEP 1996 Mathematics Report Card for the Nation and the States* (Department of Education, National Center for Education Statistics, 1997).

79. "Public Agenda Reality Check"; and Belden Russonello and Stewart and Research/Strategy/Management, *Raising Education Standards and Assessing the Results of a Public Opinion Survey* (Washington: The Business Roundtable, August 2000).

80. Louis V. Gerstner, "Don't Dumb Down Education Standards," *USA Today*, January 3, 2000, p. 19A.

128 *Brookings Papers on Education Policy: 2001*

81. *National Education Summit Action Statement*, 1999 National Education Summit, October 1, 1999.

82. See, for example, Berman, Weiler Associates, *Improving Student Performance in California: Recommendations for the California Roundtable* (Berkeley, Calif., 1982).

83. National Commission on Excellence in Education. *A Nation at Risk*.

84. David C. Berliner and Bruce J. Biddle, *The Manufactured Crisis: Myths, Fraud, and the Attack on America's Public Schools* (Reading, Mass.: Addison-Wesley, 1995).

85. Chester E. Finn Jr. and Michael J. Petrilli, *The State of State Standards 2000* (Washington: Thomas B. Fordham Foundation, 2000).

86. Bill Moyers and the Corporation for Entertainment and Learning, *The Image Makers* (Alexandria, Va.: PBS Video, 1984), videorecording.

87. Diane Ravitch, *National Standards in American Education: A Citizen's Guide* (Brookings, 1995), pp. 12–14.

88. Gerald W. Bracey, "We Crush Children under Unrealistic Standardized Tests," *USA Today*, September 2, 1999, p. 17A.

89. See, for example, Linda M. McNeil, "Contradictions of School Reform: Educational Costs of Standardized Testing," in Michael W. Apple, ed., *Critical Social Thought* (New York: Routledge, 2000).

90. Eric A. Hanushek, "Throwing Money at Schools," *Journal of Policy Analysis and Management,* vol. 1, no. 1 (1981), pp. 19–41; Eric A. Hanushek, "The Economics of Schooling: Production and Efficiency in Public Schools," *Journal of Economic Literature,* vol. 24, no. 3 (1986), pp. 1141–77; Eric A. Hanushek, "The Impact of Differential Expenditures on School Performance." *Educational Researcher,* vol. 18, no. 4 (1989), pp. 45–65; Eric A. Hanushek, "When School Finance 'Reform' May Not Be a Good Policy," *Harvard Journal on Legislation,* vol. 28, no. 2 (1991), pp. 423–56; and Eric A. Hanushek, and others, *Making Schools Work: Improving Performance and Controlling Costs* (Brookings, 1990).

91. Larry V. Hedges, Richard D. Laine, and Rob Greenwald. "Does Money Matter? A Meta-Analysis of Studies of the Effects of Differential School Inputs on Student Outcomes," *Educational Researcher,* vol. 23, no. 3 (1994), pp. 5–14; and Alan B. Krueger, "Economic Considerations and Class Size," Working Paper 447, Princeton University, Industrial Relations Section, September 2000.

92. Alfred North Whitehead, *The Aims of Education and Other Essays* (Free Press, 1967).

93. Here I draw on the thoughts of John Dewey in *Experience and Education* (New York: Collier, 1965).

94. Alex Molnar, "Cashing In on Kids: The Second Annual Report on Trends in Schoolhouse Commercialism," University of Wisconsin-Milwaukee, Center for the Analysis of Commercialism in Education, 1999.

95. Here I am drawing on the ideas of Paul Goodman in *Growing Up Absurd: Problems of Youth in the Organized System* (Random House, 1960), and *New Reformation: Notes of a Neolithic Conservative* (Random House, 1969).

96. Mary Zey, Alvin Luedke, and Steven Murdock, *Changing Employment Demands and Requirements for College Graduates: Focus Group Interviews with Industry, Agency, and School District Representatives in Texas* (Texas A&M University System, Strategic Policies Research Group, January 1999), pp. 22–23.

97. "Is the Graduating Class of 2000 Prepared for Jobs of the New Millennium?" *ACT Information Brief,* No. 99-1.

98. Texas Education Agency, *Annual AEIS Reports* (www.tea.state.tx.us).

99. Texas Education Agency, *Assessments Results* (www.tea.state.tx.us).

100. "TAAS Helps Kids!" communication from the Texas Business and Education Coalition to the Texas legislature, April 19, 1999.

101. "Strengthening the Statewide Assessment Program," a policy goal statement of the Texas Business and Education Coalition, November 1996.

102. "TAAS Helps Kids!"

103. Rob Hotakaninen, "Texas Graduation Test Unbiased, Court Says," *Star Tribune*, January 8, 2000, p. A10.

# State Academic Standards

CHESTER E. FINN JR. *and*
MARCI KANSTOROOM

S tandards-based reform has been America's premier education
strategy for more than a decade. Its many backers seek stronger
school and student performance and more equal opportunities for children,
especially disadvantaged youngsters. Every state in the union claims to be
engaged in this challenging and high-minded quest. Under both Republicans
and Democrats, Congress and the White House have recast federal policy to
support standards-based reform. Business leaders, school officials, newspaper editors, and teacher unionists all pledge their allegiance to this ambitious
approach to educational renewal.

Hopeful signs abound. Some states are boosting their scores, children are
learning more, teachers are using surer methods of instruction. Education is
attracting more high-level attention and political energy than ever before. Yet
standards-based reform also faces genuine peril. Its enemies' ranks are growing. Its allies sometimes falter. Careless implementation has produced snafus.
The future for standards-based reform is uncertain. But the price of failure
would be high.

## Background

Most people trace the roots of today's academic standards movement to
the 1983 report *A Nation at Risk*. As dismay deepened over faltering student
performance and the poor performance of American children on international
assessments, attention began to shift from school inputs (for example,
resources, programs, and facilities) as indicators of education quality to academic outcomes. As has been known since the 1966 report by James Cole-
man, *Equality of Educational Opportunity*, no sure link exists between what

131

goes into a school and what comes out. By stirring the nation's awareness of the inadequacies of its K–12 education system, the National Commission on Excellence in Education began to press educators and policymakers to focus on results. The National Governors' Association gave this effort a boost in the mid-eighties. And the 1989 summit held in Charlottesville, Virginia, yielded America's first-ever set of national education goals, six targets to be met by the year 2000. The third of these called for students to "demonstrate competency in challenging subject matter, including English, mathematics, science, history and geography." Framing so broad a goal, however, turned out to be the easy part. What, exactly, were "competency" and "challenging subject matter"? Who was to decide? What would be the measures of performance? These questions turned out to be far harder to answer.

Even before Charlottesville, the National Council of Teachers of Mathematics (NCTM) had embarked on standard setting in its field. Post-Charlottesville, others joined this effort, including the National Science Teachers Association, the American Association for the Advancement of Science, the National Council for the Social Studies, the National History Standards Project, the Geography Standards Education Project, the New Standards Project, and more.

The national efforts yielded mixed reviews. Some provoked intense controversy. The national history standards proved to be a political lightning rod. In English, the national standards project was defunded in 1994 by the U.S. Department of Education because the draft produced by the National Council of Teachers of English and the International Reading Association was so weak. The NCTM math standards are probably the best known of these efforts, but even they caused dissension as critics referred to them as "fuzzy math" and "rain forest math." (They have recently been revised.)

Some disciplines were riven by disputes over how and what students should be taught. In English, proponents of phonics instruction and whole language battled about how children learn to read. In the higher grades, educators debated whether students should be exposed to the Western literary canon. In math, they quarreled over whether classrooms should focus on basic skills or real-world problems (that pupils can solve with a calculator).

As the national efforts stumbled, individual states largely had to set their own standards. In 1994 Congress passed Goals 2000 legislation, which provided federal funds to assist them with this process. Congress also refashioned the Title I program for disadvantaged students to link it with the standards-based strategy. The idea was to reorient the giant compensatory education program so that it focused on results instead of services. States would have five years to develop academic standards and tests to measure the academic gains of poor children served by Title I. By June 2000, all but one of the states had written standards and claimed to be developing tests aligned with those standards—though many still had a distance to go.

## The Theory of Standards-Based Reform

Standards are the first leg of the accountability tripod on which the standards-based reform strategy rests. The way to improve results is not just to stipulate the results wanted, but also to devise reliable means of evaluating progress toward them and to create tangible incentives and disincentives for all participants in the education process.

No improvement (save for the random kind) is apt to occur without standards that spell out intentions and create benchmarks by which to assess progress. As the Cheshire cat told Alice, if you do not care where you want to get to, "then it doesn't matter which way you go." Standards are the target that gives people a place to aim their arrows and a means by which to gauge how hard they must pull on the bowstring. Standards allow mileage markers to be erected, so that how far one has come and how far one still has to go can be measured. They make it possible to track progress. At least as important, they create additional motivation or incentive to improve.

A behaviorist aspect to this reform strategy discomfits some educators, yet it is the way most of the world works. Knowing that someone is watching makes a difference to one's performance. Knowing that a nearby school has 60 percent of its students at standard might make teachers try harder with their pupils. And knowing what is expected can save wasted motion. Standards are neither a panacea nor a mechanism of change, but they do boost the likelihood of change and they point in the direction that change should carry educators and schools.

Putting the entire reform tripod into operation is difficult. Good standards are difficult to develop; good tests are more difficult to devise; and real consequences, being the most politically sensitive, are hardest to bring about. Still, some states and communities have all these elements in place, and early evidence indicates that they are making a difference. Without them, hundreds of thousands of youngsters would be left to fall further and further behind, rather than hustled into remediation, summer school, or intensive tutoring in phonics. Without them, today's heightened emphasis on teacher quality, preparation, knowledge, and pay would be far less likely. Without them, troubled schools would be far less apt to be reconstituted. Principals would hold onto their schools whether their results were strong or weak. Families would have fewer education choices. Preschool and after-school programs would be fewer and skimpier. Many of the new whole school designs that are being piloted would never have been developed.

A long list could be made of desirable education changes under way today that are inextricably linked to the emphasis on standards, assessments, and accountability for results. Which of them will work remains unknown, but much is being tried. Furthermore, instead of being tried randomly, because something feels good or looks glitzy or accords with someone's pet theory, many of today's reforms have at least a plausible link to the attainment of higher academic standards.

Most important, fewer children are falling through the cracks. Absent standards, it was too easy to ignore the millions of youngsters who were learning very little—many of them poor and minority children from troubled communities—or to settle for providing them with extra services that, all too often, turned out to have little to do with academic achievement. That is far harder to do in the standards era. Standards make good things happen for needy students.

### Will Standards-Based Reform Yield Academic Gains?

In the seventies, more than thirty states adopted minimum competency tests in response to agitation from parents, employers, and policymakers who were upset about worthless diplomas and weak student skills.

At the time, Diane Ravitch called the movement for minimum competency tests "as close to grassroots rebellion against the education profession as we've had in this country." It was led by parents who saw signs that their children were not learning as much as they should and sometimes could not even read their own diplomas.[1] Many educators denounced this movement, claiming that its tests were unreliable and biased against minorities. But ample evidence shows that the tests did what they were meant to do: make minimum competence in basic skills nearly universal among U.S. high school graduates. Perhaps a modest and overdue accomplishment, but a worthy one.

Barbara Lerner explains the impact of such tests in Florida:

> On the first few tries, 80 to 90 percent of Florida's minority students failed the test. But they were not crushed, as the experts predicted they would be, and they did not give up and drop out in droves without diplomas. They kept trying and their teachers did too, working hard to help them learn from failure and, ultimately, to master

the skills they needed to graduate. By the fifth try, better than 90 percent of them did just that. They left school not just with a piece of paper, but in possession of basic skills that prepared them better for life than their older siblings had been when they left the same schools in the early 1970's. Not yet well prepared, but significantly better prepared.[2]

In Virginia, the results were similar. When the minimum competency test was first given, 17.8 percent of sophomores failed, including almost 42 percent of black students. Students who failed were given extra help in special classes or with tutors. The failure rate for the class of 1981 was down to 0.46 percent for blacks and 0.05 percent for whites by the spring of their senior year.[3]

Lerner believes that the reason minimum competency testing succeeded was that it set a clear standard, linked it to a single test, and tied the test outcome to a powerful incentive: high school graduation. The message was "You need these skills to be a contributing member of our society. . . . All of the other worthy goals you and your teachers may have must be pursued in addition to, not instead of, achievement of minimum competence in reading and arithmetic."[4]

## Standards-Based Reform in North Carolina and Texas

Most of today's efforts at standards-based education reform reach considerably higher than minimum competence. This poses a greater challenge, yet some states have embraced it with determination and, in a few cases, have shown early signs of success. The experience of two states that were among the first to develop full-blown accountability systems can illumine what other states might expect when they implement standards-based reform more completely.

In 1997 North Carolina and Texas were identified by the National Education Goals Panel as having posted gains on the largest number of indicators linked to the national education goals. These states had also made the largest gains in National Assessment of Educational Progress (NAEP) scores between 1992 and 1996. The goals panel commissioned a report to determine what factors could explain the success of the two states. Spending on schools, class size, and teachers' education level and experience were ruled out as explanations by the report's authors, David Grissmer and Ann Flanagan of RAND. The study concluded that the most plausible explanation for the gains was the creation of an aligned system of standards, curriculum, and assessments in these states, with schools held accountable for the improvement of all students.[5]

This is not to say that the implementation of standards-based reform in these two states has lacked controversy. A recent study by the Harvard Civil Rights

Project argues that Texas's heavy emphasis on the Texas Assessment of Academic Skills (TAAS) is causing test-prep activities to usurp the substantive curriculum in many classrooms. A survey of elementary school teachers in North Carolina found that teachers were being directed by their principals to teach more reading, writing, and math, subjects that are covered by the state assessment, even if that means teaching less science and social studies.[6]

Whether teaching to the test is truly harmful depends on how good the test is. If the test is well designed, then teaching to it means simply teaching pupils the intended curriculum. If the test is too rudimentary, teaching to it may squeeze out other worthwhile instruction. But intensive work on basic skills may be needed before students can benefit from more sophisticated classroom activities. One thing standards and tests have clearly accomplished in Texas and North Carolina is focusing attention on children who are not meeting the standards, children who may have been half-visible to policymakers before.

### Key Attributes of Good Standards

Standards are the foundation of the eponymous reform strategy, and much depends on their quality. But what distinguishes good standards from bad? Good standards get both form and content right. Form involves three essential qualities: clarity, specificity, and measurability. (Content begins with completeness and rigor.) Although these three qualities often go hand in hand, they are not the same.

Clear standards are written in plain English; teachers and parents can easily understand them. They make sense to ordinary people. (Some say, "They pass the barbershop test.")

Specific standards communicate exactly what is being asked of students. They give real guidance to teachers and parents (and to pupils themselves). If standards are too general and abstract, they do not help people to know what is supposed to be taught and learned in, say, third-grade math. They do not narrow the possibilities enough to ensure that all students will learn the same core content. Specificity signals what is most important for everyone to learn.

Measurable standards are amenable to assessment, to feedback mechanisms by which one can ascertain how one's child, one's student, one's class, or one's school (or state) is doing as compared with benchmarks.

### Clear, Specific Standards versus Vague, Abstract Standards

The difference between vague, abstract standards and clear, specific standards is not always self-evident, but with a bit of effort it can generally be detected. A vague English standard might say, "Students use the correct forms of personal and public writing for a variety of purposes and audiences." A more specific standard says, "Students write a persuasive essay that contains engaging introductory and clincher statements; presents a definite point of view; and fully develops that view with powerful and pertinent facts, evidence, arguments, and descriptions." In math, a vague standard states, "Students know how to measure geometric objects." A specific standard reads, "Students know, use and derive formulas for the perimeter, circumference, area, surface area and volume of many types of figures including cubes, pyramids, cylinders, cones, and spheres."[7]

### Measurable Standards

If there is no way to determine whether a certain objective has been achieved, then that objective is not a standard. "Students utilize mathematical reasoning skills in other disciplines and in their lives" might be a commendable educational goal but it is difficult to imagine a teacher or state being able to determine whether it has been accomplished.[8]

If standards are not clear, specific, and measurable, they are more like hopes and dreams than usable benchmarks for schools, parents, teachers, districts, and states. Clarity and measurability are sought by most standards-writers, but pressures arising from politics and hyper-participatory processes often work against specificity. Unless states make tough choices about what is essential for their students to know and be able to do, they will be unable to design fair assessments that can be linked to the standards. Abstract, vague standards make it likely that students will be tested on material they have never been taught—and thus that the test-maker will function as de facto standards-setter for teachers and schools in that jurisdiction.

### Comprehensive Standards

Standards must not only be clear, specific, and measurable. Form is necessary but not sufficient. Good standards must also contain the right content. Getting the content right means different things in different subjects, but in general comprehensiveness and rigor are sought. The discipline should be covered thoroughly—that portion of it which is suitable for K–12 students—which generally means blending well-selected knowledge with important skills. Good standards synthesize the two; they recognize that knowledge is to skills as bricks are to mortar. Cognitive skills are best developed in the context of mastering worthy subject knowledge.

The state of Washington's social studies standards say, "The student will identify social issues and define problems to pose historical questions," which (loosely) describes a skill but is divorced from any content material.[9] The standards can be neither taught nor assessed. By contrast, Virginia's history standards ask high school students to "analyze and explain the importance of World War I in terms of: the end of the Ottoman Empire and the creation of new states in the Middle East; the declining role of Great Britain and the expanding role of the United States in world affairs; political, social and economic changes in Europe and the United States; and the causes of World War II." Such a standard requires students to develop analytical skills through the study of specific historical events.

### Rigorous Standards

The comprehensiveness of standards is generally easier to appraise than their rigor. To gauge rigor with certainty, the state assessments that are (it is hoped) aligned with the standards and the cut scores or passing levels on those tests should be examined. If the standard calls for a student to "write and solve one-step linear equations in one variable," one still needs to know how many such equations a student must solve correctly to be judged to have mastered the prescribed skill. (Getting two problems out of ten right is far different from being expected to solve nine out of ten correctly.) If a student is expected to write a persuasive letter, how persuasive must it be, how elaborate, and how many spelling and grammar errors can it contain and still be deemed to have met the standard? Without knowing the level of work that is required to succeed on an assessment, how lofty the state's expectations are cannot be determined. Unfortunately, few states have made their assessments and cut scores available for outside analysis.

A more easily detected aspect of rigor is progressivity. The content included in standards should be as demanding as the society needs its graduates to have mastered, yet presented at a level appropriate to students of various ages. A clear progression or cumulation of content and skills should be evident at different grade levels. What is expected of high school students should be different from—and harder than—what is expected in the primary grades.

Kansas's standards for English and language arts illustrate the absence of such progressivity. They state that "learners will demonstrate skills in reading for a variety of purposes." Under this heading, elementary school students are expected to "3) comprehend extended passages of technical, exposition, persuasion, and complete episodes of narration; 4) reflect on and interpret what is read; 5) critically analyze and evaluate information and messages presented through print; [and] 6) identify their own purposes through reading." Kansas middle school students will "3) comprehend and summarize extended passages of technical, exposition, persuasion, and complete episodes of narration; 4) reflect on, interpret and evaluate what is read; 5) interpret and critique with increasing sophistication information and messages presented through print; [and] 6) identify a variety of purposes for reading." Kansas high school students will "3) comprehend, summarize and analyze extended passages of technical, exposition, persuasion, and complete episodes of narration; 4) reflect on, interpret and evaluate what is read; 5) critically analyze and evaluate information and messages presented through print and consider the truth or fallacy of what they read; [and] 6) identify and evaluate a variety of purposes for reading." Scant difference exists in the expectations for different grade levels.[10]

California's English standards for "literary response and analysis" much more clearly demonstrate an increasing level of difficulty through the grades. First graders should "identify and describe the story elements of plot, setting and characters, including the story's beginning, middle, and ending." Sixth graders should "explain the effects of key literary devices in a variety of fictional and nonfictional texts (e.g. symbolism, imagery, metaphor)." Eighth graders are expected to "evaluate the structural elements of the plot (e.g. subplots, parallel episodes, climax), the plot's development, and how (and whether) conflicts are (or are not) addressed and resolved." Ninth and tenth graders should be prepared to "interpret and evaluate the impact of ambiguities, subtleties, contradictions, ironies, and incongruities in text" and to "identify and describe the function of dialogue, scene design, soliloquies, and asides and character foils in dramatic literature."[11]

## Good Standards in Specific Subjects

The three qualities of form (clarity, specificity, and measurability) and the two qualities of content (comprehensiveness and rigor) are essential characteristics of good standards in all subjects. But each field also has unique elements. In English, for example, standards should include systematic acquisition of phonics skills and phonemic awareness in the primary grades, because research shows that students must master these decoding skills to read well. In math, students must master basic arithmetic skills but also need to understand the interconnections among the procedures and be able to use these procedures to solve problems. In history, important events, individuals, and issues in United States, European, and world history should be taught in context and in ways that avoid dogma. In science, lists of subjects to be covered should be supplemented by inclusion of the underlying principles of all the sciences and the connections among them.

## Quality of Today's Standards

How good are state academic standards today? Several careful efforts have been made to evaluate them in relation to detailed, subject-specific criteria. The Thomas B. Fordham Foundation (TBF) published an evaluation of state English standards in 1997. It was followed in 1998 with reports on standards in history, geography, mathematics, and science and also a summary report, *The State of State Standards*. The foundation returned to state academic standards in early 2000, with a new appraisal of those that had changed since the first round. They were evaluated by the same experts in each field: Sandra Stotsky (English), David Warren Saxe (history), Susan Munroe and Terry Smith (geography), Ralph Raimi and Lawrence S. Braden (mathematics), and Lawrence S. Lerner (science).[12]

Each evaluator developed criteria for rating state standards in the appropriate subject in consultation with other experts in the field. In math, for example, evaluators identified seven separate criteria; in geography, eight; in history, fifteen; in science, twenty-five; and in English, thirty-four. These criteria were applied to the standards for different grades (or clusters of grades), and points were assigned based on how well the standards met the criteria for the particular grade or cluster of grades. These point totals were used to assign overall grades to a state's standards.

The American Federation of Teachers (AFT) and the Council for Basic Education (CBE) have also published such evaluations. (CBE did this only once. AFT now does it annually.) After the first rounds of grades were issued, some policymakers professed to be confused by the different ratings from the three organizations. It turns out that the grades diverged because of different views about what a high-quality standard looks like and about what is particularly important for individual subjects to impart to students.

A 1998 paper by Douglas Archbold, commissioned by the National Education Goals Panel, explored the differences in criteria used by the three organizations. While he found more agreement than not, he identified sizable discrepancies.[13] Archbold wrote, "The extensive attention to content standards and their widespread acceptance belies the significant lack of consensus on how state standards should be organized, how specific they should be, and how they are supposed to transform instruction."[14]

The AFT review, Archbold found, "focused more on readily observable features of form than on the specifics of content. . . . [It] did not make judgments about . . . whether the standards were covering the 'right' material. Rather, [it] asked if the statements of goals, topics and skills were presented in a well-organized fashion . . . and were reasonably specific in stating expectations."[15] (In grading standards almost exclusively on their clarity and specificity, which continues to be its primary focus, though some content expectations have crept in, the AFT stresses that state standards must communicate to teachers exactly what is required of them.) The CBE developed its own content standards at two grade levels and judged state standards by the extent to which they conformed. The TBF reviews, Archbold recognized, were more comprehensive, weighing the quality of standards' content in addition to their clarity of organization and specificity.

*The Grades*

While no consensus has been reached about "standards for standards," the Fordham reviewers provided the clearest picture and most accurate judgments about the essential elements of high-quality academic standards in the five core subjects. These grades are not scientific, however; they merely represent the views of an author or a pair of like-minded scholars whose judgment TBF trusts.

When TBF published its first reports on state standards in 1997 and 1998, the news was generally glum. Though standards-based reform was certainly in vogue, most states had produced disappointing expectations for their schools and children: vague, sprawling, timid, full of dubious pedagogical advice, and generally not up to the task at hand. The reviewers gave them an average grade of D-plus (see table 1). A more detailed report card showing state-by-state grades appears in table 2.

The news in 2000 was a bit brighter. The average grade rose to C-minus on the scale developed by the Fordham evaluators. States are writing stronger

**Table 1. Grades for State Academic Standards, 1998 and 2000**

| Subject | 1998 | | 2000 | |
|---|---|---|---|---|
| | Average grade | Number of honor roll states | Average grade | Number of honor roll states |
| English | D+ | 6 | C- | 19 |
| Geography | D | 6 | C- | 15 |
| History | D | 4 | D+ | 10 |
| Math | D+ | 12 | C | 18 |
| Science | C | 13 | C | 19 |
| All states | D+ | 3 | C- | 9 |

Source: Chester E. Finn Jr. and Michael J. Petrilli, eds., *The State of State Standards 2000* (Washington: Thomas B. Fordham Foundation, 2000), p. ix.

**Table 2. National Report Card**

| State | English | Geography | History | Math | Science | Cumulative GPA | Grade average | 1998 grade |
|---|---|---|---|---|---|---|---|---|
| Alabama | A | B | B | B | D | 2.80 | B- | C- |
| Alaska | F | C | F | D | — | 0.75 | D- | D+ |
| Arizona | B | B | A | B | A | 3.40 | B+ | B+ |
| Arkansas | D | F | F | D | F | 0.40 | F | F |
| California | A | C | A | A | A | 3.60 | A- | B |
| Colorado | F | A | D | D | D | 1.40 | D+ | D+ |
| Connecticut | D | D | D | D | B | 1.40 | D+ | C- |
| Delaware | C | C | D | C | A | 2.20 | C+ | D+ |
| District of Columbia | A | A | F | B | — | 2.75 | B- | C- |
| Florida | B | B | C | D | F | 1.80 | C- | D+ |
| Georgia | B | D | C | B | F | 1.80 | C- | C- |
| Hawaii | F | F | F | C | D | 0.60 | D- | D+ |
| Idaho | — | — | — | — | — | — | — | — |
| Illinois | B | D | F | D | B | 1.60 | C- | C- |
| Indiana | F | A | C | C | A | 2.40 | C+ | C+ |
| Iowa | — | — | — | — | — | — | — | — |
| Kansas | F | A | B | A | F | 2.20 | C+ | D- |
| Kentucky | F | F | D | B | D | 1.00 | D | F |
| Louisiana | B | A | C | F | C | 2.20 | C+ | C- |
| Maine | B | F | D | D | D | 1.20 | D+ | D- |
| Maryland | B | B | B | C | D | 2.40 | C+ | F |
| Massachusetts | A | D | B | D | A | 2.60 | B- | C |
| Michigan | F | B | F | F | D | 0.80 | D- | D- |
| Minnesota | F | F | F | F | A | 0.80 | D- | F |
| Mississippi | C | D | C | A | F | 1.80 | C- | D |
| Missouri | F | B | C | F | C | 1.40 | D+ | D- |
| Montana | F | — | — | D | D | 0.66 | D- | F |

**Table 2. Continued**

| | | | | | | | | |
|---|---|---|---|---|---|---|---|---|
| Nebraska | A | F | C | C | B | 2.20 | C+ | F |
| Nevada | B | C | C | C | C | 2.20 | C+ | — |
| New Hampshire | D | B | C | C | F | 1.60 | C- | C- |
| New Jersey | F | D | F | C | A | 1.40 | D+ | D+ |
| New Mexico | D | F | F | F | F | 0.20 | F | F |
| New York | C | D | D | B | C | 1.80 | C- | D+ |
| North Carolina | B | C | D | A | A | 2.80 | B- | C |
| North Dakota | F | F | F | D | F | 0.20 | F | F |
| Ohio | D | D | D | A | B | 2.00 | C | C- |
| Oklahoma | D | C | B | B | F | 1.80 | C- | D- |
| Oregon | F | F | B | D | B | 1.40 | D+ | D |
| Pennsylvania | C | — | F | C | — | 1.33 | D+ | D- |
| Rhode Island | F | — | — | F | A | 1.33 | D+ | C |
| South Carolina | B | A | C | B | B | 3.00 | B | D |
| South Dakota | C | C | C | A | B | 2.60 | B- | F |
| Tennessee | F | F | D | F | F | 0.20 | F | D- |
| Texas | B | A | B | B | C | 3.00 | B | B |
| Utah | C | C | C | B | B | 2.40 | C+ | C+ |
| Vermont | D | F | F | C | B | 1.20 | D+ | D+ |
| Virginia | B | D | A | B | D | 2.40 | C+ | C+ |
| Washington | D | F | F | F | B | 0.80 | D- | D- |
| West Virginia | B | B | C | B | F | 2.20 | C+ | C |
| Wisconsin | A | F | F | C | C | 1.60 | C- | D+ |
| Wyoming | D | F | F | D | F | 0.40 | F | — |
| United States | C- | C- | D+ | C | C | 1.72 | C- | D+ |

Source: Chester E. Finn Jr. and Michael J. Petrilli, eds., *The State of State Standards 2000* (Washington: Thomas B. Fordham Foundation, 2000), p. x.
Note: GPA = grade point average. The dash (-) means that there were no standards to evaluate.

standards with more detail, clearer content, and fewer digressions into matters better left to the judgments of schools and teachers. Eight states (and the District of Columbia) have solid enough standards to earn honors grades when averaged across the subjects. (That compares with just three in the previous round.)

This means that forty-two states still hold mediocre or inferior expectations for their K–12 students. Hence seventeen years after *A Nation at Risk*, eleven years after the Charlottesville summit, and in the same year that the national education goals were supposed to have been met, most states have not successfully completed even the first step of standards-based reform.

*Some Agreement across Graders*

While only eight states and the District of Columbia get honors from TBF, the AFT lists twenty-two states on its honor roll for standards that are clear, specific, and grounded in particular content. The AFT not only considers different criteria when evaluating state standards, but it also calculates its ratings in a different way. They are based on whether a state has high-quality standards at three different grade levels (elementary, middle, and high school) in four subjects (English, math, science, and social studies). This makes twelve indicators (three grade levels times four subjects). If a state is judged to have met the AFT's criteria for nine of the twelve, then it is deemed to have quality standards overall.

While the AFT awarded more honors grades, it is worth examining whether AFT and TBF graders ranked states in the same order. To compare the overall grades given to states, the total number of AFT criteria (out of twelve) met by a state's standards and the average of the five grades given by TBF evaluators were examined. The correlation between the overall grades given to states by the AFT and the grades given to states by TBF is .64, which means that today's two rating systems are generally identifying the same states as having good and bad standards, though considerable variation remains. For history and social studies standards, the correlation between the two sets of grades was .75; for English, .58; for math, .41; and for science, .33.

A state with exemplary standards in one or two subjects may have shoddy standards in other fields. Looking across the Fordham ratings, the correlation between state grades for math standards and history standards is .50; between history and English, .44; and between English and math, .43. Geography and history are the most strongly correlated at .52. Grades for science standards were not correlated with grades in other subjects, which suggests either that producing good science standards is very different from producing sound standards in other subjects or that the science appraisals are off base.

*Modest Improvements*

State standards are getting better, as indicated by three welcome trends:

1. Standards are becoming more specific and measurable. In English, for example, the percentage of states earning acceptable ratings for "measurability" from the TBF evaluator rose 24 percent. In geography, the average score for "guidance to teachers" rose 38 percent. And in math, the average score for "clarity" rose 40 percent.

2. Content is making a comeback. States' reluctance to specify particular knowledge may be starting to dissipate. That is certainly the case in history and in geography, where the "comprehensiveness and rigor" scores rose 15 percent. In math, scores for "content" gained 20 percent since 1998.

There are two big exceptions, however. In English, most states still refuse to identify any important literary works or authors that all children should read. (Only one jurisdiction in four shows the resolve to list literary benchmarks.) The other exception is the evasion of evolution in many science standards. The Kansas example is well known, but many other states have taken pains to avoid the "e" word—and sometimes the entire concept on which modern biology rests—throughout their standards.

3. States are less enamored of politically correct models. The standards developed by national organizations in English, history, and mathematics tended to get caught up in trendiness, which in turn afflicted state standards in those jurisdictions that patterned their own expectations for students on those of the national groups. In all three subjects, however, a constructive reaction is emerging. In English, 45 percent of states now insist on systematic phonics instruction in the early grades—up from 32 percent in 1997—though this requirement remains anathema to the International Reading Association and the National Council of Teachers of English. In history, rising scores on the Fordham evaluation reflect mounting rejection of standards promulgated by the National Council of the Social Studies as well as the troubled national history standards of a few years back. (History seems to be making a modest comeback as a subject in its own right, emerging from the murky stew called social studies.) And in math, more states are embracing the principles found in California's fine standards and rejecting the precepts of the National Council of Teachers of Mathematics (which, after much criticism, have recently been revised, mostly in directions favored by TBF's math reviewers).

### Forces Working against Good Standards

Some states are commonly acknowledged to have strong standards. Arizona, California, Massachusetts, and Texas regularly turn up on lists of states that have managed to produce solid standards in most subjects. The list is short, however, because of the daunting obstacles to writing strong standards.

In most states, the groups charged with writing standards encounter difficulty reaching consensus about which skills and knowledge are most important. They tend to try to solve that problem either by moving to a high level of generality—thus producing vague, soft standards—or by throwing everything but the kitchen sink into their standards. Consensus may thus be purchased at a high cost.

Many states seem to have intentionally written nebulous standards. Embracing vagueness is one way to sidestep controversy. Standards-writers may be reluctant to get drawn into the culture wars and so avoid identifying the books that students should read in English class and the events they should study in history. While many people agree that passing on the shared culture is a central aim of education in a liberal democracy, which books and events are at the core of this common culture remains subject to intense debate. Many states seek to sidestep this controversy altogether by refusing to identify specific examples from history and literature of knowledge that is essential for students to learn. These states seem to fear that even hinting at a literary canon will expose them to charges of cultural insensitivity. As a result, students may be required to read "a variety of traditional and contemporary literature"— but it does not seem to matter what they read.

Some states defend their decision to keep their academic standards vague by arguing for deference to local control or to the teacher's judgment. Deep analysis is not required, however, to recognize that these are essentially arguments against standards themselves, against the idea that all students should be expected to master a body of knowledge that is by necessity defined in advance. The consequence is generally that students in some schools are taught a rich curriculum while pupils in other schools miss out.

Other states have gone to the opposite extreme. Their standards require more knowledge and skills than any teacher can reasonably impart in 180 days of forty-five-minute periods; more, too, than nearly any student can reasonably learn.

Where does this overload come from? The committee process that typically generates state academic standards tends to include everyone with an opinion on schooling or an organizational interest that may be affected by what is taught to children: experts from colleges of education, classroom teachers, curriculum specialists, civic activists, minority and ethnic associations, public school administrators, politicians, employers, parents, business leaders, and more. (George Eliot wrote that the ultimate goal in life is "to influence the standards of mankind for generations to come," and in many states, this aspiration would seem to be widely shared.) All kinds of inconsistent and incompatible things may be included in the standards to placate various factions and satisfy individual enthusiasms, and the result, too often, is shapeless, sprawling standards.

Another common problem that states encounter is the tendency to focus standards on skills rather than content. This may arise from an understandable, if misguided, attempt to avoid controversy about lists of books and facts, but it may also represent a belief that what matters is developing children's powers of cognition, not mastering any particular knowledge. This position is fashionable in colleges of education, where the learning of "mere facts" is suspect and an ideal school is thought to be one that encourages children to develop naturally. This romantic view of education aims at cultivating students who love learning and who, it is said, can always "look it up on the Internet" if they have a need for specific information.

Yet, thinking skills are seldom useful absent something to think about. Moreover, knowledge, including factual information, makes further learning possible. Without a base of acquired knowledge, children lack the intellectual scaffolding to understand what they see around them or to integrate new information into their understanding. Children who lack initial knowledge will fall further and further behind—a particular problem for poor and disadvantaged youngsters. E. D. Hirsch Jr. writes, " A systematic failure to teach all children the knowledge they need in order to understand what the next grade has to offer is the major source of avoidable injustice in our schools."[16]

All these forces and more work against the creation of strong standards. They are difficult to avoid or surmount, but some states have managed that feat. The process of standards-writing varies enormously. Sometimes the differences among states are driven by legal requirements and legislative mandates. In some states, decisions about who serves on the standards commission and which grades are covered by the standards are spelled out in statutes. Elsewhere, laws prohibit standards-writers from doing anything that might interfere with the curriculum chosen by districts.

Who is involved in standards-writing makes a big difference. Including teachers in the process is surely important, preferably proven master teachers (rather than self-nominated teachers or individuals chosen to represent racial, ethnic, political, or geographic constituencies). In some states, only employees of the Department of Education, who may lack classroom experience, are involved in the process. In other jurisdictions, hundreds of teachers and curriculum specialists are included (which is probably too many).

Involving scholars who teach various subjects at the university level can bring to the process a good sense of what students emerging from high school should know and be able to do in those subjects. They can also sniff out ped-agogical trends that are based on mistaken views of the disciplines. Repre-sentatives of the business community bring another important perspective; they also have clear expectations for high school graduates. Relying on teacher educators, however, can be a mistake. They, along with K–12 curriculum development specialists, are largely responsible for the vexed attempts to develop national standards.

Veteran standard-setters warn that having too many people involved in the writing process is a recipe for disaster. Many states envision standards-writ-ing as a democratic and participatory process and thus enlist a cast of thou-sands to help write them. Some states fret that their standards will not be accepted unless every possible constituency and stakeholder is included in the process. But a large group cannot write anything coherent. Experience indi-cates that it is better to have a small group do the drafting and then ask a larger body to review drafts and offer guidance. The broader public should be offered a chance to comment on the standards, but this is best done after a draft has been prepared.

Writing good standards—and revising bad ones—is difficult, and not all states have been up to the task. Many, however, are sensitive to the reviews that their standards have been getting from a variety of outside evaluators, and most are under mounting pressure to boost student achievement. States with inadequate standards should be prodded by the examples of those that are doing a good job of this, especially states that are beginning to see some results.

### Today's Accountability Systems

Standards are just the first step. Getting serious about standards-based reform means attaching worthy assessments and palpable consequences, the other two essential legs of the accountability tripod.

When it comes to tests and accountability, the devil, as always, lurks in the fine print. Forty-two states claim to use criterion-referenced assessments aligned to their academic standards (according to *Quality Counts 2000*), yet often that is not true. The assessments that many states use, says University of California at Los Angeles (UCLA) testing expert W. James Popham, "more often than not . . . look like warmed-over versions" of standardized tests taken from a testing company's warehouse.[17] "Alignment is mostly a farce," argues Eva Baker, the director of the federally funded testing center at UCLA.[18] Using tests that do not mesh carefully with the state's standards undermines the entire reform strategy. Standards can have little traction if students' progress toward mastering them is not faithfully and honestly measured. What is taught should be assessed, and what is assessed should be taught.

Many states are growing more serious about accountability measures. Thirty-five states issue report cards to schools that include test scores, eleven states rate all their schools on the basis of academic performance, and eighteen states recognize or reward successful schools.[19] A number of states identify failing schools but few then do anything about them. While eighteen states have the authority to make major changes to failing schools, only five states had exercised it as of October 1999.[20] (At least one more has since taken steps to reconstitute or outsource some of its failing schools.)

Together, these five features—report cards for schools, ratings for schools, rewards for successful schools, authority to reconstitute (or make major changes to) failing schools, and the exercise of these sanctions—would make a solid school-level accountability system. (That is, the kind of accountability that touches schools and adults, not the children themselves.) But only a third of the states are assembling these pieces. Just seventeen jurisdictions have in place three or more of the five elements, and only two have all five.[21]

*Mismatching Standards and Accountability*

What happens when states erect tough, high-stakes accountability systems atop dubious standards? What happens in states that have great standards but no real accountability for attaining them? Is it not likely that both situations will yield only the illusion of reform?

Juxtaposing what is known about the quality of state standards against what is known about the adequacy of states' school-based accountability systems is illuminating. States can be sorted by three levels of academic standards (solid, mediocre, inferior) and two kinds of accountability (strong and weak). The results are worrying. Just five states—four of them in the South—turn out to combine solid standards with strong accountability systems. Three more states have solid standards but only weak accountability systems to go with them. A dozen jurisdictions rest high-stakes accountability systems upon mediocre or inferior standards. Thirty states display a combination of mediocre to awful (or no) standards and weak accountability (see figure 1).

Alabama, California, North Carolina, South Carolina, and Texas have solid standards and strong accountability systems. They exemplify the theory and

**Figure 1. Standards versus Accountability**

Standards

| | Solid (A or B average) | Mediocre (C average) | Inferior or none (D or F average or incomplete) |
|---|---|---|---|
| **Strong** | *The Honor Roll*<br>Alabama<br>California<br>North Carolina<br>South Carolina<br>Texas | *Shaky Foundations*<br>Florida<br>Illinois<br>Indiana<br>Kansas<br>Maryland<br>Nevada<br>New York<br>Oklahoma<br>Virginia<br>West Virginia | *Trouble Ahead*<br>Kentucky<br>New Mexico |
| **Weak** | *Unrealized Potential*<br>Arizona<br>Massachusetts<br>South Dakota | *Going through the Motions*<br>Delaware<br>Georgia<br>Louisiana<br>Mississippi<br>Nebraska<br>New Hampshire<br>Ohio<br>Utah<br>Wisconsin | *Irresponsible States*<br>Alaska<br>Arkansas<br>Colorado<br>Connecticut<br>Hawaii<br>Idaho<br>Iowa<br>Maine<br>Michigan<br>Minnesota<br>Missouri<br>Montana<br>New Jersey<br>North Dakota<br>Oregon<br>Pennsylvania<br>Rhode Island<br>Tennessee<br>Vermont<br>Washington<br>Wyoming |

(Accountability is the vertical axis.)

Source: Chester E. Finn Jr. and Michael J. Petrilli, eds., *The State of State Standards 2000* (Washington: Thomas B. Fordham Foundation, 2000).

practice of standards-based reform and thereby prove that putting all the essential elements into place is possible.

Note, though, how tiny this group is, and contrast it with this excerpt from the action statement agreed to at the 1999 education summit on standards-based reform: "The commitments made by the nation's governors and business leaders at the 1996 National Education Summit—commitments to higher standards, better assessments, and tougher accountability measures—have clearly become central elements in a nationwide campaign to improve school performance." This is most charitably described as wishful thinking. It is deceiving for governors, educators, and business leaders to claim that the country has embraced standards-based reform when only five states have melded good standards with real accountability.

Four states have solid standards but have yet to attach meaningful consequences to them. So, their standards, exemplary though they may be, do not count for much, particularly from the standpoint of the adults who work in their public schools.

A larger group of states attaches high-stakes accountability systems to mediocre standards. That combination may lead to some worrisome outcomes. Cheating is apt to become more widespread, as frustrated educators fail to find reliable guidance about what to teach, even as they know that their students must pass the statewide tests.

With high stakes attached to inferior standards, two states (Kentucky and New Mexico) run the even greater risk of undermining good schools and encouraging the spread of dubious academic content.

An astonishing twenty-one states cannot honestly claim to be serious about standards-based reform. Their academic standards—at least in most subjects—are vague, vapid, and misleading (or missing altogether). Their education systems rarely punish (or reward) schools that produce bad (or good) results.

A few of these states (most prominently Iowa) have decided on principle not to join the push for statewide standards and accountability, preferring to leave such decisions to individual communities. Others, though, have told their citizens that they have embarked on standards-based reform at the state level. This turns out to be an empty claim. They have neither the solid standards nor the tough-minded accountability systems that must accompany such a claim if it is to be taken seriously.

### The Accountability Backlash

If standards-based reform remains a wishful claim in some states, in others it has already yielded signs of backlash. In several jurisdictions, the advent of high-stakes testing has meant that children are beginning to be held back, sent to summer school, or denied diplomas. In a few places, teachers' and principals' jobs or salaries are being tied to student and school performance. This has provoked some angry responses. However, while media accounts of backlash are plentiful, the extent and seriousness of this opposition are not clear. Though veteran education writer Peter Schrag contends that this backlash "touch[es] virtually every state that has instituted high-stakes testing," nobody has yet quantified this phenomenon or done any responsible research.[22]

Examples of backlash can be split between two main categories: those that represent opposition to the fundamental concept of standards-based reform, and those that represent objections to the way that standards, tests, or accountability measures are being implemented in a particular place at a particular time.

### Hostility to the Basic Concept

Efforts to set external academic standards, measure pupil and school performance with tests, and attach consequences to that performance have had a long history of opposition in America. The view that no test is a good test seems to be deeply rooted in U.S. colleges of education. Many educators sympathize with the idea that a regime of high-stakes testing interferes with creative teaching, serious learning, and the healthy development of children. They believe that youngsters learn best when they explore subjects at their own pace and construct their own meaning from classroom activities. They believe that the teacher's role is to impart the skills, knowledge, and habits of inquiry that he or she deems to be most worthwhile, and to do so on his or her own schedule and via methods and materials of his or her own choosing. In an atmosphere of high-stakes assessment, test preparation usurps the curriculum and blocks children from developing a true love of learning and gaining higher-order thinking skills.

This view of education is at least as old as Rousseau and dominated American education for most of the twentieth century. Hirsch terms this system of ideas the Romantic Thoughtworld. It does not conform to what is known about human learning, motivation, or effective schooling, particularly for disadvantaged youngsters, but it does occupy a well-worn place in the pantheon of education theories and can be held by honorable people.

Such philosophical hostility to standards-based reform underlies much of the backlash. A shelf of recent books by veteran antitesting activists and new recruits conveys the antitesting view with fair clarity. In *One Size Fits Few*,

Susan Ohanian defies the very idea that all students should master the same material and urges teachers to refuse to teach to the state's academic standards or to administer the state's tests. One encounters similar sentiments in Alfie Kohn's *The Schools Our Children Deserve: Moving Beyond Traditional Classrooms and 'Tougher Standards'* and Peter Sacks's *Standardized Minds: The High Price of America's Testing Culture and What We Can Do to Change It.*[23]

Journalists writing about standards often turn to a small coterie of testing critics for comments on the reforms. In addition to those just named, familiar figures are affiliated with an advocacy group called FairTest (the National Center for Fair and Open Testing, which essentially opposes all standardized tests), with the Center for Research on Evaluation, Standards, and Student Testing (CRESST, headquartered at UCLA), or with the Center for the Study of Testing, Evaluation, and Educational Policy (CSTEEP, at Boston College). All three are organizations composed of testing experts who, for the most part, do not think much of testing in general and high-stakes testing in particular.[24]

In response to a report of a cheating incident in Potomac, Maryland, Monty Neill, the director of FairTest, said, "Schools are turning into test coaching centers, caught up in this frenzy of trying to look their best."[25] Alfie Kohn, in a Richmond *Times-Dispatch* article on the implementation of Virginia's Standards of Learning, argues, "This is not about helping kids become critically [sic], curious, creative thinkers. It's about cramming forgettable details in short-term memory, or else."[26] While such commentators are often presented as if they were fair-minded experts, most have consistently opposed standards and tests for many years.

While the Romantic Thoughtworld is nearly always found on the political left, philosophical opposition to standards-based reform also sometimes comes from libertarians and conservatives who believe ardently in local control, marketplace mechanisms, and school-level pluralism as governing principles for education and who do not trust the state to decide what all children should learn. Mary O'Brien, a parent who is leading a grassroots protest against the Ohio proficiency tests, contends that the state should not be trying to control the curriculum of local schools.

Whether it comes from left or right, however, this sort of backlash does not have much to do with high-stakes testing or standards-based reform as these are being implemented in America today. Rather, it is grounded in ideological rejection of state-prescribed standards, tests, and accountability in general.

Furthermore, the backlash needs to be kept in perspective. Though such people are typically loquacious, prolific, energetic, and persistent, they do not represent the views of most Americans when it comes to education reform. A recent Public Agenda study found that solid majorities of employers (87 percent), college professors (79 percent), parents (79 percent), and schoolteachers (60 percent) were in favor of high-stakes tests for promotion.[27] Clear majorities of all these groups say it is better for a child to repeat a grade than to be promoted to the next level without having learned the requisite skills.

A major reason for the strong support for standards among employers and college faculty is concern over the meager skills of high school graduates. Though today's vigorous economy masks the problem, many young Americans are not acquiring necessary skills and knowledge from their schooling. Three out of four employers and college professors say that contemporary graduates have only fair or poor skills in grammar and spelling and the ability to write clearly.[28] Majorities give similar ratings for basic math skills.

While two-thirds of high school parents told Public Agenda that their child will have the skills to succeed on the job, only 33 percent of employers say that the young people they see have what it takes.[29] And while two-thirds of parents believe that getting a high school diploma signifies that a youngster has mastered at least basic skills, just 39 percent of employers and 33 percent of college professors concur. The latest figures suggest that a third of college freshmen must take at least one remedial class in reading, writing, or math. This split between relatively complacent parents and mostly alarmed employers and college professors helps to paint the backdrop for the current debate about standards-based reform and high-stakes testing.

Opponents of such reform often seek to portray the public as rejecting standards and tests—and they may resort to questionable means of documenting this position. The American Association of School Administrators (AASA) held a press conference in June 2000 to announce the results of a survey that the organization claimed showed that Americans do not believe in one-size-fits-all tests. "Registered voters and public school parents value individual talents and contributions," said AASA executive director Paul Houston. "The idea that every child should be treated the same is a profoundly un-American idea." Yet the questions posed by this survey seemed to be deliberately phrased to elicit opposition. Respondents were asked, for example, whether they agree or disagree that "A student's progress for one school year can be accurately summarized by a single standardized test." That 42 percent of voters strongly disagree with that statement or that an additional 20 percent somewhat disagree is not surprising. But standards and accountability need not reduce a student's performance to a single test score. Few of its proponents contend that it should.

When asked such questions fairly, the public continues to signal strong support for standards, tests, and accountability. Even on the AASA survey, 79 percent of parents agreed that "we need a standardized test to measure what our children are learning and judge our schools," the same percentage that favored high-stakes testing in the Public Agenda study. And given the stark choice between a school that focused on test scores and one that "emphasized discovery and joy of learning," 52 percent of the parents favored the test-oriented school.[30] A question asking parents whether they prefer a school that emphasizes the mastery of knowledge and skills would surely have turned up even stronger backing for the standards and accountability approach.

In the face of solid public support for standards-based reform, some opponents have resorted to simply scoffing at what the public says it wants. The author of a recent *Phi Delta Kappan* article bashing standards-based reform writes dismissively, "The standards movement has a lot going for it. . . . The movement has massive political and corporate backing. Educators who oppose the movement are not well organized. . . . Perhaps most important, it meshes well with simplistic, popular views of what educating is all about."[31]

Principled opposition to standards and tests is not confined to education's elite circles. It is also articulated by teachers who believe that high-stakes testing will force them to focus their instruction on the skills that tests measure at the expense of other things that they believe are more important to teach (for example, creativity, deep knowledge, higher-order skills). Many teachers have strong philosophical commitments to the pedagogy they imbibed at colleges of education, and teaching the curriculum that will be tested may preclude them from teaching the things they want their students to learn. Similar objections are heard from alternative schools that historically have not had to participate in statewide tests or graduation requirements but are now being required to. They say, in effect, that external standards and tests will cramp their style and undermine their distinctiveness.

Objections to the standards-based approach to education are not always philosophical; sometimes they are grounded in narrower self-interest. The prospect of new accountability arrangements alarms many who work in schools today. The lead article on the front page of the Sunday *Washington Post* on June 25, 2000, declared, "School principals across the Washington region are protesting, resigning and, in some cases, retiring in the face of increased accountability for high test scores and better schools."

It is a gripping tale, which is why it—and similar stories arising in other parts of the country—has consumed so much newsprint and airtime. However, the amount of turmoil and turnover occasioned by new accountability obligations may not be as great as it might seem. The *Post* acknowledged, for example, that two-thirds of secondary school principals in Maryland will be eligible for retirement within five years and that one local school system had changed 42 percent of its principals over the past three years. But the onset of standards-based accountability, with an administrator's own reputation (or job security) tied to the performance of his or her school vis-à-vis statewide academic standards, is apt to upset people who have spent decades working under a different sort of regimen.

The principal's job is undeniably getting harder within the framework of standards-based reform. A different sort of person may be needed in these key posts, someone prepared and compensated in different ways and equipped with the necessary tools to be an effective executive. Discontent among aficionados of the old arrangement may not be a bad thing, and the departure of school leaders who cannot or will not adjust to the obligation to produce measurable academic gains among their students may not be regrettable.

Distinguishing principled from self-interested opposition often can be difficult. This is particularly the case when it comes to the student protesters who have grabbed the limelight in a few states. A few hundred students in Massachusetts organized test boycotts ("Be a Hero, Take a Zero"), rallies, and a petition demanding that Governor Paul Cellucci take the new Massachusetts Comprehensive Assessment System tests. (In Colorado, too, students demanded that the governor take the test.) The complaints of student protesters echo the antitesting ideology they have picked up from some of their teachers. The protesters show a somewhat predictable unhappiness with having to take a test that matters.

Media accounts of backlash must be kept in perspective, however. Less than 1 percent of Massachusetts youngsters boycotted the state test in 1999–2000. The millions of students who take tests without complaint are rarely heard from. While some teachers complain about the reforms, hundreds of thousands of conscientious, hard-working educators are doing their best to prepare children to succeed on high-stakes tests and to usher their schools into the age of accountability. They seem generally willing—sometimes relieved, even eager—to be held responsible for their effectiveness. A 1999 survey by the American Federation of Teachers found that teachers favored the standards-based approach by a four-to-one margin. A similar survey of principals in four states also found nearly universal support for standards.[32]

Some parents likely have a view of standards-based reform that parallels their well-known view of schools. (Some careful research in this area would be beneficial.) Surveys regularly show that parents tend to give low marks to schools in general while awarding high marks to their own child's school. Similarly, some parents who profess allegiance to standards-based reform in the abstract probably get skittish when it begins to affect their own kids and schools. High standards are a fine thing until one's own children do not meet them.

*Implementation Problems*

A second category of backlash might be termed dismay over the implementation of such reforms in particular places. Though some overlap exists with the philosophical and self-interested objections, and some strategic advantage is found in using the principled argument as a foil for the implementation argument, the distinction is nonetheless important. Many states are experiencing glitches, and much of the anxiety that accompanies standards-based reform is grounded in legitimate concerns with the way this new regimen is being installed and operated. Given the mess that some states have made of getting worthwhile standards, tests, and accountability mechanisms into place, even those who favor such reforms in principle can reasonably object to their handling in practice. As with principled opposition, however, more than a little opportunism is at work.

TESTS BEFORE STANDARDS. Parents in Ohio are upset about new state tests, and with good reason. In the Buckeye State, students in fourth, sixth, ninth, and twelfth grade take state proficiency tests, and students cannot receive a diploma without passing the ninth-grade test. The state recently introduced a Fourth-Grade Guarantee: Students who do not pass a reading proficiency test will not be promoted to fifth grade beginning in 2002 unless the teacher and principal both certify that the student is ready for fifth-grade work.

In response, parents have orchestrated grassroots campaigns to keep children home on testing days and are organizing a ballot initiative to eliminate the testing system. Among their complaints is that the fourth-grade exam is too difficult. Ohio teachers say that they warned the state about problems with the fourth-grade test, but that their feedback was ignored. Many teachers also say that they have not been given clear information about what material is covered by the test.

This is a particularly acute problem considering the shortcomings of Ohio's present accountability system. Today, the state does not have standards as that term is construed elsewhere. Instead, Ohio uses "learning outcomes" and "model competency programs." The former are distressingly vague and lack important content, according to an external review conducted by Achieve Inc., a bipartisan organization formed by governors and chief executive officers to support standards-based reform. The model competency programs provide far more detail, but unlike the standards that most states have, they are voluntary. Perhaps as a result, they are not widely used or even known. Nor are they well aligned with the state's proficiency testing program.[33]

Where there are no real academic standards or where the assessments are not closely aligned with them, the test—the only operative standard visible in most schools and classrooms—becomes the de facto standard. This is more weight than most tests can, or should be expected to, bear. Ohio superintendent Susan Tave Zelman acknowledged to a reporter that the state "did it backward," putting high-stakes tests into place when districts were not yet able to determine what material their students were expected to master and to revise their curricula accordingly.[34]

Failing to provide everyone involved in the K–12 system with clear, accurate signals as to both the academic content and the level of performance that the state expects of its children and its schools is one way to get standards-based reform wrong. Until states develop good academic standards and align their assessments to these standards, parents and teachers are right to object to the introduction of rewards and sanctions based on test scores.

RELYING ON A SINGLE TEST SCORE. Another implementation complaint contends that relying on a single test score to make important decisions about a student's future is unfair, an argument that has lately gotten considerable play in Virginia. The Commonwealth's Standards of Learning (SOLs) program tests children on tough new standards approved by the state board of education in 1995. Students take tests in third, fifth, and eighth grades and in high school. They cover English, math, science, and history. Starting in 2007, at least 70 percent of a school's pupils must pass the tests for a school to remain accredited. In the first round of testing, which took place during the 1998–99 school year, only 2.2 percent of the state's public schools in the state met the accreditation requirement. Beginning in 2004, high school seniors will have to pass at least six of the eleven high school-level tests to graduate.

Polls show strong support for accountability testing in the Old Dominion, but dissatisfaction with some specific aspects of the testing program.[35] A group called Parents Across Virginia United to Reform SOLs was formed, among other things, to demand that multiple criteria be used to evaluate students, not just test scores. Six bills were introduced in the legislature in 2000 stipulating that state tests would not be the only basis for deciding whether students will graduate. So far, the state board of education has rejected the idea, insisting that it will not support any proposal that allows students to graduate without passing rigorous tests.

A single test score ought not determine one's life prospects. Students should have multiple opportunities to take the test, and other factors should be weighed besides the test score. In Indiana, for example, high school students face a high-stakes exit exam, but those who fail it may still graduate if they have received a grade of C or better in core academic courses during their high school careers. Students who do not meet these criteria may still file an appeal under certain specialized circumstances. States may go too far in this direction, thus turning a high-stakes test into a no-stakes test. Still, it is reasonable for them not to hang huge decisions on slender pegs.

THE SPECIAL CASE OF CHEATING. Whether for reasons of high principle or mundane self-interest, whether grounded in philosophical objections or implementation anxiety, cheating on tests is a bad thing. But the issue has gotten much attention lately, particularly near the end of the school year when much high-stakes testing is done. A middle school teacher in Reston, Virginia, was suspended for preparing his students for a state social studies exam using questions from an improperly obtained copy of the test. The principal of a top-ranked elementary school in Maryland resigned in the face of allegations that she violated state rules by coaching students, giving them answers and granting them extra time to correct answers on the Maryland School Performance Assessment Program. An investigator for the New York City school system has alleged that sixty-one principals and teachers violated testing regulations by handing out answers or revising students' test sheets. Those are just a few of the more colorful examples that surfaced in the 1999–2000 school year.

It is inexcusable for any educators to turn to cheating to improve their students' scores. But the subject is like police blotter items; the millions of people in the city who obey the law do not make it onto TV, while the few who misbehave are all over the news. A tiny percentage of teachers has been involved in cheating episodes. But no one should overreact to a few high-profile cases.

Some have used these incidents to argue against high-stakes testing in general. They say that tests and accountability measures encourage the wrong kind of competition, and they suggest that too much pressure is being placed on students and schools. Some go as far as to suggest that society ought not even hold cheaters responsible, because society placed them in this high-stakes situation. "We don't have the luxury of piously condemning individual teachers when the real villain here is an overemphasis on test scores at the expense of real learning," argues Alfie Kohn.[36] Any high-stakes situation creates incentives for misbehavior, which is why, for example, Olympic athletes are tested for performance-enhancing drugs. But no one suggests abolishing the Olympics.

Cheating is undeniably wrong. But it is also a clue that something good is happening. Standards-based reform is gaining traction, causing schools and teachers (and students) to change their behavior. That was the whole point, after all: to induce teachers to teach differently and students to learn differently. If it had no effect on behavior, standards-based reform would be a waste of time.

### What to Conclude from the Backlash?

The testing experts object not just to how standards-based reform is being put into place, but also to the broader concept of standards-based reform. For them, the impact of standards and tests is more painful than they are willing to bear. But they must realize that some pain and friction will result as people adjust to what is, in essence, a behaviorist effort to bring about change in teaching and learning via rewards and interventions. To make standards-based reform work, many will have to change their ways, work harder, and be held to account for their results. But considerable public benefit should accrue over the long term from doing this reform right and just about everyone thinks that that benefit is worth attaining.

Those who think the state is not implementing standards-based reform properly do have legitimate concerns. Some backlash is thus warranted. These complaints are worth taking seriously, and any reform-minded state should be dedicated to fixing the conditions that give rise to the complaints.

### Getting It Right

What should a state do to ensure that standards-based reform runs as smoothly as possible? Creating solid standards and high-quality tests aligned to those standards are the first two steps. Coming up with a fair accountability mechanism is third. Developing a reasonable timetable is fourth. Fifth and last is to stay the course.

Developing clear, specific, measurable, comprehensive, rigorous standards is the cornerstone of getting standards-based reform right. Aligning assessments with standards is also fairly straightforward, though the final step of test development—setting the bar at the right level—can be a challenge. Citizens in some states fear that the bar has been set too high. In Massachusetts, for instance, over 50 percent of tenth graders have failed the new Massachusetts Comprehensive Assessment System tests, including 80 percent of black students and 85 percent of Hispanic students.[37] In other jurisdictions, however, the bar seems to be too low. Thus the percentage of students who are judged by a state assessment to be proficient in particular subjects is much higher than the percentage of youngsters found to be proficient on the NAEP. For instance, in Wisconsin, 88 percent of fourth graders were said to meet state reading goals in 1997, yet only 35 percent of the Badger State's fourth graders met NAEP's proficient standard on the most recent test.[38]

Some worry that, because academic ability is unevenly distributed, some students will never be able to meet high standards and that any standard meant to apply to all students will have to be a low standard. One way to address this is to create multilevel standards, or more than one cut score. Many states today offer an advanced diploma in addition to their regular diploma.

Some states (such as Texas) have opted to start with relatively low cutoff scores that are gradually raised. Linking the exit standards to external norms (what businesses and colleges expect high school graduates to be able to do) could provide a valuable benchmark for states that are attempting to determine how high is too high. Such a benchmark could be more compelling for parents and voters, and more difficult for educators to challenge.

The accountability system—rewards for meeting standards and, especially, sanctions for not doing so—is apt to attract the most attention and to provoke the loudest outcry if not handled well. High-stakes consequences ought not to rest solely on the outcome of a single test. Disaggregating test scores for poor and minority students can be a way of focusing the efforts of schools on the students most likely to be left behind.

Beyond that, the only truly fair accountability system is one that includes consequences for both children and adults. The best way to prevent children from being punished for failing to master material that they were never taught is to ensure that teachers and schools face strong incentives to cover the necessary material. In many states, the rewards and sanctions attached to the tests apply only to students, not to educators or school systems. The proficiency tests may yield data that enable the state to identify districts in trouble, but nothing then happens. Report cards for schools and school systems generally lead to no real consequences, neither rewards for the successful nor interventions in cases of failure and malpractice. The principals and teachers in highly effective schools get no bonuses and the superintendents of failing districts do not lose their jobs. This is wrong.

The timing of implementation is important, too. Rushing too fast to install standards-based reform is bound to create problems. The standards must be communicated to those who need to understand and operate them before schools can fairly be held accountable for meeting them. Veteran teachers may need help in preparing to teach to high standards, and the programs that prepare new teachers may need to be retooled to conform to those standards. Systems must be in place to ensure that struggling students have access to the help they need. All involved should be given advance notice as to the consequences.

One way to ease the blow of consequences is to phase accountability mechanisms in gradually. Instead of suddenly penalizing today's high school students for problems that have accumulated over twelve years of schooling, a state might start by holding this year's first graders to promotion standards. Next year, the standards would apply to second graders, then third graders, and this would continue until all grades were covered.

But lollygagging is at least as vivid a risk as excessive speed. According to a recent Public Agenda study, only 42 percent of teachers say that they receive most of their curricular guidance from state standards. Just 44 percent say that they expect more from students because of state (or district) standards.

Standards-based reform is penetrating American K–12 education, but it is penetrating slowly and unevenly. That is why perhaps the most important advice to be given to standards-minded states is to muster the resolve to stay the course. People will not change in response to standards-based reform unless they are convinced that the system is not going away anytime soon. States should be steadfast about the concept and key elements of the reform, while figuring out how to make midcourse corrections without vacillating.

## Prospects

Standards-based reform is at a crossroads. State standards are improving but few are good. Most states think they have accountability systems, yet few can honestly boast that they have combined good standards with tough consequences. Still, governors, federal officials, business leaders, and platoons of educators insist that American children now live and attend school in an age of standards-based reform. What to make of all this?

That a handful of states are doing it right proves that it can be done. Yet eleven years after the first national education summit and the setting of national education goals, standards-based reform is not well established in the United States. Some people seem content to let it plod on. For example, an effort is being made to remove the deadline from the national goals that were not attained. That will allow all the standards-setters, enforcers, testers, monitors, and analysts to maintain full employment and will enable elected officials to continue to claim that they and their states are fully engaged in standards-based reform, notwithstanding the skimpy evidence that this effort is causing their students to learn more.

We are not that patient or that willing to mislead parents and cheat kids. If only a handful of states have got it right after a decade of trying to impose top-down, standards-based accountability on a public school system that is doing its best to resist, then policymakers who are serious about boosting achievement might think twice about putting all their eggs in this one reform basket. Standards-based reform is not easy to get through legislatures and state boards of education, much less to implement in the face of tenure laws, collective bargaining agreements, an alphabet soup of vested interests, vast bureaucratic inertia, and grassroots backlash fanned by disgruntled educators. Isn't it time for states to put some other arrows in their reform bows?

Fortunately, a whole separate reform strategy is marching across America in tandem with standards-based reform. Market-based reform comes in myriad shapes and sizes, including charter schools, open enrollment, public school choice, and vouchers. This strategy embraces diversity, pluralism, and competition.

These two major reform strategies complement one another. Both ask individual schools to achieve the desired results using whatever strategy they deem best. Focusing on academic results, as standards-based reform seeks to do, allows states to ease up on rules, regulations, and the preoccupation with inputs.

Each of these strategies is apt to improve the other. Choice, after all, will work well only when reliable, standards-based consumer information is available. Standards will ensure that some commonality of content will be evident in the diverse schools that children may attend if given a choice, which should be some reassurance to those who fear that introducing choice will lead to cultural or ethnic balkanization. However, standards-based reform is incomplete if children who attend schools that do not meet the standards are not offered other options. Hybrids of the two strategies are in places such as Texas and North Carolina, where vibrant charter school programs operate in tandem with statewide standards, tests, and top-down accountability structures.

Standards-based reform done poorly, however, can damage market-style reform. Consider charter schools. In the thirty-one states that today have both mediocre-to-inferior academic standards and charter school laws, these new schools are finding themselves being held accountable for reaching standards that are probably not worth reaching. Bad standards could force otherwise exemplary charter schools to become worse, thus ruining a second reform strategy while perpetrating fraud in the name of the first strategy. That cannot be good for anyone.

Our criticism of inadequate state standards and our alarm over their weak link with systemic accountability is no rejection of standards-based reform. Nor is it some sort of half-veiled argument for a laissez-faire system of unbridled competition with no public accountability. We favor solid statewide academic standards. We favor serious statewide results-based school accountability that rewards success and penalizes failure on the part of children and adults alike. We also favor market-style reform that gives families choices among schools and obligates schools to satisfy their clients as well as their supervisors. We favor two-way accountability—to the statewide system and to the school's customers—within a framework of high-quality academic standards in core subjects for every child and school in the state.

We are not part of the standards backlash; we are close to the opposite. Our worry is that, after all this time and effort, few academic standards have been set high enough and few accountability systems are robust. In those few places, much is to be commended. But most of the United States still has a long way to go.

---

## Comment by Richard Rothstein

Commenting upon the paper by Chester E. Finn Jr. and Marci Kanstoroom is difficult because it is ambivalent about its own goals. In some aspects, the paper is a polemic and does not pretend to dispassionate analysis. All nuance must be lost, for example, when the authors rank states' standards and accountability systems with grades of A through F and find some states on the honor roll while others are irresponsible or only going through the motions. The paper also includes a balanced discussion of many contradictions and shortcomings of the standards movement, but disconnected from its condemnations of other critics who make essentially similar points. The most jarring aspect of the paper is a condemnation of the standards movement's opponents, followed by acknowledgment that these opponents' criticisms are, in large measure, correct. And examination of the grades Finn and Kanstoroom give to state standards reveals that many of those states getting high grades are guilty of policy distortions that the authors rightly condemn, but that are not accounted for in the calculation of grades and rankings.

Finn and Kanstoroom properly trace the contemporary standards movement to ideas of systemic reform that led to the Charlottesville, Virginia, education summit's adoption of six national education goals in 1989. But the authors err when they describe systemic reform as a tripod of linked standards, assessment, and accountability. There was a fourth leg.

Marshall Smith and Jennifer O'Day, who coined the term *systemic reform*, were clear in their writings that adequate resources were also an essential part. Smith and O'Day's particular concern was that school improvement could result in middle-class children learning new, higher-order thinking skills while poor children, with more poorly trained teachers, inadequate facilities, laboratories, and instructional materials, and less access to challenging courses, would be judged solely on how they performed on multiple-choice assessments of basic skills. Truly raising standards, Smith and O'Day feared, would simply cause more disadvantaged children to fail. They termed the fourth leg, a guarantee of fully qualified teachers and other quality resources, "opportunity to learn."[39]

In negotiations with the Bush administration for the 1989 summit, Arkansas governor Bill Clinton represented the Democratic governors. Accompanied at these meetings by Marshall Smith, Clinton urged that opportunity to learn standards be included in the new program.[40] He proposed, for example, a national commitment to reduce the proportion of low birth weight infants to 5 percent.[41] But the Bush administration resisted, fearing this would open the door to big federal expenditure obligations for preschool, child health, and compensatory education programs. Clinton backed down. The agreement released by President George Bush and the governors set a goal of all children entering school ready to learn, but specified no new programs to achieve it. "We understand the limits imposed on new spending by the Federal deficit," the president and governors agreed. "However," they added, "we urge that priority for any further funding increases be given to prepare young children to succeed in school."[42]

Despite a failure to fund it, however, getting all children ready to learn, with an adequate menu of health care and early childhood education, was one of the six national education goals that led to the contemporary standards movement. The subsequent suppression of discussion of this goal, in both the Bush and Clinton administrations, has predictably led to many of the conflicts around standards that exist today and that the authors properly term a "backlash." The original conception of higher standards had a carrot-and-stick philosophy. But the contemporary standards movement, and particularly the wing of it represented by Finn and Kanstoroom, wants a stick to do the entire job. Thus, in their rankings of states, no mention is made of whether children are prepared to achieve high standards, but only of whether the bar is set high enough. Fear of sanctions alone is deemed sufficient to raise standards.

Thus, when Finn and Kanstoroom say that in the contemporary standards movement "attention began to shift from school inputs (for example, resources, programs, and facilities) as indicators of education quality to academic outcomes," they are only partially correct. The standards movement properly added a focus on results to what had been an excessive focus on inputs alone. But it was not the intention at Charlottesville to supplant a concern about whether children had adequate resources with one about whether they had adequate standards, tests, and sanctions for poor performance. All four are needed.

A proper ranking or evaluation of state standards, therefore, should take account of whether states assure all children the opportunity to learn to higher standards. Is public preschool provided to low-income children, and is the preschool of adequate quality? Are uncertified or otherwise unqualified teachers disproportionately recruited or assigned to classrooms with low-income children? Does the state enroll high proportions of poor children in the federal Child Health Insurance Program (CHIP) to make it more likely that they attend school ready to learn? Has the state organized adequate professional development programs to ensure that all teachers are prepared to deliver curriculum aligned with higher standards? Are advanced placement and other high-quality courses made available to all students or only to those in wealthier communities? These resource issues should not be the only ingredients of a state ranking system, nor even the major ones. But they should be included, as the Charlottesville goals require.

In this connection, it is worth noting that the authors misinterpret a recent report that finds that North Carolina and Texas had the greatest score gains on National Assessment of Educational Progress (NAEP) exams from 1990 to 1996. Finn and Kanstoroom report that "spending on schools, class size, and teachers' education level and experience were ruled out as explanations by the report's authors, David Grissmer and Ann Flanagan of RAND. The study concluded that the most plausible explanation for the gains was the creation of an aligned system of standards, curriculum, and assessments in these states, with schools held accountable for the improvement of all students."

This misinterpretation is not entirely, or even largely, the fault of Finn and Kanstoroom. The RAND authors have promoted their own findings in a distorted fashion, and the press has been eager to expand upon them. However, a careful reading of the report cited by Finn and Kanstoroom, as well as the underlying study upon which the cited report was based (it should be emphasized that the underlying study was released after the Finn and Kanstoroom paper was prepared), shows that Grissmer and Flanagan have a more complex explanation.[43] They do attribute gains from 1990 and 1996 to a strong accountability system. But they also find that these gains continued a pattern, particularly in Texas, that began before 1990. And they attribute the beginnings of this pattern (and the high starting point of Texas scores in 1990) to resource applications, in particular to the widespread availability of public prekindergarten (required for districts with low-income children since 1984), teachers' reports of having adequate curricular resources, and the organization of opportunities for professional development. Again, standards, accountability, and assessment cannot successfully function without attention to resources or opportunity to learn.

Another difficulty with Finn and Kanstoroom's discussion of standards is not unique to their approach, but inherent in the standards movement generally. They say: "Unless states make tough choices about what is essential for their students to know and be able to do, they will be unable to design fair assessments that can be linked to the standards." But this formulation ducks the toughest choice. Are the authors referring to what *all* students should know and be able to do or only some of them? Are their standards minima, that all must meet, or goals that only some will achieve?

Too often, standards advocates fail to make this distinction, leaving the impression that, if only standards are high enough and the sanctions for not meeting them tough enough, all students can and will meet them. But there is little that *all* students can know and be able to do. A distribution of outcomes will always be evident in many academic areas. At the present time, that distribution is very wide. For example, on most NAEP exams, fourth-grade students with scores one standard deviation above the mean have scores that are at the eighth-grade mean or above. The distribution is correlated with differences in student background, but not entirely so. A wide distribution would still exist if all socioeconomic difference were eliminated. On international comparison tests (such as the Third International Mathematics and Science Study), distribution of scores in other industrialized nations (including the high-scoring nations) is as wide, or nearly as wide, as that in the United States. The entire distribution in these nations is shifted to the right, compared with that in the United States, but the distribution exists nonetheless.

If Americans want to reform schools and improve education, one goal should be to narrow that distribution, particularly to bring up the left tail, and to make sure that many fewer eighth-grade students who are below the mean for eighth graders are not at the fourth-grade level. So efforts should be made to tighten the distribution as much as possible.

And Americans should also want to move the whole distribution up, to make sure that the fourth-grade mean is higher than it used to be and that the eighth-grade mean is higher than it used to be.

But the notion that these efforts can eliminate the distribution entirely and leave all students—as the authors say and as is implicit in most discussions of standards—meeting the same standard means either that the standards movement is not serious or that it is posing a standard that is at the left tail of the remaining distribution, even after it has been narrowed. When education has improved to its maximum potential, a standard that all, or almost all, students can achieve must be a very low standard.

That seems absurd. That is not a standard. It is a minimum. It is not a goal for all students.

So to have serious standards reform in the United States, the concept of standard must be redefined. Two standards, at least, are needed. One is a minimum standard, perhaps a standard that students who are one standard deviation below the mean are expected to meet. And the other is a higher standard, a goal that is a realistic expectation for the typical student. The authors state that "standards are the target that gives people a place to aim their arrows and a means by which to gauge how hard they must pull on the bowstring." This is true. But if the target is also defined as one that every marksman, every time, will hit, the bull's-eye will have to be so large that it represents no challenge to most marksmen, most of the time.

To talk about a minimum standard, on the one hand, and about an expectation of high achievement for typical students, on the other, in the same breath and with the same word, is to guarantee failure. It ensures the kinds of problems being faced now in places such as Massachusetts, New York, and Virginia, states that established a standard for all students that was previously the standard for students who were going to an academic four-year college. In New York, the Regents' minimum competency tests have been abolished, and all students are required to pass the college-bound Regents exams to graduate. This guarantees the kind of backlash the authors decry. New York inevitably either will have an unacceptably high number of failures or, more likely, will reduce the level of the Regents so more students can pass. In fact, at the present time, both are happening. What New York should have done is gradually raise the academic content level of both the minimum competency tests and the academic Regents exams. This would have been meaningful education reform.

Presently, nationwide, about one-quarter of the young people graduate from a four-year college. The education reform movement wants to increase that. Say it increases to 35 percent, which is an enormous, almost inconceivable, increase for the near future. Do policymakers really want to say that unless all students—not 25 percent, not 35 percent, but all—achieve that level, then elementary and secondary schools have failed?

That is where New York is heading. A train wreck is coming, and no one knows what the wreckage will look like. New York cannot have standards-based reform if that reform means a single standard for all students—unless New York wants a minimal standard that is much lower than the standards currently being discussed. If a backlash can send this standards movement back to the drawing board before the train wreck occurs, Finn and Kanstoroom ought to welcome, not condemn, that protest. It can only improve the chances of true standards-based reform, after a new start.

The authors acknowledge this point but in a way that is disconnected from the core of their analysis. They write:

> Some worry that, because academic ability is unevenly distributed, some students will never be able to meet high standards and that any standard meant to apply to all students will have to be a low standard. One way to address this is to create multilevel standards, or more than one cut score. Many states today offer an advanced diploma in addition to their regular diploma. . . . Rushing too fast to install standards-based reform is bound to create problems.

But whether states have created multilevel standards, or more than one cut score, is not a consideration for Finn and Kanstoroom when states' standards are graded and ranked. Also not considered is whether a state offers an advanced diploma in addition to its regular one or whether a state has set standards at lower grade levels so that either half of all students must fail or that most students pass only because the standard is a minimum and not a goal. Without such criteria, determining the significance of the authors' state rankings is difficult. California and Texas, for example, both make the authors' honor roll. But California has adopted the absurd goal of having all students achieve at the ninetieth percentile of a national distribution. And Texas's state assessment is more like a minimum competency exam that large numbers of students should eventually be able to pass. It is an inadequate goal for most.

Notwithstanding their agreement that multiple cut scores are appropriate, the authors cite with approval a Public Agenda poll finding that "clear majorities . . . say it is better for a child to repeat a grade than to be promoted to the next level without having learned the requisite skills." Most public discussion of the abolition of social promotion assumes a single cut point—grade level. Grade level conventionally means the achievement at the fiftieth percentile. Even if grade level is defined as standards-referenced, not norm-referenced, are the authors opposing the promotion of students below grade level or below some lower cut point? The authors' grading and ranking of states for their standards and accountability systems take no account of whether the cut point for promotion is appropriate.

Almost all of the backlash against standards about which Finn and Kanstoroom are concerned is not a backlash against standards. It is a backlash against another leg of their tripod—the assessment through standardized tests of whether students are meeting the standards. The authors again condemn critics of testing, while at the same time endorsing most of the critics' specific complaints and failing to incorporate these admittedly valid complaints into their grading and ranking of states.

Finn and Kanstoroom may be correct that many critics (such as Susan Ohanian, Alfie Kohn, and Peter Sacks) "have consistently opposed standards and tests for many years." But it is poor public policy to denounce critics who have a valid message because their motives may be suspect. A better approach is to address the valid criticisms, leaving inappropriate motives fully exposed.

Finn and Kanstoroom are in agreement with most of the specific claims being advanced by the named critics:

—"A single test score ought not determine one's life prospects. Students should have multiple opportunities to take the test, and other factors should be weighed besides the test score."

—"Using tests that do not mesh carefully with the state's standards undermines the entire reform strategy. Standards can have little traction if students' progress toward mastering them is not faithfully and honestly measured."

—"Parents in Ohio are upset about new state tests, and with good reason. . . . Among their complaints is that the fourth-grade exam is too difficult. . . . Where there are no real academic standards or where the assessments are not closely aligned with them, the test—the only operative standard visible in most schools and classrooms—becomes the de facto standard. This is more weight than most tests can, or should be expected to, bear. . . . Until states develop good academic standards and align their assessments to these standards, parents and teachers are right to object to the introduction of rewards and sanctions based on test scores."

—"Rushing too fast to install standards-based reform is bound to create problems. . . . One way to ease the blow of consequences is to phase accountability mechanisms in gradually. Instead of suddenly penalizing today's high school students for problems that have accumulated over twelve years of schooling, a state might start by holding this year's first graders to promotion standards. Next year, the standards would apply to second graders, then third graders, and this would continue until all grades were covered."

Little advocated by the most militant backlash leaders is not encompassed by the four critiques just summarized. But Finn and Kanstoroom, while giving lip service to these critiques, proceed to grade and rank states without regard to them. Multiple opportunities to take tests play no role in the rankings. (While some states permit high school students multiple opportunities to take exit exams before denial of diplomas, I am aware of no state where multiple opportunities to take tests are offered before individual high-stakes decisions, such as social promotion, or systemwide accountability decisions are made.) Nor have states included other measures, such as student work portfolios, in high-stakes accountability systems for students, although some states utilize attendance and dropout data to supplement test scores for schoolwide accountability. Senator Paul Wellstone (D-Minn.) has introduced legislation that would prevent states from basing high-stakes decisions such as promotion on only a single test. From their arguments, Finn and Kanstoroom might be expected to endorse the Wellstone bill. Do they?

Meshing tests with standards is even a bigger problem and this, too, is not taken into account in the authors' ratings. Several states have excellent standards, but they are meaningless because the states' standardized tests (in most cases, off-the-shelf commercial tests or derivatives) are incapable of assessing the higher-order thinking skills that good standards include. The Smith and O'Day conception of systemic school reform was specifically intended to encompass higher quality curriculum. As Finn and Kanstoroom state, "most of today's efforts at standards-based education reform reach considerably higher than minimum competence." Yet in many cases, tests are little different from the minimum competency exams of the 1970s. The authors acknowledge that Texas exams are of this sort ("start[ing] with relatively low cutoff scores that are gradually raised"). So if Texas standards are, as the authors state, excellent, then state tests are not assessing whether students achieve them. The test becomes, in the authors' words, the "de facto standard." This may be good policy. The authors praise the minimum competency testing of the 1970s, but when it comes to the contemporary drive for higher standards, such practice should not earn a state honor roll kudos.

The authors' recommendation that states implement standards-based accountability over a twelve-year period, one grade at a time, is nowhere reflected in their grading or ranking of states. This is not because no alternative exists to the present system of unaligned assessments, high-stakes decisions based on single measures, and attempts to impose a single standard on all variants of student ability. Other ways are available to hold schools accountable, but not in a single test. For example, in most states, accreditation systems are weak and without teeth. Beefing up those accreditation systems would be a simple matter, so that, for example, they were not incestuous peer reviews but included outside reviewers from business, political bodies, and university consumers of secondary graduation standards, as well as other teachers and administrators.

Test data should be one of the indicators in a serious accreditation system, but so should a much broader range of data about the quality of schools that is available and that would be available to a sophisticated accreditation team— student work portfolios, for example, or employment and college outcomes. These are not input data. They are outcomes, but more sophisticated outcome indicators than a standardized test.

A standards and accountability system worthy of honor roll citation would also make a clear distinction between accountability at a school level and accountability at an individual level. There can be high stakes for schools on the basis of a single test, provided that the test is properly aligned with standards and with the curriculum and that the schools have been given the resources necessary to deliver it. But no valid policy reason exists to have individual-level accountability testing. If states want to hold schools accountable for value-added, testable achievement, states can do this with the kind of matrix sampling done in the NAEP, and individual students would not need to be tested. Such a testing strategy permits, in terms of both time consumed and expense to grade, a more sophisticated assessment of higher-order skills than the kind of inexpensive fill-in-the-bubble tests currently used to generate individual and school scores at once.

Some may argue that individual-level testing is needed to motivate students, to give them incentives to learn. Even if this is desirable (and it is), this still does not lead to the desirability of asking that standardized tests for school accountability do double duty. High-stakes tests at the classroom level are nothing new in the contemporary standards movement. Albert Shanker used to say that the American students' favorite question was, "Will it be on the test?"

All students experienced high-stakes tests (even weekly quizzes) in school. But they do not have to be standardized. Teachers are capable of constructing high-stakes tests for their students. If they exist simultaneously with high-stakes standardized tests at the school level, no need, no reason, and no justification can be offered for trying to administer them at the student level. They provide little valid information that cannot be generated by combining the other two types of information, the teacher evaluations based on their own classroom high-stakes tests and the statewide evaluations, which tell whether schools are functioning properly.

The authors should make a choice about whether they want to transform the direction of the standards movement in ways they carefully set forth (no accountability based on single tests, no testing not aligned with higher standards, no adoption of accountability in a hurried fashion, no single cut score for all students, and so on), or whether they want to insist that the most vocal advocates of these positions are enemies of the standards movement and that those who implement standards in violation of these conditions are its friends.

If Finn and Kanstoroom continue to take the latter position, they will be increasingly embarrassed as the backlash, which they should support, gains traction and as the flaws of the standards movement, as presently conceived, become more conspicuous and unavoidable. For the time is not far off when courts will prohibit the continued administration of high-stakes tests because of the flaws in these tests, and in their relationship to higher standards, that Finn and Kanstoroom acknowledge.

The main basis of these court decisions will be the unacceptable unreliability of single administrations of standardized tests as guides to underlying ability. The chances of false negatives on a single test are too high. In Texas, a state court recently ruled against a suit by the Mexican American Legal Defense Foundation that claimed Texas's high school exit exams were unconstitutional. But the court's reasoning was based largely on the fact that students could take the exit exam over and over again if they did not pass. What if a similar suit were brought against a state that retained fourth- or eighth-grade students based on a single test, where multiple tries are not permitted? If a state retained students who scored below a level equivalent to a thirtieth percentile showing, any testing expert could easily prove that establishing a cut score anywhere above the fifteenth percentile would entail an unacceptable number of false failures (students whose true ability was at the thirtieth percentile, but whose score on a particular administration was much lower). Such court decisions could set back the cause that Smith and O'Day and the Charlottesville goals-setters worked so hard to promote.

If Finn and Kanstoroom used their considerable influence to reform the standards, assessments, and accountability systems before they are banned by the courts, the authors could make a big contribution to saving a movement with the potential to truly reform American education. But they would have to ally themselves with critics they despise and to delink this cause from others that they hold dear.

---

## Comment by Bill Honig

Chester E. Finn Jr. and Marci Kanstoroom examine the states' academic standards, which have been the progeny of the standards-based reform movement in the United States. According to them, the essential trinity of this reform is the adoption of specific curriculum and performance standards, assessment of how many students meet the standards, and then adoption of either negative (takeovers) or positive (school or teacher bonuses) consequences. The assumption underlying this reform strategy is that assessments will reflect the standards and signal success or failure and that consequences will drive schools and districts to increase performance.

Finn and Kanstoroom correctly point out that for this trinity to work, standards have to be not only consistent with the best thinking about that particular discipline but also detailed enough to drive instruction in the right way. They found few states had drafted standards with this kind of specificity.

An example of the level of specificity and accuracy Finn and Kanstoroom admire is California's reading and language arts standards that delineate as its first standard for first grade that students should be able to look at an unencountered simple word in print, generate the sounds from all the letters and letter combinations, and blend those sounds into a recognizable word (assuming that the word is in the student's oral vocabulary). This skill is called decoding, and an overwhelming body of research and best practice find that the ability to decode is an essential tool in becoming automatic with words and thus learning to read. Weak decoding skills are implicated in 85 percent of reading failure. Yet, few of the current state reading and language arts standards mention the ability to decode.

The failure to include this instructional objective renders a set of reading standards fatally flawed. Finn and Kanstoroom are justified in bemoaning the fact that so few of the standards meet their criteria. The trinity loses its coherence and power if, initially, vague standards confuse implementation.

Unfortunately, evidence shows that the steps Finn and Kanstoroom recommend—the adoption of detailed and accurate standards, conducting assessment geared to those standards, and providing consequences—will by themselves produce only limited improvements in student performance.

First, even in the California standards, giving each child the ability to decode is only one among a welter of standards. The standards do not necessarily make decoding a priority for instruction. Second, while the result of decoding—higher comprehension—is assessed, a specific decoding test is usually not part of the assessment and must be left for local diagnostics. Third, and most important, the triad—standards, assessment, and consequences—may not be the most important set of reform components. The assumption seems to be that lack of motivation is the culprit in preventing improvement. Thus, with powerful rewards or sanctions, teachers and administrators will figure out what to do and produce results, or, more likely, alternative forms of schooling (such as charter schools) will spring up and be responsive to quality concerns. This assumption is valid for some. Educators will strive harder for rewards or fear of sanctions. Their careers are at risk if they fail to do so.

However, most teachers and administrators passionately desire that their students read and compute better. The major impediment to improvement in their schools is the lack of capacity to improve instruction. Most schools do not know enough about the specifics of reading or math instruction—what are the key components, why students have difficulty mastering these components, and the focus and leadership—to assure that instructional practice reflects these specifics. Even though newly created charter schools are freed from most bureaucratic restraints, on the whole they do not offer instruction that is much different from existing public schools. Charter schools also need more intelligent attention to effective instruction.

Thus, while standards, assessment, and consequences are important, even more important to improving achievement is an implementation triad—teacher knowledge, quality instructional materials, and site and district leadership. When these three components are done well, achievement skyrockets. What teachers should know is defined by quality standards, and thus standards are a sine qua non. For example, in California, under staff development legislation for reading and math, providers of instruction for teachers must be certified to assure that their training is based on the standards. But translating standards into effective staff development is a crucial step usually missing in policy debates.

Similarly, textbooks in California are adopted under criteria based on the standards. A tremendous amount of work has gone into assuring that reading and math textbooks accurately reflect the curriculum contained in the standards. Broad statewide assessments prove whether the implementation is working or not. But a missing link is the diagnostic benchmarks that should be adopted by schools and districts. If decoding is important and should be learned by mid-first grade, then any school serious about reading improvement will give students a simple decoding test at mid-first grade to determine who can decode so that instruction can be intensified for those who cannot.

The bread and butter of improvement is found in staff development. Teachers and administrators must understand the standards and know how best to implement them, how to select and use materials that reflect the standards, and what to do to put into place these instructional details and make improvement an operational priority.

Take decoding as an example. Decoding is crucial in learning to read. Some students pick it up easily; most have to be taught it in an organized fashion. Learning to decode takes most students about a year and a half, starting in kindergarten and ending in mid-first grade. It is important to know why some students do not learn to decode.

First, some cannot hear and process the discrete sounds in spoken words (phonemic awareness) at basic levels early enough so that they can learn phonics. (Students need to be able to identify the first and last sound in spoken words for phonics instruction to take, a skill that students should possess by the end of kindergarten.)

Second, some students, while phonemically aware, get confused about the basic linguistic ways of representing sound in English; that is, phonics. They have not been taught in a systematic way from late kindergarten through first grade and have gaps in knowledge of basic letter and sound combinations.

Third, some students can generate the sounds of individual letters or letter combinations but they cannot use that knowledge successfully in sounding out a whole word. They need to be taught to blend.

Finally, students may possess all these tools, but they have not read enough text in which they can practice these skills in figuring out new words. To avoid utter confusion, text should match the instructional sequence of the phonics lessons (decodable text) so that students can successfully apply what they have learned.

This complex set of interlocking components should guide instruction, diagnostics, and accountability. Both teachers and administrators need to be familiar with these ideas and use them to guide adoption of books and implementation of assessment and instruction. Most instructional strategies in schools (public, charter, or private) are not that focused.

Similarly, in the mathematics area, a body of knowledge exists about the specifics underlying basic arithmetic concepts and computation (usually much more complex than is generally understood), where students have difficulty learning these ideas, and instructional delivery. Most classrooms do not reflect this knowledge. A large amount of research has demonstrated that investments in teacher understanding of math combined with materials designed under these principles and in an administration that supports the implementation of these ideas produce significant results.

A hidden assumption of Finn and Kanstoroom seems to be that schools as presently constituted lack the will to improve. Thus, they believe that standards, assessment, and consequences are necessary to encourage alternatives to bureaucratic organizations, which are distracted by internal political issues and impervious to considerations of quality. Although the standard, assessment, and consequence triad will help improve schools, if these elements are combined with the implementation triad, then major improvements can be expected in the variety of organizational patterns that currently exist.

### Notes

1. Lawrence Feinberg, "High School Competency Tests Viewed as Too Easy," *Washington Post*, December 8, 1981, p. A1; and Jean Seligman, "A Really Final Exam," *Newsweek*, May 28, 1979, p. 97.

2. Barbara Lerner, "Good News about American Education," *Commentary*, March 1991, pp. 22–28.

3. Feinberg, "High School Competency Tests Viewed as Too Easy," p. A1.

4. Lerner, "Good News about American Education."

5. David Grissmer and Ann Flanagan, *Exploring Rapid Achievement Gains in North Carolina and Texas* (Washington: National Education Goals Panel, November 1998).

6. M. Gail Jones and others, "The Impact of High-Stakes Testing on Teachers and Students in North Carolina," *Phi Delta Kappan*, November 1999, pp. 199–203.

7. This example was suggested by Leslye Arsht, president and cofounder, StandardsWorks.

8. New Jersey Standard 4.4, by the end of grade eight, cited in Ralph A. Raimi and Lawrence S. Braden, *State Mathematics Standards* (Washington: Thomas B. Fordham Foundation, 1998).

9. Examples taken from Lynn Olson, "Rating the Standards," *Quality Counts 99*, January 11, 1999, pp. 107–109, based on analysis by Matthew Gandal and Jennifer Vranek of Achieve Inc.

10. Examples taken from Sandra Stotsky, *State English Standards* (Washington: Thomas B. Fordham Foundation, 1997).

11. Example taken from Olson, "Rating the Standards."

12. The attributes of good standards rely heavily on the criteria developed by the experts who evaluated standards for the Thomas B. Fordham Foundation.

13. Douglas Archbold, *The Reviews of State Content Standards in English Language Arts and Mathematics: A Summary and Review of Their Methods and Findings and Implications for Future Standards Development*, ED–98–PO–2038 (Washington: National Education Goals Panel, July 1998), p. 2.

14. Archbold, *The Reviews of State Content Standards in English Language Arts and Mathematics*, p. 4.

15. Archbold, *The Reviews of State Content Standards in English Language Arts and Mathematics*, p. 16.

16. E. D. Hirsch Jr., *The Schools We Need and Why We Don't Have Them* (Doubleday, 1999), p. 33.

17. W. James Popham quoted in David J. Hoff, "Made to Measure," *Education Week*, June 16, 1999, p. 21.

18. Eva Baker quoted in Hoff, "Made to Measure," p. 21.

19. Chester E. Finn Jr., Marci Kanstoroom, and Michael J. Petrilli, *The Quest for Better Teachers: Grading the States* (Washington: Thomas B. Fordham Foundation, November 1999). All numbers are as of October 1999. Maryland's recent actions are not counted.

20. Finn, Kanstoroom, and Petrilli, *The Quest for Better Teachers*.

21. While evaluations of standards and accountability systems are included in this report, grades for assessments are missing. This is because states have generally not made their tests available to outside reviewers. Until we know how good a state's tests are, our conclusions about the state's overall accountability systems are partly speculative.

22. Peter Schrag, "High Stakes Are for Tomatoes," *Atlantic Monthly*, August 2000, p. 20.

23. Alfie Kohn, *The Schools Our Children Deserve: Moving Beyond Traditional Classrooms and 'Tougher Standards'* (Houghton Mifflin, 1999); Susan Ohanian, *One Size Fits Few: The Folly of Educational Standards* (Portsmouth, N.H.: Heinemann, 1999); and Peter Sacks, *Standardized Minds: The High Price of America's Testing Culture and What We Can Do to Change It* (Cambridge, Mass.: Perseus Books, 1999).

24. Richard Phelps, *Why Testing Experts Hate Testing* (Washington: Thomas B. Fordham Foundation, 1999).

25. Francis X. Clines, "Cheating Report Renews Debate Over Use of Tests to Evaluate Schools," *Washington Post*, June 12, 2000, p. A16.

26. Pamela Stallsmith, "Critic Says State Tests Crowd Out Creativity," Richmond *Times-Dispatch*, March 22, 2000, p. B7.

27. Public Agenda, "Reality Check 2000," *Education Week*, February 16, 2000, p. 51.

28. Public Agenda, "Reality Check 2000."

29. Public Agenda, "Reality Check 2000."

30. "Split on Testing," *Washington Post*, June 27, 2000, p. A11.

31. Marion Brady, "The Standards Juggernaut," *Phi Delta Kappan*, May 2000, pp. 649–51.

32. Lynn Olson, "Worries of a Standards 'Backlash' Grow," *Education Week*, April 5, 2000, p. 1.

33. Achieve Inc., "A New Compact for Ohio's Schools: A Report to Ohio's Educational Policy Leaders," March 1999.

34. Mark Fisher and Scott Elliott, "Proficiency: The Test Questioned," *Dayton Daily News*, March 12, 2000, p. 14A.

35. R. H. Melton, "Gilmore, Allen Concede Problems in State Tests," *Washington Post*, January 19, 2000, p. B4.

36. Quoted in William J. Bennett, "What the Schools Have Forgotten," *Washington Post*, June 22, 2000, p. A25.

37. Chris Pipho, "The Sting of High-Stakes Testing and Accountability," *Phi Delta Kappan*, May 2000, pp. 645–46; and "Critics Target Wrong Culprit as Minorities' Test Scores Lag," *USA Today*, May 30, 2000, p. 16A.

38. John F. Jennings, *Why National Standards and Tests? Politics and the Quest for Better Schools* (Thousand Oaks, Calif.: Sage, 1998), p. 178.

39. Marshall S. Smith and Jennifer A. O'Day, "Systemic School Reform," in S. Fuhrman and B. Malen, eds., *The Politics of Curriculum and Testing* (Bristol, Pa.: Falmer Press, 1991); Marshall S. Smith and Jennifer A. O'Day, "Educational Equality: 1966 and Now," in D. Verstegen and J. Ward, eds., *Spheres of Justice in Education: The 1990 American Education Finance Association Yearbook* (HarperCollins, 1991); and Jennifer A. O'Day and Marshall S. Smith, "Systemic Reform and Educational Opportunity," in S. H. Fuhrman, ed., *Designing Coherent Education Policy: Improving the System* (San Francisco: Jossey-Bass, 1993).

40. Maris A. Vinovskis, "Chapter Two: Development of the Six National Educational Goals and Creation of the Panel to Oversee Them," paper prepared for the National Education Goals Panel, November 1999.

41. Julie A. Miller, "Small Group's Inside Role in Goals-Setting Provides Clues to Education Policymaking," *Education Week*, March 14, 1990.

42. Maris A. Vinovskis, "Chapter Three: America 2000 and the National Education Goals," paper prepared for the National Education Goals Panel, September 1999, preliminary draft.

43. David Grissmer, Ann Flanagan, Jennifer Kawata, and Stephanie Wiliamson, *Improving Student Acievement: What State NAEP Test Scores Tell Us* (Santa Monica, Calif.: RAND, 2000).

# Searching for Indirect Evidence for the Effects of Statewide Reforms

DAVID GRISSMER *and* ANN FLANAGAN

States are the primary policymakers in several important areas of K–12 education. States, on average, provide approximately one-half of educational funding to school districts. Thus they are instrumental in determining how much is spent on education and how that money is used to reduce inequity in funding among school districts. States also are instrumental in determining who teaches, what is taught, and the conditions for teaching. These state policies include setting teacher certification standards, establishing maximum class-size and minimum graduation requirements, setting educational standards in subjects, and establishing methods of assessing student performance and methods of accountability for teachers, schools, and school districts. States also influence the extent of early education through kindergarten and preschool regulations and, in some states, through subsidizing prekindergarten for lower income families.

Given their dominant role in educational funding and regulation, states not surprisingly have been the primary initiators of the latest wave of educational reform starting in the mid-1980s.[1] Perhaps the most widespread initiative is a systemic reform movement that includes defining educational standards, aligning curriculum and teacher professional development to the standards, and having some form of assessment and accountability with respect to the standards.[2] While simple in concept, design and implementation are arduous, and states have made varying amounts of progress.[3] Many states have also passed legislation authorizing charter schools, school choice, or contract schools based on the assumption that public schools are unreformable without external competition and parental choice.

Having fifty states take different approaches to education can provide a long-term advantage if research and evaluation can identify successful and unsuccessful approaches. If states adopted fairly uniform policies and implemented similar reform initiatives at the same time, then evaluation would be difficult. However, the states have a wide degree of variation in their educational policies and practices, making between-state variation a significant part of total variation. For instance, two-thirds of the variance in district per pupil expenditures is between, not within, states.[4] Reform initiatives across states have also varied widely both in substance and timing of implementation, making states a potentially valuable source of evidence about the effects of resources and reforms.

## Analyzing Comparative State Achievement

Until 1990, no statistically valid measures existed of the achievement of representative samples of students across states.[5] Comparative state analysis became possible when the National Assessment of Educational Progress (NAEP) tests were administered to representative samples of students across a voluntary sample of states in 1990, 1992, 1994, 1996, and 1998. Nine tests were given in reading and mathematics at either the fourth or eighth grade. Each test was given to approximately twenty-five hundred students, with forty-nine states administering at least one test. These tests represent the first valid, comparable measures of achievement of representative samples of children in various states. These data are unique in that they make it possible to assess comparative achievement across states.

While these tests present an opportunity to assess comparative state achievement performance, significant analytical and methodological problems arise in obtaining the kind of reliable results needed by policymakers. First, previous research would suggest that family variables would account for a substantial part of the variation of scores across states because of wide variation in their demographic composition and family characteristics. The family variables collected with NAEP are limited, and those collected are student-reported by fourth- and eighth-grade students, making their quality poor. Without accurate family control variables, the results from any analysis will be problematic. Any analysis needs to address this issue.

Second, the current methodological debate concerns whether aggregate- or individual-level analysis yields more accurate results.[6] The NAEP data can be analyzed at the individual level to yield statewide parameters or at the aggregate state level.[7] Arguments can be made for each type of analysis. Other things being equal, researchers prefer individual-level data because of the larger samples, the usually greater variation in both independent and dependent variables, and the ability to do hierarchical modeling that might include variables from individual, classroom, school, district, and state levels.

However, other things are usually not equal in models at individual and more aggregate levels. The quality of data available at different levels of aggregation is often different. With the NAEP data, the only family variables available at the individual level are the poorer quality student-reported variables, whereas, at the state level, Bureau of the Census data can be used to define a broader and more accurate set of family characteristics. Cumulative educational resource variables also can be defined at the state level, but not at the individual level. For instance, the Tennessee Student/Teacher Achievement Ratio (STAR) experiment suggests that achievement at grades four and eight is dependent on class size in grades K–3. So educational variables need to be defined that take account of the conditions at each previous grade as well as the present grade. At the state level, variables corresponding to state averages during the time in school before the NAEP tests can be obtained, but similar variables at the individual level cannot be obtained. Also with NAEP, the individual-level scores are imputed because of the matrix sampling used, but statewide averages do not depend on imputation.

Different sources of bias can also be present at different levels of aggregation, and it is not clear at what level the net bias is greater. It has been suggested that certain sources of bias such as the selectivity present in neighborhood choice, teacher choice, and teacher assignment to schools and classrooms might be greater at individual levels, but partially canceled out at higher levels of aggregation.[8]

Eventually, analysis is needed comparing results with the same data set for individual and aggregate levels of analysis and tracing any differences to the different quality of data available, differential sources of bias, or hierarchical effects. Unlike the generally null effects measured at lower levels of aggregation, previous studies using state-level data have shown consistently positive, statistically significant effects of educational resources on educational outcomes.[9] The interpretation of this disagreement has generally been that measurements using less aggregate data are more accurate and that state-level results are biased upward. However, an alternate explanation has been suggested that measurements at lower levels of aggregation may be biased downward.[10] Such an explanation is more consistent with the results from experimental data from Tennessee and Wisconsin.[11]

Third, models using nonexperimental data will be deemed more credible if they can predict results that agree with results from well-designed, -implemented, and -analyzed experimental data. The Tennessee STAR experiment shows positive and statistically significant class-size effects through eighth grade from lower class size in K–3.[12] These effects are generally larger for minority and disadvantaged students.[13] The Tennessee STAR class-size experiment has so far withstood analytical scrutiny.[14] A new quasi-experiment in Wisconsin of pupil/teacher ratio reductions also shows initial results similar to the Tennessee experiment.[15] So models using nonexperimental data need to test predictions against these results. The resource equations estimated from the aggregate state NAEP data and used in this analysis are able to predict pupil/teacher ratio effects that are in agreement with the Tennessee experiment.[16]

In this analysis, we present results using state aggregate-level data. While this allows improved family variables and use of cumulative educational characteristics, it poses other problems. The sample is small, with a lack of independence of the state scores across tests and an unequal number of tests in which states participated. Our analysis is based on five math tests—eighth-grade tests in 1990, 1992, and 1996 and fourth-grade tests in 1992 and 1996; thirty-six states are represented; and the sample has a total of 171 scores. While the standard *t*-tests can account for differences in sample size and can still be trusted to determine statistical significance, results from small samples can be more vulnerable to statistical assumptions, estimation procedures, and the influence of a few, extreme data points. A previous analysis found little sensitivity to estimation procedure or outliers.[17]

## Testing for Indirect Evidence of the Effects of State Reform

We approach the measurement of reform efforts through a series of hypotheses that can at best provide indirect or circumstantial evidence. We suggest that the following hypotheses need to be true for a viable hypothesis to be made that statewide reforms are having an effect.

—Successful state reform efforts that began in the mid-to-late 1980s and into the 1990s should result in some achievement score gains in the 1990–96 period at the fourth- and eighth-grade level.

—The pattern of achievement gains across states should show significant variation given that states vary widely in the pace, type, and implementation of reforms.

—Any state achievement gains should not be traceable to changes in resources.

—Achievement gains within states should occur in all localities within the state (central cities, suburbs, and rural areas) if statewide reform efforts are effective.

A set of findings that are consistent with these hypotheses would only suggest that statewide reforms would be a viable candidate for explaining the gains, but certainly not provide compelling evidence. However, a wide range of possible results not consistent with reform effects would make it extremely difficult to hypothesize a link between achievement gains and statewide reforms.

For instance, if NAEP scores show no gains or even declines in the 1990–96 period, one would have to hypothesize either that reform effects take longer or that other influences were driving scores downward or that reforms were ineffective. While it is too early to expect to see the full effects from reforms that started in the mid-to-late 1980s, it is not too early to expect some effects. Some educational reforms require significant changes in the behavior of organizations and large groups of individuals—a process that requires years, not months. Other reforms operate gradually because they effectively grandfather current students and teachers. For instance, changes in entrance standards for teachers will take ten years or more to affect a sizable portion of teachers, and new graduation requirements for students are usually started at least five years into the future to give students and teachers time to adapt.

Another reason for expecting gradual effects is that student scores are probably partially dependent on conditions in all previous grades, so students need to experience reforms from school entry before their full effects on scores at later grades are seen. However, some reforms may have immediate, as well as cumulative, effects on achievement. These considerations point to the possibility of some immediate effects, but also more gradual gains in scores from changing policies that may be fully realized sooner in early grades than later grades. Little empirical evidence outside of the Tennessee experiment is available to determine the expected dynamic pattern of the effects of specific changes in policies, making assumptions about the pattern of effects across grades problematic.

The fourth- and eighth-grade NAEP test-takers in the earliest test (1990 and 1992) would have experienced less reform than later test-takers (1996).

The eighth-grade group taking the 1990 math state test entered school in 1982, while the 1996 eighth-grade group entered in 1988. Thus the former group would have spent most of its years of schooling before much of the reform began, and the latter group would have experienced some reform during most of its school career. However, the latter group would experience little reform over its entire school career. The fourth graders taking the math test in 1992 would have experienced some early reforms during their schooling, while the students taking the test in 1996 would experience the reforms implemented between 1988 and 1992 over their entire schooling.

Because of the widely varying timing and substance of reforms across states, effective state reforms would be expected to show differential achievement gains across states. A set of results that showed widespread improvements, but little difference across states, would point to national rather than state effects. Also, score improvements that can be directly related to changes in specific resources would leave little room for the effects of systemic reform efforts.

Finally, improvements occurring only in suburbs or central cities would mean that reforms are differentially effective in these areas or that district policies, demographic shifts, or differential resource growth are responsible for them. Because state average scores can often be dominated by the larger populations in central cities and suburbs, it is important to determine if gains are truly statewide, occurring in populous, as well as less populous, localities.

In short, our analysis cannot provide compelling evidence but can narrow the range of viable hypotheses and provide indirect evidence of whether statewide reform remains one of those viable hypotheses. Direct tests for specific reform effects are going to be difficult for several reasons. The timing, range, and intensity of systemic reform efforts are often too complex to be characterized by single variables that can be used in multivariate models. Even if they could be, the state-by-state data are not yet readily available that can characterize such efforts. Also, more than one initiative often is implemented at the same time because legislative reform packages typically include several reform initiatives. Finally, the expected dynamic pattern of effects across grades and time is largely unknown, making fine-grained measurements problematic to interpret. Thus it may always be difficult to provide analytically compelling evidence that specific reforms are working without more focused experimentation.

This study extends a previous analysis in two ways.[18] The previous study utilized the state NAEP data to estimate trends across states, differences in scores across states for students from similar families, and the effect of differing levels and allocations of resources across states. This study extends the previous analysis by (1) estimating the trends by state that are unaccounted for by resources and (2) providing estimates of trends for central-city, rural, and suburban areas within states to provide additional evidence about the effects of statewide reforms.

## Measuring State Achievement Gains

The official state NAEP reports contain an indication of gain for each state from the previous similar test and an indication of its statistical significance based on the sampling standard errors.[19] These measures have several limitations for assessing and ranking states based on achievement gains. They do not take account of changing student populations from test to test caused by migration, changing exclusion and participation rates, and sampling variation.

For instance, states in the southeast and southwest have had significant increases in the population of Hispanic children from 1990 to 1996, while many northern states show little increase. Unless these changes are accounted for in assessing trends, it cannot be determined whether the education system is causing changes in scores or population shifts are changing scores. Besides population shifts, the participation and exclusion rates change for each state across tests and that can also affect scores. Variations also exist in the characteristics of students stemming from normal sampling variations, which need to be considered. Our estimates take these factors either partially or wholly into account.

The published measures also do not reflect whether states are making systematic gains across all tests. Estimating the gains across all tests is a more robust measure than each test individually and provides a better measure to rank state performance.

## Study Objectives, Data Sources, and Methodology

The National Assessment of Educational Progress tests began to be administered in 1990 to representative samples of students within states to compare performance of students across states. They remain the only valid measures of comparable achievement that include most states. Seven state tests have

**Table 1. Description of Seven State National Assessment of Educational Progress Reading and Math Tests Given between 1990 and 1996**

| Year | Subject | Grade level | States tested | Range of student samples | Range of school samples |
|------|---------|-------------|---------------|--------------------------|-------------------------|
| 1990 | Math    | 8 | 38 | 1,900–2,900 | 30–108 |
| 1992 | Math    | 8 | 42 | 2,000–2,800 | 28–112 |
| 1992 | Math    | 4 | 42 | 1,900–2,900 | 44–143 |
| 1992 | Reading | 4 | 42 | 1,800–2,800 | 44–148 |
| 1994 | Reading | 4 | 39 | 2,000–2,800 | 51–117 |
| 1996 | Math    | 4 | 44 | 1,800–2,700 | 51–132 |
| 1996 | Math    | 8 | 41 | 1,800–2,700 | 30–116 |

Source: C. A. Shaughnessy, J. Nelson, and N. Norris, *NAEP 1996 Mathematics Cross State Data Compendium for the Grade 4 and Grade 8 Assessment*, NCES–98–481 (Department of Education, 1998); I. V. S. Mullis and others, *NAEP 1992 Mathematics Report Card for the Nation and the States: Data from the National and Trail State Assessments* (Washington: National Center for Education Statistics, 1993); and C. M. Reese and others, *NAEP 1996 Mathematics Report Card for the Nation and the States* (Washington: National Center for Education Statistics, 1997).

been given in fourth- or eighth-grade reading or math through 1996, with five of these being math tests. We focus on the five math scores because they provide both fourth- and eighth-grade results and the widest comparison period. In the 1990–96 period, two reading tests were administered at the fourth-grade level but were given only two years apart, making it difficult to estimate a reliable trend.

The NAEP state tests are not simply multiple-choice tests measuring basic skills. The tests require responses from a few sentences to a few paragraphs, thereby testing more critical thinking skills. NAEP data collection takes students approximately ninety minutes to complete for a given subject. Matrix sampling of questions is used to allow testing a broad range of knowledge while limiting the time each student is tested. Bib spiraling of questions ensures that effects from the placement of questions within booklets and grouping of questions are minimized.

Table 1 lists descriptive characteristics of the seven state reading and math tests given from 1990 to 1996. The four tests in the 1990–92 period sampled only public school students. The 1994 reading and the 1996 fourth- and eighth-grade math tests also sampled representative private school students. Our analysis is focused only on public school scores.

The sampling is based on a multistage design that first chooses a geographical area (county, group of counties, or Metropolitan Statistical Area [MSA]), then schools within geographical areas, and then students within schools. Public school samples are stratified to achieve increased minority representation. The samples ranged from approximately two thousand to three thousand students per state and from 30 to 150 schools within states. Because participation was voluntary, the sample of states changes from test to test. There are thirty-six states in our analysis that participated in either four or five of the math tests.

Two types of exclusions from testing are allowed: limited-English proficiency (LEP) and individualized education plan/disabled (IEP/DS). Approximately 1–2 percent of students nationally is excluded for LEP and about 4–6 percent for IEP/DS. The range of variation across states for the average IEP/DS exclusion rate across tests is from 2.6 in North Dakota to 6.7 percent in Florida. The similar range for LEP exclusion is from 0.0 percent in Wyoming to 8.3 percent in California.[20]

States show a fairly stable pattern across tests in exclusion rates indicating uniformity in application of criteria over time. The cross-sectional variation in exclusion rates across states appears to arise mainly from differences in actual incidence of LEP and IEP/DS students. For instance, the variation in LEP rates is mainly accounted for by recent Hispanic immigration.

Nonparticipation also has the potential to bias results if nonrandom and significant differences exist across states. Both entire schools and students can choose not to participate. A high proportion of nonparticipation comes from school nonparticipation. Substitution is attempted in the case of nonparticipation. Nationally, participation rates after substitution are approximately 85 percent. The range of variation across states for average participation across tests is from 74 to 100 percent.

Some evidence exists that participation tends to be lower for schools with lower socioeconomic status (SES), resulting in a correlation across tests in participation rates. States with lower participation on one test tend to have lower participation in other tests. We correct for the effects of participation differences by inclusion of the participation rate in the regressions and also by weighting the family variables by the actual participation by race for each test.

*State Achievement Results*

The state scores are highly correlated across tests (at least .77 and usually above .85). So we summarize the achievement scores using the average across all tests in which each state participated (see figure 1). The pattern of scores shows that smaller, more rural northern states are disproportionately in the upper part of the distribution while southern states disproportionately appear

**Figure 1. Average State National Assessment of Educational Progress Scores across Seven Tests**

Standard deviation

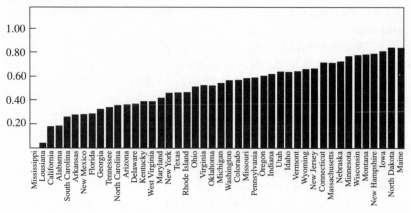

in the lower half of the rankings. Highly urban eastern, midwestern, and western states tend to be closer to the middle of the distribution. However, exceptions are present in nearly all categories. The difference between the scores for the highest and lowest state is three quarters to one standard deviation across tests. Average scores in the highest ranked state would be approximately between the sixty-second and sixty-seventh percentile nationally, while average scores from the lowest state would be around the thirty-third to thirty-eighth percentile. This represents a significant variation in test scores among students from different states.

*Model Specification and Estimation*

We estimate all models as a panel data set using a random effect specification. We use a generalized estimator with an exchangeable correlation structure for estimating the random effect models. This estimator is recommended for panels with short time series variation, and it accounts for the unbalanced panel and provides robust standard errors that account for both the lack of independence of observations within states and heteroskedasticity.[21]

We first model the average state scores as a function of state family/demographic characteristics and dummy variables for a score gain on each repeated test. The random effect equations are

$$y_{ij} = a + \Xi\, b_k\, F_{ijk} + \Xi\, g1_i\, d928th_i + \Xi\, g2_i\, d968th_i + \Xi\, g4_i\, d964th_i + h1\, d8th + r1\, p_{ij} + u_i + e_{ij}$$

in which $y_{ij}$ is the normalized test score for the $i$th state ($i = 1,36$) in the $j$th test ($j = 1,5$), $F_{ijk}$ is a set of $k$ family characteristics for the $i$th state at the time of the $j$th test, $d928th_i$ is a gain score dummy variable for improvement between the 1990 and 1992 eighth-grade math test for the $i$th state, $d968th_i$ is a gain score dummy variable for improvement from the 1990 to the 1996 eighth-grade math test for the $i$th state, $d964th_i$ is a gain score dummy variable for improvement from the 1992 to 1996 fourth-grade math test for the $i$th state, $d8th$ is a dummy variable for the eighth-grade test, $p_{ij}$ is the participation rate for $i$th state in the $j$th test, $u_i$ is the random effect for state $i$, $e_{ij}$ is the usual identical and independently distributed error term, and $a$, $b_k$, $g1_i$, $g2_i$, $g4_i$, $h1$, and $r1$ are coefficients in the regression.[22]

We also include interaction terms between family variables and the eighth-grade dummy. This allows for the possibility of different family effects for fourth- and eighth-grade students. The participation rate is included in the regressions to correct for changing participation rates of states. The dummy for the eighth-grade test allows for differences in scaling or other differences between the fourth- and eighth-grade tests.

We also estimate a single composite annualized gain measure across all tests by substituting for the individual gain dummies a single variable for each state that contains the number of years between each repeated test.[23] This variable will be a better indicator of the existence of state policies that reflect systemic gains across all grades and subjects from 1990 to 1996. In this formulation, we have combined gains at the fourth- and eighth-grade levels and treated them equally in determining the overall trend. However, the reform efforts that cause any gains at different grades might have occurred at different times.[24]

### Developing Family Control Variables

The NAEP family data are limited in scope and accuracy because fourth- and eighth-grade students report them. The NAEP collects from students the family type (single versus two parents), highest parental education level, a measure of family mobility, and race/ethnicity. In addition, it collects from administrative records the percentage of students on free lunch or eligible for Title I—proxies for family income. Previous studies compared the accuracy of student-reported NAEP data and U.S. census data for similarly aged children for five family variables for each state.[25] Not surprisingly, census and student-reported NAEP data on race/ethnicity and family type show strong agreement (correlation of .95 and above). However, major differences were found between student-reported parental education and parent-reported education from the census. For instance, fourth-grade students' reports of their parental education have 36 percent missing values. For those responding, about 57 percent report at least one parent is a college graduate compared with about 25 percent from census data for similar families.

Given the quality issues with NAEP family data, we have utilized the 1990 census data and the National Education Longitudinal Study (NELS) to develop alternate family control variables. The latter is the largest nationally representative data collection containing both achievement and family data. The NELS tested more than twenty-five thousand eighth-grade students and collected data from their parents on family characteristics.

We have developed three distinct sets of family control variables to determine if the results are sensitive to the source of family data and the methods utilized to weight the effects from different family characteristics. The first set combines data from the 1990 census and NAEP to provide parental education levels, family income, race/ethnicity, family type, and family mobility. We also develop two composite SES-like variables utilizing the NELS sample.

CENSUS AND NAEP FAMILY VARIABLES. Census data for families with children of similar age to NAEP test-takers can provide better estimates for some family variables that are inaccurately reported by students. However, census data still do not reflect the family characteristics of actual NAEP test-takers. NAEP excludes private school students, disabled students, LEP students, and nonparticipants—all of whom are contained on census files. In addition, the NAEP sample will reflect normal sampling variation and changes in population characteristics from 1990 to 1996. The census can provide estimates for only the 1990 census year.

If NAEP family variables are reported accurately, they will better describe the NAEP test-taking population than census data. Our analysis of these differences shows that the small differences in race/ethnicity and family type primarily arise from differences in the NAEP and census sample, while the differences in parental education primarily stem from inaccuracy in student reporting and bias in missing data.[26]

The most accurate set of family variables can be obtained by using a combination of NAEP and census variables. NAEP variables appear to be accurately reported for race/ethnicity, family type, and family mobility. Census data appear to be better for parental education and family income. However, the census variables can also be made to more closely reflect the actual NAEP sample by taking into account the actual racial/ethnic composition of the NAEP test-takers for each test.

We first generate from census data for families having children either eight to ten years of age (fourth graders) or twelve to fourteen years of age (eighth graders) their parental education and family income by racial/ethnic group within each state. We then utilize the racial/ethnic composition of each NAEP test by state as weights to develop an estimate of the parental education and income of the families of NAEP test-takers.

For instance, the census data may show that 35 percent of non-Hispanic white Indiana parents with children age eight to ten are college graduates; 15 percent for similar black parents; and 10 percent for similar Hispanic parents. If 80 percent of NAEP test-takers in Indiana for the 1990 test were white, 12 percent black, and 8 percent Hispanic, the estimates for NAEP families in the state would be $(.35 \times .80) + (.15 \times .12) + (.10 \times .08) = .306$. The estimated percentage of NAEP test-takers in Indiana who have a college graduate parent is 30.6.

This method provides family variables that partially reflect the changing characteristics of NAEP test-takers resulting from changing private school participation, exclusion rates, participation rates, population shifts over time, and normal sampling variation. To the extent that these factors shift the race/ethnicity of students taking NAEP, our variables will reflect such changes. However, the method will not reflect that part of changing family characteristics that affects within-race/ethnicity changes.

We have used this composite set of family variables from NAEP and the census for one set of family controls (hereafter Census/NAEP). These variables are race/ethnicity (NAEP), single parent (NAEP), highest parental education (census adjusted by NAEP race/ethnicity), family income (census adjusted by NAEP race/ethnicity), and family mobility (NAEP).

COMPOSITE SES FAMILY CONTROL VARIABLES. Entering the Census/ NAEP variables in the achievement regressions will generate coefficients for the family variables that essentially provide estimates for how much of the score gains should be attributable to changing family characteristics. The weakness of these approach is that these coefficients are estimated using only the 171 data points from state scores. Besides having a small sample size, these data have much less variation in family characteristics than available at the individual level. We developed a second approach to derive family control variables that uses the much larger sample of individual-level data from the NELS to develop SES-like variables that weight the influence of each family characteristic.[27]

We develop equations from NELS relating math achievement to eight family characteristics: highest education level of each parent, family income, family size, family type, age of mother at child's birth, mother labor force status, and race/ethnicity. These equations essentially develop weights for the influence of each family characteristic and estimate how much of the gains in scores can be attributable to changing student characteristics.

We then utilize these equations to predict a score for each child in a census sample drawn from each state of families with similarly aged children as the NAEP test-takers. We then obtain the mean predicted score for three racial/ethnic groups in each state. We then use the actual race/ethnic composition taking each NAEP test to weight the race/ethnic mean predicted scores to obtain a state-level predicted score based on the family characteristics of NAEP test-takers. This SES variable may contain more accurate information about family influence than the Census/NAEP variables because it has used the larger individual-level sample in its development. We refer to this composite family control variable as SES.

We want the family control variables to reflect the influence of family only. However, the NELS equations containing family variables only may still reflect some influence of school variables because of the correlation between family and school variables. To address this, we develop a third SES-like variable that utilizes NELS achievement equations with family variables and added school fixed effects. This equation introduces a dummy variable for the approximately one thousand schools in NELS that further reduces any influence of school variables in the family coefficients. The family coefficients from these equations are then similarly utilized as in SES to develop a score for each census student with ages similar to NAEP. We refer to this family control variable as SES-FE. When using the SES variables, we also include the measure of family mobility from NAEP because this variable is not included in the SES composite.

## Results

We present estimates of national gains, state gains, and locality gains within states.

### Estimated Gains across All Participating States

We report estimates for the three random effect models using different family control variables. The family control variables always have the appropri-

**Table 2. Estimated Score Gains from Random Effect Models for Each Repeated Test, Controlling for Differences in Student Populations and State Participation Rates**

Standard deviation units

| Family variable | 1990–92 eighth-grade math | 1990–96 eighth-grade math | 1992–96 fourth-grade math |
|---|---|---|---|
| SES | .104* | .229* | .096* |
| SES-FE | .104* | .230* | .095* |
| Census/NAEP | .126* | .242* | .094* |

*Statistically significant at 1 percent level.

ate sign usually with strong statistical significance.[28] The trends change little across the three family variables.

The data in table 2 show the estimated national gains for each repeated test controlling for the changing student characteristics of the NAEP samples and participation changes. The results show statistically significant differences for each test with little difference across models. The largest gains have occurred for eighth-grade math tests in which composite gains from 1990 to 1996 are about one quarter of a standard deviation or 8–9 percentile points. Smaller gains of approximately .10 standard deviation or 3 percentile points occurred in fourth-grade math from 1992 to 1996.

## Estimating Gains Unaccounted For by Resource Variables

The separate gains from each test converted to an estimated annualized gain in combined fourth- and eighth-grade math scores are presented in table 3. The results in the first row indicate statistically significant average annual gains in math scores (regardless of grade) of about .03 standard deviation or about 1 percentile point a year from 1990 to 1996. The last row contains the annualized gain variables after resource variables are entered.

Our educational resource variables focus mainly on the major variables that account for differences in resource expenditures across states.[29] We utilize pupil/teacher ratio, teacher salary (adjusted for cost-of-living differences), teacher-reported adequacy of resources (some or none, most, or all), and the percentage of children in public prekindergarten. These four categories of expenditures (together with a per pupil transportation, special education, and limited proficiency measure) account for 95 percent of the variance in per pupil expenditures across states and thus capture the different levels and utilization of almost all state expenditures.

**Table 3. Estimated Annualized National Gains in Math Scores with and without Resource Variables**

| Model | Random SES | SES-FE | Census/NAEP |
|---|---|---|---|
| Annual gain (no policy variables) | .032* | .032* | .032* |
| Annual gain (policy variables included) | .029* | .028* | .025* |

*Statistically significant at 1 percent level.

Another desirable variable in our equations would be one that measures the change in the variance of district per pupil expenditures within each state. Evidence suggests that spending increases disproportionately benefit disadvantaged students.[30] If equal expenditure increases have higher achievement effects on some districts, then states that shifted funding formulas across districts could show average score gains even if total expenditures remained the same. This variable would also need to be measured cumulatively beginning with data in 1982. We currently do not have such data available. However, equalization of spending within states has been a slow process with limited success.[31] While a portion of score gains for individual states that have moved more rapidly toward equalization might be accounted for by such shifts, trend estimation is likely to remain unaffected for most states. However, the gains after controlling for changing resources should be interpreted as arising from structural reform or funding equalization effects or both.

We define our education measures as averages over the time in school before the NAEP test. So pupil/teacher ratio is the state average for the years the student has attended school before the NAEP test. For instance, for the 1990 eighth-grade test we average pupil/teacher ratio for 1983–90. The public prekindergarten variable corresponds to the state participation in the year in which the tested group was four years old. The only variable not defined during the time in school is the NAEP-reported level of teacher resources that is recorded at the time of each test, so it may be biased downward.[32]

All resource variables have the appropriate sign and, except for teacher salary, are generally significant at the 10 percent level or better when national trend variables are included.[33] The coefficient of pupil/teacher ratio when interacted with family variables provides results that are in agreement with the Tennessee STAR experiment. However, the resource variables weaken when a full set of state trend variables are included. Only pupil/teacher ratio at lower grades remains statistically significant. In view of the small sample and the loss of degrees of freedom associated with the trend dummies, some weakening is not surprising.

The educational resource variables included in the analysis do not explain much of the trend in scores. Resources that would affect 1990–96 scores have changed only marginally. When these variables are also included in the regression (last row of table 3), the trend coefficients are only slightly reduced. Thus much of the math increases have to be explained by factors outside our resource variables. Reform efforts of various kinds unrelated to per pupil expenditure, pupil/teacher ratio, teacher characteristics, and teaching resources would be a leading candidate to explain these gains with the possibility of equalization of resources across school districts also playing a role in gains. The pattern of gains across states can provide further evidence about the source of these gains.

*Estimated Annual Gains by State*

The estimated annualized gains for individual states are summarized in table 4. The state results are presented by the coefficients across models and the statistical significance for each model. Over three quarters of states show consistent statistically significant annual gains on math tests. However, the rate of gains varies markedly across states from being flat to as much as .06 to .07 standard deviation per year (approximately 2 percentile points). The size of these latter gains is far above what has been experienced over the NAEP period from 1971 to 1990, when annual gains are around .01 standard deviation per year or less. Thus significant evidence exists that many states are experiencing math score gains far above historical averages, and some states are producing gains significantly above those of other states.

North Carolina and Texas, the states showing the largest rate of improvement, were the subject of a case study to determine if their state-administered test scores showed similar gains and to try to identify plausible reasons for such large gains.[34] The state-administered tests given to all students statewide showed large gains in approximately the same time period in math scores.

The case study concluded that the small changes in key resource variables and teacher characteristics that occurred in the states could not explain any significant part of the gains. The study identified a set of similar systemic reform policies implemented in both states in the late 1980s and early 1990s as being the most plausible reason for the gains.[35] These policies included developing state standards by grade, assessment tests linked to these standards, good data feedback systems to teachers and principals, some accountability measures,

**Table 4. Estimated Annualized Gains in Math Scores on National Assessment of Educational Progress Tests from 1990 to 1996**

| State | SES-FE | SES | Census/NAEP | Average |
|---|---|---|---|---|
| North Carolina | 0.070* | 0.070* | 0.073* | 0.071 |
| Texas | 0.061* | 0.061* | 0.061* | 0.061 |
| Michigan | 0.057* | 0.057* | 0.060* | 0.058 |
| Indiana | 0.050* | 0.050* | 0.050* | 0.050 |
| Maryland | 0.047* | 0.046* | 0.053* | 0.049 |
| West Virginia | 0.041* | 0.042* | 0.044* | 0.042 |
| New Jersey | 0.038* | 0.038* | 0.045* | 0.040 |
| Minnesota | 0.040* | 0.041* | 0.040* | 0.040 |
| Connecticut | 0.039* | 0.038* | 0.042* | 0.040 |
| Colorado | 0.039* | 0.040* | 0.041* | 0.040 |
| Florida | 0.040* | 0.040* | 0.040* | 0.040 |
| Kentucky | 0.038* | 0.039* | 0.041* | 0.039 |
| Rhode Island | 0.037* | 0.038* | 0.042* | 0.039 |
| California | 0.037* | 0.037* | 0.040* | 0.038 |
| Wisconsin | 0.038* | 0.038* | 0.038* | 0.038 |
| New York | 0.037* | 0.036* | 0.038* | 0.037 |
| South Carolina | 0.035* | 0.034* | 0.038* | 0.036 |
| Nebraska | 0.035* | 0.035 | 0.032* | 0.034 |
| Arizona | 0.032* | 0.032* | 0.036* | 0.033 |
| Tennessee | 0.030* | 0.030* | 0.038* | 0.033 |
| Louisiana | 0.031* | 0.031* | 0.032* | 0.031 |
| New Mexico | 0.031* | 0.032* | 0.029* | 0.031 |
| Alabama | 0.030* | 0.030* | 0.032* | 0.031 |
| Arkansas | 0.028* | 0.029** | 0.033* | 0.030 |
| Virginia | 0.027* | 0.026* | 0.029* | 0.027 |
| Mississippi | 0.025** | 0.026** | 0.029* | 0.027 |
| Massachusetts | 0.023** | 0.022** | 0.027* | 0.024 |
| Maine | 0.023** | 0.023** | 0.023** | 0.023 |
| Pennsylvania | 0.024 | 0.024 | 0.022*** | 0.023 |
| Iowa | 0.023** | 0.023** | 0.022** | 0.023 |
| Missouri | 0.022** | 0.022** | 0.023** | 0.022 |
| North Dakota | 0.020** | 0.020** | 0.018** | 0.019 |
| Delaware | 0.017*** | 0.016*** | 0.019** | 0.017 |
| Utah | 0.016 | 0.018*** | 0.017*** | 0.017 |
| Georgia | 0.014 | 0.013 | 0.015*** | 0.014 |
| Wyoming | -0.005 | -0.005 | -0.004 | -0.005 |

* Statistically significant at better than 1 percent level.
** Statistically significant at better than 5 percent level.
*** Statistically significant at better than 10 percent level.

and deregulation of the teaching environment. However, much research across all states is needed before any conclusions about the cause of these gains can become compelling.

While the results clearly show that many states in the top portion of the ranking have statistically significant differences from those near the bottom, groups of states more closely ranked cannot be distinguished with any precision. So while North Carolina and Texas show the largest gains, their gains cannot be statistically separated from states ranked in the next thirteen positions.

The corresponding estimated gains after inclusion of resource variables in the equations are presented in table 5. For almost all states, shifts in resources can account for only a small part of gains.

## Results for Mathematics Trends by Locality

The pattern of gains within each area of a state can provide evidence about the source of the gains. If all areas of a state are improving at nearly equal rates, state policies would be a likely explanation for the gains. However, large differences in gains across areas would point to district policies, differential resource changes, or demographic shifts as a likely candidate to explain gains.

The NAEP state samples for 1992, 1994, and 1996 are stratified within each state to allow the reporting of scores for three mutually exclusive location types for most states: central city, urban fringe/large town, and rural/small town.[36] Central cities are the central cities of the Standard Metropolitan Statistical Areas (SMSAs) as defined by the Office of Management and Budget (OMB). Suburban areas include densely settled places and areas within SMSAs classified as urban by OMB, but outside central cities and large towns (non-SMSAs) with a population of more than twenty-five thousand. Rural areas include small towns outside SMSAs with a population of less than twenty-five thousand and all places with a population of less than twenty-five hundred outside SMSAs. In 1992 approximately 32 percent of K–12 students were in central cities; 42 percent, in suburban areas; and 26 percent, in rural areas. These percentages vary considerably by state as do the characteristics of each type of region across states.

Because the characteristics of central-city localities vary markedly by state, we have classified states into three groups based on regional and population density criteria (see table 6). We first classify states as northern or southern, and we subdivide northern states into those containing large urban areas and those mainly rural states having only relatively small cities. These groupings

**Table 5. Estimated Annualized Gains Unaccounted for by Resource Changes in Math Scores on National Assessment of Educational Progress Tests from 1990 to 1996**

| State | SES-FE | SES | Census/NAEP | Average |
|---|---|---|---|---|
| North Carolina | 0.063* | 0.062* | 0.066* | 0.064 |
| Michigan | 0.055* | 0.056* | 0.056* | 0.056 |
| Texas | 0.053* | 0.054* | 0.046* | 0.051 |
| Indiana | 0.047* | 0.048* | 0.048* | 0.047 |
| Maryland | 0.044* | 0.044* | 0.048* | 0.046 |
| Florida | 0.040* | 0.040* | 0.039* | 0.040 |
| Minnesota | 0.040* | 0.040* | 0.038* | 0.039 |
| California | 0.038* | 0.039* | 0.040* | 0.039 |
| Connecticut | 0.037* | 0.037* | 0.042* | 0.039 |
| Colorado | 0.039* | 0.039* | 0.038* | 0.039 |
| West Virginia | 0.037* | 0.038* | 0.039* | 0.038 |
| Rhode Island | 0.035* | 0.036* | 0.041* | 0.037 |
| Wisconsin | 0.034* | 0.034* | 0.031* | 0.033 |
| Kentucky | 0.032* | 0.033* | 0.032* | 0.033 |
| Nebraska | 0.033* | 0.034* | 0.030* | 0.032 |
| New York | 0.032* | 0.032* | 0.033* | 0.032 |
| Pennsylvania | 0.030** | 0.032** | 0.032** | 0.031 |
| New Jersey | 0.028*** | 0.029*** | 0.037** | 0.031 |
| South Carolina | 0.031* | 0.031* | 0.033* | 0.031 |
| Tennessee | 0.028* | 0.029* | 0.037* | 0.031 |
| Arizona | 0.031* | 0.031* | 0.032* | 0.031 |
| New Mexico | 0.029* | 0.029* | 0.025* | 0.028 |
| Louisiana | 0.025* | 0.025* | 0.025* | 0.025 |
| Massachusetts | 0.022** | 0.022** | 0.026* | 0.023 |
| Virginia | 0.022** | 0.022** | 0.025* | 0.023 |
| Arkansas | 0.024** | 0.024** | 0.022** | 0.023 |
| Alabama | 0.023** | 0.023** | 0.023* | 0.023 |
| Iowa | 0.023** | 0.023** | 0.019** | 0.022 |
| Maine | 0.020** | 0.020*** | 0.021** | 0.020 |
| Missouri | 0.020** | 0.020** | 0.020** | 0.020 |
| Delaware | 0.017*** | 0.017*** | 0.021** | 0.018 |
| Utah | 0.019*** | 0.019*** | 0.016 | 0.018 |
| Mississippi | 0.017 | 0.016 | 0.017 | 0.017 |
| North Dakota | 0.016*** | 0.017*** | 0.012 | 0.015 |
| Georgia | 0.009 | 0.009 | 0.012 | 0.010 |
| Wyoming | -0.012 | -0.013 | -0.010 | -0.012 |

* Statistically significant at better than 1 percent level.
** Statistically significant at better than 5 percent level.
*** Statistically significant at better than 10 percent level.

**Table 6. Classification of States**

| Northern urban | Northern rural | Southern |
|---|---|---|
| California | Iowa | Alabama |
| Colorado | Maine | Arizona |
| Connecticut | Montana | Arkansas |
| Indiana | Nebraska | Delaware |
| Maryland | North Dakota | Florida |
| Massachusetts | Utah | Georgia |
| Michigan | Wyoming | Kentucky |
| Missouri | | Louisiana |
| New Jersey | | Mississippi |
| New York | | New Mexico |
| Oregon | | North Carolina |
| Pennsylvania | | South Carolina |
| Rhode Island | | Tennessee |
| Washington | | Texas |
| Wisconsin | | Virginia |
| Minnesota | | West Virginia |

include the states with the largest cities among the northern urban or southern states.

Unlike our state-level analysis, our census variables that define localities within states are currently estimated only for 1990. Thus the results do not reflect differential migration effects across localities. The interpretation of results must take this into account.

The results show that statistically significant math gains are occurring in almost all major regions and localities (central city, suburban, rural). The gains by state groups and localities are presented in table 7. The size of math gains bears no strong relationship to region or locality and cannot be characterized easily by type of student. Both regions and localities with disproportionately high- and low-scoring students appear to be making significant gains, as are regions and localities with both large and small proportions of minority and lower SES students.

## Math Gains for Localities within States

The gains in each locality by state are compared in table 8. Sixteen states are making statistically significant gains in suburban localities, compared with nine in rural and central-city localities. Only three states—North Carolina, Texas, and Michigan—have statistically significant gains in all localities. Thir-

**Table 7. Estimated Annualized Math Achievement Gains in Central City, Suburban, and Rural Areas of State Groups**

| State group | Northern urban | Southern | Northern nonurban |
|---|---|---|---|
| Central city | 1.02* | .86* | .33 |
| Suburban | 1.31* | .94* | 1.36* |
| Rural | .92* | 1.22* | .73*** |

Note: Unit of measure is National Assessment of Educational Progress (NAEP) points, not standard deviation units. A NAEP point is approximately equal to a percentile point.
* Statistically significant at better than 1 percent level.
*** Statistically significant at better than 10 percent level.

teen states have statistically significant gains in two or three localities, while only five show gains in a single locality. Sixteen states show no statistically significant gains in any locality. These data show that states that have insignificant gains in one locality are far more likely to have insignificant gains in the other localities and that states with significant gains in one locality are far more likely to have gains in one or both other localities.

Perhaps these results should not be surprising given that the state is probably the only common influence over school systems in these diverse localities. But it does suggest that at least a few states may have statewide reform efforts that can raise achievement across diverse localities of the state.

### Evidence of the Effects of Reform

Our assumptions in this analysis were that four conditions needed to be met for statewide systemic or structural reforms to be considered viable hypotheses for improving achievement. These assumptions were that the 1990–96 period was not too early for some effects to be evident at the fourth- and eighth-grade level, that these effects show differential gains across states that cannot be explained by resource effects, and that gains occur in all three localities (central city, suburban/large town, and rural/small towns).

We utilized the state NAEP scores to test these assumptions. This analysis could have produced a wide range of results that were inconsistent with the hypothesis that statewide reform efforts are increasing achievement, making it difficult to maintain statewide reform as a viable candidate for improving educational outcomes. However, the results show evidence that significant math achievement gains did occur at the fourth- and eighth-grade levels, and the size of the gains were markedly different across states ranging from little to

**Table 8. Estimated Math Gains by Locality within States**

| State | Central city | Suburban | Rural | Average |
|---|---|---|---|---|
| North Carolina | 2.92* | 2.08* | 2.48* | 2.49 |
| Texas | 2.05* | 2.14* | 3.19* | 2.46 |
| Missouri | 0.31 | 2.99* | 3.17* | 2.16 |
| Michigan | 2.51* | 1.74** | 1.38*** | 1.88 |
| Mississippi | 1.87** | 2.3* | 0.95 | 1.71 |
| Indiana | 2.19* | 1.5** | 0.98 | 1.56 |
| Maine | 1.48*** | 2.14* | 0.62 | 1.41 |
| Kentucky | 1.68** | 1.34*** | 1.04 | 1.35 |
| Wisconsin | 0.21 | 2.03* | 1.7** | 1.31 |
| West Virginia | 0.65 | 1.56*** | 1.51*** | 1.24 |
| Arkansas | 1.29*** | 1.15*** | 1.22 | 1.22 |
| Nebraska | 0.14 | 2.59* | 0.84 | 1.19 |
| Tennessee | 0.07 | 1.74** | 1.61** | 1.14 |
| New York | 2.05* | 1.26*** | 0.05 | 1.12 |
| Connecticut | 0.72 | 1.58 | 0.79 | 1.03 |
| Minnesota | 0.89 | 1.05 | 0.85 | 0.93 |
| Florida | 0.52 | 0.31 | 1.9** | 0.91 |
| Rhode Island | 0.62 | 0.86 | 0.97 | 0.82 |
| Alabama | 0.32 | 0.96 | 1.08 | 0.79 |
| Maryland | -0.02 | 1.1 | 1.2 | 0.76 |
| Massachusetts | 1.15 | 0.7 | 0.27 | 0.71 |
| Colorado | 1.06 | 0.73 | 0.27 | 0.69 |
| Virginia | 0.34 | 0.8 | 0.76 | 0.63 |
| Louisiana | 0.15 | 0.76 | 0.8 | 0.57 |
| Iowa | 0.06 | 1.24*** | 0.2 | 0.5 |
| North Dakota | 0.49 | -0.38 | 1.03 | 0.38 |
| Arizona | 0.07 | 1.06 | -0.09 | 0.35 |
| South Carolina | 1.17 | -0.3 | 0.03 | 0.3 |
| Utah | -0.39 | 0.17 | 0.92 | 0.23 |
| Delaware | 0.47 | -0.24 | 0.44 | 0.22 |
| New Mexico | 0.34 | -1 | 1.05 | 0.13 |
| Georgia | -0.68 | 0.15 | 0.5 | -0.01 |
| Wyoming | -0.98 | n.a. | -0.45 | -0.48 |
| California | -0.08 | 0.66 | -2.07** | -0.5 |

Note: Unit of measure is National Assessment of Educational Progress (NAEP) points, not standard deviation units. A NAEP point is approximately equal to a percentile point.
* Statistically significant at better than 1 percent level.
** Statistically significant at better than 5 percent level.
*** Statistically significant at better than 10 percent level.

no gain to over 2 percentile points a year. Only a small portion of the gains could be traced to changing resource levels or patterns of utilization. Finally, several states that were making among the largest gains show statistically significant gains in all localities or in two localities with above average gains in the third locality.

Three states—North Carolina, Texas, and Michigan—have among the largest estimated nonresource-related gains along with statistically significant gains in all three localities. Several more states have statistically significant gains, which are among the larger gains among states with statistically significant gains, in two localities with a large, but statistically insignificant, gain in the third locality. These states include Mississippi, Indiana, Kentucky, and Arkansas.

For a consistent explanation to emerge from this analysis, one would have to judge that these states, on average, have the more effective statewide reforms compared with the remaining states in the sample. However, it is too early to make such judgments without extensive case studies backed up by multivariate analysis with specific reform variables that show consistent effects across all states in the sample. Such analysis will not be easy because of the difficulty of defining simple variables that need to characterize often complex, multidimensional reforms and the imprecision of specifying the timing of how each reform will affect the achievement of children at different grades.

More state NAEP tests from 1998 and 2000 will allow reading to be included in the trend analysis and longer-term, and probably more reliable, math trends to emerge. Comparable analysis is also needed using individual-level NAEP data with a variety of family defined variables from NAEP, the census, and other sources. However, such analysis will likely provide only indirect evidence. In the long run, compelling evidence can come only from theories of the processes involved in reform that are supported by a consistent set of empirical evidence that relies partly on experimentation.

Perhaps more important, time is needed to determine if achievement gains registered at lower grades can translate into higher achievement, higher high school graduation rates, and college entrance rates. Long-term gains are important, and time will tell if the cohorts registering gains at lower levels also perform better in the long term.

---

## Appendix A

Table A-1 contains brief definitions of variables in the analysis.[37] We provide two regression results using only the socioeconomic status (SES) family variable because results are similar across models. Regression results controlling for family factors with the state trend variables are presented in table A-2. Highly significant family effects are evident at both the fourth- and

**Table A-1. Definitions of Variables**

| Variable | Definition |
|----------|-----------|
| SES-FE | Family control variable derived from National Education Longitudinal Study and Census analysis |
| SES-FE X 8 | Interaction of socioeconomic status and eighth grade |
| Migrat | Migration variable defined as percent of children in state not moving in last two years |
| Migrat X 8 | Interaction of Migrat and grade eight |
| Partic | State participation rate in National Assessment of Educational Progress |
| Pre-k | Proportion of children who attended public prekindergarten |
| Pre-k MS | Missing value dummy for pre-K |
| Pup/tch14 | Estimated pupil/teacher ratio in grades one through four for regular students since school entry |
| Pup/tch58 | Estimated pupil/teacher ratio in grades five through eight for regular students since school entry |
| SM RES | Percentage of teachers stating lowest level for adequacy of resources |
| MS RES | Percentage of teachers stating middle level for adequacy of resources |
| Salary | Cost-of-living-adjusted average teacher salary since school entry |

eighth-grade levels. Migration has the appropriate sign (higher migration associated with lower scores) but is not statistically significant. It is stronger at the fourth-grade level than at the eighth-grade level. Participation rate is insignificant.

The data in table A-3 show the regression results including resource variables. Each of the resource variables except *pup/tch58* shows the appropriate sign and statistical significance in regressions without state trend variables (not shown here). However, the addition of trend variables together with the small sample size leaves only pupil/teacher ratio in grades one through four as statistically significant.

**Table A-2. Regression Results Using SES Family Variable and No Resource Variables**

| Variable | Coefficient | Standard error | t-value |
|---|---|---|---|
| Math 8 | .1657543 | .1426886 | 1.162 |
| SES-FE X 8 | .3938796 | .1094957 | 3.597 |
| Migrat X 8 | -.0021783 | .0018911 | -1.152 |
| SES-FE | 2.035218 | .1886709 | 10.787 |
| Migrat | .002942 | .0020562 | 1.431 |
| Partic | -.0001979 | .0014717 | -0.134 |
| _al | .029579 | .0095173 | 3.108 |
| _az | .0316479 | .0099543 | 3.179 |
| _ar | .0278936 | .0117515 | 2.374 |
| _ca | .0367304 | .0095022 | 3.865 |
| _co | .0390878 | .0095801 | 4.080 |
| _ct | .0394347 | .009302 | 4.239 |
| _de | .0166991 | .0093678 | 1.783 |
| _fl | .0396503 | .009373 | 4.230 |
| _ga | .0137887 | .009441 | 1.461 |
| _in | .0499645 | .0093249 | 5.358 |
| _ia | .0230342 | .0097577 | 2.361 |
| _ky | .0380975 | .0093752 | 4.064 |
| _la | .0307633 | .0093495 | 3.290 |
| _me | .0230644 | .0110435 | 2.089 |
| _md | .046503 | .0099258 | 4.685 |
| _ma | .0228114 | .0105862 | 2.155 |
| _mi | .057065 | .0095376 | 5.983 |
| _mn | .0403991 | .0093629 | 4.315 |
| _ms | .0253555 | .0108143 | 2.345 |
| _mo | .0218783 | .0106093 | 2.062 |
| _nb | .0350814 | .0096757 | 3.626 |
| _nj | .0380681 | .0162847 | 2.338 |
| _nm | .0314021 | .0095753 | 3.279 |
| _ny | .036831 | .0093639 | 3.933 |
| _nc | .069961 | .0093552 | 7.478 |
| _nd | .0196395 | .0093485 | 2.101 |
| _pa | .0235906 | .0149498 | 1.578 |
| _ri | .0371184 | .0093416 | 3.973 |
| _sc | .0349429 | .0112646 | 3.102 |
| _tn | .0300438 | .0105668 | 2.843 |
| _tx | .0608845 | .0095564 | 6.371 |
| _ut | .0163193 | .0108139 | 1.509 |
| _va | .0266978 | .0093135 | 2.867 |
| _wv | .0412171 | .0093227 | 4.421 |
| _wi | .03773 | .010316 | 3.657 |
| _wy | -.004787 | .0138291 | -0.346 |
| _cons | -.1430117 | .1875799 | -0.762 |

**Table A-3. Regression Results Using SES Family Variable and Resource Variables**

| Variable | Coefficient | Standard error | Z |
|---|---|---|---|
| Math X 8 | -.0958318 | .1802354 | -0.532 |
| SES-FE X 8 | .2510509 | .1085145 | 2.314 |
| Migrat X 8 | .0005133 | .0019856 | 0.258 |
| SES-FE | 1.912927 | .1814407 | 10.543 |
| Migrat | .0003299 | .0021167 | 0.156 |
| Partic | -.0001342 | .0014072 | -0.095 |
| Pre-k | .0017036 | .0017584 | 0.969 |
| Pre-k MS | -.0018513 | .0224975 | -0.082 |
| Pup/tch14 | -.0223897 | .0054167 | -4.133 |
| Pup/tch58 | .0054708 | .0035312 | 1.549 |
| Salary | .0003195 | .0016462 | 0.194 |
| SM RES | .0003468 | .0013151 | 0.264 |
| MS RES | .0015869 | .0015744 | 1.008 |
| _al | .0226697 | .0091153 | 2.487 |
| _az | .0305599 | .0095726 | 3.192 |
| _ar | .0236479 | .0118699 | 1.992 |
| _ca | .0380835 | .0090936 | 4.188 |
| _co | .03855 | .0090126 | 4.277 |
| _ct | .0371844 | .0088708 | 4.192 |
| _de | .0168658 | .0087682 | 1.924 |
| _fl | .0397925 | .0088547 | 4.000 |
| _ga | .0094946 | .0091611 | 1.036 |
| _in | .0471741 | .0087517 | 5.390 |
| _ia | .0225505 | .0092622 | 2.435 |
| _ky | .0324594 | .0094206 | 3.446 |
| _la | .0250868 | .0089352 | 2.808 |
| _me | .019982 | .0103469 | 1.931 |
| _md | .0443275 | .0094405 | 4.695 |
| _ma | .0222328 | .0098951 | 2.247 |
| _mi | .0552718 | .0090566 | 6.103 |
| _mn | .0400017 | .0087593 | 4.567 |
| _ms | .016594 | .0111745 | 1.485 |
| _mo | .0198353 | .0100363 | 1.976 |
| _nb | .0331712 | .0090534 | 3.664 |
| _nj | .0280754 | .0156126 | 1.798 |
| _nm | .0286538 | .0090542 | 3.165 |
| _ny | .03181 | .0088515 | 3.594 |
| _nc | .0625436 | .0093101 | 6.718 |
| _nd | .0163816 | .0088707 | 1.847 |
| _pa | .0303262 | .0148288 | 2.045 |
| _ri | .0354713 | .0087433 | 4.057 |
| _sc | .030791 | .0105949 | 2.906 |
| _tn | .0284307 | .0099766 | 2.850 |
| _tx | .0528761 | .0102466 | 5.160 |
| _ut | .018615 | .0107085 | 1.738 |
| _va | .0222918 | .0088107 | 2.530 |
| _wv | .0369601 | .0087689 | 4.215 |
| _wi | .0339381 | .0098091 | 3.460 |
| _wy | -.0116974 | .0131212 | -0.891 |
| _cons | .3095933 | .2778234 | 1.114 |

# Comment by Philip Uri Treisman and Edward J. Fuller

It is a long way from the statehouse to the schoolhouse, and not all of the distance can be measured in miles. Despite nearly two decades of efforts to make state education systems more coherent, these systems remain complex enterprises, shaped by deeply rooted and competing visions of schooling.[38] Further, the American tradition of local control of school governance—and the associated principle that those closest to children should shape the content and character of their education—provides a formidable counterweight to state-level education policy initiatives. Consequently, any effort to draw a causal link between changes in state policy and gains in student performance will face many hurdles.

Deep disagreements remain among policy analysts about the consequences of shifting educational decisionmaking away from local communities. Some researchers argue that an increase in state influence will negatively affect teacher practice and student learning.[39] They assert that state-developed content standards and other state-level policies affecting instruction are likely to reflect political compromises that reduce curriculum standards to the lowest common denominator. Low standards, they argue, will most negatively affect students in predominantly poor and minority schools. They contend that, in contrast, standards in wealthy school districts will be kept high by strong community pressure to offer college-preparatory curricula. In short, these researchers believe that state usurpation of the traditional local role in standards setting will have a markedly adverse effect on student achievement.

Meanwhile, other researchers argue that a coherent approach to education policymaking at the state level will obviate the creation of curricula shaped—at least in some school districts—by cultural stereotypes or low expectations.[40] Such locally created shallow curricula have historically impeded the upward mobility of those most dependent on a quality education, the poor and the disenfranchised. As Marshall S. Smith and Jennifer O'Day have written:

> The potential advantage of a systemic strategy is that the policy coherence around a common set of challenging standards could insure that, at a minimum, teachers and schools receive consistent signals about what is important for them to teach and for students to learn. And these signals would be the same for all schools and students, thus countering trends toward a dual curriculum with high expectations for advantaged youth and much lower ones for everybody else.[41]

In her analysis of school reform and state policymaking, Susan Fuhrman argues that growing evidence shows that state policymakers can, despite substantial obstacles, enact rigorous curriculum standards and support them with coherent, coordinated policies.[42] But she also argues that powerful incentives exist—such as the election cycle and the daunting complexity of educational problems—for legislators to focus their policymaking on the short term and on the direct, immediate interests of their constituents. This natural political process works against the creation of the long-term, stable educational policies on which successful school reform depends. School improvement is a slow process and is easily derailed by frequent changes in curriculum requirements and standards for performance.

Yet, whatever the arguments for or against setting curriculum policy at the state level, almost all states have moved in this direction. In 1998, forty states had statewide curriculum standards, forty-eight states assessed student learning, and thirty-six published annual "report cards" on individual schools.[43] Thus, it behooves scholars to conduct an earnest search for evidence regarding the effectiveness of systemic reform.

In their paper, David Grissmer and Ann Flanagan have taken an important step toward that goal. Using adjusted state-level National Assessment of Educational Progress (NAEP) mathematics scores as their measuring rod, they estimate, state by state, the effects on student learning of education reform efforts begun in the mid-1980s. The adjustments they make to average NAEP scale scores address important deficiencies in student-level NAEP data. These deficiencies stem from the fact that students are poor judges of some demographic information collected by NAEP, including, for example, their parents' levels of education and of income, which are important variables to take into account when assessing overall state educational performance.

By using aggregate state scores, instead of individual student performance data, Grissmer and Flanagan lose information that comes from larger sample sizes—for example, greater variation in both the dependent and independent variables under study. But they argue compellingly that problems in the quality of the student-level data justify their choice.

The decision to work with aggregate state data permits Grissmer and Flanagan to control for many characteristics of the educational systems that have been the target of state-level reforms, such as average student/teacher ratios, average teacher salaries, teachers' perceptions of the adequacy of resources, and the percentage of students enrolled in prekindergarten programs. They take into account family characteristics, as well as examination participation and exclusion rates. Their analysis of the NAEP data shows that most states are making statistically significant gains—at least in mathematics perfor- mance—but that some states are doing far better than others, even after the researchers control for differences in resources allocated to education.

By looking at the performance of urban, suburban, and rural students within each state, Grissmer and Flanagan are able to partially recapture some of the information lost by aggregation. In effect, they triple their $n$. But this disag- gregation by geographic locality is especially important for policy analysis because it illuminates a canonical legislative process; namely, the legislature's need to balance the competing interests of rural, urban, and suburban con- stituencies. The researchers hypothesize that "achievement gains within states should occur in all localities within the state . . . if statewide reforms are effec- tive." They show that only three states—North Carolina, Texas, and Michi- gan—had significant gains in achievement for rural, urban, and suburban students. Thus, by Grissmer and Flanagan's standard, only three states have effectively implemented statewide systemic reform.

A natural extension of Grissmer and Flanagan's argument involves disag- gregating NAEP data by race and ethnicity, variables available in the NAEP data set and reported reliably by students. As is true for geographic locality, race and ethnicity are politically potent variables, and, certainly, balancing the competing interests of various racial and ethnic groups is also central to leg- islative policymaking. Examining the performance of racial and ethnic sub- populations should thus be central to evaluating the effectiveness of systemic educational reform, given that the systemic reform movement has as a cen- tral tenet the idea that *"all children can learn challenging content and com- plex problem-solving skills."*[44]

While we did not (as did Grissmer and Flanagan) make statistical adjust- ments for demographic variables in the aggregate state data, we have exam- ined the NAEP achievement gains of African American, Hispanic, and white children, as reported by the National Center for Education Statistics (NCES).[45] Modifying Grissmer and Flanagan's working hypothesis, then, we assert that if statewide reforms are effective, then achievement gains should occur for all ethnic groups within the state.

We find that for students in grade four, Texas was the only state with sta- tistically significant average scale score gains from 1992 to 1996 for African American, Hispanic, and white students. North Carolina, Michigan, and Indi- ana also had statistically significant average scale score gains from 1992 to

1996, but only for white and African American students. Grissmer and Flanagan identify Texas, North Carolina, and Michigan as the three top-performing states in their study, with Indiana following closely behind in their next tier of high-performing states.

For students in grade eight, only Texas, North Carolina, and Colorado in 1996 had statistically significant average scale score gains from the earlier assessments in 1990 and 1992 for all three subpopulations. Seven other states, including Michigan, had statistically significant average scale score gains from 1990 or 1992 to 1996 for two of the three major racial or ethnic subpopulations. Thus, many of the states identified by NCES data as having high levels of achievement for students for all racial and ethnic groups also appear in the list of states identified by Grissmer and Flanagan as having high levels of achievement in all three localities. This concurrence provides corroborative evidence that state systemic reform policies are having their intended effects on mathematics achievement in at least a few states.

In a related study, Grissmer and Flanagan conclude "that the most plausible explanation for the test score gains [in Texas and North Carolina] is found in the policy environment established in each state."[46] By "policy environment," they mean legislation related to curriculum, testing, and accountability. The term also includes the intensity and stability of business support for educational reform.[47] Grissmer and Flanagan show that certain other factors influenced by state policy and presumed to affect student achievement—for example, real per pupil spending, pupil/teacher ratios, the proportion of teachers with advanced degrees, and average levels of teacher experience—could not explain the large gains in achievement on either the NAEP or on state tests.

Our experience in Texas resonates with Grissmer and Flanagan's key finding that both long-term advocacy from the business community and state-level systemic reform policies can be potent forces in shaping local schools and the achievement of their students. But, as is true for so many domains, the details matter, and Grissmer and Flanagan's analysis cannot shed light upon such details.

In Texas, the business community, through multiple vehicles, including the Texas Governor's Business Advisory Panel and the Texas Business and Education Coalition, has been the guardian of a master plan for educational reform that was created in the early 1980s by a commission appointed by the governor and headed by prominent businessman Ross Perot. The Perot commission reforms included, among others, smaller class sizes and vastly expanded prekindergarten programs. These changes profoundly increased instructional capacity in Texas school districts, especially those serving poor children.

Perot understood that Texans would not increase funding for education unless they could be assured that their money would be used wisely and that it would, in particular, lead to increased student learning. Perot's epiphany became the organizing principle for business involvement in Texas education. This insight is the basis for the state's standards-based accountability system and its heavy reliance on student testing.

But legislative and gubernatorial actions were not driven solely by the business community's vision of educational improvement. Shortly after the Perot commission issued its report—and organized various business and political leaders to support it—an oil crisis (a cyclical occurrence in Texas) curtailed the state's financial capacity to enact reforms on the scale envisioned by the commission. Most severely affected were proposals to modernize the state's school funding system. Successful school finance litigation—for example, the 1987 *Edgewood Independent School District* v. *Kirby* case and its progeny— forced the legislature in 1989 to enact a large tax increase and, in subsequent sessions, to essentially equalize school funding.

The issue of funding equalization is not addressed by Grissmer and Flanagan, although they acknowledge its possible importance. As they note, "another desirable variable in our equations would be one that measures the change in the variance of district per pupil expenditures within each state. Evidence suggests that spending increases disproportionately benefit disadvantaged students." William Hussar and William Sonnenberg provide useful state-by-state data on disparities in per pupil funding levels.[48] Their data show a substantial decrease in the variation of per pupil funding levels across Texas school districts from the mid-1980s to 1994. The consequence, according to one Texas policy analyst, was "that lower-wealth schools were finally able to offer better quality educational programs—long taken for granted in the state's more affluent suburbs—[and this] has contributed to the overall improvement of student achievement throughout most of the state."[49] This view is supported by recent research that shows that funding equalization in Texas has substantially reduced the effect of district wealth on how well students perform on state assessment instruments. Specifically, researchers at Texas A&M University found that student performance on the Texas Assessment of Academic Skills, or TAAS, can no longer be predicted by the wealth of their district.[50]

In short, the courts have played a role as important as that of business in strengthening and modernizing Texas education. In the 1980s, the combination of successful business-led education initiatives and successful finance litigation on behalf of resource-poor school districts led to significant changes in state-level educational policies and substantial increases in state financial support for education. The effect was an increase in the instructional capacity of school districts, which allowed these districts to respond constructively to a high-stakes, standards-based accountability system.

The mutually reinforcing pressures on the legislature generated by the business community and the courts (and, not incidentally, by a politically powerful lieutenant governor) created what is arguably a singular moment in Texas history. In this moment, it was both necessary and possible to create a far-reaching education accountability system that addressed long-standing issues of equity. This system has multiple features, including two that may be of particular interest for policymaking and analysis.

The first concerns mechanisms for incremental improvement. Bluntly put, because of powerful business support, the legislature was able to initialize the education system with relatively low standards; that is, standards that a large majority of schools could meet with only modest increases in resources. For example, in the 1993–94 academic year, for schools to avoid a rating of "low performing," only 25 percent of their students (in each of several subpopulations) had to pass that year's examination. A system with such low standards was clearly vulnerable to attacks from those who opposed any significant state role in setting curriculum standards. But with the strong support of business, legislators could build a "ratcheting-up" feature into the accountability system, giving schools time to develop the necessary capacity to help a higher percentage of their students to succeed. In particular, they designed the system so that the minimum percentage of students required to pass the test for a school or district to receive an acceptable rating would rise by 5 percentage points a year for seven years.

The legislature also gave the state education agency flexibility to allow districts to respond effectively to raised curriculum standards. For example, as the state curriculum frameworks are made more rigorous, test items reflecting new curriculum content are gradually phased in to the state assessments by the state agency. This allows school systems time to prepare for change so that they might achieve increasingly high levels of success. In summary, then, continuous, incremental improvement is an organizing theme of the Texas education system.

The second feature of the Texas system of interest to policymakers is its sophisticated mechanism for addressing equity. Specifically, the accountability rating of a school or school district depends on the achievement of its lowest-performing subpopulation on tests in mathematics, reading, and writing.[51]

The five subpopulations whose performance is tracked in the Texas account-ability system are African American, Hispanic, white, economically disad-vantaged, and all students. The fact that schools know that their state-assigned ratings—which are widely reported in the press—depend not just on the aver-age performance of all their students, but also on the performance of each (proper) subpopulation, has a powerful effect on how schools allocate their resources. The effect is that poor and minority students can receive a far bet-ter education than previously offered, with achievement results that are dis-cernable in Grissmer and Flanagan's analysis.

To see the power of this system, consider 1994–95 mathematics perfor-mance data from two Texas high schools. Grant High School is a suburban school serving a relatively affluent and predominantly white population, while Lee High School is an inner-city school serving an economically disadvan-taged and predominantly minority population. (Grant High School and Lee High School are pseudonyms.)

As can be inferred from the data in table 1, Grant and Lee both received an accountability system rating of "low performing," because in both schools less than 30 percent of the African American students passed the mathemat-ics portion of the exit TAAS exam. African American students in both schools passed this section of TAAS at roughly the same rate, and the same is true for Hispanic, white, and economically disadvantaged students. Were the account-ability system ratings based—as is the case in most states—on only the pass-ing rates of all students, Grant would not receive a low rating. Disaggregating student performance data and using the passing rate of the lowest-performing subpopulation to determine school ratings sends a clear equity message: Texas schools must educate all of their students.[52]

The Texas accountability system specifies particular subpopulations that must achieve at defined levels  as well as the subjects in which they must achieve. In the early years of the Texas accountability system, mathematics was the subject most likely to be responsible for a school rating of "low per-forming." Consequently, many school districts, and especially those at risk of receiving a low rating, focused their instructional capacity-building efforts on this subject—a clear response to a clear policy signal.

The logic of Grissmer and Flanagan's analysis suggests that another way to test for the effectiveness of state reforms is to assess student performance state by state in specific subject domains. Certainly, if state policy is having a positive effect on student learning, then that learning should be reasonably broad-based and should include reading and mathematics, as these are core

**Table 1. Texas Assessment of Academic Skills Results in Mathematics, Grant and Lee High Schools, 1994–95 Academic Year**

| Student subpopulation | Grant High School | | | Lee High School | | |
|---|---|---|---|---|---|---|
| | *Number of students* | *Number proficient* | *Percent proficient* | *Number of students* | *Number proficient* | *Percent proficient* |
| All students | 607 | 406 | 66.9 | 214 | 63 | 29.4 |
| African American | 27 | 6 | 22.2 | 124 | 30 | 24.2 |
| Hispanic | 70 | 23 | 32.9 | 79 | 24 | 30.4 |
| White | 510 | 377 | 73.9 | 11 | 9 | 81.8 |
| Economically disadvantaged | 63 | 26 | 41.3 | 125 | 38 | 30.4 |

Note: In 1994–95 at least 30 percent of the students in each subpopulation had to pass the Texas Assessment of Academic Skills for the school to avoid a state rating of "low-performing." To pass the exam, a student had to successfully answer approximately 70 percent of the test items.

subjects for every state's reform efforts. Grissmer and Flanagan proposed such an analysis, but at the time of their study, they had NAEP reading data only for the 1992 and 1994 administrations of the exam. In their view (and ours), it was too short a time span to measure improvements that might be caused by changes in state-level education policy. So, again, we turn to NCES reports, which include data on 1992, 1994, and 1998 administrations of the NAEP reading examination.[53] Our study of the data in these reports raises fundamental questions about Grissmer and Flanagan's conclusions.

According to NCES reading data, thirteen states made statistically significant gains between 1992 and 1998 on the fourth-grade NAEP reading assessment. In comparison, NCES data show that sixteen states made statistically significant gains between 1992 and 1996 on the fourth-grade NAEP mathematics assessment. Only six states showed statistically significant gains in both subjects. Of the five states found by Grissmer and Flanagan to have the greatest (and statistically significant) gains in mathematics—North Carolina, Texas, Michigan, Indiana, and Tennessee—only North Carolina had statistically significant gains in reading, and then only for white students.

Examining NAEP reading data for differences by locality—that is, rural, urban, or suburban—only Connecticut made statistically significant gains in two of the three. No other state made gains in more than one locality. Of Grissmer and Flanagan's top tier of states, Texas showed statistically significant gains in reading only for rural students; no locality in North Carolina or Michigan showed statistically significant gains.

Looking at the reading performance of African American, Hispanic, and white students, again only Connecticut showed statistically significant gains for all three subpopulations, while Maryland, Delaware, and Colorado showed statistically significant gains for two subpopulations. Grissmer and Flanagan's top performers, North Carolina and Texas, showed statistically significant gains only for white students. In Michigan, none of these three subpopulations showed statistically significant gains.

The NCES-reported NAEP reading data constitutes a clear threat to Grissmer and Flanagan's findings. Aggregate NAEP data may provide too coarse a measure to pick up achievement gains or, perhaps, state reforms are not sufficiently powerful to affect basic reading skills. To explore these possibilities, we examine TAAS data on mathematics and reading performance from 1994 to 1999. (The data for 1994 and 1999 are shown in figure 1.) Grissmer and Flanagan have argued compellingly that state policy has made a substantial and positive difference in Texas and North Carolina.[54] Thus, Texas provides a natural context for looking at these questions and, more broadly, at the dynamics of state policy systems and their effects.

Specifically, we examine the changes in school-level student performance from 1994 to 1999 on the fifth-grade reading and mathematics TAAS tests. We measure the relationship between the percentage of a school's economically disadvantaged students and a school's Texas Learning Index (TLI) score. The TLI is "a [standardized] score that describes how far a student's performance is above or below the passing standard."[55] A TLI score of 70 indicates that a student is at the passing standard.

The correlation between a school's percentage of economically disadvantaged students and a school's average fifth-grade mathematics TLI decreased substantially from 1994 to 1999, while little change was evident in the relationship between a school's percentage of economically disadvantaged students and a school's average fifth-grade reading TLI. More important, the change in the slope of the regression line for mathematics between 1994 and 1999 suggests that the correlation between a child's economic circumstances and his or her mathematics performance has become weaker. This does not, however, appear to be true for reading skill. The TAAS data for the intervening years (1995, 1996, 1997, and 1998) show a consistent pattern—a steady increase in mathematics performance and a steady decrease in the explanatory power of adverse economic circumstances. This pattern is not seen in the reading data; the graphs are largely the same from year to year. Thus, for our analysis, Texas state data provide the same general picture of Texas performance as the NCES-reported NAEP data and, at least in mathematics, as Grissmer and Flanagan's analysis.

**Figure 1. Average Texas Learning Index (TLI) Scores for All Fifth-Grade Students by the Percentage of Economically Disadvantaged Students Enrolled in a School, in Reading and Mathematics, 1994 and 1999**

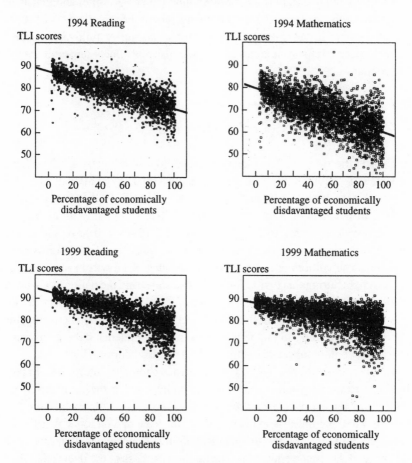

Note: Percentage of variation in TLI scores explained by the percentage of economically disadvantaged children enrolled in a school, for 1994 reading, 0.5559; 1994 mathematics, 0.4018; 1999 reading, 0.5346; and 1999 mathematics, 0.2913.

In summary, the above data suggest what data almost always suggest to researchers: the need for more research. Such research should examine the ways in which states, and various groups within states, have organized their efforts to build school capacity. Gains in student mathematics performance in Texas and gains in student reading performance in Connecticut should receive special attention, as these gains—as measured both by NAEP and by state-level examinations—appear to be large and broadly distributed across sub-populations and geographic localities. In their paper, Grissmer and Flanagan assert "it is too early to make . . . judgments [about the effectiveness of state-level reforms] without extensive case studies backed up by multivariate analysis with specific reform variables that show consistent effects across all states." We concur.

## Comment by Robert H. Meyer

David Grissmer and Ann Flanagan sought to test indirectly for the effects of statewide reform efforts on student achievement by analyzing the state National Assessment of Educational Progress (NAEP) tests in mathematics at the fourth- and eighth-grade levels from 1990 to 1996. The authors assume that statewide reform efforts begun in the mid-1980s will have stimulated growth in student achievement during the 1990–96 period if the reforms were effective. The authors produce estimates of rates of growth in mathematics achievement during this period for individual states and the nation as a whole, controlling statistically for differences across states and over time in the demographic mix of students. Grissmer and Flanagan find that, after controlling for differences over time in the demographic mix of students, national average test scores in the fourth and eighth grades increased during 1990–96.

In this comment I discuss how this evidence should be interpreted. In particular, I examine whether this evidence indicates that the productivity of American education has increased over the last decade.[56] I conclude the following. First, the information contained in the state and national NAEP data for 1990–96 is too limited to support definitive conclusions about the productivity of American education. The major weakness of the data is that they do not contain information on the achievement growth of multiple cohorts of students. As a result, analyzing the data using conventional value-added models of student achievement and school productivity is not possible. I draw on NAEP data for the period 1973–86 to show how more extensive data can be used to conduct such analyses. Second, I show that despite the limitations of the NAEP data for 1990–96, the data can be analyzed or interpreted within the value-added framework. My analysis supports the conclusion that national productivity growth in grades five through eight most likely increased during the late 1980s and declined during the mid-1990s.

Before turning to the weaknesses of the state and national NAEP data for 1990–96, I should note that the NAEP data do have some major strengths. First, the NAEP is regarded as a high-quality assessment that covers a broad domain of mathematics skills. Second, the NAEP is not a high-stakes examination, and thus it cannot be argued that improvements in NAEP test scores are the product of narrow teaching to the test.[57]

The basic problem with the state NAEP data (for the period 1990–96) is that they do not permit tracking of achievement growth of different cohorts of students. Information on achievement growth is currently available for only a single cohort of students, those who were fourth graders in 1992 and eighth graders in 1996. As a result, using conventional value-added models of achievement growth to estimate the effectiveness of state educational policies with these data is not possible.[58] Instead, the authors estimate the rate of growth in fourth- and eighth-grade achievement (controlling for differences across states and over time in the demographic mix of students). In previous research I have demonstrated that changes in the level of student achievement often provide a misleading picture of changes in the efficacy of schools and school policies.[59]

What are some of the problems that arise from not having data on achievement growth for different cohorts? One major problem is that researchers cannot control for what students know when they enter school in kindergarten or first grade. As a result, changes in the average level of student achievement could reflect differences that existed before students start traditional schooling. For example, increases in eighth-grade achievement could reflect improvements in the quality of preschool education that occurred a decade earlier. In the absence of data on student achievement measured soon after students begin their schooling, it is difficult, if not impossible, to disentangle the contributions of schooling and other resources received before and after the beginning of conventional schooling.

A second problem is that, without data on achievement at different grade levels and at different times, identifying when successful educational policy interventions were made is impossible. In particular, rising eighth-grade test scores could reflect earlier improvements in middle school education or later improvements in early elementary school education. To evaluate particular educational reforms, the effectiveness of these reforms must be measured at particular times (that is, when these reforms were being implemented).

To illustrate the practical significance of getting the timing right, consider the national NAEP trend data on mathematics for the period 1973 to 1986.[60] As indicated in panel A of table 1, NAEP scores for eleventh grade (age sev-

**Table 1. National Assessment of Educational Progress Mathematics Data, 1973–86**

A. Average test scores by age and year

| Age | 1973 | 1978 | 1982 | 1986 |
|-----|------|------|------|------|
| Nine | 219.1 | 218.6 | 219.0 | 221.7 |
| Thirteen | 266.0 | 264.1 | 268.6 | 269.0 |
| Seventeen | 304.4 | 300.4 | 298.5 | 302.0 |

B. Average test score gain from year to year for each cohort

| Age | 1973 to 1978 | 1978 to 1982 | 1982 to 1986 |
|-----|------|------|------|
| Nine to thirteen | 45.0 | 50.0 | 50.0 |
| Thirteen to seventeen | 34.4 | 34.4 | 33.4 |

Source: J. A. Dossey, I. V. Mullis, M. M. Lindquist, and D. L. Chambers, *The Mathematics Report Card: Are We Measuring Up?* (Princeton, N.J.: Educational Testing Service, 1988).

enteen) exhibit sharp declines from 1973 to 1982 and then partial recovery between 1982 to 1986. The eleventh-grade data, by themselves, are fully consistent with the premise that academic reforms in the early and mid-1980s generated substantial gains in academic achievement. An analysis of the data based on a gain indicator (a value-added type indicator) instead of an average test score suggests the opposite conclusion (see panel B of table 1).

The gain indicator is similar to a true value-added indicator in that it controls for differences among students in prior achievement. It does so in a simple and intuitive way: Gain is the change in average test scores over time (and across grades) for the same cohort of students. For example, the gain in test scores for students who were eleventh-grade students in 1986 is given by the average test score of eleventh-grade students in 1986 minus the average test score for seventh-grade students (age thirteen) in 1982 (four grades and four years earlier); that is, $302.0 - 268.6 = 33.4$. Unfortunately, the gain indicator, unlike the value-added indicator, does not control for differences in student, family, and neighborhood characteristics that contribute to growth in student achievement. As a result, the gain indicator reflects possible changes over time in the composition of the population as well as changes in school productivity. Nonetheless, it is instructive to compare the gains in achievement experienced by different cohorts.[61]

As indicated in panel B, the achievement growth of high school students (from seventh to eleventh grade) during the 1982 to 1986 period was no better than achievement growth during previous periods. The gain from the seventh to eleventh grades was slightly lower during the 1982 to 1986 period than in previous periods. The rise in eleventh-grade math scores from 1982 to 1986 stems from an earlier increase in achievement growth for that cohort, not from an increase in achievement growth over grades seven to eleven. In short, these data provide no support for the notion that high school academic reforms generated significant increases in test scores during the mid-1980s. Moreover, they illustrate the methodological point that, to properly evaluate programs and policies, data that support a value-added-type analysis must be available.

Returning to the state NAEP data, their major weakness is that they contain longitudinal data (data over time) for only a single cohort of students, the students who were fourth graders in 1992 and eighth graders in 1996. (In contrast, the national NAEP data in table 1 contain longitudinal data for three separate cohorts.) As a result, these data are inadequate to support a conventional value-added or gain analysis. The key question is, what can be learned from these data, if anything, about the productivity of American education?

In the remainder of this comment, I demonstrate how to use a value-added framework to interpret the NAEP mathematics data for the period 1990–96. To keep the analysis simple I focus only on the national data for this period. One advantage of these data is that they include fourth-grade students in 1990 as well as all of the observation points in the state NAEP data. A second advantage is that the national NAEP represents the population of all fourth- and eighth-grade students, whereas the state NAEP covers only students in public schools and students in states that participated in the state NAEP.I estimate the average four-year gain in achievement for the cohorts who were eighth-grade students in 1990, 1992, and 1996, given alternative assumptions about the pattern of fourth-grade achievement before 1990. (The latter data are not included in the NAEP data for 1990–96.) This analysis parallels the analysis reported in table 1. The objective of this analysis is to determine whether conclusions about the pattern of average gains in mathematics achievement are sensitive to alternative assumptions about trends in fourth-grade achievement before 1990.

The first step in the analysis is to project fourth-grade achievement in 1986 and 1988, given the data from 1990–96. Figure 1 depicts the results of four alternative methods for projecting these data: (1) quadratic trend, (2) linear trend, (3) flat trend (no change from 1986 to 1990), and (4) mean of the data from 1990, 1992, and 1996 (see also panel A of table 2). The trend variables do the best job of preserving (and projecting) the pattern observed in the 1990–96 data, in particular the positive slope of the data. But, in the absence

**Figure 1. Projected Fourth-Grade Achievement before 1990 Given Different Models**

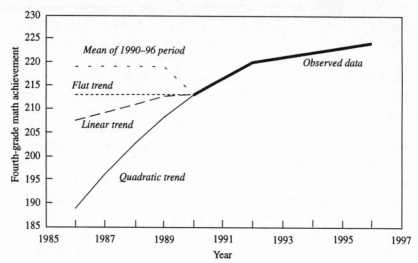

of other information, there is no reason to believe that the trend from 1986–90 mirrors the trend from 1990–96.[62] As a result, I have included two other projections that exhibit much higher values of fourth-grade achievement. Note that the projected levels of fourth-grade achievement vary by as much as thirty points in 1986. As a result, the sensitivity of the analysis to different assumptions about student achievement before 1990 can now be checked.

Estimates of average test score gains, given the different projection methods, are presented in panel B of table 2. A perhaps surprising result of the analysis is that for three of the projection methods (the methods that I believe are most credible) test score gains were lower during the 1992–96 period than the previous period. At face value, these results indicate that the productivity of American schools in grades five through eight declined during the mid-1990s. The analysis based on the quadratic trend indicates declining productivity dating back to the mid-1980s. The other three projection methods, however, provide evidence of rising productivity during the mid-to-late 1980s. All things considered, I believe that the analysis supports the conclusion that national productivity growth in grades five through eight most likely increased during the late 1980s and declined during the mid-1990s.

This brief analysis reveals the value of interpreting test score data within a value-added framework. Even in the absence of data required to conduct a conventional value-added (or gain) analysis, the data may be analyzed or inter-

**Table 2. National Assessment of Educational Policy (NAEP) Projected and Actual Mathematics Data, 1986–96**

A. Average test scores by grade and year

| Grade or projection method | Projected data | | Actual data | | |
|---|---|---|---|---|---|
| | *1986* | *1988* | *1990* | *1992* | *1996* |
| Grade four | | | 213 | 220 | 224 |
| Projection method | | | | | |
| Mean of 1990–96 data | 219 | 219 | | | |
| Flat trend | 213 | 213 | | | |
| Linear trend | 208 | 211 | | | |
| Quadratic trend | 189 | 203 | | | |
| Grade eight | | | 263 | 268 | 272 |

B. Average test score gain from fourth grade to eighth grade for each cohort

| Projection method | Projected data | | Actual data |
|---|---|---|---|
| | *1986 to 1990* | *1988 to 1992* | *1992 to 1996* |
| Mean of 1990–96 data | 44 | 49 | 52 |
| Flat trend | 50 | 55 | 52 |
| Linear trend | 55 | 57 | 52 |
| Quadratic trend | 74 | 65 | 52 |

Source: Actual NAEP data, C. M. Reese, K. E. Miller, J. Mazzeo, and J. A. Dossey, *NAEP 1996 Mathematics Report Card for the Nation and the States* (Department of Education, National Center for Education Statistics, 1997). Projected data estimated by author.

preted using the value-added approach. In both of the data sets examined here, the value-added analyses yielded conclusions that differed from the trend analyses based only on average test scores. It is surprising, but true: Rising average test scores may not be evidence of rising productivity (at least over periods of time less than a decade) and vice versa.

More generally, the analysis suggests the importance of using adequate data to evaluate the impact of educational policies and interventions. Given the limitations of NAEP data (even augmented by additional years of data), relying on state and district data to evaluate educational policies and interventions may be more fruitful. Many states and districts have assessment programs that would support conventional value-added analyses of student achievement and school productivity.

# Notes

1. Richard F. Elmore, *Restructuring Schools: The Next Generation of Educational Reform* (San Francisco: Jossey-Bass, 1990); Chester E. Finn Jr. and Theodor Rebarber, eds., *Education Reform in the '90s* (Macmillan, 1992); and Diane Massell and Susan Fuhrman, *Ten Years of State Education Reform, 1983–1993*, CPRE Research Reports Series RR–028 (Rutgers University, Consortium for Policy Research in Education, 1994).

2. The phrase *systemic reform* is used to refer to an imprecisely defined set of reform initiatives. For an excellent discussion of the origin of the concept, its utilization, and a critique, see Maris A. Vinovskis, "An Analysis of the Concept and Uses of Systemic Educational Reform," *American Educational Research Journal*, vol. 33, no. 1 (Spring 1996). See also Marshall S. Smith and Jennifer O'Day, "Systemic School Reform," in Susan Fuhrman and Betty Malem, eds., *The Politics of Curriculum and Testing: The 1990 Yearbook of the Politics of Education Association* (London, England: Falmer, 1990), pp. 233–67; and Jennifer A. O'Day and M. S. Smith, "Systemic Reform and Educational Opportunity," in S. Fuhrman, ed., *Designing Coherent Education Policy* (San Francisco: Jossey-Bass, 1993), p. 251.

3. Margaret E. Goertz, Robert E. Floden, and Jennifer O'Day, *Studies of Education Reform: Systemic Reform*, vol. 1: *Findings and Conclusions* (Rutgers University, Consortium for Policy Research in Education, 1995); David K. Cohen, "Standards-Based School Reform: Policy, Practice, and Performance," in Helen Ladd, ed., *Holding Schools Accountable* (Brookings, 1996); Richard F. Elmore, C. H. Abelmann, and S. F. Furman, "The New Accountability in State Education Reform: From Process to Performance," in Helen Ladd, ed., *Holding Schools Accountable* (Brookings, 1996); and Diane Massell, Michael Kirst, and Margaret Hoppe, *Persistence and Change: Standards-Based Reform in Nine States* (University of Pennsylvania, Graduate School of Education, Consortium for Policy Research in Education, 1997).

4. William N. Evans, Sheila Murray, and Robert Schwab, "Schoolhouses, Courthouses, and Statehouses after *Serrano*," *Journal of Policy Analysis and Management*, vol. 16 (January 1997), pp. 10–31.

5. The average Scholastic Assessment Test (SAT) score is sometimes used to compare state outcomes. Research has shown that differences in average SAT scores at the state level primarily reflect different participation rates among students in the state. See Brian Powell and Lala Carr Steelman, "Bewitched, Bothered, and Bewildering: The Use and Misuse of State SAT and ACT Scores," *Harvard Educational Review*, vol. 66 (Spring 1996), pp. 27–59; and David Grissmer, "The Use and Misuse of SAT Scores," *Journal of Psychology, Law, and Public Policy* (forthcoming). State participation rates vary from less than 5 percent to more than 80 percent of seniors. These differences in participation do not reflect only differing abilities to succeed in college because some of the states with the highest National Assessment of Educational Progress (NAEP) scores have the lowest SAT participation. The states of Iowa, Minnesota, Nebraska, North Dakota, Oklahoma, South Dakota, and Wisconsin score above state averages on NAEP tests but have among the lowest SAT participation rates—less than 10 percent.

6. David Grissmer, Ann Flanagan, Jennifer Kawata, and Stephanie Williamson, *Improving Student Achievement: What State NAEP Scores Tell Us*, MR–924 (Santa Monica, Calif.: RAND, 2000).

7. See Stephen Raudenbush, "Synthesizing Results from the NAEP Trial State Assessment," in David Grissmer and Michael Ross, eds., *Analytic Issues in the Assessment of Student Achievement* (Washington: National Center for Education Statistics, 2000) for an example of individual-level NAEP analysis using the 1992 eighth-grade test. This analysis provides a definitive hierarchical linear modeling approach to analysis of the state NAEP data using a single test.

An extension of this approach using all NAEP state tests and introducing trends would allow a comparative analysis to the aggregate analysis done here.

8. Grissmer, Flanagan, Kawata, and Williamson, *Improving Student Achievement*.

9. Eric A. Hanushek, Steven G. Rivkin, and Lori L. Taylor, "Aggregation and the Estimated Effects of School Resources," *Review of Economics and Statistics* (Fall 1996), pp. 611–27.

10. Grissmer, Flanagan, Kawata, and Williamson, *Improving Student Achievement*.

11. Jeremy Finn and C. Achilles, "Tennessee's Class Size Study: Findings, Implications, and Misconceptions," *Educational Evaluation and Policy Analysis*, vol. 20, no. 2 (Summer 1999); Alex Molnar and others, "Estimated Achievement and Teacher Time Allocation Effects from a Quasi-Experimental Class Size Reduction in Wisconsin," *Educational Evaluation and Policy Analysis*, vol. 20, no. 2 (Summer 1999); and David Grissmer, "Assessing the Evidence on Class Size: Policy Implications and Future Research Agenda," *Educational Evaluation and Policy Analysis*, vol. 20, no. 2 (Summer 1999).

12. E. Word, J. Johnston, and H. P. Bain, *Student Teacher Achievement Ratio (STAR): Tennessee's K–3 Class Size Study, Final Summary Report 1985–1990* (Nashville: Tennessee Department of Education, 1990); E. R. Word, J. Johnston, and H. P. Bain, *The State of Tennessee's Student/Teacher Achievement Ratio (STAR) Project: Technical Report 1985–1990* (Nashville: Tennessee State Department of Education, 1994); C. M. Achilles and others, "The Lasting Benefits Study (LBS) in Grades 4 and 5 (1990–1991): A Legacy from Tennessee's Four Year (K–3) Class Size Study (1985–1990), Project STAR," paper presented at the North Carolina Association for Research in Education, Greensboro, North Carolina, January 14, 1993; Jeremy D. Finn and Charles M. Achilles, "Answers and Questions about Class Size: A Statewide Experiment," *American Educational Research Journal*, vol. 27, no. 3 (Fall 1990), pp. 557–77; Finn and Achilles, "Tennessee's Class Size Study"; B. A. Nye, L. Hedges, and S. Konstantopoulos, "The Effects of Small Class Size on Academic Achievement: The Results of the Tennessee Class Size Experiment," University of Chicago, Department of Education, 1999; Barbara Nye, Larry V. Hedges, and Spyros Konstantopoulos, "The Long Term Effects of Small Classes: A Five-Year Follow-up of the Tennessee Class Size Experiment," *Educational Evaluation and Policy Analysis*, vol. 20, no. 2 (Summer 1999); and A. B. Krueger, "Experimental Estimates of Education Production Functions," *Quarterly Journal of Economics*, vol. 114 (1999), pp. 497–532.

13. Krueger, "Experimental Estimates of Education Production Functions"; and Finn and Achilles, "Tennessee's Class Size Study."

14. Grissmer, "Assessing the Evidence on Class Size."

15. Molnar and others, "Estimated Achievement and Teacher Time Allocation Effects from a Quasi-Experimental Class Size Reduction in Wisconsin."

16. Grissmer, Flanagan, Kawata, and Williamson, *Improving Student Achievement*.

17. Grissmer, Flanagan, Kawata, and Williamson, *Improving Student Achievement*.

18. Grissmer, Flanagan, Kawata, and Williamson, *Improving Student Achievement*.

19. C. A. Shaughnessy, J. Nelson, and N. Norris, *NAEP 1996 Mathematics Cross State Data Compendium for the Grade 4 and Grade 8 Assessment*, NCES–98–481 (Department of Education, 1998); I. V. S. Mullis and others, *NAEP 1992 Mathematics Report Card for the Nation and the States: Data from the National and Trail State Assessments* (Washington: National Center for Education Statistics, 1993) ; and C. M. Reese and others, *NAEP 1996 Mathematics Report Card for the Nation and the States* (Washington: National Center for Education Statistics, 1997).

20. See Grissmer, Flanagan, Kawata, and Williamson, *Improving Student Achievement*, for more discussion of exclusion and participation rates by state.

21. All estimation was done in STATA using the GEE estimator with exchangeable correlation structure.

22. The earliest state scores in each test category (1990 eighth-grade math and 1992 fourth-grade math) are converted to variables with a mean of zero and divided by the standard deviation of national scores. The later tests in each category are subtracted from the mean of the earlier test and divided by the same national standard deviation. This technique maintains the test gains within each category and allows the results to be interpreted in terms of changes with respect to national scores.

23. We develop a single variable whose value is zero for the first application of each test and is the number of years between the first application and each subsequent application for remaining values. The order of our *j* tests is as follows: 1990 eighth-grade math, 1992 eighth-grade math, 1992 fourth-grade math, 1996 eighth-grade math, and 1996 fourth-grade math. So the annualized gain variable entries for each state would be (0,2,0,6,4). The regression coefficient for this variable is the annualized gain across all tests.

24. Because it is largely unknown how much specific state reforms might cause immediate gains at all grades or cumulative gains that start at school entry, our method simply provides a gross measure of whether evidence exists that scores at fourth and eighth grade are increasing and the rate of increase. For instance, the eighth-grade gains could be caused by early reform efforts between 1982 and 1988 if they are cumulative or reforms causing immediate gains between 1988 and 1996. The fourth-grade gains could be from cumulative effects of reforms between 1988 and 1992 or immediate effects from 1992 to 1996. It is possible that the gains might also stem from changes in earlier preschool experience.

25. Grissmer, Flanagan, Kawata, and Williamson, *Improving Student Achievement*; and David W. Grissmer, Ann Flanagan, and Jennifer Kawata, *Assessing and Improving the Family Characteristics Collected with the National Assessment of Educational Progress*, DRR–1914–IET (Santa Monica, Calif.: RAND, August 1998).

26. Grissmer, Flanagan, and Kawata, *Assessing and Improving the Family Characteristics Collected with the National Assessment of Educational Progress*.

27. D. W. Grissmer and others, *Student Achievement and the Changing American Family* (Santa Monica, Calif.: RAND, 1994).

28. Grissmer, Flanagan, Kawata, and Williamson, *Improving Student Achievement*, contains the regression results for the state trends equations. The socioeconomic status (SES) variables derived from the National Education Longitudinal Study (NELS) are strongly significant and have *t*-values greater than 8. The five family variables entered in the Census/NAEP regressions almost always have the appropriate sign and are statistically significant. However, the trend results do not appear to be sensitive to which family variables are included.

29. See Grissmer, Flanagan, Kawata, and Williamson, *Improving Student Achievement*, for more detailed definitions of the resource variables.

30. David Grissmer, A. Flanagan, and S. Williamson, "Does Money Matter for Minority and Disadvantaged Students: Assessing the New Empirical Evidence," in William Fowler, ed., *Developments in School Finance: 1997*, NCES 98–212 (Department of Education, 1998).

31. Evans, Murray, and Schwab, "Schoolhouses, Courthouses, and Statehouses after *Serrano*"; and William N. Evans, S. Murray, and R. Schwab, "The Impact of Court-Mandated School Finance Reform," in Helen Ladd, Rosemary Chalk, and Janet Hansen, eds., *Equity and Adequacy in Education Finance* (Washington: National Academy Press, 1999).

32. Grissmer, Flanagan, Kawata, and Williamson, *Improving Student Achievement*, has detailed definitions of the variables together with means and standard deviations.

33. The low effectiveness of direct investment in salaries from this analysis may have three explanations, and further research should be undertaken to help identify the reason. The results could reflect the inefficient structure of the current teacher compensation system. The current system rewards experience and education, but neither seems to be directly related to produc-

ing higher achievement. If the system could distinguish and provide higher compensation for higher quality teachers and those teachers who are more effective with lower scoring students where more leverage exists for raising scores, then one would expect a dollar of compensation to be more effective. However, in the current system, another dollar of compensation is used to reward experience and degrees and to raise all salaries—rewarding high- and low-quality teachers as well as teachers of both low- and high-scoring students. With such a compensation system, its lack of cost-effectiveness may be understandable.

However, another explanation is that interstate differences in salary may be less sensitive to achievement than intrastate salary differences. The primary teacher labor markets may be within states where interdistrict salary differentials may affect the supply and distribution of higher quality teachers much more than interstate differences. A similar analysis across school districts within a state might show stronger compensation effects.

A third explanation is that teacher salary is the most highly correlated schooling characteristic with family SES variables, and part of the salary effect may appear as social capital. If teachers strongly prefer to teach children of similar SES levels as their own, other things being equal, then separating salary effects from social capital effects may be difficult.

34. David Grissmer and Ann Flanagan, "Exploring Rapid Score Gains in Texas and North Carolina," commissioned paper, National Education Goals Panel, Washington D.C., 1998.

35. These policies seemed to have their origin in the business community in each state that was instrumental in generating the agenda for reform and its passage in the legislature, and in the systemic reform ideas generated in the educational research community. See Smith and O'Day, "Systemic School Reform"; and O'Day and Smith, "Systemic Reform and Educational Opportunity."

36. Unfortunately, the 1990 eighth-grade math test did not have locality defined similarly to the tests after 1990. So these results contain only the four math tests in 1992–96.

37. More detailed definitions are contained in Grissmer, Flanagan, Kawata, and Williamson, *Improving Student Achievement.*

38. See David B. Tyack, *The One Best System* (Harvard University Press, 1974).

39. See, for example, Linda McNeil, *Contradictions of Control* (New York: Routledge and Kegan, Paul, 1986); Linda McNeil, "Creating New Inequalities: Contradictions of Reform," *Phi Delta Kappan*, vol. 81 (July 2000), pp. 729–34; and Arthur Wise, *Legislated Learning* (University of California Press, 1979).

40. See, for example, David Cohen and James Spillane, "Policy and Practice: The Relations between Governance and Instruction," in Susan Fuhrman, ed., *Designing Coherent Educational Policy: Improving the System* (San Francisco: Jossey-Bass, 1993); Consortium for Policy Research in Education, *Putting the Pieces Together: Systemic School Reform*, CPRE Policy Briefs (New Brunswick, N.J., 1991); and Andrew Porter, "National Equity and School Autonomy," *Educational Policy*, vol. 8, no. 4 (1994), pp. 489–500.

41. Marshall S. Smith and Jennifer O'Day, "School Reform and Equal Opportunity: An Introduction to the Education Symposium," *Stanford Law and Policy Review* (Winter 1992–93), p. 17.

42. Susan Fuhrman, *Politics and Systemic Education Reform*, CPRE Policy Briefs, RB–12–04/94 (Rutgers University, Consortium for Policy Research in Education, 1994), pp. 1–7.

43. Craig Jerald and Ulrich Boser, "Taking Stock," *Education Week: Quality Counts '99*, vol. 18, no. 17 (January 11, 1999), pp. 81–101.

44. Smith and O'Day, "School Reform and Equal Opportunity," pp. 15–20, italics in original.

45. C. M. Reese, K. E. Miller, J. Mazzeo, and J. A. Dossey, *NAEP 1996 Mathematics Report Card for the Nation and the States* (Department of Education, National Center for Education

Statistics, 1997); and Ina V. S. Mullis, John A. Dossey, Eugene H. Owen, and Gary W. Phillips, *NAEP 1992 Mathematics Report Card for the Nation and the States* (Department of Education, National Center for Education Statistics, 1993).

46. David Grissmer and Ann Flanagan, *Exploring Rapid Achievement Gains in Texas and North Carolina* (Washington: National Education Goals Panel, 1998), p. i.

47. Grissmer and Flanagan, *Exploring Rapid Achievement Gains in Texas and North Carolina*.

48. William Hussar and William Sonnenberg, *Trends in the Disparities in School District Level Expenditures per Pupil* (Department of Education, National Center for Education Statistics, 2000).

49. Albert Cortez, "Why Better Isn't Good Enough: A Closer Look at TAAS Gains," *IDRA Newsletter,* vol. 27 (March 2000), pp. 2–10.

50. Kenneth Meier, *Examining the Effects of School Finance Reform in Texas* (Texas A&M University, Center for Excellence in Education, 1999).

51. For more information on the Texas accountability system, see Texas Education Agency, *Texas Education Agency Accountability Manual 2000–2001* (Austin, Texas, 2000).

52. Both Grant High School and Lee High School were eventually able to earn acceptable ratings. By the 1998–99 academic year, Grant's passing rates increased to 94.2 percent overall, 84.8 percent for African American students, 87.8 percent for Hispanic students, 98.4 percent for white students, and 81.9 percent for economically disadvantaged students. In 1998–99 Lee's passing rates increased to 75.9 percent overall, 83.9 percent for African American students, 67.6 percent for Hispanic students, 85.7 percent for white students, and 76.7 percent for economically disadvantaged students.

53. Patricia L. Donahue, Kristin E. Voelkl, Jay R. Campbell, and John Mazzeo, *NAEP 1998 Reading Report Card for the Nation and the States* (Department of Education, National Center for Education Statistics, 1999).

54. Grissmer and Flanagan, *Exploring Rapid Achievement Gains in Texas and North Carolina*.

55. Texas Education Agency, *Texas Education Agency Technical Digest 1997–1998* (Austin, Texas, 1998), p. 8.

56. To simplify the discussion I focus on interpreting the evidence on national test scores. Similar issues arise with respect to state data.

57. However, because how students perform on the NAEP does not matter, it could be argued that students do not take the test seriously. From an evaluation perspective, it would be worse if student willingness to take the test seriously has changed over time, perhaps in response to growing emphasis on the importance of standardized testing.

58. See Robert H. Meyer, "Value-Added Indicators of School Performance," in Eric A. Hanushek and Dale W. Jorgenson, eds., *Improving America's Schools: The Role of Incentives* (Washington: National Academy Press, 1996), pp. 197–223.

59. Meyer, "Value-Added Indicators," pp. 197–223.

60. This analysis is taken from Meyer, "Value-Added Indicators," pp. 197–223. See Paul E. Barton and Richard J. Coley, *Growth in School: Achievement Gains from the Fourth to the Eighth Grade* (Princeton, N.J.: Educational Testing Service, Policy Information Center, 1998), for a similar analysis that focuses on gains in student achievement for students age nine to thirteen from 1978 to 1996.

61. NAEP was originally designed to permit this type of analysis. In mathematics, the tests have generally been given every four years at grade levels spaced four years apart. For this illustrative analysis, I assume that average test scores in 1973 are comparable to the unknown 1974 scores.

62. Information from the NAEP national trend data indicates that fourth-grade test scores increased over the period 1986–90. See J. R. Campbell, C. M. Hombo, and J. Mazzeo, *NAEP 1999 Trends in Academic Progress: Three Decades of Student Performance*, NCES 2000–469 (Department of Education, Office of Educational Research and Improvement, National Center for Education Statistics, 2000). I have not included these data in this analysis because my focus is on what can be learned from a short span of data. In addition, the samples used for the two types of data are somewhat different, so the test score data are not strictly comparable.

# The Controversy over the National Assessment Governing Board Standards

MARK D. RECKASE

T HIS PAPER PROVIDES an analysis of the controversy surrounding the standard setting process conducted by ACT Inc. for the National Assessment Governing Board (NAGB).[1] This process is the most thoroughly planned, carefully executed, exhaustively evaluated, completely documented, and most visible of any standard setting process of which I am aware. Extensive research was conducted to determine how best to develop each step in the process.[2] A distinguished team of experts guided the process through its development and implementation.[3] And, the process has been open to scrutiny with evaluators observing the design and implementation of every step.

Any process can be improved with experience and with continuing research and development. Better methods for setting standards likely will be created in the future. Until such developments occur, however, this process—called the achievement levels setting (ALS) process by NAGB—is the model for how standard setting should be done. The question I attempt to answer here is: If the standard setting process is of such high quality, why are the standards set by the process so controversial?

Although I think extremely well of the NAGB standard setting process, interpreting the results of the ALS process is a very complex undertaking. A difference has become evident between the technical accuracy of the standards and the clarity of meaning for the standards that were set. The technical quality of the standards is very high. Statistical analyses have shown that the standards are well within the accepted bounds for amount of error in the estimated cutscores, and follow-up validity studies have provided supportive

231

evidence for the technical quality of the standards.[4] Cutscores are points on the score scale used for reporting that separate levels of performance such as pass/fail or, in this case, the achievement level categories. Further, the standards are based on the reasoned judgments of a carefully selected group of qualified individuals.[5] These individuals reviewed the outcomes of their work and endorsed the resulting standards as being reasonable and representing their best efforts.[6]

But as important as the technical and procedural quality of the standards is, the clarity of information communicated by the standards-based reporting is at least as important. As the Committee on the Evaluation of National and State Assessments of Educational Progress concluded: "Standards-based reporting is intended to be useful in communicating student results to the public and policy makers. However, sufficient research is not yet available to determine how various audiences interpret and use NAEP's [National Assessment of Educational Progress's] achievement-level results."[7]

NAGB reports three standards of performance for many content areas included in the National Assessment of Educational Progress. NAGB calls these standards achievement levels (ALs). NAGB policy defines three ALs with these labels: Basic, Proficient, and Advanced. For content areas with ALs, NAEP reports the numerical value of the cutscores that delimit the three ALs on the NAEP score scale and the percentage of students in tested grade levels that are above each cutscore. Interpretive aids for the results include descriptions of skills and knowledge for students estimated to be in ranges on the score scale defined by the ALs and examples of items with estimated levels of performance for each AL.[8] An AL is the range of the score scale from an AL boundary to the next higher AL. For example, the Basic level ranges from the lowest score for Basic to just below the start of Proficient. The Advanced level ranges from just above Proficient to an unspecified maximum possible level of performance. In practice, the Advanced level does not have an upper boundary. Three AL ranges correspond to the standards for Basic, Proficient, and Advanced. To be determined is whether the method for reporting NAEP results communicates useful information about the levels of educational achievement of students in the United States.

I am not a disinterested party in the standards setting process, nor is anyone who can knowledgeably discuss the issues that are involved. NAEP is too complex a program for anyone to intelligently discuss without having been directly involved with it at some time, as either a proponent or a critic. I coauthored the original ACT Inc. proposal to NAGB for work on the project and was an internal consultant to the project for many years. I still serve on the Technical Advisory Committee for Standard Setting (TACSS), which gives advice to ACT Inc. and NAGB about standard setting issues. All opinions expressed here are my own, however, and they may or may not reflect the positions of ACT Inc. or NAGB.

## The Standard Setting Process

Everyone who works in the area of standard setting agrees that setting standards is a judgmental process. As a result, no standards are right or wrong. Judgments of what standards should be can vary widely. Examples are the differences in judgments made by teenagers and their parents about standards of dress, music, and so on. An ongoing debate is being conducted in the United States about standards of behavior, safety, quality, and so on, because they are judgments. The nature of standards makes it important that the qualifications of the persons making judgments be open to scrutiny so that their perspectives are understood.

Standards for ALs were formally set when NAGB set the policy for the standards. The standards are the words *basic*, *proficient*, and *advanced* and the definitions that elaborate on the meaning of those words. NAGB in 1990 formally approved the policy that led to the ALs and thereby set the ALs. Everything that has happened since that time is part of translating the standards that were set by policy into content descriptions and numerical values on the NAEP score scale. The persons who set the standards were the members of NAGB at the time that the AL policy was developed and approved. The members of NAGB at the time of approval of the policy are listed in table 1.

Not all persons working in standard setting agree with the conception of standard setting as translation of policy onto a numerical scale. Others argue that the groups of people who are brought together to rate test performance, test items, or individual performance are the people setting the standards instead of those who set the policy. For example, L. A. Shepard says that "standard setters look at items on the tests and decide how many should be passed to reflect minimal proficiency."[9] Individuals who participate in the process are called panelists. They perform the ratings but are not allowed to freely choose any standard they wish. They are given the policy, and the decisions they make are expected to be consistent with that policy. The procedures they are to follow are specified and the information they receive as feedback is determined

**Table 1. Members of NAGB at the Time of Approval of Achievement Levels Concept**

| Name | Title | Organization[1] |
|---|---|---|
| Chester E. Finn Jr., chair | Professor of education and public policy | Vanderbilt University |
| Phyllis Williamson Aldrich | Curriculum coordinator | Saratoga-Warren B.O.C.E.S., Saratoga Springs, N.Y. |
| Francie Alexander | Associate superintendent | California Department of Education |
| David Battini | High school history teacher | Cairo-Durham High School, Cairo, N.Y. |
| Richard A. Boyd | Executive director | Martha Holden Jennings Foundation |
| Bruce E. Brombacher | Teacher | Jones Middle School, Upper Arlington, Ohio |
| Michael N. Castle[2] | Governor | State of Delaware |
| Saul Cooperman[2] | Commissioner of education | State of New Jersey |
| Antonia Cortese | First vice president | New York State United Teachers |
| Wilhelmina F. Delco[2] | Representative | Texas House of Representatives |
| Victor H. Ferry | Principal | Southwest School, Waterford, Conn. |
| Michael S. Glode | Member | Wyoming State Board of Education |
| Dale E. Graham | Principal (retired) | Carmel High School, Carmel, Ind. |
| Elton Jolly | President and chief executive officer | Opportunities Industrialization Centers of America |
| Carl J. Moser | Acting director | Lutheran Church—Missouri Synod |
| Mark D. Musick | President | Southern Regional Education Board |
| Carolyn Pollan | Representative | Arkansas House of Representatives |
| Matthew W. Prophet Jr. | Superintendent | Portland (Ore.) school district |
| William T. Randall[2] | Commission of education | State of Colorado |
| Dorothy K. Rich | President | Home and School Institute |
| Richard W. Riley | Attorney | Nelson, Mullins, Riley, and Scarborough, Atlanta, Ga. |
| Thomas Topuzes | Attorney | Law Office of Frank Rogozienski (Calif.) |
| Herbert J. Walberg | Professor of education | University of Illinois |
| Christopher T. Cross (ex-officio) | Assistant secretary for educational research and improvement | U.S. Department of Education |

Source: National Assessment Governing Board (NAGB).
1. Affiliations were current as of April 1990.
2. Not present when achievement level policy was adopted.

by policy. Those who rate performance as part of a standard setting process are doing an important task, but it is one of accurate translation of policy, not setting policy.

## *Foundations for the Process*

NAGB was created in 1988 with a charge from Congress to develop standards for performance on the National Assessment of Educational Progress. Specifically, the legislation states: "The National Assessment Governing Board . . . shall develop appropriate student performance levels for each age and grade in each subject area to be tested under the National Assessment of Educational Progress."[10] NAGB interpreted this charge to mean that it should determine score points on the NAEP score scale that define benchmarks for performance on the NAEP assessments. NAGB policy in 1990 defined three benchmarks for reporting performance (labeled Basic, Proficient, and Advanced), and NAGB crafted the definition of performance for each level.[11]

> *Advanced.* This higher level signifies superior performance beyond proficient grade-level mastery at grades 4, 8, and 12. For the 12th grade the advanced level will show readiness for rigorous college courses, advanced technical training, or employment requiring advanced academic achievement. As data become available, it may be based in part, on international comparisons of academic achievement and may be related to Advanced Placement and other college placement exams.
>
> *Proficient.* This central level represents solid performance for each grade tested—4, 8, and 12. It will reflect a consensus that students reaching this level demonstrated competency over challenging subject matter and are well prepared for the next level of schooling. At grade 12 the proficient level will encompass a body of subject-matter knowledge and analytical skills, of cultural literacy and insight, that all high school graduates should have for democratic citizenship, responsible adulthood, and productive work.
>
> *Basic.* This level, below proficient, denotes partial mastery of knowledge and skills that are fundamental for proficient work at each grade—4, 8, and 12. For 12th grade this will be higher than minimum competency skills (which normally are taught in elementary and junior high schools) and will cover significant elements of standard high school-level work.

These policy definitions provide some contextual information to aid in understanding the intentions of NAGB as it set the policy. However, while this information may facilitate the interpretation of the ALs, it also may open the ALs to criticism. For example, the Advanced definition mentions "readiness for rigorous college courses." The question then arises: Are twelfth-grade students at the Advanced level ready to succeed in rigorous college level courses? The question is reasonable, but given the context of NAEP, it is very difficult, if not impossible, to answer. To answer the question, the performance on the NAEP that is consistent with the translation of the Advanced policy definition to the score scale must be related to the specified level of performance in college. Verifying whether this relationship exists is not possible because NAEP does not report scores for individual students. Therefore, it is not possible to identify twelfth-grade students who scored at the Advanced level and track those students to determine how well they performed in college-level courses. The number of students at various levels of performance can be inferred by making strong assumptions. The best case would be that the number of students at the Advanced level was the same as the number that succeeded in rigorous college-level courses. Unfortunately, determining whether the students in those two groups are the same students is impossible. Strong empirical support cannot be obtained for the connection between NAEP performance and performance in college-level courses.

NAGB later changed the policy definitions so that they did not suggest connections between external performance and NAEP results. These changes provided more defensible definitions for the ALs but reduced the interpretive context for the standards. The revised policy definitions are:

> *Proficient*: This level represents solid academic performance for each grade assessed. Students reaching this level have demonstrated competency over challenging subject matter, including subject-matter knowledge, applications of such knowledge to real world situations, and analytical skills appropriate to the subject matter.
> *Advanced*: This level signifies superior performance.
> *Basic*: This level denotes partial mastery of prerequisite knowledge and skills that are fundamental for proficient work at each grade.[12]

A comparison of the two sets of AL policy definitions shows the tension between meaningful communication and technical accuracy. The latter definitions can be more readily supported by data because they do not make strong predictions. The former gives more interpretive context, but the definitions cannot be supported with straightforward analyses.

The translation from the policy definitions to the numerical values on the NAEP score scale does not occur in one step. The policy definitions are generic. They refer to academic performance, but they do not focus on specific academic areas. The NAEP assessments are specific to areas of study within the educational system in the United States. Before cutscores can be determined, the specific content domains that are the focus of the standards must be defined.

Over the last ten years, the domains of interest have included mathematics, science, reading, writing, U.S. history, geography, and civics.[13]

The description of a domain is called a framework. NAGB framework documents guide not only the standard setting but also the design and development of the NAEP assessment. The frameworks are general descriptions of what is expected of students for that curriculum area. For example, the 1998 NAEP civics framework document lists its goals as:

—Specify the civic knowledge and skills that students should possess at grades four, eight, and twelve.

—Describe the desired characteristics of the 1998 assessment of civics.

—Present preliminary descriptions of the three levels of achievement—Basic, Proficient, and Advanced—by which students' performance should be judged and reported in that assessment.[14]

The description of the knowledge and skills that students should possess covers eighteen pages of the framework document. The description is organized around five questions and three intellectual skills. The five questions are:

1. What are civic life, politics, and government?

2. What are the foundations of the American political system?

3. How does the government established by the Constitution embody the purposes, values, and principles of American democracy?

4. What is the relationship of the United States to other nations and to world affairs?

5. What are the roles of citizens in American democracy?[15]

The intellectual skills are: identifying and describing; explaining and analyzing; and evaluating, taking, and defending a position.

The framework also indicates the basic design for the NAEP assessment. For example, at the fourth-grade level, the NAEP civics assessment should include 25 percent of exercises on "What are civic life, politics, government?" and only 10 percent on "What is the relationship of the United States to other nations and to world affairs?" At fourth grade, 40 percent of the exercise pool should assess "identifying and describing" skills.

A final component of the framework document is a translation of the policy definitions for the ALs to content descriptions. These are called preliminary achievement level descriptions (ALDs). An example of preliminary ALDs from the 1998 NAEP civics framework is:

Fourth-grade students at the Proficient level should be able to:
—Explain the importance of government in the classroom, school, community, state, and nation.

—Assess the strengths and weaknesses of a school rule or a law.

—Explain how rule of law protects individual rights and the common good.

—Explain how politics helps people make decisions about the ways they live together.

—Explain ways groups in schools and communities can manage conflict peacefully.

—Explain what the national government is and what it does.

—Explain how holidays and symbols (e.g. flag, Statue of Liberty) reflect common American values.

—Evaluate, take, and defend a position on why it is important for people to participate in civic life.

—Identify heads of executive branches of their local, state, and national governments.

—Describe ways in which nations interact with one another and try to resolve problems.

—Explain that students are citizens of their classroom, community, state, and nation.

—Describe rights and responsibilities of a citizen.[16]

The fourth grade also has achievement level descriptions for the Basic and Advanced levels. ALDs are included for eighth and twelfth grades as well.

Any academic content area covers a broad domain. The framework document delimits the part of the content area domain that is the focus of the NAEP assessment and the ALs. The specification of the NAEP exercise pool limits the domain even further because some aspects of the domain are impossible to assess in paper-and-pencil form under timed testing conditions. This most limited domain of the potential NAEP exercise pool is partitioned by the application of the policy definitions into four parts: the skills and knowledge expected of students at the Basic, Proficient, and Advanced levels, and those that are below the level of Basic. Students at an AL are expected to be able to demonstrate the skills at their AL and those below it. Figure 1 is a graphic representation of the relationship between the content domain, framework, item pool, and ALs for the 1998 NAEP civics assessment.

NAEP standards are set within the context of the policy definitions and the frameworks. Thus, the ALs are constrained to indicate what students should know and be able to do within the domain defined by these documents. Interpretations cannot go beyond the academic material defined in the frameworks or the content that can legitimately be included on the NAEP assessment. Further, the test produced from the framework for a particular year is one representation of what the framework means in practice. With each developmental cycle, a new set of tests is produced. Each of these tests is another sampling

**Figure 1. Relationship between the Civics Content Domain and the National Assessment of Educational Progress (NAEP) Framework**

Civics domain

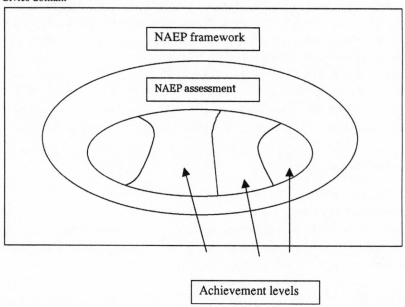

of tasks designed to elicit information about the skills and knowledge acquired by students about the restricted domain covered by NAEP. This domain is extensive, despite the constraints. NAEP uses a matrix sampling approach to testing so that a large number of test exercises can be administered.[17]

All of these features of the achievement levels setting process—policy, frameworks, and tests—circumscribe the domain that is the reference for the achievement levels. The standards cannot be set beyond the content that is the intersection of the three. If a topic is not mentioned in the framework, test items will not be developed to measure the topic, and standards cannot consider the topic. The equivalent in the health arena would be to set standards for the amount of protein in the adult diet. The standard is limited to the amount of protein, not sugar, fat, exercise, or vitamin requirements. Those dietary and health requirements are covered in other frameworks. Also, the standard for protein would be guided by a policy for the standard. Is it for minimum requirement for health? Is the requirement for maximum length of life? These are statements of policy that guide the determination of the standard.

NAGB sets policy, and the policy sets the standards. The policy is generic and must be translated to academic content. The content does not include the broad domain of a curriculum area such as civics but is limited by what is included in a framework document. The framework is based on judgments about what is important for students to know and be able to do in the content domain. Practical aspects of large-scale paper-and-pencil testing further limit the domain specified in the framework. Achievement level descriptions subdivide the test domain into skill and knowledge clusters that represent what the students who match the policy definitions of Basic, Proficient, and Advanced know and what they are able to do. All of this is accomplished before the formal procedure, typically called standard setting, is put into practice.

*The Panelists*

Standard setting would be a relatively easy task if it were possible to determine the score on the test score scale directly from the policy definitions and the ALDs given in the framework document. Unfortunately, that is not the case. The language of policy and descriptions of content are far less precise than even moderately reliable test scores. Language is open to many different interpretations. As elaborate and carefully considered as NAGB policy and frameworks are, human judgments are still needed to determine a test score that is consistent with the dictates of policy.

The persons who translate policy into standards on the NAEP score scale need to have a number of qualifications. First, they must be knowledgeable about the subject matter. Second, they must be familiar with the capabilities of the grade group for which the standard is being set. Finally, they must understand the educational system of the United States and appreciate the diverse approaches to educating students. In addition to these characteristics, NAGB requires that the persons who translate policy into numerical standards be representative of the country as a whole and certain stakeholder groups.

NAGB policy requires that participants in the ALS process be broadly representative of teachers, nonteacher educators, and the general public. The policy specifies that teachers make up approximately 55 percent of the panelists; nonteacher educators, 15 percent; and the general public, 30 percent. NAGB also requires that minority groups make up about 20 percent of the panelists, that the NAEP regions are proportionally represented, and that males and females participate in roughly equal numbers.[18] ACT Inc. suggested the additional content and experience qualifications, and NAGB approved them. Panelists needed to have appropriate content knowledge and experience with students from the grade level for their panel. Meeting the aggregate of these requirements poses a challenging recruiting task. In addition to the NAGB policy requirements, ACT Inc. recommended that the selection of panelists be replicable so that the panels for field trials, pilot tests, and operational ALS would have similar characteristics.[19]

In addition to all of these requirements, panelists were nominated as exemplary individuals in their stakeholder category. Teachers were well credentialed and had national reputations. They also taught the grade levels that were the focus of the standards. Many had awards for teaching excellence and had worked on the design and scoring of state assessments. General public representatives included school board members and journalists and others knowledgeable about educational issues and the content areas. They also had experience with the grade-level groups either as parents of that age group or from active work with the student population. Nonteacher educators included curriculum experts from state departments of education and other education officials as well as university faculty. As with the other groups, the nonteacher educators had to be familiar with the student population for the grade level they would be considering. Overall, the panelists were exemplary groups with knowledge of the content domain and familiarity with the student population. Twenty-seven to thirty-one panelists were involved in the standard setting activities at each grade level for the 1998 NAEP civics ALS process; eighty-seven panelists served in all.[20]

The intellectual power of the group of panelists collectively provides the mechanism for converting the policy definitions and the ALDs to numerical values on the NAEP score scale. This is done through the process of judging the expected level of performance for students at the borderline of the ALs on the test questions on the NAEP assessment. The panelists are not expected to do this task without substantial guidance and training.

## Converting Policy to the NAEP Score Scale

The process for converting the policy definitions to points on the NAEP reporting score scale is elaborate. It involves training panelists about NAEP and the rating processes used to convert policy and content into numerical scores. It involves a variety of rating processes through multiple rounds with feedback on the results of the process between rounds. Also, the panelists are provided with a variety of types of background information at carefully selected points in the process so that it will not overwhelm or confuse them. Full documentation of the process can be obtained in a number of ACT Inc. reports.[21]

The basic components of the process need to be understood as they relate to the interpretation of the results. The achievement levels setting process is an elaborate operation. The first element is "Providing a Common Understanding of the Purposes for Setting Achievement Levels and the Procedures to Follow in the Civics ALS Process." This element alone takes four-and-a-half hours. The entire process takes almost five days to complete. Panelists also receive materials that explain the purpose of the meeting, describe the tasks to be done, and define the terms used during the process prior to the achievement levels setting meeting.

Of all of the elements in the process, three are important for understanding the results. First, before the panelists do any rating of test items they are well trained about NAGB policy, the NAEP framework, the NAEP assessments, and the ALDs. The NAEP assessment is administered to them so they will have direct experience with the timing of the examination and the demands on the students. By the end of the process, the panelists know as much or more about the NAEP assessment as many of the people who work on developing it. This training provides a solid background for the rest of the process.

The second element is the rating process. Panelists begin the translation of policy to numerical scores on the NAEP scale by description of the knowledge and skills needed to be considered just above the lower boundary of the AL category. The knowledge and skills in the description must be a subset of those in the preliminary ALD. Once they reach consensus on the descriptions, the panelists begin the rating process. The rating process is slightly different for items that are scored correct or incorrect (0, 1) from those that are scored with a rating scale. For the former set of items, the panelists indicate the proportion of one hundred examinees who match the borderline descriptions who will answer each test question correctly. This activity requires an understanding of the borderline description and the relationship of the item being rated to the description.

For the items scored using a multipoint rating scale, the panelists specify the mean score for each item for one hundred examinees whose skills are described by the borderline description. Panelists are divided into two groups when they perform the ratings. Each group rates half of the items in the NAEP pool so that the accuracy of the standards can be estimated by comparing the standards from the two groups.[22] For both item types, the values specified by the panelists reflect the match of the items to the ALDs and the borderline descriptions that in turn are tied back to the policy definitions. The ratings typically are moderately related to the difficulty of the items, but the ratings do not have to be related to difficulty. The ALDs and borderline descriptions tell what students should know and be able to do while the difficulty of the item represents what the students can do. If the developers of the ALDs believe that students should improve in a specific area, the rating may be high even though the items are difficult for the examinee sample. The rating process is not a difficulty estimation process; it is a means of translating policy and ALDs onto a numerical scale.

The third important element is the process of refining the translation of the standards to the numerical score scale. The first round of ratings provides a starting point on the NAEP score scale for the rest of the process. After the first round, the panelists are told the location of the cutscores that they have set, and they are given additional information about the difficulty of the items, feedback on their performance of the process, and student booklets that match the standard set by their group. This information has two purposes. The first is to help the panelists improve their understanding of what they are doing. A number of different types of process feedback are provided for that purpose. The second purpose is to keep the panelists grounded in the realities of student capabilities. Saying that all students should be able to do everything is easy. The information about the difficulty of items and examples of student performance on NAEP test booklets helps panelists keep in touch with what can reasonably be expected of students. In later rounds of the process, the panelists are told the proportion of students who exceed each cutscore. Throughout the process, the focus is on helping the panelists understand what they are doing and informing them of the relationship between the results and student performance.

The first round of ratings is often characterized as being a modified Angoff rating process because the ratings of the items are similar to probabilities of correct response for borderline groups.[23] After the first round of ratings, panelists are provided with holistic feedback that gives them a broader context than the typical modified Angoff process. Panelists perform a fourth round of ratings by directly making changes to the cutscores on the NAEP score scales without considering individual items. With the gradual shift from item-by-item rating to holistic rating, continuing to characterize this process as modified Angoff seems improper.[24]

*The Results of the Standard Setting*

The ALS process translates policy to numerical score values on the NAEP score scale. Multiple steps are involved in the process. Policy definitions are mapped to content descriptions. The lower bound of the content related to each achievement level is defined, and the result is used to guide the rating of test items. Through four rounds of rating, the connection between policy, ALD, and the score scale is refined. The result is an estimate of a cutscore that indicates the borderlines between ALs on the NAEP score scale. Each of grades four, eight, and twelve has a cutscore for the lower borderline of Basic, Proficient, and Advanced. These cutscores with information about their reliability and the proportion of students above them are given to NAGB for final approval. The entire process is advisory to NAGB, which can accept, reject, or modify the standards. NAGB sets the standards through the initial policy and determines whether the numerical cutscores are consistent with its intentions.[25]

The ALS process yields four other products. The first is a refined and reviewed set of ALDs. Panelists are not allowed to revise the ALDs to any great extent, but they can make suggestions for rewordings and other minor improvements. These ALDs serve as verbal descriptions of the AL ranges on the NAEP score scale. The second product is a set of exemplar items. At the end of the ALS process, panelists select items from those that more than half of the students in an AL range answered correctly as examples of what the students can do. The number of exemplar items is limited because only a portion of the NAEP item pool is made public. The exemplar items provide a concrete representation of the skills and knowledge given in the ALDs.

The third product is an evaluation of the process. Panelists evaluate the functioning of the process at seven points. These evaluations usually show that the process is working well, but occasionally they point out areas that are in need of improvement.[26] At the end of the process, panelists are asked if they recommend the cutscores to NAGB as a representation of policy and the ALDs. About 90 percent of the panelists indicate that they would recommend that the results of the process be used by NAGB.[27]

The results of a series of validity studies are the fourth product of the ALS process. At NAGB's request, ACT Inc. performs studies to determine if the students who fall in the AL ranges can do the academic tasks suggested by the achievement level descriptions. These studies show that students estimated to be in the AL ranges answer items judged to match the ALDs 60 to 70 percent of the time. Also, teachers tend to classify their own students into higher ALs than they scored but evaluate the work of students from other teachers into lower ALs than they were placed by the NAEP score.[28] The studies also show that the ALs set by the panelists are precise (have small standard errors of estimation) and that panelists' ratings are moderately related to the difficulty of test items. Collectively, these studies support the conclusion that the cutscores set on the NAEP scale are reasonable and accurately reflect the intentions of the panelists.[29]

## The Interpretation of the Results

The interpretation of the ALs hinges on the strength of evidence for the accuracy of the translation of NAGB policy to cutscores on the NAEP score scale. If the translation was done properly, then it can be inferred that the students who are estimated to be in an AL category have demonstrated the characteristics described in the policy definitions. Further, these students have demonstrated at least a sampling of the knowledge and skills described in the ALDs. They also can answer at least half of the items that measure the knowledge and skills in the ALDs correctly. Validity evidence suggests that they can answer 60 to 70 percent correctly.[30]

The evidence that these interpretations are correct is predominantly procedural. NAGB, the panelists, and special independent content groups carefully review the connections between the policy definitions and ALDs.[31] The connection between policy definitions and content descriptions is uniformly judged to be strong. The connection between ALDs and borderline descriptions is carefully developed during the ALS process. This is one of the reasons that the process takes five days.[32] The connection among policy, ALDs, borderlines, and item ratings is refined over three rounds of ratings with multiple checks on consistency and reasonableness. Final adjustments are made directly on the score scale. The vast majority of panelists endorse the results and report that they understand the process and the wealth of information that was used to support the process. On procedural grounds, the entire process is tightly interwoven with strong connections between every component part. Each activity is carefully reviewed by the TACSS before implementation. The process is also documented in great detail in numerous ACT Inc. reports.

*The Context of the NAEP*

Assuming that the process works as designed, what can be said about the skills and knowledge possessed by students in each of the AL categories? For example, on the 1990 NAEP mathematics assessment, 2.8 percent of the twelfth-grade students demonstrated performance that was equivalent to the Advanced policy definition and the twelfth-grade Advanced ALD. Does that mean that only 2.8 percent of the twelfth-grade student population can do Advanced-level work as defined by NAGB?

The answer depends on the context under which the performance information is collected. NAEP collects data from a stratified random sample of target students. When twelfth-grade Advanced is considered, these students include not only those who are taking a full load of mathematics courses, but also those who only took one or two courses and then decided to take no more. The selected students take what has been called a drop-from-the-sky assessment. They have no preparation, and they receive no feedback on how well they performed on the test. Their teachers do not receive results, nor do any school staff. At most, the school might receive information about how the students from their state performed on the test.

Each student tested responds to a relatively small proportion of the items. Each student takes a set of items that requires about an hour to complete. The results from each student's responses are combined using statistical procedures to estimate how well the entire population of students would do if they had taken all of the questions. The 2.8 percent of twelfth-grade students above Advanced for NAEP mathematics is the statistical estimate of the proportion of students who would demonstrate performance above the Advanced cutscore if they took the entire set of NAEP mathematics items.

*Student Motivation*

Student motivation to do well has been a continuing concern for NAEP because of the drop-from-the-sky nature of the assessment and the lack of any personal consequences related to the performance. At a meeting several years ago, Eugene Johnson and I developed a hypothetical motivation scale called the Tiger Scale.[33] This scale was never used in practice, but, if it were, students would be asked to go from one end of a football field to another. Motivation would be measured by how long it took them to make the trip. The following phrases describe different rates of movement.

1. The slow meander, possibly with a rest on the grass along the way. Crossing the football field might take hours.

2. Directed walk. Walking at a normal pace from one end to the other.

3. Fast walk. Trying to get from one end to the other quickly.

4. Jog. Slow run.

5. Run. Run, but not to obtain best time.

6. Fast run. Try to get personal best.

7. Run to catch a plane or train. Run as fast as possible because missing the plane means staying the night in the airport.

8. Running to save your life. A tiger is chasing you and safety is at the other end of the field.

After developing this scale, I asked Eugene Johnson to identify the levels (rates of movement) that corresponded to NAEP performance. He estimated that NAEP performance motivation varied by student at levels 1, 2, or maybe 3. In comparison, we judged performance on the American College Test (ACT) or Scholastic Assessment Test (SAT) college admissions tests to be at the 5, 6, or 7 level. These differences in motivation would most likely show up on the items that demand the most mental effort, especially open-ended items that require extended responses.

If this analysis of student motivation to perform on NAEP is accurate, then motivational level must be taken into account when interpreting NAEP results. The 2.8 percent Advanced students on 1990 NAEP mathematics means that 2.8 percent of students exhibited Advanced performance when they were not trying hard. Most likely a higher proportion would be above the Advanced cutscore if they put in the effort that they do to prepare for the SAT and ACT. The most direct implication is that the percentages above the cutscores are lower bounds on the level of performance that could be exhibited if a reason existed to try harder. This could explain why teachers tend to classify their own students into higher ALs than NAEP test scores do. The teachers know how well the students can perform if they are motivated to do well.

Another factor that enters into the interpretation of the NAEP results is the match between the content of the NAEP assessment and the curriculum at the state and local level. The NAEP assessment indicates how well students perform on the material within the NAEP framework. If that framework matches the curriculum in a school, NAEP indicates the skills and knowledge that students have learned. If significant mismatch exists between the framework and the curriculum, the NAEP results reflect that students have not learned what they have not been taught. This does not mean that students could not learn the material, but that they have not been exposed to it. Low proportions above an AL cutscore could mean that the material in the framework is not included in the curriculum.

The two factors of motivation and curriculum match suggest that a careful interpretation of NAEP results is required. A proper interpretation of the 1990 NAEP mathematics results would be that 2.8 percent of the sample of students in twelfth grade at that time demonstrated Advanced performance without trying hard on the content that may or may not have matched their local curriculum. Further, a large proportion of the students may not have been taking a mathematics course at the time the test was administered. While 2.8 percent does not seem like a high proportion under normal school conditions, it seems high if it were equivalent to the percent of people who could run one hundred yards in less than ten seconds without trying hard and with little prior training.

### The Criticisms of the Achievement Levels

The ALs and the supporting reporting have been criticized as being inaccurate by a number of evaluation teams over the years. These criticisms are summarized in the National Research Council book *Grading the Nation's Report Card.*[34] The criticisms are of five basic types.

1. The standards are set too high. More students exhibit the skills and knowledge in the frameworks than shown by the percentages above the achievement level cutscores.

2. Sufficient evidence has not been provided that students in the AL ranges can do the things listed in the ALDs. Inconsistencies exist among the policy definitions, ALDs, and exemplar items.

3. Evidence shows that the process does not work well. Open-ended items result in higher standards than multiple-choice items, and easy items result in different standards than hard items. Further, panelists cannot accurately estimate item difficulty.

4. The process must be flawed because NAGB chose to modify the recommendations for cutscores that came from the process.

5. Estimating the performance of one hundred hypothetical students at a borderline is too cognitively complex for panelists to do well. The results of a process that requires panelists to do such a task must result in questionable results.

These criticisms stem from several observations. First, small percentages of students are estimated to be above the Advanced level at all grades and in all subjects. These percentages range from about 5 to near 0 depending on grade and content area. These small proportions seem to be counter to experience and the results of other testing programs such as Advanced Placement, ACT, and SAT.[35] Also, teachers classify their own students into higher ALs than those indicated by the NAEP results. Further, the percentage below Basic tends to be fairly large, suggesting that the educational system is not functioning well. This result is counter to data on international comparisons in reading and for some grade levels in science and mathematics.

Second, a consistent finding from the ALS process is that panelists' ratings of open-ended items result in higher cutscores than those from multiple-choice items.[36] Some argue that the different item types should not result in different cutscores. That they do is cited as evidence for a flaw in the standard setting methodology. This argument is further supported by the relatively low correlations between panelists' ratings of items and item difficulty, suggesting that panelists do not understand the way that items function.

Third, the exemplar items do not represent challenging items. The students do not do well on some of the items within an AL and do very well on others. The exemplars are used to suggest that the match between NAEP and the ALDs is not good and that NAEP does not include items that stimulate advanced work. The argument is that Advanced performance is not demonstrated because Advanced items are not included in the test. Finally, some critics say that answering correctly 50 to 60 percent of the items at an AL does not indicate that students can do the work.

## Reactions to the Criticisms

The results reported for NAEP using the ALs are reasonable given the level of motivation of the students and the match between the test content and the curriculum. The results show that many students do not do Advanced-level work when they do not try hard and many students do not reach the Basic level under the same circumstances. Advanced, Proficient, and Basic work is defined by the subset of content in the framework that is covered by the NAEP tests.

The controversy over NAEP interpretations is caused by the desire to make statements about student performance from NAEP that are not supported by the data. The desired interpretation has to do with ability to compete in an international intellectual marketplace. Consumers of NAEP results want to know if students are ready for challenging work in college or on the job. Unfortunately, NAEP is not designed to answer that question. To answer it, the motivational level of the students would have to be increased by making the program high stakes and the focus of the tests different. Many do not want to make such changes because the long-term trend comparisons would not make sense if the context of the NAEP test were altered. The result is a continuing tension between what some want to say from NAEP results and what is supported by the standard setting process and the data. Reactions to specific criticisms are as follows:

1. The standards are set too high. The major evidence for this conclusion is that many students do well on the Advanced Placement and college admission tests, and teachers rate their own students higher than the NAEP results would indicate. The comparison of NAEP results with those from other tests is questionable because students do not prepare for NAEP and are highly motivated to prepare for the other tests. Advanced Placement has an entire course that is focused on the test content, and students take the test immediately following the course. College admission tests have a variety of test preparation activities, and students are highly motivated to do well on the tests. Their future careers depend on it. Those tests have motivational level 7 on the Tiger Scale.

In addition, NAEP measures different parts of the curriculum than the other tests. The SAT is not closely tied to the curriculum, and the ACT is focused on the curriculum for college-bound students. The Advanced Placement program defines its own curriculum. NAEP tries to match the common denominator of the educational programs in all states. Because of these differences in content focus, direct comparisons of the test results cannot be made. Rough comparisons of results could be offered if carefully conducted concordance studies were done to determine comparable points on the score scales for the different testing programs. To my knowledge, such studies have not been undertaken.

ACT Inc. has performed a number of studies to investigate the match between teacher ratings of student performance and NAEP results. The usual finding is that teachers rate their own students higher than the NAEP classifications of the same students, but teachers rate the papers of students from other teachers lower than the NAEP results for those students. These results seem to indicate that teachers use other information than NAEP-type performance when rating their own students. They may know how well their students can perform when motivated. It may be possible that the students' classroom work is different from that demonstrated on NAEP. Students have been known to produce pictures using the dots on the answer sheet when the test does not count instead of putting in a solid effort.

The information from all of these sources suggests that students can perform better than they do on NAEP. That does not mean that the NAEP results are inaccurate or invalid. It only means that the NAEP results have to be interpreted within the realities of the way that the testing program is administered.

2. There is not sufficient evidence for validity. Validity is a continuing process. Current thinking on validity places the emphasis on supporting the accuracy of inferences that are made from available information.[37] In the case of NAEP and the ALs, users would like to make an unlimited number of inferences, and gaining information to support all of them is impossible. Someone who wants to make an inference is responsible for collecting the data to support it.

The main inference of the ALs is that students in an AL range have the skills and knowledge listed in the ALDs. Because of the lack of student-level scores for NAEP, directly checking the validity of this inference cannot be done. Data from ACT Inc. studies have shown that students in an AL range answer 60 to 70 percent of the items that are judged to measure the skills in the ALDs correctly. These results give some evidence that the desired inferences are supported. One might question whether 60 to 70 percent is high enough to indicate that students can do the required work. Olympic high jumpers have to clear the bar only one-third of the time to say they can do the jump, but pilots are expected to land a plane every time before they are deemed capable of the task. The criteria for "can do" for students have been debated without resolution since the first ALs were set.

3. Ratings of different types of items yield different standards, thus indicating that the process does not work properly. The standard setting process does not require that open-ended and multiple-choice items yield the same standard. The process only requires that the panelists translate the ALDs into ratings of items. The difference in standards for the different sets of items likely indicates a difference in student familiarity with the different item types and the greater effort required to respond to open-ended items. Instead of indicating a flaw in the procedure, the differences in standards for different item types are an interesting research finding in their own right.

Better feedback procedures have reduced these differences somewhat, but they do not disappear even when panelists are asked to attend to the differences. The cognitive requirements of the different item types and the match to the ALDs may legitimately require differences in standards for the item types. The explanation for this phenomenon is still unknown, but it is a stable result over different content areas and does not seem to be an artifact of the standard setting procedure.

4. NAGB modified the standards so they must be flawed. NAGB sets the standards. The panelists and the entire process are advisory to NAGB. The board weighs all of the results and determines the best course of action. NAGB decided to lower some of the cutscores for the 1996 NAEP science ALs after reviewing preliminary results from the Third International Mathematics and Science Study (TIMSS). This was well within their charge. Standard setting is a judgmental process, and the board judged that the lower cutscores were more consistent with its policy statement than those recommended by the panelists. This does not mean that the process is flawed. It only means that NAGB took information into account that was not available to the panelists and used its judgment to set the standard using all of the information available.

5. The process is too cognitively complex to give meaningful results. Teachers, nonteacher educators, and members of the general public do cognitively complex tasks every day. However, cognitive complexity does not bear on whether or not the tasks can be done. The cognitive complexity does bear on how much training and background are needed to do the task. The ALD panelists were selected because of their experience with the educational system and the student population as well as their content expertise. They have the background to do the task. They were also given extensive training in every aspect of the process. Their background and training led to their own confident appraisal that they did do the required tasks well. There is no solid evidence that this was not the case.

### Conclusion

The ALS process is the most carefully developed, thoroughly researched, and frequently evaluated standard setting process that has been conducted to date. Every aspect has been given careful scrutiny. Some of the early criticisms of the process were well founded. The process has been refined to address some of the issues that have been raised by critics. The current process provides well-supported translations of NAGB policy into cutscores on the NAEP score scale. No other standard setting meets the standards of quality exhibited by the NAGB process. I enthusiastically support the results of the process.

Many challenges have been made to the interpretation of the results of NAEP and the ALS process. Because of the nature of NAEP, it does not support the kinds of inferences that some seem to want to make. NAEP is not a high-stakes testing program. It cannot tell how students will perform when they are highly motivated and well prepared for the task at hand. At best, it tells how students perform when they are not trying hard on material that may not match the course work they are taking. It is a general indicator of performance, not a focused indicator of the highest possible level of performance. A parallel from everyday life may clarify the situation. My average driving speed around town is much slower than the highest rate of speed I can safely drive on a well-constructed highway. NAEP gives equivalent academic performance to the driving around town speed. Some people want to know the equivalent to the highest safe rate of speed. The NAEP testing program was not designed for that purpose, and inferences of that type cannot be supported.

NAEP and the ALS process provide accurate results given their context. The challenge is for users to understand the context and not make more of the information than can be supported by the structure of the testing program.

---

## Comment by Michael J. Feuer

Mark D. Reckase offers an important contribution to the literature of academic standards setting, and he and his colleagues should be commended for their fine work in this field going back at least a decade. Setting reliable and valid standards in large-scale assessments is a critical activity, especially in an age of increasing reliance on such assessments for important public policy decisions affecting millions of children and the schools they attend. Although the method used to set standards for the National Assessment of Educational Progress (NAEP) can be challenged for a number of reasons, the work of Reckase and his colleagues has significantly advanced understanding of both the problems and the opportunities for standards setting not only in NAEP but also in testing more generally. In a 1999 National Research Council (NRC) report summarizing a three-year congressionally mandated evaluation of NAEP, the study committee working under the aegis of the Board on Testing and Assessment identified a number of constraints on the validity of the modified Angoff method for NAEP.[38] Although Reckase argues that they are not sufficient to undermine the whole enterprise, the committee was considerably less sanguine. One problem is the so-called method variance—the finding that judges involved in the Angoff process have generally been unable to maintain a consistent view of borderline performance for each of the levels and that significant discrepancies are found between the cut points for dichotomous (right or wrong) items and extended-response items. To the extent that identifying cut score locations is a main purpose of the standards setting activity, method variance that renders the cut scores dependent on the mix of item types in the assessment can exacerbate an already complex process and undermine the credibility of the results. This is just one example of the overwhelming cognitive complexity of the Angoff approach, which the NRC committee highlighted as one of its most fundamental shortcomings. In the committee's words, "[Requiring] raters to delineate the ways the student could answer the item, relate these to cognitive processes that students may or may not possess, and operationally link[ing] these processes with the categorization of performance at three different levels . . . represents a nearly impossible cognitive task."[39] Adding method variance to this problem only worsens matters.

Another issue that concerned the NRC committee (and other evaluators) is the observed discrepancy between student performance on NAEP—specifically, the distribution of students in the various intervals of performance—and estimates of achievement derived from other large-scale testing programs.[40] According to NAEP, for example, only 2.8 percent of twelfth graders score in the advanced category of performance. But how can this finding be squared with the 18 percent of students taking the Scholastic Assessment Test (SAT) who score at or above 600, a level considered to be roughly comparable with NAEP's advanced level? One answer, which Reckase offers, is that the SAT is taken by a self-selected group while NAEP more thoroughly samples from the whole student population. However, if none of the seniors who did not take the SAT would have scored above 600, almost 8 percent of all high graduates would have scored above 600; that is, more than three times the number estimated by NAEP to be ready for rigorous college-level work.[41] That different testing programs yield different aggregate estimates of performance does not necessarily invalidate any of them. But the credibility and validity of the interpretations that emerge from the NAEP are at risk when such discrepancies are so large, when they go unexplained, and when the results become the basis for broad policy pronouncements about the failure of the system to educate large proportions of the student population.

These and other issues warrant continued attention on the part of methodologists and policymakers seeking improved techniques for setting standards. But the policy context for this activity must be kept in focus. NAEP standards are, by law, determined by the National Assessment Governing Board (NAGB), which is essentially a political rather than a scientific body. NAGB has, over the years, correctly understood its mandate (vis-à-vis the achievement levels) as a politically judgmental one instead of a strictly scientific one. (Few NAGB members have sufficient formal training or expertise in measurement, statistics, or the methodological apparatus of standards setting to engage in any of the mathematical discussions that often erupt.) Hence, when NAGB in 1996 reviewed the results of the achievement level setting process for the science assessment and changed the distributions of students in the various categories, it was exercising its public mandate and rendering its judgment in spite of the technical results. In other words, NAGB was implicitly conceding that flaws must have existed in the way the judges identified cut scores and categorized student performance; and it saw its role as the arbiter of these results on behalf of a broad and diverse American public.

Analysts of NAEP standard setting, therefore, face more than statistical and cognitive problems, which are formidable. They need to include in their design requirements for improved methodologies explicit consideration for the overarching political and policy context in which the standards reside. Achieving a sophisticated understanding of the complex relations between science and policy is always difficult and is no less so with respect to NAEP, NAGB, and the achievement levels. Given the salience of this issue in the current debates over school reform, Reckase and his colleagues should be commended for their thorough work and for their tenacious efforts to advance the cause of improved standard setting methodologies. That their work is not over is abundantly clear, and one can only hope that continued attention to these issues will lead to continuous improvement (in American education as well as in educational testing).

---

## Comment by Edward H. Haertel

Mark D. Reckase has been closely involved in the achievement level setting (ALS) process that ACT Inc. has carried out under contract for the National Assessment Governing Board (NAGB). In his paper, he offers an overview of that process and argues that both the process and the resulting standards are sound. He then discusses interpretation of standards-based National Assessment of Educational Progress (NAEP) reports in the light of motivational context and test-curriculum match. Next, Reckase summarizes criticisms of the standards, suggests reasons for those criticisms, and offers a rebuttal. He concludes that the process is "the most carefully developed, thoroughly researched, and frequently evaluated standard setting process that has been conducted to date."

Reckase makes a number of important points, and he and I are probably in agreement on most of them. I certainly agree that standard setting is judgmental—there is no right answer waiting to be discovered. I agree that the National Assessment Governing Board is vested with the authority to establish achievement levels and that the levels are captured in NAGB's policy definitions and achievement level descriptions (ALDs). It follows that the work of the panels convened by ACT Inc. should be viewed as essentially technical. Panelists provide information used in determining points on NAEP proficiency scales that capture the policies and meanings intended by the board. Reckase might be surprised to hear me say that I think, given the history of the process and the constraints under which it is implemented, that ACT Inc. is probably doing about the best job that anyone could do. We are also in agreement that some criticisms of the achievement levels are beside the point. All that said, however, I remain among those in the field who still see fundamental flaws in the achievement level process, despite the extensive research conducted and refinements made since the first efforts of a decade ago.

## Procedural versus Substantive Aspects of Standards Validation

As Reckase acknowledges, the evidence for the soundness of the achievement levels and the interpretations they support "is predominantly procedural. . . . On procedural grounds, the entire process is tightly interwoven with strong connections between every component part." At least three other experts in the field, Michael Kane, Ronald K. Hambleton, and Gregory J. Cizek, have also argued that because standard setting is inherently judgmental, procedural validity, or the "due process" aspect of the standard-setting process, is essentially sufficient to justify the resulting standards. [42] (Psychometricians working on these problems probably number in the dozens, not the hundreds, and it is perhaps not surprising that Kane, Hambleton, and Cizek all have been involved, in one way or another, with the NAGB and ACT Inc. achievement level setting process.)

There is an alternative view, however. An explicit goal of the NAEP achievement levels is to enhance the meaningfulness of score reports. Summaries of group performance in terms of achievement levels support score-based inferences that are not possible without the achievement levels. Suppose these summaries were limited to statements such as, "NAGB believes that, in 1998, X percent of fourth graders performed as well as ought to be expected on the National Assessment in Civics."In that case, the procedural validity claim would probably suffice. But standards-based reports of NAEP performance convey substantive interpretations as well. Saying that, in 1998, X percent of fourth graders could "explain ways groups in schools and communities can manage conflict peacefully"is a claim about the state of the world that may in principle be either true or false. For that reason, I and others with serious concerns about the achievement levels see a need for an additional kind of validity evidence. Despite consensus that no one right answer can be found in standard setting, achievement level descriptions nonetheless do have a substantive component. It is a matter of judgment how Proficient should be defined, but once that definition is established, it becomes a question of fact whether students classified as Proficient by and large possess the capabilities enumerated in the definition.

## Areas of Agreement

I concur with Reckase that some of the criticisms leveled at the NAGB achievement levels are simply beside the point and that other criticisms have been obviated by changes and improvements made since the first preliminary achievement level setting efforts in 1990 and the first ACT Inc. efforts in 1992.

One such criticism concerns the alignment of the NAEP frameworks with state and local curricula or with classroom instruction. Alignment requirements differ according to intended test use. If individual students are to be held accountable, then they should be tested only on material they have had an opportunity to learn. But if the purpose is to measure achievement of the knowledge and skills set forth in the NAEP frameworks, then the test should match the frameworks, regardless of what is taught.

Another criticism that may be off the mark is that the standards are set too high. In NAGB's judgment, the Proficient achievement levels represent ambitious but reasonable goals. No one is compelled to hold the same aspirations, but neither can anyone else assert that this judgmental aspect of the policy definitions and ALDs is incorrect. At the same time, if an ALD for the twelfth-grade advanced level refers to attributes such as "readiness for rigorous college courses,"then people are entitled to ask whether the proportion of college freshmen succeeding in rigorous college courses roughly corresponds to the proportion of high school seniors designated advanced. If independent evidence suggests that these proportions differ substantially, then the cut score defining the twelfth-grade advanced level is called into question.

Reckase also argues that the percentages of students at each level should be interpreted in the light of the motivational context of the NAEP administration. This is entirely reasonable, but I do not believe that NAGB has done all that it could to encourage appropriately cautious interpretation. For example, the achievement level descriptions for writing explicitly state that they pertain to on-demand, timed writing to an unfamiliar prompt, but for most other content areas such caveats are lacking. If the context and limitations of the national assessments were made more salient, complaints that the levels are too high might subside. Reckase also used his motivational argument to help explain the low percentage of twelfth-grade students at the advanced level in mathematics. However, motivation is generally expected to be a more serious problem with twelfth-grade students than with younger students, yet the proportions classified as advanced are similar at grades four, eight, and twelve. It appears, therefore, that low motivation cannot be the whole story.

Much has also been made of the fact that judgments about open-ended versus multiple-choice items, or about easy versus hard items, imply different cut scores. The naive version of criticism reflects a misconception about the standard-setting process. Items in different formats or at different difficulty levels are generally testing different elements of knowledge and skill. The proportions of students who have attained proficiency may differ from one such element to another. If that is the case, then panelists´ judgments ought to reflect those differences. The different cut scores entailed by judgments of different item types need not imply any defect in panelists´ judgments or in the procedures they are asked to follow. However, there is still a problem. If item type one implies cut score one and item type two implies some higher cut score two, then someone needs to think hard about the status of examinees scoring above cut score one and below cut score two. These examinees are proficient with respect to some parts of the framework and not others. The current NAGB and ACT Inc. process finesses this problem by locating the performance standard somewhere between cut score one and cut score two. Exactly where depends, in some ill-specified way, on the proportions of items of types one versus two and the statistical properties of those items. So far as I know, NAGB has yet to take up the policy question of how examinees exhibiting such uneven performance should be classified. In the absence of a clearer policy, there is no basis for refining the achievement level setting process. For now, ACT Inc. is doing the best that can be done, but with clearer policy guidance from NAGB, the process might be improved.

Finally, the NAGB and ACT Inc. process has been criticized on the grounds that NAGB has sometimes modified the standards recommended by standard-setting panels. Reckase offers a benign account of one such modification, reporting that "NAGB decided to lower some of the cutscores for the 1996 NAEP science ALs [achievement levels] after reviewing preliminary results from the Third International Mathematics and Science Study (TIMSS). This was well within their charge."I concur with Reckase that "NAGB [may take] information into account that was not available to panelists and [use] its judgment to set the standard using all the information available."In this case, however, NAGB modified seven of the nine achievement levels set for science in 1996, moving some up and others down, not just because of TIMSS, but also because the overall pattern of cut scores across grade levels defied common sense. Moreover, the panelists who engaged in that standard-setting effort reported markedly lower levels of confidence and satisfaction than had panelists in earlier level setting processes. After NAGB modified the science levels, in response to criticism that it had thereby invalidated the warrant for the achievement level descriptions, another panel was convened to rewrite the descriptions to match the new standards. In another case, following the 1992 standard setting in reading and mathematics, NAGB was criticized not just because it chose to adjust the mathematics levels downward by one standard error, but also because that adjustment was applied after the fact, in mathematics but not in reading. As shown by these cases, even if NAGB is acting well within its charge when it modifies ALS recommendations, there is a risk that, in so doing, NAGB may jeopardize even claims of procedural validity.

## Areas of Disagreement

Reckase states, "The main inference of the ALs is that students in an AL range have the skills and knowledge listed in the ALDs."He goes on to say that because NAEP does not provide student-level scores, this inference cannot be tested directly, but that "Data from ACT Inc. studies have shown that students in an AL range answer 60 to 70 percent of the items that are judged to measure the skills in the ALDs correctly."I am at something of a disadvantage here, because I am not sure exactly what studies are referred to. The only

ACT Inc. study I know of in which items were classified according to the match of their content to the knowledge and skills listed in the ALDs was done in 1999 using data from the 1998 assessment in civics. In that study, the average difficulty of items classified as Below Basic, Basic, Proficient, and Advanced did show the expected increasing pattern, and students in each achievement level range answered over half the corresponding items correctly. However, there was substantial variability within each set of items. For various items classified as Proficient, for example, the probabilities of correct responses by Proficient students ranged from about 5 percent to about 95 percent. In other words, focusing just on the items that appeared to measure what the ALDs said Proficient students could do, some turned out to be trivially easy for these students and others were extremely difficult. Independent studies along the same lines, conducted about five years ago by the NAEP Validity Studies Panel convened by the Center for Research on Evaluation, Standards, and Student Testing, found similar disparities. The commonsense interpretation of the standards holds that if an achievement level description says that Proficient students can do such and such a thing, and if an item clearly appears to require doing that thing, then students in the Proficient score range should have a decent chance of getting that item right. The evidence I have seen indicates that depending on the item, this may or may not be so.

Reckase also observes that people do cognitively complex things all the time, and that is certainly true. I cannot speak for everyone who has claimed that the Angoff task was impossibly complex, but I would like to try to explain what I mean by that criticism.

In carrying out the core judgmental process that defines the Angoff procedure, panelists are asked to imagine a hypothetical group of minimally competent examinees, inspect a test item, infer the knowledge and skills required to answer that test item correctly, compare those skill requirements to the skill profile of the hypothetical borderline examinees, and state the proportion of such examinees who would answer the item correctly. They may or may not be expected to take guessing into account. I believe that, in the ACT Inc. standard-setting process, panelists merely estimate the proportion "able to solve"the item and some adjustment is then applied to correct for the possibility of guessing on selected-response items.

That no human being, in principle, could ever learn to estimate such conditional probabilities accurately is a strong claim. My analysis in support of that claim is specific to contexts such as NAEP, in which Angoff judgments are made as part of a translation process, mapping the policy judgment embodied in an ALD onto a score scale. A different analysis would be required if the Angoff task were used as originally intended—to capture panelistsí value judgments without reference to anything more than a very sketchy prior definition.

The essence of my argument is that the hypothetical borderline examinees not only do not exist, but also do not even resemble any real-world examinees. They possess the set of skills in the borderline description derived from the ALD. They are perfectly marginal in all respects. If such examinees were found at any point along the trajectory of typical student development, then a point on the NAEP proficiency scale would correspond to their performance. The fact that, empirically, different elements of borderline performance map onto different points along the NAEP scale necessarily implies that no one point on the proficiency scale represents the border between categories. Moreover, the fact that the hypothetical borderline examinee does not possess any pattern of proficiencies found in the real world implies that panelistsí experience with real students, however extensive, cannot suffice to inform their judgments. Panelists are told about imaginary students who can and cannot do some mix of things unlike any real student, then they are asked the likelihood that these imaginary students could do still other things not even referred to in the achievement level descriptions. Estimating conditional probabilities is difficult enough when one has good data. In this case, I believe it is impossible.

## Conclusion

If the search for a better method means the search for some method that will give more defensible cut scores on the NAEP proficiency scale, with no other changes in the procedures for developing achievement level descriptions, the claims made for the meaning of the standards, or the methods of standards-based reporting, then I believe that search is probably futile. Substituting some similar judgmental method for the Angoff procedure would not address the fundamental problem posed by borderline achievement level descriptions that characterize students unlike any in the real world. More promising standard-setting approaches either would rely on empirical studies to project meaningful, real-world task performances onto the NAEP scale or would use achievement level descriptions based directly on the empirically determined locations of items on the NAEP proficiency scales. Either of these approaches would result in achievement level definitions that were much more strongly informed by empirical data concerning studentsí typical patterns of knowledge and skill acquisition. Borderline examinees would resemble real students, and borderline performance would correspond to a point or a narrow region on the NAEP proficiency scale. To assert that ALDs need to be better grounded in reality is not to imply that standards should be lowered. With ALDs better informed by real patterns of skill acquisition, and with clearer policy direction concerning students who do not fit neatly within a level, better substantive as well as procedural arguments could be made for the validity of standards-based score interpretations.

## Notes

1. ACT Inc. has performed standard setting processes for the National Assessment Governing Board (NAGB) in eight content domains. The process has evolved over nine years of work. These remarks refer specifically to the standard setting process for 1998 National Assessment of Educational Progress (NAEP) in civics and writing. A summary description of the process is given in ACT Inc., *Developing Achievement Levels on the 1998 NAEP in Civics and Writing: Design Document* (Iowa City, Iowa: ACT Inc., 1997).

2. A complete list of references to research on the process is too extensive to include here. NAGB has compiled an extensive bibliography of publications that summarizes this work. At last count it included 101 references, not including ACT Inc. reports of the achievement levels setting (ALS) process.

3. ACT Inc. has formed an external Technical Advisory Committee for Standard Setting consisting of eleven experts on standards setting and an internal Technical Advisory Team. These two groups provide guidance to the project on technical matters.

4. A summary of the technical work on the ALS process is given in Mark D. Reckase, *The Evolution of the NAEP Achievement Levels Setting Process: A Summary of the Research and Development Efforts Conducted by ACT* (Iowa City, Iowa: ACT Inc., 2000).

5. The selection process for panelists is given in detail in the design documents for the process. A recent example is ACT Inc., *Developing Achievement Levels on the 1998 NAEP in Civics and Writing.*

6. The reactions of panelists to the results of the ALS process are summarized in final reports of the studies. A recent example is ACT Inc., *Setting Achievement Levels on the 1996 National Assessment of Educational Progress in Science.* Final report, volume III: *Achievement Levels Setting Study* (Iowa City, Iowa: ACT Inc., 1997).

7. J. W. Pellegrino, L. R. Jones, and K. J. Mitchell, eds., *Grading the Nation's Report Card: Evaluating NAEP and Transforming the Assessment of Educational Progress* (Washington: National Academy Press, 1999), p. 182.

8. For example, see National Center for Education Statistics, *NAEP 1994 U.S. History: A First Look; Findings from the National Assessment of Educational Progress* (Department of Education, 1995).

9. L. A. Shepard, "Setting Performance Standards." in R. A. Berk, ed., *A Guide to Criterion-Referenced Test Construction* (Johns Hopkins University Press, 1984), p. 174.

10. Improving America's Schools Act (P.L. 103–328).

11. National Assessment Governing Board, *Setting Appropriate Achievement Levels for the National Assessment of Educational Progress: Policy Framework and Technical Procedures* (Washington, May 1990).

12. National Center for Education Statistics, *NAEP 1994 U.S. History.*

13. NAEP assesses performance in other areas of study such as the arts, but ALs have not been developed for these areas.

14. National Assessment Governing Board, *Civics Framework for the 1998 National Assessment of Educational Progress* (Department of Education, 1998).

15. National Assessment Governing Board, *Civics Framework for the 1998 National Assessment of Educational Progress,* p. 18.

16. National Assessment Governing Board, *Civics Framework for the 1998 National Assessment of Educational Progress,* p. 43.

17. NAEP does not have a test form as such. There are many different booklets composed of blocks of items. Each student takes a number of blocks of items, but no student takes more than a small fraction of the total. The booklets share some blocks in a regular pattern. From the pattern of overlap, performance of the full set of students on the full set of items can be estimated.

18. National Assessment Governing Board, *Setting Appropriate Achievement Levels for the National Assessment of Educational Progress.*

19. American College Testing, *Design Document for Setting Achievement Levels on the 1992 National Assessment of Educational Progress in Mathematics, Reading, and Writing* (Iowa City, Iowa, January 1992).

20. A full description of the characteristics of the panelists is given in the ACT Inc. report of the ALS studies for a NAEP content domain. The report for 1998 NAEP civics was in preparation at the time this article was written.

21. For example, see ACT Inc., *Setting Achievement Levels on the 1996 National Assessment of Educational Progress in Science.*

22. The sets of items rated by the two groups have a small number of items in common. This allows direct comparison of ratings on those items.

23. W. H. Angoff, "Scales, Norms, and Equivalent Scores," in R. L. Thorndike, ed., *Educational Measurement,* 2d ed. (Washington: American Council of Education, 1971).

24. A more extensive presentation of this argument is given in Mark D. Reckase, "The ACT/NAGB Standard Setting Process: How 'Modified' Does It Have to Be before It Is No Longer a Modified-Angoff Process?" paper presented at the annual meeting of the National Council on Measurement in Education, New Orleans, La., April 2000.

25. NAGB accepted most of the cutscores from the process without change. However, the mathematics and science cutscores were adjusted somewhat and cutscores from the first writing ALS were not approved because of concerns about their technical quality.

26. The eighth-grade panelists for the 1996 NAEP science ALS were reconvened partially because of their evaluations of the part of the process. For details of the evaluations, see ACT Inc., *Setting Achievement Levels on the 1996 National Assessment of Educational Progress in Science.*

27. For the 1998 NAEP civics ALS, 88.5 percent of the panelists indicated that they would definitely (63 percent) or probably (25 percent) recommend the use of the standards.

28. Validity studies cannot be performed directly with NAEP data because no student level scores are reported. Special lengthened forms to NAEP are used for these studies so reliable estimates of student performance can be obtained.

29. NAGB has produced a bibliography of reports of research on the ALS process. It contains more than one hundred entries and continues to grow. This paper cannot summarize the full scope of this work. For a more complete summary, see Reckase, *The Evolution of the NAEP Achievement Level Setting Process.*

30. See Reckase, *The Evolution of the NAEP Achievement Level Setting Process,* pp. 46–49.

31. P. L. Hanick and S. C. Loomis, "Setting Standards for the 1998 NAEP in Civics and Writing: Using Focus Groups to Finalize the Achievement Levels Descriptions," paper presented at the annual meeting of the National Council on Measurement in Education, Montreal, Canada, April 1999.

32. The current process allocates approximately ten hours to understanding the ALDs and producing borderline descriptions.

33. The development of the scale was stimulated by discussions at a workshop hosted by the National Research Council Committee on the Evaluation of National and State Assessments of Educational Progress. The meeting took place during May 1997. At that time, Eugene Johnson was responsible for psychometric analyses for NAEP and had detailed information about performance on NAEP.

34. Pellegrino, Jones, and Mitchell, *Grading the Nation's Report Card,* chapter 5.

35. Direct comparisons cannot be made between these tests because they do not use the same score scales and they are not parallel forms. Critics define their own standard on the tests and argue that the differences in percent above the standard indicate flaws in the ALS. These interpretations are themselves flawed, and they are not supported by sound technical studies.

36. This has been a consistent finding for many NAEP content areas. For example, see L. Bay, "Comparing Student Performance on Different Items Relative to Achievement Level Cutpoints," paper presented at the annual meeting of the National Council of Measurement in Education, San Diego, Calif., April 1998.

37. S. Messick, "Validity," in R. L. Linn, ed., *Educational Measurement,* 3d ed. (New York: American Council on Education and Macmillan, 1989).

38. I relied heavily in this comment on the findings in Pellegrino, Jones, and Mitchell, *Grading the Nation's Report Card: Evaluating NAEP and Transforming the Assessment of Educational Progress.* Though I was involved in the management of the study, I was not one of its authors. My comments do not necessarily reflect the position of the council or the board. See also James Pellegrino, Lauress Wise, and Nambury Raju, "Guest Editors' Note," *Applied Measurement in Education,* vol. 11, no. 1 (1998), pp. 1–7; and Robert Linn, "Validating Inferences from National Assessment of Educational Progress Achievement-Level Reporting," *Applied Measurement in Education,* vol. 11, no. 1 (1998), pp. 23–48.

39. Pellegrino, Jones, and Mitchell, *Grading the Nation's Report Card,* p. 166.

40. See, for example, Robert Linn and others, *The Validity and Credibility of the Achievement Levels for the National Assessment of Educational Progress in Mathematics* (University of California at Los Angeles, Center for the Study of Evaluation, 1991); Daniel Stufflebeam, Richard M. Jaeger, and Michael Sriven, *Summative Evaluation of the National Assessment Governing Board's Inaugural 1990–91 Effort to Set Achievement Levels on the National Assessment of Educational Progress* (Washington: National Assessment Governing Board, 1991); Robert Glaser, Robert Linn, and George Bohrnstedt, eds., *Assessing Student Achievement in the States* (Stanford, Calif.: National Academcy of Education, 1992); Robert Glaser, Robert Linn, and George Bohrnstedt, eds., *Setting Performance Standards for Student Achievement* (Stanford, Calif.: National Academcy of Education, 1993); Robert Glaser, Robert Linn, and George Bohrnstedt, eds., *The Trial State Assessment: Prospects and Realities* (Stanford, Calif.: National Academcy of Education, 1993); Robert Glaser, Robert Linn, and George Bohrnstedt, eds., *Quality and Utility: The 1994 Trial State Assessment in Reading* (Stanford, Calif.: National Academcy of Education, 1996); and General Accounting Office, *Educational Achievement Standards: NAGB's Approach Yields Misleading Interpretations,* GAO/PEMD–93–12 (1993).

41. Lorrie Shepard, "Evaluating Test Validity," *Review of Research in Education,* vol. 19 (1993), pp. 405–50.

42. Michael Kane, "Validating the Performance Standards Associated with Passing Scores," *Review of Educational Research*, vol. 64 (1994), pp. 425–61; Ronald K. Hambleton, "Setting Performance Standards on Achievement Tests: Meeting the Requirements of Title I," in L. Hansche, ed., *Handbook for the Development of Performance Standards* (Department of Education and the Council of Chief State School Officers, 1998), pp. 87–114; Gregory J. Cizek, "Reconsidering Standards and Criteria," *Journal of Educational Measurement*, vol. 30 (1993), pp. 93–106; and Gregory J. Cizek, "Standard Setting as Psychometric Due Process: Going a Little Further Down an Uncertain Road," paper presented at the annual meeting of the National Council on Measurement in Education, San Francisco, April 1995.

# The Role of End-of-Course Exams and Minimum Competency Exams in Standards-Based Reforms

JOHN H. BISHOP, FERRAN MANE,
MICHAEL BISHOP, *and* JOAN MORIARTY

EDUCATIONAL REFORMERS and most of the American public believe that most teachers ask too little of their pupils. These low expectations, they believe, result in watered-down curricula and a tolerance of mediocre teaching and inappropriate student behavior. The result is that the prophecy of low achievement becomes self-fulfilling.

Although research has shown that learning gains are substantially larger when students take more demanding courses, only a minority of students enroll in these courses.[1] There are several reasons for this. Guidance counselors in many schools allow only a select few into the most challenging courses. While most schools give students and parents the authority to overturn counselor recommendations, many families are unaware they have that power or are intimidated by the counselor's prediction of failure in the tougher class. As one student put it: "African-American parents, they settle for less, not knowing they can get more for their students."[2]

In part the problem is ignorance. Students appear to be unaware of just how important courses such as algebra and geometry are for getting into and completing college. Even though 80 percent of tenth graders in 1988 expected to go to college, and 53 percent aspired to a professional or technical job, only 20 percent of eighth graders in 1989 thought they would need geometry and only 24 percent said they would need algebra "to qualify for [their] first choice job."[3]

267

A second source of the problem is that most students prefer courses that have the reputation of being fun and not requiring much work to get a good grade. In the 1987 Longitudinal Survey of American Youth, 62 percent of tenth graders agreed with the statement, "I don't like to do any more school work than I have to."[4] Many parents support their children's preference for easier courses. Even in wealthy communities, they often demand that their child switch to courses in which good grades are easier to get. As one guidance counselor described:

> A lot of . . . parents were in a "feel good" mode. "If my kids are not happy, I'm not happy." . . . Probably . . . 25 percent . . . were going for top colleges. They were pushing their kids hard. The rest—75 percent (I'm guessing at the numbers)—said "No, that's too hard, they don't have to do that." . . . If they [the students] felt it was too tough, they [the parents] would back off. I had to hold people in classes, hold the parents back. [I would say] "Let the kid get C's. It's OK. Then they'll get C+'s and then B's." [But they would demand,] "No! I want my kid out of that class!"[5]

Teachers are aware of student preferences and adjust their style of teaching and their homework assignments with an eye to maintaining enrollment levels. Guidance counselors, students, and parents avoid rigorous courses largely because the rewards for the extra work are small for most students. While selective colleges evaluate grades in the light of course demands, many colleges have, historically, not factored the rigor of high school courses into their admissions decisions. Trying to counteract this problem, college admissions officers have been telling students that they are expected to take the most rigorous courses offered by their school. This effort has been partly successful. More students are taking chemistry, physics, and advanced mathematics. But apparently many students have not gotten the message and still think taking easy courses is a good strategy. One student told a reporter:

> My counselor wanted me to take Regents history and I did for a while. But it was pretty hard and the teacher moved fast. I switched to the other history and I'm getting better grades. So my average will be better for college. Unless you are going to a college in the state, it doesn't really matter whether you get a Regents diploma.[6]

Consequently, the bulk of students who do not aspire to attend selective colleges rationally avoid rigorous courses and demanding teachers.

When teachers try to set high standards, they often get pressured to go easy. The following story is from southern Texas in the early 1980s.

> In the first grading period I boldly flunked a number of students, including the daughter of an administrator of a local elementary school and a star fullback who was also the nephew of a school board member. Shortly thereafter I was called in to meet

with my principal and the aggrieved parents. Such was my naivete that I actually bothered to bring evidence. I showed the elementary administrator her daughter's plagiarized book report and the book from which it had been copied, and I showed the fullback's father homework bearing his son's name but written in another person's hand writing. The parents offered weak apologies but maintained that I had not treated their children fairly.

My principal suddenly discovered a number of problems with my teaching. For the next few weeks he was in my class almost daily. Every spitball, every chattering student, every bit of graffiti was noted. When there were discipline problems my superiors sided with the offending students. Teaching became impossible.

So I learned to turn a blind eye to cheating and plagiarism and to give students, especially athletes, extra credit for everything from reading orally in class to remembering to bring their pencils. In this way I gained the cooperation of my students and the respect and support of my superiors.[7]

This story is not an isolated example. Thirty percent of American teachers say they "feel pressure to give higher grades than students' work deserves." Thirty percent also feel pressured "to reduce the difficulty and amount of work you assign."[8]

*Nerd Harassment*

Interviews John H. Bishop conducted of middle school boys in Ithaca, New York, in 1996 and 1997 revealed that most of them internalized a norm against "sucking up" to the teacher. How does a boy avoid being thought a "suck up"? He

—Avoids giving the teacher eye contact,
—Does not hand in homework early for extra credit,
—Does not raise his hand in class too frequently, and
—Talks or passes notes to friends during class (this signals that he values friends more than his reputation with the teacher).

Similarly, Laurence Steinberg, B. Bradford Brown, and Sanford M. Dornbusch's 1996 study of nine high schools in California and Wisconsin concluded that

less than 5 percent of all students are members of a high-achieving crowd that defines itself mainly on the basis of academic excellence. . . . Of all the crowds the "brains" were the least happy with who they are—nearly half wished they were in a different crowd.[9]

Why are the studious called suck ups, dorks, and nerds or accused of "acting white"? In part, it is because many teachers grade on a curve and this means trying hard to do well in a class is making it more difficult for others to get top grades. When exams are graded on a curve or college admissions are based on rank in class, joint welfare is maximized if no one puts in extra effort. In the repeated game that results, side payments (friendship and respect) and punishments (ridicule, harassment, and ostracism) enforce the cooperative "don't study much" solution. If, by contrast, students are evaluated relative to an outside standard, they no longer have a personal interest in getting teachers off track or persuading each other to refrain from studying. Peer pressure demeaning studiousness should diminish.

## Teacher Quality and Out-of-Field Teaching

The standards for getting into secondary school teaching are low. Most states using the National Teachers Examination/Praxis test have set remarkably low minimum passing scores.[10] Despite the low cut scores, failing these tests is not an absolute bar to entering the profession. Principals routinely fill open positions with uncertified teachers. School administrators are also remarkably willing to hire and assign staff to teach subjects that are outside their field of expertise and training. More than half of secondary school history classes are taught by teachers who neither majored nor minored in history in college. More than half of chemistry and physics students are taught by teachers who did not major or minor in a physical science or engineering in college.[11]

## The Signals Sent by the Labor Market

Employers also have an important role in encouraging higher academic standards. American employers, however, have a difficult time getting information on student achievement in school so they seldom consider the rigor of high school courses or externally assessed student achievement when making hiring decisions. If a student or graduate has given written permission for a transcript to be sent to an employer, the Federal Education Rights and Privacy Act obligates the school to respond. Many high schools are not, however, replying to such requests. In Columbus, Ohio, for example, Nationwide Insurance sent more than twelve hundred requests for transcripts signed by job applicants to high schools in 1982 and received only ninety-three responses. An additional barrier to the use of high school transcripts in selecting new employees is that high schools take a great deal of time to respond, if they do at all. In most high schools, the system for answering transcript requests has been designed to meet the needs of college-bound students rather than the students who seek jobs immediately after graduating. The result is that a 1987 survey of a stratified random sample of small- and medium-size employers who were members of the National Federation of Independent Business (NFIB) found that transcripts had been obtained before the selection decision for only 14.2 percent of the high school graduates hired.[12] Only 15 percent of the employers had asked high school graduates to report their grade point average. The absence of questions about grades on most job application forms probably reflects the low reliability of self-reported data, the difficulties of verifying them, and the fear of equal employment opportunity challenges to such questions.[13] Tests are available for measuring competency in reading, writing, mathematics, science, and problem solving. But, after the 1971 *Griggs* v. *Duke Power Co.* decision, almost all firms were forced to stop employment testing by Equal Employment Opportunity Commission guidelines that made it prohibitively costly to demonstrate test validity.[14] The 1987 NFIB survey found that basic skills tests had been given in only 2.9 percent of the hiring decisions studied.

These problems in signaling student achievement to employers are probably important reasons that tests assessing skills have only modest effects on the wages and earnings of men and women under the age of twenty-five.[15] Over time, however, employers learn which employees are the most competent by observing job performance. Those judged most competent are more likely to get further training, promotions, and good recommendations when they move on. Poor performers are encouraged to leave. Because academic achievement in high school is correlated with job performance, the sorting process results in basic skills assessed during high school having a much larger effect on the labor market success of thirty-year-olds than of nineteen-year-olds even when contemporaneous measures of completed schooling are held constant.[16]

Joseph Altonji and Charles Pierret's study of how scores on the Armed Forces Qualification Test (AFQT) taken while a teenager affect subsequent labor market success provides estimates of the magnitude of these effects in the late 1980s and early 1990s. Controlling for a contemporaneous measure of completed schooling, they found that a one standard deviation (four to five grade level equivalent [GLE]) higher AFQT score was associated with only a 2.8 percent increase in wage rates the first year out of school but a 16 percent increase eleven years later.[17] By contrast, the percentage impact of a year of schooling decreased with time out of school from 9.2 percent for those out just one year to 3 percent for those out for twelve years.

The long delays before the benefits of academic achievement in high school start accruing can send students the wrong signals. Teenagers are very aware that getting a college degree will yield substantial benefits. They can see in their community and on TV that college-educated adults have good jobs and live in large attractive houses.

How, by contrast, do youngsters assess the rewards for taking tough courses and studying hard in high school? Those who aspire to attend competitive colleges realize they have to work hard in high school. But most students plan to attend the local state college or community college, not a competitive state university or a selective private college. Their own experience tells them that this objective can be achieved without taking tough courses or working hard.[18] They do not know whether the successful adults they see in their community took rigorous courses and studied hard in high school. They may, however, know more about older siblings and other recent graduates. What lessons would they draw from observing their success in the labor market? They will observe almost no relationship between academic achievement of their older siblings and friends and the quality of their jobs. So youngsters would reasonably conclude that while credentials are rewarded by employers, learning is not. If that is the conclusion they draw, the best strategy for the bulk of students is to study just hard enough to get the diploma and be admitted to college, but no harder. One student put it succinctly: "Why should I do the extra work, if I don't have to?"[19]

## Policy Responses to Low Standards and Students' 'Doing the Minimum'

State-level political and educational leaders have been concerned about the low standards and weak incentives for hard study for decades. The traditional policy instruments—budgetary support for schools and school construction, teacher certification rules, and so on—did not address learning standards, so other instruments were sought. Five different strategies have been pursued: increased graduation requirements; achievement tests, school report cards, and stakes for schools, teachers, and administrators; minimum competency exam (MCE) graduation requirements; voluntary end-of-course examinations (EOCEs); and compulsory EOCEs. The latter four strategies are collectively referred to as standards-based reforms (SBRs). The first, third, fourth, and fifth are collectively referred to as stakes-for-students policies.

1. INCREASED GRADUATION REQUIREMENTS. While most school districts have local graduation requirements that exceed state-set minimums, the subject-specific nature of the state mandates appears to be binding for many stu-

dents. During the past two decades many states have increased the number of core academic courses that students must take to graduate from public high schools. Possibly as a result, enrollment in college preparatory mathematics and science classes has been rising as well. The increase in graduation requirements may, however, have the unintended consequence of inducing some students to drop out of high school altogether.

2. ACHIEVEMENT TESTS, SCHOOL REPORT CARDS, AND STAKES FOR TEACHERS AND ADMINISTRATORS. Another approach has been to develop content standards for required core academic courses, administer tests assessing that content to all students across the entire state, and then publish the results—district by district and school by school. Thirty-seven states now publish school report cards for all or almost all of their schools.[20] The hope is that publicly identifying low-performing schools will spur administrators and school boards to take remedial action. Nineteen states have special assistance programs to help failing schools turn themselves around. If improvements are not forthcoming, eleven states have the power to either close down, take over, or reconstitute failing schools. Positive reinforcements are also being tried. Nineteen states have a formal mechanism for rewarding schools either for year-to-year gains in achievement test scores or for exceeding student achievement targets.[21]

3. MINIMUM COMPETENCY EXAM GRADUATION REQUIREMENTS. A growing number of states are applying stakes to students as well as to teachers. In 1996, seventeen states and a number of urban districts were awarding high school diplomas only to students who had passed a minimum competency exam. Table 1 presents 1980–82 and 1992 data from a survey of principals on the proportion of high school students who faced such a requirement. MCE graduation requirements were often established in response to a popular perception that the state or district's K–12 education system had failed. Generally, southern states and states and districts with large urban populations have established MCEs. As a result, students from low socioeconomic backgrounds and students with low test scores are more likely to attend schools with MCEs. In 1992 about 40 percent of the nation's public school students lived in states that imposed an MCE graduation requirement at public high schools. Another 20 percent of the nation's public high school students live in districts that have established their own MCE and set their own passing standard.[22]

MCEs raise standards, but probably not for everyone.[23] The standards set by the teachers of honors classes and advanced college prep classes are not changed by an MCE. Students in these classes pass the MCE on the first try without special preparation. Typically high school transcripts report only who

**Table 1. High Schools Requiring Passage of a Minimum Competency Exam to Graduate**
Proportion of seniors who attend

| Year(s) | Socioeconomic status | | | Reading and math scores | | |
|---|---|---|---|---|---|---|
| | Low | Medium | High | Low | Medium | High |
| 1980–82 | .560 | .503 | .487 | .547 | .515 | .466 |
| 1992 | .647 | .557 | .442 | .643 | .565 | .457 |

Source: Tabulations of High School and Beyond and National Education Longitudinal Study of 1988 principal survey responses weighted by the number of students sampled at the high school. Both surveys oversampled schools with large minority populations.

has passed the MCE, not how far above the passing standard the student got. The higher standards are experienced by the students who are in the school's least challenging courses. Students pursuing the "Do the Minimum" strategy are told they must work harder if they are to get the diploma and go to college. School administrators will not want to be embarrassed by high failure rates, so they are likely to focus additional energy and resources on raising standards in the early grades and improving the instruction received by struggling students. In most states, science, history, and civics or government are not covered by the MCE, so its impact on achievement in these subjects is indirect. Presumably it raises achievement in reading, writing, and mathematics, and this then helps students do better in history and science classes and on tests covering these subjects.

MCEs typically set a low minimum standard. In 1996 only four of the seventeen states with MCEs targeted their graduation exams at a tenth-grade proficiency level or higher. Failure rates for students taking the test for the first time varied a great deal: from a high of 46 percent in Texas, 34 percent in Virginia, 30 percent in Tennessee, and 27 percent in New Jersey to a low of 7 percent in Mississippi. However, because students can take the tests multiple times, eventual pass rates for the class of 1995 were much higher: 98 percent in Louisiana, Maryland, New York, North Carolina, and Ohio; 96 percent in Nevada and New Jersey; 91 percent in Texas; and 83 percent in Georgia.[24] Because the tests are designed to determine who falls below a low standard, they typically do not assess material that college-bound students study in tenth and eleventh grade (for example, algebra 2 and geometry proofs).

4. VOLUNTARY END-OF-COURSE EXAMINATIONS. End-of-course exams are different from MCEs in that they typically assess more difficult material and are taken by students nearing the end of a specific course or sequence of courses—for example, biology, French, American history, or calculus.[25] They are very much like the final exams that teachers give at the end of the year.

Teachers are inevitably viewed as responsible, at least in part, for how well their class does on the exam. EOCEs signal a student's achievement level in the subject, not just whether a student exceeds or falls below a specific cut point that all high school graduates are required to surpass. Consequently, all students, not just those at the bottom of the class, have an incentive to study hard to do well on the exam and, thus, an EOCE is more likely to improve classroom culture than an MCE.[26] The stakes tend to be different as well. For voluntary EOCEs, the stakes are typically getting an A instead of a B in a course or getting college credit for a high school course. For MCEs, the stakes are getting a high school diploma. To summarize, compared with MCEs, the standards are higher with voluntary EOCEs and the stakes are lower but they largely apply equally to all students in a particular class, though sometimes not to all students in a school.

*Advanced Placement Courses and Exams.* The number of students taking Advanced Placement (AP) examinations has been growing at a compound annual rate of 9 percent per year. In 1999, 686,000 students, about 11 percent of the nation's juniors and seniors, took one or more AP exams.[27] Despite this success, however, 44 percent of the high schools do not offer even one AP course, and many others allow only a tiny minority of their students to take these courses.

*North Carolina End-of-Course Tests.* The Elementary and Secondary Reform Act of 1984 authorized the North Carolina Department of Education to develop end-of-course exams for ten core high school subjects. EOCEs were introduced between 1988 and 1991 for algebra 1 and 2, geometry, biology, chemistry, physics, physical science, U.S. history, social science, and English 1. Except for a four-year interlude in which some tests were made a local option, all students enrolled in these courses were required to take the state tests. Easier versions of these courses not assessed by a state test do not exist, so virtually all North Carolina high school students take at least six of these exams. Test scores are reported separately on the student's transcript. Most teachers have been incorporating EOCE scores into their course grades, and a state law now mandates that, starting in the year 2000, the EOCE scores must have at least a 25 percent weight in the final course grade.

*California's Golden State Exams.* California introduced voluntary EOCEs in algebra 1 and geometry in 1987, U.S. history and economics in 1990, biology and chemistry in 1991, written composition in 1996, government in 1997, reading/literature in 1998, and physics and Spanish in 1999. By 1993 about 31 percent of California high school students were taking the algebra exam,

20 percent were taking the geometry exam, and 14 percent were taking the U.S. history and biology exams.[28] Outstanding achievement on each exam is recognized by the state and appears on the student's transcript but is not part of the grade that the student receives from his or her teacher. Students who earn high honors, honors, or recognition designations on six Golden State exams get a special Golden State diploma from the state. In 1998 about 1 percent of the state's graduates received such a designation.

*Regents Courses and Exams.* Begun in the 1860s, New York state's curriculum-based Regents examination system is the oldest American example of end-of-course examinations. Sherman Tinkelman, assistant commissioner for examinations and scholarships, described the system in a 1966 report:

> The Regents examinations are closely related to the curriculum in New York State. They are, as you can see, inseparably intertwined. . . . These instruments presuppose and define standards. . . . They are a strong supervisory and instructional tool— and deliberately so. They are effective in stimulating good teaching and good learning practices.[29]

They are taken throughout one's high school career. A college-bound student taking a full schedule of Regents courses would typically take Regents exams in mathematics and earth science at the end of ninth grade; mathematics, biology, and global studies exams at the end of tenth grade; mathematics, chemistry, American history, English, and foreign language exams at the end of eleventh grade; and a physics exam at the end of twelfth grade. To accommodate summer school students and courses ending in January, the exams are given three times a year.

These external exams have substantial effects on teachers. Because they grade the Regents exams of the students in their own classes, they can see the kinds of mistakes their students are making and use that information to improve their coverage of the material the following year. Essays are generally graded by more than one teacher, and this results in feedback and discussions among colleagues that are an excellent professional development experience for most participants. The exams also provide a benchmark against which the teacher, his or her departmental colleagues, and administrators may judge teaching effectiveness. On occasion, examinations have been deliberately revised to induce changes in curriculum and teaching.

> For years our foreign language specialists went up and down the State beating the drums for curriculum reform in modern language teaching, for change in emphasis from formal grammar to conversation skills and reading skills. There was not very great impact until we introduced, after notice and with numerous sample exercises,

oral comprehension and reading comprehension into our Regents examinations. Promptly thereafter, most schools adopted the new curricular objectives.[30]

Publication of school-level results puts administrators under pressure to hire teachers who have deep knowledge of their subject and to introduce whole school reform programs that upgrade instruction in the early grades.

For students the stakes attached to Regents exams were low. Each district decides whether Regents exam grades are to be a part of the course grade and how much weight to assign to them. While almost all districts count Regents exam results as a final exam grade, teachers or departments generally give their own final as well. When grades on finals are averaged in with quarterly marking period grades, Regents exam scores seldom account for more than an eighth of the student's final grade in a course. Eligibility for a Regents diploma as opposed to a local diploma depends on passing the Regents exams, but the benefits of getting a Regents diploma are small. While Regents exam grades appear on high school transcripts, college admissions decisions depend primarily on grades and Scholastic Assessment Test (SAT) scores, not Regents exam scores or Regents diplomas.[31] Many students saw an advantage in taking easier non-Regents classes to enhance their grade point averages (GPAs).

AP and Regents exams raise standards through a variety of mechanisms. First, in the classes in which they are used, they push up teaching standards and help motivate students to study and to cooperate with each other. Students are no longer competing for a limited number of A's and B's. Now everyone in the class can be recognized for excellence in the subject. Second, the external exam creates a signal of competence that colleges use in making admissions and placement decisions, and this increases the rewards for learning and makes them more visible and immediate. This also increases student motivation. Third, the honors and college credits that are awarded to those who demonstrate and signal their achievement attract students into the more challenging and demanding courses that prepare them for these examinations. In many districts, this effect operates as far back as sixth grade, when decisions about whether to accelerate in mathematics effectively determine whether a student can take AP calculus in his or her senior year. Fourth, the share of students taking the externally examined courses and the results of those exams affect the community's perception of school quality and of the performance of the school district's teachers and administrators. Property values respond to these perceptions. School administrators will thus face strong incentives to focus on the school's core academic mission.

The power of these incentives depends on the share of students taking externally examined courses. Unfortunately, during the 1980s and early 1990s many students were not taking Regents courses and exams. In 1992 the most popular exam, course 1 mathematics, was taken by 62 percent of students, the global studies exam was taken by 57 percent of students, and the English and biology exams were taken by 50 percent of students. Only 38 percent of graduates earned Regents diplomas, signifying completion of a sequence of Regents courses, in 1992–93.[32] New York state dealt with this problem by creating and expanding a system of Regents competency tests (RCTs) in reading, writing, math, science, global studies, and U.S. history that set a minimum standard for those not taking Regents courses.

5. COMPULSORY END-OF-COURSE EXAMINATIONS. The RCTs were low-level tests. The mathematics RCT, for example, assumed no exposure to algebra or geometry. Concern grew that large numbers of students particularly in New York City were wasting their time in watered-down courses. Ramon Cortines, chancellor of New York City school system, for example, declared:

> The easy way out is the road to nowhere. If achievement in our schools is to improve, we must raise our expectations for students and staff. Our system will fail in its obligation to this community unless we equalize educational opportunity and raise standards in all of our schools.[33]

Under Cortines's leadership the New York City Board of Education decided that, starting with those entering ninth grade in the fall of 1994, all students would have to take three Regents-level math and three Regents-level science courses before graduating. With this step, New York City was abolishing the bottom track. Students were taught much more demanding material, but they did not have to pass the Regents exams to get credit for the course. That was their teacher's decision.

Two years later the state Board of Regents decided to raise the bar for the entire state. Students would not only be required to take Regents-level courses, but they also would have to pass the Regents exams for these courses. Specifically, students entering ninth grade in 1996 or later were required to take a new six-hour Regents English examination and pass it at the 55 percent level. The class of 2001 has the additional requirement of passing an examination in algebra and geometry. The class of 2002 must pass Regents examinations in global studies and American history as well. When laboratory science exams come on stream, the phase-in of all five new required Regents exams will be completed with the graduating class of 2003. While passing cut scores were lowered by ten points, the content of the exams was not watered down.[34] The one-half of New York students who had been getting through high school taking unchallenging local courses will now be forced to demonstrate a level of mastery in the five core subjects that is close to the minimum standard that had in the past applied to college preparatory classes. Supporting changes were also made in the elementary school curriculum.

The anticipated shift to an all-Regents curriculum appears to have induced many districts to expand enrollment in Regents courses by students who will graduate before the graduation requirements kick in. The percentage of the state's high school students who took and passed Regents English (at the 65 percent level) rose from 42 percent in 1993 to 58 percent in 1997. During that four-year interval, the share taking and passing Regents exams rose from 40 to 47 percent in biology, from 52 to 59 percent in course 1 mathematics, and from 40 to 49 percent in U.S. history.

While New York state has the most comprehensive system of compulsory end-of-course exams, a number of other states appear to be shifting toward EOCEs. North Carolina has had compulsory end-of-course exams since the early 1990s. Arkansas, California, Maryland, Mississippi, Oklahoma, Tennessee, and Virginia are phasing in compulsory end-of-course exams in key subjects. Maryland, Tennessee, and Virginia have plans for the EOCEs to eventually replace the MCE.

### The Effects of Standards-Based Reform and Course Graduation Requirements

What have been the effects of the standards-based reforms and increased high school graduation standards? A good deal of comparative international evidence shows that comprehensive systems of end-of-course examinations—or curriculum-based external exit exam systems (CBEEES)—are associated with higher student achievement.[35] This suggests that increasing the rewards for student achievement can have positive effects. However, the most popular student stakes policies in the United States—minimum competency exams and higher course graduation requirements—are very different from CBEEES. The school stakes policies that are being adopted in a growing number of states are also different from CBEEES. Thus, the policies being pursued in most states are not likely to have the same effects on student outcomes that CBBEES in Europe and Canada have had.

The impact of these policies must be studied in the cultural and institutional context—the United States—in which they are being implemented. States have introduced different packages of standards-based reform initiatives. This cross-state variation in SBR policies creates an opportunity to assess their impacts on student achievement and labor market success after high school.

## Impacts of Higher Standards on Dropout Rates and Graduation Rates

Theory predicts that an increase in the number of courses required to graduate is likely to induce some students to give up on getting a diploma and drop out of high school. Consider the situation facing students who have failed a number of courses and have therefore accumulated only eight Carnegie units by the end of their sophomore year. If the state requires sixteen Carnegie units to graduate (as Illinois did in 1992), getting a high school diploma looks feasible. If the state requires twenty-three Carnegie units to graduate (as Louisiana and the District of Columbia did in 1992), getting a diploma starts looking very difficult. Reduced enrollment rates and graduation rates are likely to result. Therefore,

Hypothesis 1: *Enrollment rates and graduation rates will be lower in states that set higher Carnegie unit graduation requirements minimums.*

Minimum competency exams are different from Carnegie unit graduation requirements and, consequently, may have different effects.[36] In our view, failing an MCE test the first or second time it is taken is rarely going to lead the student to give up and drop out. People tend to attribute bad outcomes to external factors, bad luck, and other temporary circumstances ("I was feeling sick," "the test didn't cover the material I studied," or "I didn't try") rather than to their innate ability.[37] As a result, they are likely to be optimistic about their chances of passing the next time. Only 4.3 percent of the tenth graders in New Jersey, New York, and Ohio who were questioned after failing an MCE expressed a fear that they would not graduate. Most reacted by "studying harder next year" (24 percent), taking summer school courses (29 percent), repeating the same course next year (24 percent), taking a special course the next year (9 percent), and getting tutoring help (30 percent).[38] Incentives to stay in school to get the diploma will rise if the signal sent by MCEs makes academic achievement or the diploma more valuable in the labor market. Nevertheless, educators are very concerned about the possibility that MCEs will increase dropout rates of students with poor grades and low test scores, so that is the hypothesis that will be tested.

Hypothesis 2A: *Enrollment rates will be lower and dropout rates higher at schools with MCEs.*

Hypothesis 2B: *Any negative effect of MCEs on enrollment rates will be confined to the students with below average eighth-grade GPAs.*

Conventional wisdom predicts that a minimum competency exam will cause graduation rates to fall. But this, too, is not necessarily the case. Economic theory makes an unambiguous prediction of lower graduation rates only for when the rewards for getting a diploma and for effective teaching are unaffected by establishing an MCE. This, however, is not likely to be the case. Minimum competency exams improve the information signaled by the diploma, so the economic payoffs to getting a diploma and to academic achievement are likely to increase. The publicity that inevitably attends the publication of school results on medium- and high-stakes tests will make teachers and administrators more accountable for the achievement of at-risk students. If the returns to greater student effort and to increased focus on teaching at-risk students do not diminish too rapidly, learning might improve so much that graduation rates rise when an MCE is established. The policy debate, however, is dominated by concerns that higher standards will lower graduation rates, so that hypothesis is tested. Therefore,

Hypothesis 3A: *MCEs will increase the number of students who graduate more than four years after completing eighth grade.*

Hypothesis 3B: *An MCE graduation requirement will increase the likelihood of students getting a general equivalency diploma (GED) instead of a regular diploma. Because getting a GED also involves passing a test, it is not clear which types of students are more likely to be induced to pursue that option by an MCE.*

Hypothesis 3C: *MCEs will increase the number of students who have not obtained a diploma or GED within six years of completing eighth grade.*

Hypothesis 3D: *Any negative effect of MCEs on high school completion rates will be confined to the students with below average eighth-grade GPAs.*

A number of studies have examined the effect of MCEs and Carnegie unit graduation requirements on enrollment and graduation rates. Dean Lillard and Phillip DeCicca found that enrollment rates were reduced by increases in the number of courses necessary to graduate but not by MCEs. Their analyses of the National Education Longitudinal Survey of 1988 (NELS-88) found that different specifications produced different estimates of their impact on dropout rates. Models that controlled for state fixed effects and examined the introduction of a state MCE tended to find no effect.[39] Two independent sources of data—

state aggregate data obtained from the U.S. Census Bureau and the National Center for Education Statistics (NCES), and NELS-88—are analyzed below.

*Cross Section of States*

State-level data on enrollment rates and high school graduation rates for the early 1990s were analyzed. The dependent variables were the 1990 enrollment rate of seventeen-year-olds and the high school graduation ratio (the ratio of the number of high school diplomas awarded in the state to the number of seventeen-year-olds). We were interested in assessing the effects of four state policies: compulsory attendance laws, state-mandated minimum course graduation requirements, state minimum competency exams, and the hybrid EOCE/MCE system of New York state. The demographic background of the students in the state was accounted for by including five control variables— an index of parents' education, the child poverty rate, percentage foreign born, the share of African American students, and the share of Hispanic students— in the model. A complete description of the variables and the regression results (table A-1) can be found in Appendix A. The main findings are summarized in bar-graph form in figure 1.

School attendance laws appear to have the desired effect, but the magnitude is small. States requiring seventeen-year-olds to attend school had higher enrollment rates, and the relationship was statistically significant in one of the two enrollment rate regressions.

States that set high course graduation requirements have significantly lower school enrollment rates. A four-unit increase in requirements is associated with enrollment rates being 0.7 to 1.2 percentage points lower.

The MCEs that existed at the beginning of the 1990s had no tendency to lower aggregate enrollment and graduation rates. None of the coefficients on the MCE variable was significant, and some of the point estimates were, contrary to conventional wisdom, positive.

Finally, New York state's voluntary Regents exams also had no significant effects on dropout rates or graduation rates

*NELS-88 Analysis of Dropout Rates and Noncompletion of High School*

NELS-88 is a longitudinal data set that followed a nationally representative sample of eighth graders in 1988 through the year 1994. The survey contractor for NELS-88 made extensive efforts to find and interview dropouts. Shortened interviews where conducted with 1,082 dropouts in 1990 and 2,156 dropouts in 1992.

**Figure 1. Effects of State Policies on School Attendance and Graduation Rates**

Percentage point increase

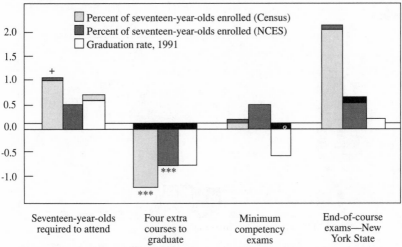

Source: Analysis of state data from National Center for Education Statistics (NCES), *Education in States and Nations* (Department of Education, 1991); and the 1990 census.
+ Statistically significant at 1 percent level on a one tail test.
*** Statistically significant at 1 percent level on a two tail test.

We used the restricted data set that identifies the state in which the student's high school was located. From this source we created our key variable, MCESTATE, which was equal to one for students in states that required them to pass a minimum competency exam to graduate in 1992 (Alabama, Florida, Georgia, Hawaii, Louisiana, Maryland, Mississippi, Nevada, New Mexico, New Jersey, North Carolina, South Carolina, Tennessee, and Texas) and zero elsewhere.[40] Because of the Regents exam system, New York state was treated as a special case. A separate New York dummy variable was included in the model to measure the effect of combining end-of-course and minimum competency exams, and all New York high schools were given a value of zero on the MCE variable. The final policy variable was the minimum number of Carnegie units required to get a diploma set by state law.

We expect MCEs to have most of their impact on high school students who are at risk of failing them. Consequently the effects of state minimum competency exams were captured by two variables: a dummy variable for states with an MCE graduation requirement and an interaction between the MCE dummy variable and the student's eighth-grade GPA. The interaction variable was defined as MCE*(GPA-2.91). By deviating GPA from its mean of 2.91

**Figure 2. Probability of Not Getting a Diploma or GED by Eighth-Grade GPA and State MCE**

Percent

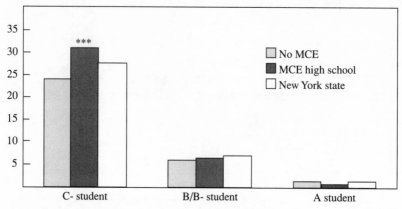

Source: Analysis of National Education Longitudinal Study of 1988 with controls for attitudes, socioeconomic status, grade point average and test scores in eighth grade, and state and high school characteristics.
Note: GED = general equivalency diploma; MCE = minimum competency exam.
*** Statistically significant at 1 percent level on a two tail test.

before constructing the interaction variable, the coefficient on the MCE dummy variable becomes an estimate of the impact of MCEs on students who have a B/B- average in eighth grade.

Logit models were estimated predicting whether the student drops out at any time during high school, whether the student obtains a GED certificate, whether the student fails to get either a GED or a high school diploma, whether the student gets his or her diploma late, and whether he or she gets it ahead of schedule. Appendix B provides details of the specification and a comprehensive list of the control variables. Results are presented in table B-1. We summarize the most important findings in the text below and in three graphs. Figure 2 presents predicted noncompletion rates for students with different eighth-grade achievement levels by whether their state has an MCE graduation requirement. Figure 3 presents results for delays in graduation and early graduation; figure 4, getting a GED.

Dropout rates and high school noncompletion rates of students with A averages in eighth grade were no greater when they lived in states with MCE graduation requirements. B students living in MCE states were not more likely to drop out and not more likely to fail to get a diploma or GED, but they were more likely to graduate late and more likely to finish with a GED when they

**Figure 3. Probability of Getting Diploma Late or Early by Eighth-Grade GPA and State Minimum Competency Exam (MCE)**

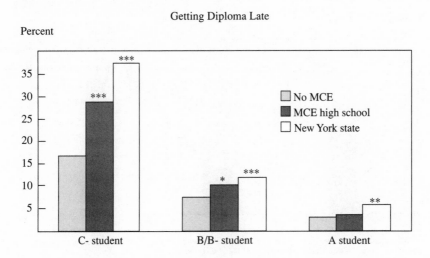

Getting Diploma Late

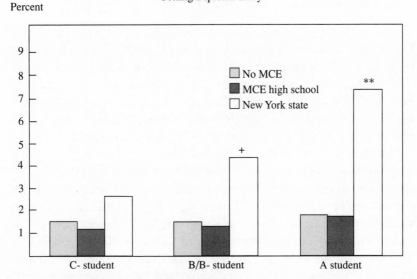

Getting Diploma Early

Source: Analysis of National Education Longitudinal Study of 1988 with controls for attitudes, socioeconomic status, grade point average and test scores in eighth grade, and state and high school characteristics.
+ Statistically significant at 10 percent level on a one tail test
* Statistically significant at 5 percent level on a one tail test
** Statistically significant at 5 percent level on a two tail test
*** Statistically significant at 1 percent level on a two tail test.

**Figure 4. Probability of Getting a GED by Eighth-Grade GPA and State Minimum Competency Exam (MCE)**

Percent

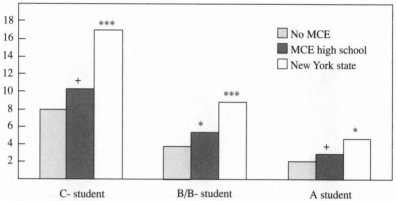

Source: Analysis of National Education Longitudinal Study of 1988 with controls for attitudes, socioeconomic status, grade point average and test scores in eighth grade, and state and high school characteristics.
Note: GED = general equivalency diploma.
+ Statistically significant at 10 percent level on a one tail test
* Statistically significant at 5 percent level on a one tail test
*** Statistically significant at 1 percent level on a two tail test.

lived in an MCE state. C students do not have higher dropout rates when they live in MCE states, but their graduation rates are affected.[41] We estimate that for C- students, noncompletion rates were 31 percent when the state had an MCE graduation requirement and 24 percent when it did not. Twenty-eight percent of C- students living in MCE states took longer to graduate from high school; 17 percent delayed their graduation in non-MCE states. Ten percent of C- students in MCE states got a GED; only 7.8 percent in non-MCE states.

New York's unique policy environment appears to have had substantial effects on dropout rates and on when students graduate from high school. Compared with students in states without an MCE, New York students were significantly more likely to drop out, more likely to get a GED, more likely to graduate early, and more likely to graduate late. For A students, early graduations were about four times more likely in New York. Regardless of GPA, New York students were twice as likely to get a GED and twice as likely to have their graduation delayed. Nevertheless, failing to graduate or get a GED before spring 1994 was not more likely in New York. This pattern suggests that while some New York students are failing many courses and must take five years to finish high school, another group of students are taking accelerated courses and graduating early.

State-set minimum course graduation requirements significantly increase dropout rates and the probability of getting a GED but had no effect on delayed diplomas or not getting a diploma or GED.[42]

*Dropout Rate Trends*

Over the last few decades, many states have introduced MCEs or increased course graduation requirements or both. The state cross-section regressions imply that the increases in Carnegie unit graduation requirements should have, ceteris paribus, decreased enrollment rates of seventeen-year-olds by about 1 percentage point. Data on trends in dropout rates are presented in table 2. Despite these policy shifts, event dropout rates for African Americans fell from 10.47 percent in 1972–74 to 5.40 percent in 1990–92 and 5.37 in 1996–98. Hispanic dropout rates fell from 10.23 percent in 1972–74 to 7.73 percent in 1990–92 and then rose slightly to 8.47 percent in 1996–98. Event dropout rates also fell for whites. Status dropout rates also declined during the period when MCEs were being introduced and graduation requirements were being increased. Clearly, if tougher graduation standards do tend to increase dropout rates, their effects were counterbalanced by other forces that reduced dropout rates, such as growing incomes, the rising payoff to high school completion and college attendance, and the introduction in eighteen states of policies that make driver's licenses conditional on regular school attendance.[43]

The decline in dropout rates, however, does not appear to have led to increases in diplomas awarded. This stems in part from students substituting GEDs for high school diplomas. But adding the American Council on Education's reports of GEDs awarded to youth under age twenty to administrative reports of diplomas awarded by public and private schools does not change the conclusion. When this sum is divided by the number of seventeen-year-olds (last column of table 2), this ratio is stable in the 1970s and 1980s and declines in the 1990s.[44] These data are consistent with the hypothesis that rising graduation requirements are lowering graduation rates even while they leave dropout rates unchanged.

**Effects of Standards-Based Reforms on Student Achievement**

Past studies of the effects of statewide testing tied to curriculum frameworks with stakes attached to school results, minimum competency tests for graduating, or both have found positive effects on student achievement. Bar-

Table 2. Trends in Dropout Rates by Ethnicity

| Years | Event dropout rate, grades ten to twelve | | | Status dropout rate, fifteen- to seventeen-year-olds | | | Status dropout rate, eighteen- to twenty-four-year-olds | | | Diploma + GED LT20/ seventeen-year-olds |
|---|---|---|---|---|---|---|---|---|---|---|
| | White | Black | Hispanic | White | Black | Hispanic | White | Black | Hispanic | Total |
| 1972–74 average | 5.80 | 10.47 | 10.23 | 6.83 | 7.90 | — | 14.63 | 25.93 | 38.83 | 77.3 |
| 1981–83 average | 5.07 | 8.10 | 9.97 | 5.70 | 5.47 | 10.83 | 14.53 | 21.73 | 35.17 | 76.6 |
| 1990–92 average | 3.87 | 5.40 | 7.73 | 4.27 | 4.90 | 9.47 | 13.30 | 15.67 | 32.87 | 77.8 |
| 1996–98 average | 4.37 | 5.37 | 8.47 | 4.07 | 4.07 | 7.17 | 12.87 | 16.67 | 29.63 | 74.7 |

Source: Bureau of the Census, *Current Population Reports*, various issues (Department of Commerce); and National Center for Education Statistics, *Digest of Educational Statistics: 1999* (1999), tables 104, 107.

Note: The event dropout rate is the percent of tenth- to twelfth-grade students in October of one year who are not enrolled in high school or graduated the following October. The status dropout rate is the percent of fifteen- to seventeen-year-olds and eighteen- to twenty-four-year-olds in the civilian noninstitutionalized population who have not graduated from high school and are not attending high school currently. The last column is the ratio of the sum of the three-year average (the number of high school diplomas awarded plus the number of general equivalency diplomas [GEDs] awarded to people under twenty years of age) to the number of resident seventeen-year-olds for that year. The increases in event dropout rates over the course of the 1990s have apparently been caused largely by changes in Current Population Survey interviewing and editing procedures that increased reporting of dropout events.

bara Lerner and the New Jersey Office of Educational Assessment found that test scores of students increased after the introduction of minimum competency exams and that the increases were greatest for minority students, for central city students, and for students in the bottom half of the test score distribution.[45] E. Mangino and M. A. Babcock's study found that test scores of low-achieving students had risen the most after the introduction of the Texas Assessment of Basic Skills in the Austin Independent School District. This was particularly true for the items assessing higher-level skills.[46]

Norman Fredericksen's study is the most valuable because he had access to confidential data on 1978 and 1986 National Assessment of Educational Progress (NAEP) test scores of public school students together with the location of the school they were attending. This enabled him to classify NAEP test takers in 1978 and 1986 by whether they lived in a state with high-stakes testing, moderate-stakes testing, or no- or low-stakes testing in 1986. His 1978 base year was before the introduction of minimum competency testing systems. Student data for both 1978 and 1986 were available for twenty-seven states. The "High Stakes" category was composed of states that Fredericksen judged "had not only mandated the use of MCTs [minimum competency tests]; they also required school officials and teachers to set standards in terms of MCT scores for granting diplomas and promoting students to the next grade." Ten of the twenty-seven states were considered to have a "High Stakes" testing system. The "Moderate Stakes" states had MCTs but "professed to use the MCTs for such purposes as monitoring student performance, remediation of simple faults, or coaching those students who badly need assistance." Seven states were placed in the moderate-stakes category. The remaining eleven states were placed in the low-stakes category. Three states had no MCTs. None of the others "mandated the use of MCT scores for any specific purpose…. Some states allowed local options regarding the use of MCTs by county, by district or by individual school."

Fredericksen selected NAEP mathematics items that had been administered in both years and classified them into routine items (generally simple computation) and nonroutine items (assessing higher-order thinking skills). Using a difference of differences methodology, he compared the 1978 to 1986 change in percent correct for high-stakes states with the change in percent correct for low-stakes states. Because stakes applied to promotion decisions, graduation, schools, and individual students, he studied all three of the age groups assessed by NAEP. He found that 1978 to 1986 gains in percent correct for routine items were 7.9 percentage points higher for nine-year-olds, 3.1 points higher for thirteen-year-olds, and 0.6 points higher for seventeen-year-olds in high-stakes states than in low-stakes states. On nonroutine items the high-stakes state advantage was 4.5 points for nine-year-olds, 4.6 points for thirteen-year-olds, and 1.9 points for seventeen-year-olds. With the exception of the routine items given to seventeen-year-olds, these are substantial differentials. Except in primary school the response appears to be greater for test items assessing higher-level skills than for simpler test questions.[47]

Two different data sets were analyzed regarding the effects of standards-based reform strategies: (1) cross sections of state mean NAEP fourth- and eighth-grade test scores in reading, mathematics, and science in 1992, 1994, 1996, and 1998 and (2) NELS-88 data on test score gains from eighth grade to twelfth grade for individual students. The first data set allows examination of the effects of various standards-based reform initiatives on the achievement of primary school and middle school children. The second data set permits analysis of the effect of minimum competency exams on learning gains after eighth grade and allows disaggregation of the analysis by the student's eighth-grade GPA.

### Cross Section of States

The analysis of state cross-section data provides estimates of the effects on statewide student achievement of six different but complementary standards-based reform strategies:

1. Minimum competency exams.

2. Voluntary end-of-course exams combined with minimum competency exams; that is, the New York/North Carolina policy mix during the middle of the 1990s.[48]

3. School-by-school reporting of the results of statewide testing.

4. Rewards for schools that improve on statewide tests or exceed targets set for them.

5. Sanctions for failing schools—threats of closure, reconstitution, loss of accreditation, and so on.

6. Assistance programs for low-performing schools.

The dependent variables were state-level means for fourth- and eighth-grade NAEP tests in 1992, 1994, 1996, and 1998 in reading, mathematics, and science. The models estimated all had updated versions of the following demographic controls—the parental education index, poverty rate for children, percent of public school students who are African American, percent of students who are Hispanic, and percent of students who are Asian. The control variables are described at greater length in Appendix A and the source notes of this paper's tables.

IMPACTS OF STAKES FOR STUDENTS. We began by examining the effects of stakes for students—state minimum competency exams and end-of-course exams combined with MCEs—on test scores. Because only two states, New York and North Carolina, had a comprehensive system of end-of-course exams during this period, the EOCE/MCE variable is a dummy that equals one for New York and North Carolina and a zero otherwise. At the beginning of the decade the Regents exams were voluntary and the North Carolina EOCEs had been in place for only a year or so. As the end of the decade approached, the New York students taking NAEP tests were facing the prospect of being compelled to take the Regents exams in high school and to pass five of them to graduate. The MCE variable is a one for states that had or were phasing in a minimum competency exam graduation requirement (that is, students are taking pilot tests even if stakes are not yet being applied to high school seniors) and the students taking the NAEP test were going to be subject to the MCE requirement.

The results are presented in table A-2. We found that the New York/North Carolina policy mix, a hybrid MCE/end-of-course exam system, had large and significant effects on reading, mathematics, and science achievement in 1994, 1996, and 1998. The effects were large, ranging from a half to three quarters of a grade level. Looking over time, the effect of attending school in an EOCE/MCE state grew substantially. When we estimated models with separate effects for New York and North Carolina, we found that the growing size of the EOCE/MCE effects was almost entirely a North Carolina phenomenon. This is reasonable because EOCEs were phased in between 1988 and 1991 so the students taking NAEP tests in 1992 should have had only a year or so of exposure to the backwash effects of EOCEs on teaching in earlier grades.

The estimated effects of minimum competency exams were also positive but smaller. Our point estimates imply that fourth graders in MCE states were 30 to 40 percent of a GLE ahead of students in non-MCE states. Eighth graders were 12 percent of a GLE ahead in reading and about a quarter of a GLE ahead in math and science.

This pattern of larger effects for younger students suggests that the MCE variable may be a proxy for other correlated features of the policy environment. And SBR policies do tend to cluster. Figure 5 presents a matrix of the correlations among our five SBR policy indicators. States that have MCE exams

**Figure 5. Correlations between State Standards-Based Reform Strategies**

|  | Minimum competency exam | School report cards | Rewards for successful schools | Penalties for failing schools | Assistance for failing schools | Rewards+ penalties index |
|---|---|---|---|---|---|---|
| Minimum competency exam in 1996 | 1.00 | .271 | .448 | .411 | .316 | .554 |
| School report cards | .300 | 1.00 | .442 | .356 | .575 | .414 |
| Rewards for successful schools | .333 | .278 | 1.00 | .205 | .169 | .668 |
| Penalties for failing schools | .544 | .457 | .429 | 1.00 | .709 | .839 |
| Assistance for low-performing schools | — | — | — | — | 1.00 | .605 |
| Rewards + penalties index | .526 | .442 | .822 | .867 | — | 1.00 |

Note: Numbers below the diagonal are the correlations between averages of 0-1 indicator variables reported in the January 1997 and January 1998 "Quality Counts" issues of *Education Week*. Numbers above the diagonal are for policy intensity variables constructed from the detailed description of accountability systems in the January 1999 "Quality Counts." The minimum competency exam variable is a 0-1 variable that counts New York state as a minimum competency exam state. Hawaii is excluded. Information on the policies of the District of Columbia was obtained by interviewing the *Washington Post* reporters who cover District of Columbia schools.

tend to also have well-developed school report card systems. They are also more likely to reward schools that have improved significantly or exceeded achievement targets, to provide assistance to schools that are failing, and to sanction failing schools that do not improve. Fifteen of the sixteen states with MCEs either reward successful schools or sanction failing schools. Nine of the MCE states do both. Those nine states are Georgia, Louisiana, Mississippi, New Jersey, New Mexico, North Carolina, South Carolina, Tennessee, and Texas. Only six of the thirty-four non-MCE states do both. Nineteen of the non-MCE states have not adopted any of the school-oriented SBR initiatives except for school report cards. These states tend to be small, middle class, and largely white. Their students tend to score above the national average on nationally normed tests, so state politicians probably do not feel the same need to impose a state accountability system intended to push reluctant local school administrators to raise standards. Most of these states have also not felt the need to identify a group of low-performing schools and then provide special assistance to help these schools turn themselves around.

School-focused SBR strategies also tend to cluster. States that sanction failing schools are much more likely to have programs that assist failing schools to get better and more likely to reward successful schools.

IMPACTS OF STAKES FOR SCHOOLS. What are the impacts of school-focused SBR strategies—school report cards, rewards for success, and sanctions for failure—on student achievement? Information on which states were pursuing these SBR strategies was taken from the 1997 and 1998 "Quality Counts" special issue of *Education Week*. Because the information on SBR initiatives was only available for the late 1990s, we ran regressions predicting mathematics and science achievement in 1996 and fourth- and eighth-grade reading achievement in 1998. As a first step, each policy variable was entered alone into the standard specification in which NAEP test scores are predicted by the parental education index, the child poverty rate, percent two-parent families, percent African American, percent Asian, and percent Hispanic or Native American.

The results are presented in table 3. School report cards and other public reporting strategies appear not to have significant or consistently positive relationships with the NAEP test scores. SBR strategies that involve rewards and consequences for schools, by contrast, do appear to have positive relationships. Students in states pursuing the rewards strategy are significantly better in math and reading in fourth grade. Students in states pursuing the consequences strategy are significantly better in math and reading in fourth grade and also better in science in eighth grade. Point estimates of the differences between states with and without these strategies tend to be less than 15 percent of a GLE for eighth-grade achievement levels and about 40 percent of a GLE for fourth-grade reading achievement.

When all three SBR policy indicators were entered simultaneously, the rewards and consequences variables continued to have positive effects, but the school report card variable became unstable and lost significance. We, therefore, dropped public reporting from future specifications of the model.

The coefficients on the rewards and consequences indicators were not significantly different from each other, so we imposed the assumption that they are equal and used a sum of the two variables in our preferred specifications. In these models, the rewards + consequences SBR variable is a significant predictor of four of the five test scores. Adding indicator variables for minimum competency exams and for the EOCE/MCE policy mix has almost no effect on the estimated effect of school rewards and consequences on test scores.

We also ran models that provided separate estimates of the effect of each policy: rewards, consequences, minimum competency exams, and hybrid end-of-course/MCE exams. The results of these estimations are presented in figures 6 and 7. An examination of these figures reveals that states that have implemented both policies—rewards for success and sanctions for failure—have fourth-grade reading scores that are 63 percent of a GLE greater than demographically similar states that have implemented neither policy and

Table 3. Effects of Stakes for Teachers and Students on Reading and Mathematics Achievement in Fourth and Eighth Grade

| Subject, year, and grade | Stakes for schools and teachers | | Minimum competency exam | | EOCE/MCE, New York and North Carolina | | Adjusted R square | RMSE | Number of observations |
|---|---|---|---|---|---|---|---|---|---|
| | Coefficient | Standard error | Coefficient | Standard error | Coefficient | Standard error | | | |
| *Public reports* | | | | | | | | | |
| Reading, 1998, fourth grade | 3.90 | 3.32 | | | | | .731 | 4.60 | 39 |
| Reading, 1998, eighth grade | 4.83+ | 3.00 | | | | | .662 | 3.34 | 35 |
| Math, 1996, fourth grade | 1.95 | 2.09 | | | | | .765 | 4.14 | 43 |
| Math, 1996, eighth grade | -1.41 | 1.94 | | | | | .879 | 3.77 | 40 |
| Science, 1996, eighth grade | -.31 | 1.56 | | | | | .907 | 3.02 | 40 |
| *Rewards* | | | | | | | | | |
| Reading, 1998, fourth grade | 4.61** | 2.25 | | | | | .753 | 4.41 | 39 |
| Reading, 1998, eighth grade | 1.67 | 1.78 | | | | | .641 | 3.44 | 35 |
| Math, 1996, fourth grade | 2.26+ | 1.50 | | | | | .774 | 4.06 | 43 |
| Math, 1996, eighth grade | .98 | 1.48 | | | | | .879 | 3.77 | 40 |
| Science, 1996, eighth grade | .33 | 1.18 | | | | | .907 | 3.02 | 40 |
| *Consequences* | | | | | | | | | |
| Reading, 1998, fourth grade | 5.08** | 1.93 | | | | | .770 | 4.25 | 39 |
| Reading, 1998, eighth grade | 2.07 | 1.89 | | | | | .645 | 3.42 | 35 |
| Math, 1996, fourth grade | 2.65* | 1.53 | | | | | .778 | 4.02 | 43 |
| Math, 1996, eighth grade | 1.71 | 1.49 | | | | | .882 | 3.72 | 40 |
| Science, 1996, eighth grade | 2.30* | 1.14 | | | | | .917 | 2.85 | 40 |

*Rewards + consequences*

| | | | | | | | | | |
|---|---|---|---|---|---|---|---|---|---|
| Reading, 1998, fourth grade | 3.76*** | 1.23 | | | | | .784 | 4.12 | 39 |
| Reading, 1998, eighth grade | 1.43 | 1.12 | | | | | .650 | 3.40 | 35 |
| Math, 1996, fourth grade | 1.89** | .92 | | | | | .785 | 3.96 | 43 |
| Math, 1996, eighth grade | 1.09 | .94 | | | | | .882 | 3.72 | 40 |
| Science, 1996, eighth grade | 1.05+ | .74 | | | | | .912 | 2.93 | 40 |
| Reading, 1998, fourth grade | 3.65*** | 1.24 | -.01 | 2.12 | 5.87* | 3.17 | .797 | 4.00 | 39 |
| Reading, 1998, eighth grade | 1.33+ | 1.01 | .84 | 1.78 | 7.44*** | 2.50 | .728 | 3.00 | 35 |
| Math, 1996, fourth grade | 1.85** | .86 | 2.21 | 1.76 | 8.12*** | 3.09 | .818 | 3.64 | 43 |
| Math, 1996, eighth grade | 1.16 | .93 | .34 | 2.05 | 4.93* | 2.86 | .886 | 3.66 | 40 |
| Science, 1996, eighth grade | 1.07+ | .72 | 1.03 | 1.58 | 4.78** | 2.24 | .919 | 2.82 | 40 |

Source: Authors' analysis of National Center of Education Statistics data from the National Assessment of Educational Progress (NAEP) reading, mathematics, and science report cards in 1996 and 1998. In the math 1996 and science 1996 regressions, the indicators of state policy came from the January 1997 "Quality Counts" issue of *Education Week*, which used as a primary source *Bending without Breaking*, a 1996 publication of the Education Commission of the States.

Note: For the reading 1998 regressions, the policy indicators in the 1997 and 1998 "Quality Counts" issues were averaged. The reward + consequences variable in the bottom two panels is the sum of the reward dummy and the consequences dummy. All of the regressions controlled for the following demographic characteristics of the state's students: the incidence of poverty for children under eighteen (averaged from 1990 to 1996), the percent of children in two-parent families, the percent of 1996 public school students African American, the percent of 1996 public school students Hispanic or Native American, the percent of 1996 public school students Asian, and a parents' education index. The education index was defined as the average of the percent of 1990 parents who have a secondary high school diploma and the percent of parents who have a university degree. Hawaii was not included in the analysis because we could not control for the effects of Pacific Islander ethnicity. About half of Hawaiian students say they are Pacific Islanders, and these students do significantly less well on NAEP tests than local whites and Asians. The EOCE/MCE (end-of-course exam/minimum competency exam) variable is a dummy = 1 for New York and North Carolina. RMSE stands for root mean square error or alternatively the standard error of the estimate.

+ Statistically significant at 10 percent level on a one tail test.
* Statistically significant at 5 percent level on a one tail test.
** Statistically significant at 5 percent level on a two tail test.
*** Statistically significant at 1 percent level on a two tail test.

**Figure 6. Effects of Standards-Based Reform Initiatives on Fourth-Grade Reading and Math Ability**

Percent of a grade level equivalent

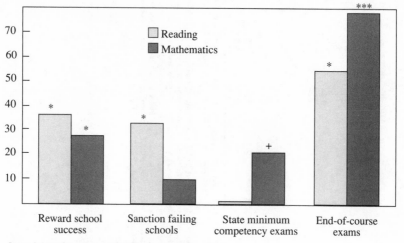

Source: Information on state policies, Education Commission of the States.
+ Statistically significant at 10 percent level on a one tail test
* Statistically significant at 5 percent level on a one tail test
*** Statistically significant at 1 percent level on a two tail test.

fourth-grade math scores about 32 percent of a GLE greater. Their eighth-grade test scores are about 20 percent of a GLE greater.

EFFECTS OF EOCES AND MCES CONTROLLING FOR STAKES FOR SCHOOL INI-TIATIVES. Adding the school rewards and consequences variable to the models containing EOCE and MCE variables leaves the coefficient on the end-of-course/MCE strategy variable (the New York/North Carolina dummy) essentially unchanged. We conclude, therefore, that our earlier finding that the New York/North Carolina student stakes policy mix has a large effect on achievement is not changed by including controls for other SBR initiatives.

Adding the school rewards and consequences variable does reduce our estimates of the backwash effects of minimum competency exams on achievement in fourth and eighth grades. The biggest change is in the model predicting fourth-grade reading achievement where the estimated effect disappears. The estimated effects of MCEs on reading and science achievement in eighth grade are reduced by 20 to 33 percent. Point estimates imply that, when other SBR policies are held constant, eighth-grade students in MCE states are less than 10 percent of a GLE ahead of students in states without MCEs.[49] If this were to be the only effect of MCEs, most advocates for the policy would probably

**Figure 7. Effects of Standards-Based Reform Initiatives on NAEP Eighth-Grade Test Scores**

Percent of a grade level equivalent

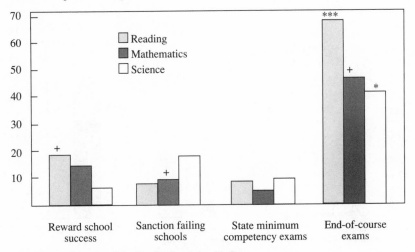

Source: Information on state policies, Education Commission of the States.
Note: NAEP = National Assessment of Educational Progress.
+ Statistically significant at 10 percent level on a one tail test
* Statistically significant at 5 percent level on a one tail test
*** Statistically significant at 1 percent level on a two tail test.

be disappointed. But we have not yet looked at the effect of MCEs on learning during the high school years. We have also not looked at the effects of MCEs on college attendance and labor market success. One would expect the effects of MCEs to be greatest on students who are approaching graduation or who have graduated.

*Analysis of Longitudinal Data on Test Score Gains during High School*

Models were estimated predicting test score gains during the full four-year period from 1988 to 1992 for each of the four subject matter tests and for the mean of the test score gains. Students who dropped out of high school were given the tests along with those who remained in school, so the negative effects on learning that come from students dropping out of school are taken into account. The specification of the model and the results are fully described in Appendix B and table B-2.[50] The main findings are summarized in figure 8.

Our first finding is that state minimum course graduation requirements had no effect on test score gains from eighth to twelfth grade. Our second finding

**Figure 8. Effects of Graduation Requirements on Eighth- to Twelfth-Grade Test Score Gains by GPA in Eighth Grade**

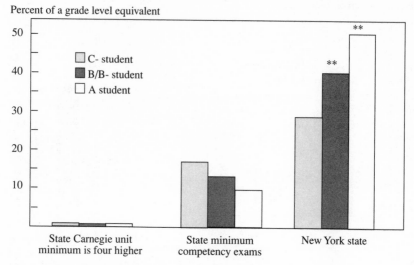

Source: Analysis of National Education Longitudinal Study of 1988 with controls for attitudes, socioeconomic status, grade point average and test scores in eighth grade, and state and high school characteristics.
** Statistically significant at 5 percent level on a two tail test.

is that MCEs had some small positive effects. Students with average grades had significantly larger gains in math and social studies when they lived in MCE states. When the gains on all four tests were averaged, however, achievement gains were only slightly and nonsignificantly greater in MCE states. We also found no evidence that students with below average grades were more effected by MCEs than students with high GPAs.

Our third finding is that end-of-course exams combined with MCEs—or something else in the New York state policy mix—appears to have had large significant effects on learning during high school. For students with average grades, test score gains in New York were a significant 38 percent of a GLE greater on the test composite, 72 percent of a GLE greater in science, and 29 percent of a GLE greater in mathematics. This occurred even though dropout rates are higher in New York than in most other states and dropouts learn considerably less than students who stay in school. NELS-88 students who had dropped out of school were tested in 1992 along with everyone else. Those who stayed in school learned enough extra to counterbalance the negative effects of New York's higher dropout rate.

The fourth major finding is that the positive effects of the New York policy mix on learning between eighth and twelfth grade were not limited to students with low GPAs in eighth grade. The estimated impacts were larger and more significant for high and average GPA students than for low GPA students. This is what one would expect from a system of state-sponsored end-of-course exams that serve as a final in many of the courses students are taking in high school. Unlike MCEs, which focus all their incentive effects on students who are doing poorly in school, end-of-course exams such as the Regents strengthen incentives for students in the middle and top of the class as well. Theory predicts that everyone should try harder.

### The Effects of State Graduation Requirements on College Enrollment Rates

If tougher high school graduation requirements raise the achievement of high school graduates, as intended, they are likely to increase the proportion of high school graduates who attend and complete college. Analyzing High School and Beyond (HSB) data, John H. Bishop and Ferran Mane in 1999 found that high school graduates coming from high schools with an MCE graduation requirement (as reported by the principal) were significantly more likely to be in college during the four-year period immediately following high school graduation. Effects were largest for students in the middle and bottom of the test score distribution and tended to be greater in the second and third years out than in the first, fourth, and subsequent years out. Opponents of MCEs concede this point but argue that it is accomplished by reducing the number of high school graduates, not by increasing the numbers attending and completing college.

What needs to be studied, therefore, is the college enrollment and completion rates of eighth graders living in MCE states, not the college going rates of high school graduates in MCE states. Opponents of MCEs predict that the reductions in high school graduation rates they expect MCEs to cause will then lower the proportion of eighth graders with low GPAs who eventually attend college. Proponents of MCEs disagree. They argue that MCE tests assess very basic skills and that students who cannot, after many tries, pass such tests are not prepared for college-level work. Open-door institutions will admit them, but they will need extensive remedial course work and are unlikely to complete any course of study. It is better, they argue, for high schools to hold all students to higher standards and that poorly prepared students be told of their deficiencies early in high school when there is time to do something about it. The result, they argue, will be an increase in the number of high school graduates who have the skills and knowledge necessary to succeed and thrive in college. They, therefore, would predict that, even when MCEs delay or prevent some from graduating from high school, the proportion of eighth graders who enter college on schedule in fall 1992 will not decline and a year or so later college enrollment rates will be higher in MCE states. The positive effect of MCEs on college enrollment rates is delayed because some enter college one year later because of the extra time required to complete high school and because MCEs increase college retention rates.

Logistic regressions were estimated predicting college enrollment in the fall of 1992, spring of 1993, fall of 1993, and the spring of 1994 of students who were in eighth grade in the spring of 1988. The model specifications were the same as those used in the dropout and high school completion models.[51] The results are presented in table B-3 and figure 9. Higher state minimum course graduation requirements significantly reduced college attendance. A four Carnegie unit increase in graduation requirements reduced college enrollment rates by 1.2 to 2.1 percentage points in fall 1992, spring and fall 1993, and spring 1994.

State MCEs had no effects on overall college entry rates in the fall of 1992. However, this result hides equal and opposite effects on students with good and bad grades in eighth grade. We estimate that A students in MCE states were 2.8 percentage points more likely to be in college in fall 1992 than A students in non-MCE states, while C- students were 2.7 percentage points less likely to be in college than C- students in non-MCE states.

One year later in fall 1993, however, all students, regardless of GPA, were more likely to be attending college when they grew up in an MCE state. The positive effect of state MCEs on college enrollment in 1993–94 was not significantly different for students with good and bad GPAs in eighth grade. Thus, state MCEs apparently delayed the graduation of some eighth graders with C- GPAs, and this delayed their entry into college. But one year later college attendance rates of C- students were 2.3 percentage points higher in MCE states than non-MCE states. Attendance was also higher for other students. Our regressions also predict that B students were 4.4 points more likely and A students were 3.3 points more likely to be attending college in MCE states.

The New York state policy mix also appears to have had significant positive effects on college attendance in the fall of 1993. The statistically signifi-

**Figure 9. Effects of State Minimum Competency Exams (MCEs) and New York State on the Probability of Eighth Graders Attending College Five to Six Years Later**

Change in probability (percent)

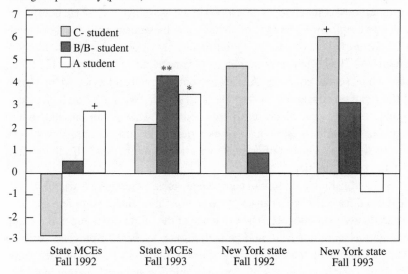

Source: Analysis of National Education Longitudinal Study of 1988 with controls for socioeconomic status, grade point average and test scores in eighth grade, and state and high school characteristics.
+ Statistically significant at 10 percent level on a one tail test
* Statistically significant at 5 percent level on a one tail test
** Statistically significant at 5 percent level on a two tail test.

cant New York state effect is a 6 percentage point greater likelihood of college attendance by students with C- GPAs in eighth grade. New York students with average grades were 3 percentage points more likely to be in college, but this differential was not large enough to be statistically significant.

## Effects of MCE Graduation Requirements on Wages and Employment after High School

MCEs are hypothesized to improve job opportunities in three ways. The first way is, by improving student achievement, they raise worker productivity.[52] Even when this does not immediately raise workers' earnings, the effect of academic achievement on wages grows with time and eventually becomes very large.[53]

The second way MCEs improve job opportunities is by sending a signal to employers that "all the graduates of this high school meet or exceed your hiring standards." The fact that they have passed the MCE is the proof. In most communities, competencies developed in the local high school are poorly signaled to employers. The lack of signals of achievement in high school tends to make employers with the best jobs reluctant to risk hiring recent high school graduates. They often carry in their head very negative stereotypes regarding recent high school graduates. A black personnel director interviewed for a CBS-TV special on educational reform proudly stated, "We don't hire high school graduates any more, we need skilled workers."[54] They prefer, instead, to hire workers with many years of work experience because an applicant's work record serves as a signal of competence and reliability that helps them identify the most qualified.

By establishing a minimum competency exam, therefore, a school district or state education system can try to overcome this signaling problem and help its graduates get good jobs. The existence of the minimum competency exam graduation requirement should be well known to local employers. With the MCE requirement, the school's diploma now signals more than just seat time; it signals meeting or exceeding certain minimum standards in reading, writing, mathematics, science, and social studies. Because of pooling, all high school graduates should benefit from an MCE regime, not just the students with low achievement levels in eighth grade.

The third way that MCEs can affect job opportunities is by improving the quality of the information that employers have on the academic achievement of recent high school graduates. If employers become better able to assess the academic achievement of job applicants, they will give these traits greater weight in the selection decisions and rewards for academic achievement will rise. Regents exam scores appear on student transcripts, so New York employers should be better informed about high school achievement than employers in other states and offer larger rewards for that achievement. In other MCE states, transcripts indicate whether the student has passed the MCE, but MCE test scores are not typically reported.

The foregoing logic generates a number of testable predictions regarding the graduates of high schools with an MCE graduation requirement. Holding constant socioeconomic status (SES), eighth-grade test scores, eighth-grade GPA, working during eighth grade, attitudes in eighth grade, whether the individual gets a diploma or a GED, current and past college attendance, and a complete set of other individual and school characteristics:

Hypothesis 4A: *Rewards for academic achievement will be significantly greater in New York state.*

Hypothesis 4B: *Students at MCE high schools will obtain higher wage rates and higher earnings than students at schools without MCE graduation requirements.*

### Results Using NELS-88 Data

Analyzing High School and Beyond data and controlling for college attendance and a host of other variables, John H. Bishop, Joan Moriarty, and Ferran Mane in 1998 found that females graduating from high schools with a minimum competency exam graduation requirement (student report) earned more than women graduating from schools without an MCE. Concern about the accuracy of student reports of the existence of an MCE at their high school led Bishop and Mane in 1999 to reanalyze HSB data using principal reports of the existence of an MCE graduation requirement. They found even larger effects. Principal reports of an MCE graduation requirement had positive effects (significant in some, but not all, years) on wage rates of male and female graduates and on the earnings of graduates four and five years after graduation. The wage rate effects of MCEs appeared to be larger for students in the bottom three quarters of the test score distribution.

Here we analyze data from NELS-88 and use the policy of the state in which the high school is located to define the MCE variable. Models were estimated predicting six indicators of early labor market outcomes: earnings in calendar 1993, average monthly earnings when working, monthly earnings in January and February 1994, the hourly wage rate, the total number of months worked, and the total number of months unemployed during the twenty-one-month period following high school graduation. The estimations are a decided improvement over the analyses previously conducted in High School and Beyond data because the use of restricted data allows us to include controls for the unemployment rate in the state and the average earnings in manufacturing and retailing for the state.

Table B-4 presents our analysis of the relationship between state MCE graduation requirements and the earnings and employment of high school graduates and dropouts. The regressions control for whether students graduated from high school and whether they attended college, so we are measuring the short-run effects of graduation requirements on labor market success net of effects

**Figure 10. Effect of Minimum Competency Exams (MCEs) on Monthly Earnings of Workers in 1992–94**

Dollars

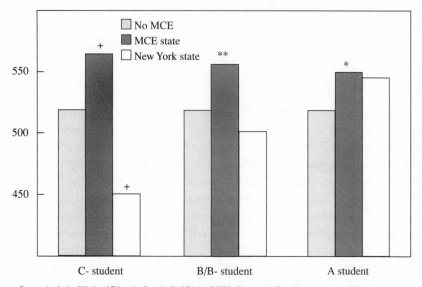

C- student          B/B- student          A student

Source: Analysis of National Education Longitudinal Study of 1988 with controls for college attendance, high school comple- . tion, socioeconomic status, grade point average and test scores in eighth grade, and state and high school characteristics.
Note: GED = general equivalency diploma.
+ Statistically significant at 10 percent level on a one tail test
* Statistically significant at 5 percent level on a one tail test
** Statistically significant at 5 percent level on a two tail test.

that operate through the probability of graduating or attending college. Regression specifications and control variables are described in Appendix B.

Our first finding is that higher state course graduation requirements have no tendency to increase the employment and earnings of recent high school graduates. To the contrary, they are associated with graduates getting lower wage rates.

Relationships between earnings, academic achievement, and types of exit examination systems are graphed in figures 10, 11, and 12. In states without MCE graduation requirements, academic achievement had no large or significant effect on monthly earnings in 1992–94, total earnings in 1993, or hourly wage rates in 1993. Students who had one standard deviation higher test scores and one point higher eighth-grade GPA were paid 1.3 percent more per hour but earned 1.3 percent less in 1993. This pattern of negligible rewards for academic achievement also prevailed in MCE states. In New York state, however,

**Figure 11. Effect of Minimum Competency Exams (MCEs) on Annual Earnings of Workers in 1993**

Dollars

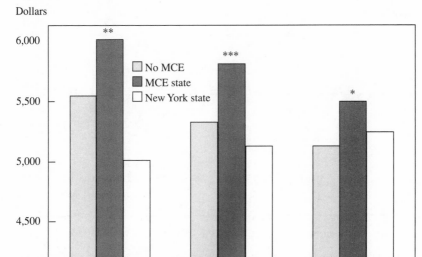

Source: Analysis of National Education Longitudinal Study of 1988 with controls for college attendance, high school completion, socioeconomic status, grade point average and test scores in eighth grade, and state and high school characteristics.
* Statistically significant at 5 percent level on a one tail test
** Statistically significant at 5 percent level on a two tail test.
*** Statistically significant at 1 percent level on a two tail test.

achievement differentials of the same magnitude were associated with a statistically significant 13 percent increase in monthly earnings in the first quarter of 1994, a 4.8 percent increase in 1993 earnings, and a 4.2 percent increase in hourly wage rates. In the earnings and wage regressions, all four coefficients on the New York state*GPA interaction were positive and two were significantly positive. The effect is so strong it apparently results in low GPA students being paid significantly less per month. Our interpretation of this result is that it reflects the improved signaling to employers of student achievement in high school that results from putting Regents exam scores on high school transcripts (see hypothesis 4A).

Consistent with hypothesis 4B, minimum competency examinations had positive effects on the earnings of students of all ability levels. The state MCE coefficient was positive in all four of the models predicting wage rates and earnings and was significant in two. Students with average grades from states

**Figure 12. Effect of Minimum Competency Exams (MCEs) on Hourly Wage Rates in 1993**

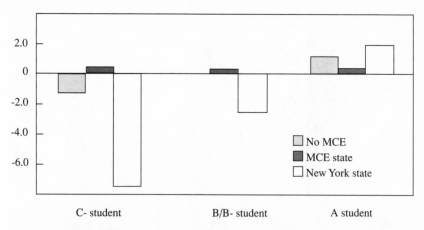

Source: Analysis of National Education Longitudinal Study of 1988 with controls for college attendance, high school completion, socioeconomic status, grade point average and test scores in eighth grade, and state and high school characteristics.

with MCEs earned 7 percent more per month and 9 percent more during calendar 1993 than students from states without MCEs. Effects were slightly larger for low GPA students, but not significantly so. Going to a high school in a state with an MCE was, by contrast, not associated with more months employed or fewer months unemployed for students with average grades.

These are striking findings. The effects of MCEs are large and appear to have grown since 1981. Bishop and Mane's 1999 analysis of the effects of MCEs on the 1981–82 labor market outcomes of 1980 graduates found no effects on annual earnings and statistically insignificant effects (of about 1.6 percent) on wage rates. These regressions predicting the 1993–94 labor market outcomes of people who were eighth graders in 1988 get much larger effects on monthly earnings and annual earnings of all students and on employment of low GPA students.

Why did the impact of MCEs grow? Three explanations come to mind. First, in 1981–82 most state-level MCE graduation requirements were new and employers had probably not fully adapted their hiring policies to the innovation. Second, during the 1980s employers began to recognize that jobs were becoming more cognitively complex and started to give cognitive skills more emphasis in hiring. The payoff to years of schooling and test scores rose, and a rising premium for graduating from an MCE high school may be part of the same phenomenon.[55] Finally, starting in 1989, the American Federation of Teachers (AFT) and a number of blue-ribbon panels began urging employers to reward achievement in high school.[56] In MCE states this may have led employers to offer all recent high school graduates better jobs. In New York state, where Regents exam scores are on student transcripts and AFT president Albert Shanker's column appeared regularly in the *New York Times*, it may have led employers to seek the transcripts of job applicants and use them as a factor in hiring.

### Summary and Conclusions

We looked at the effects of one old-style educational reform—higher course graduation requirements—and five standard-based reforms—school report cards, rewards for school improvement, sanctions for failing schools, minimum competency examinations, and hybrid MCE/end-of-course examinations. For state course graduation requirements, state minimum competency exams, and end-of-course exams, we studied effects on eight outcomes—high school dropout rates, high school graduation rates, test scores, college attendance rates, employment, unemployment, wage rates, and earnings. For school-based SBR policies, only test scores were studied. Our results are summarized in table 4.

CAVEATS. The large number of cells in table 4 with a '—' display our current ignorance and lay out an agenda for future research. Findings were not always consistent across data sets. While a host of individual, school, and state characteristics were controlled, treating our estimates of differences between MCE states and non-MCE states as unbiased estimates of the causal impact of MCEs or EOCEs is risky. MCEs and EOCEs may be correlated with other important but unmeasured determinants of the outcome of interest. If so, our regression coefficients would be biased estimates of the true causal impacts of these policies. In future research we plan to try to fill in some of table 4's empty cells and to deal with omitted variable and selection bias problems by studying the effects of changes in policy regime.

IMPACTS OF SBR POLICIES ON TEST SCORES. States with minimum competency exams tend to have also been early adopters of school accountability systems that reward high-achieving schools or sanction failing schools that do not improve. This means that unbiased estimates of the effect of a particular SBR initiative are possible only when the presence or absence of other

Table 4. Effects of Standards-Based Reform Initiatives on Enrollment Rates, Graduation Rates, Test Scores, College Attendance, and Labor Market Success

| | Four extra courses required to graduate | Minimum competency exam | End-of-course and state MCEs CBEEES | School report cards | Sanction failing schools | Reward school success | Assist failing schools |
|---|---|---|---|---|---|---|---|
| *State cross sections* | | | | | | | |
| Enrollment at age seventeen | -.010** | .003 | .013 | — | — | — | — |
| High school graduation | -.007 | -.005 | .003 | — | — | — | — |
| Reading, 1998, fourth grade | t = 0 | .00 | .51* | 0 | .33*** | .33*** | 0 |
| Reading, 1998, eighth grade | t = 0 | .07 | .65*** | 0 | .12+ | .12+ | 0 |
| Math, 1996, fourth grade | t = 0 | .19 | .71*** | 0 | .16** | .16** | — |
| Math, 1996, eighth grade | t = 0 | .03 | .43* | 0 | .10 | .10 | — |
| Science, 1996, eighth grade | t = 0 | .10 | .46** | 0 | .10+ | .10+ | — |
| | | | | | | | |
| *Longitudinal for eighth graders in 1988* | | | | | | | |
| Test gain 1988 to 1992 (GPA is C-) | .006 | .155 | .28 | — | — | — | — |
| Test gain 1988 to 1992 (GPA is B/B-) | .006 | .116 | .39** | — | — | — | — |
| Test gain 1988 to 1992 (GPA is A) | .006 | .081 | .49** | — | — | — | — |
| Ever dropped out (GPA is C-) | .025** | .014 | .084+ | — | — | — | — |
| Ever dropped out (GPA is B/B-) | .013** | .005 | .051** | — | — | — | — |
| Ever dropped out (GPA is A) | .004** | .001 | .023* | — | — | — | — |
| Neither diploma nor GED (GPA is C-) | .000 | .071*** | .051 | — | — | — | — |
| Neither diploma nor GED (GPA is B/B-) | .000 | .005 | .013 | — | — | — | — |
| Neither diploma nor GED (GPA is A) | .000 | -.002 | .003 | — | — | — | — |
| Late diploma (GPA is C-) | .010 | .111*** | .200*** | — | — | — | — |
| Late diploma (GPA is B/B-) | .004 | .027* | .091*** | — | — | — | — |
| Late diploma (GPA is A) | .002 | .003 | .036** | — | — | — | — |
| Got GED (GPA is C-) | .016* | .025+ | .092*** | — | — | — | — |

| | | | | | | | |
|---|---|---|---|---|---|---|---|
| Got GED (GPA is B/B-) | .009* | .014* | .048*** | — | — | — | — |
| Got GED (GPA is A) | .005* | .008+ | .025* | — | — | — | — |
| College in fall 1992 (GPA is C-) | -.013** | -.027 | .047 | | | | |
| College in fall 1992 (GPA is B/B-) | -.021** | .007 | .008 | | | | |
| College in fall 1992 (GPA is A) | -.012** | .028+ | -.026 | | | | |
| College in fall 1993 (GPA is C-) | -.016*** | .023 | .061+ | | | | |
| College in fall 1993 (GPA is B/B-) | -.020** | .044** | .030 | | | | |
| College in fall 1993 (GPA is A) | -.014** | .033* | -.010 | | | | |
| Earnings in 1993 (GPA is C-) | -1.0% | 11.2%*** | -10.5% | — | — | — | — |
| Earnings in 1993 (GPA is B/B-) | -1.0% | 9.3%**** | -3.6% | — | — | — | — |
| Earnings in 1993 (GPA is A) | -1.0% | 7.5%* | 3.1% | — | — | — | — |
| Average earnings per month (GPA is C-) | 0.0% | 9.0%* | -13%+ | — | — | — | — |
| Average earnings per month (GPA is B/B-) | 0.0% | 7.1%** | -4% | — | — | — | — |
| Average earnings per month (GPA is A) | 0.0% | 5.6%+ | 5% | — | — | — | — |
| Hourly wage rate (GPA is C-) | -1.6%** | 1.3% | -4.9% | — | — | — | — |
| Hourly wage rate (GPA is B/B-) | -1.6%*** | 0.3% | -1.9% | — | — | — | — |
| Hourly wage rate (GPA is A) | -1.6%*** | -0.6% | 0.6% | — | — | — | — |
| Number of months employed in 1993-94 | -1.0% | 2.0% | 1.0% | — | — | — | — |

Note: MCEs = minimum competency exams; CBEEES = curriculum-based external exit exam system; GPA = grade point average; GED = general equivalency diploma. For dropout rates, graduation rates, and college attendance rates, table entries are estimates of the effect of a policy on the probability of being enrolled or of not completing high school. For test score outcomes, the figures in the table are in grade level equivalents. For labor market outcomes, table entries are percentage increases or decreases associated with the policy.

+ Statistically significant at 10 percent level on a one tail test.

\* Statistically significant at 5 percent level on a one tail test.

\** Statistically significant at 5 percent level on a two tail test.

\*** Statistically significant at 1 percent level on a two tail test.

— = Data were not available for testing this hypothesis.

$t = 0$ indicates the relationship was assumed to be zero a priori.

initiatives is taken into account. Our analysis of the state cross sections of NAEP test scores handles this problem by controlling for other SBR policies. The number of students tested is also large, and one can repeat the analysis for different subjects and for different years. These features of the state cross-section analysis probably make it our best estimate of the overall effects of individual SBR policies.[57]

The policy that clearly has the biggest effects on test scores is the hybrid end-of-course/minimum competency exam system that has been in place in New York state since the early 1980s and in North Carolina since about 1991. In comparison to students in states without MCEs or EOCEs, eighth graders in New York and North Carolina were about 45 percent of a grade level equivalent ahead in math and science and 65 percent of a GLE ahead in reading. In addition, test score gains from eighth to twelfth grade were nearly 39 percent of a grade level equivalent greater in New York state. This confirms and extends earlier findings that New York state did significantly better on SAT tests and the 1992 eighth-grade NAEP math tests than other states with demographically similar populations.[58] This policy package is also often referred to as a curriculum-based external exit exam system. Most countries have such systems and studies have found that young people living in provinces and countries with such systems have higher reading, math, and science achievement than students in jurisdictions that lack CBEEES.[59]

The next most powerful intervention appears to be state-imposed stakes for teachers and schools, particularly when rewards for successful schools were combined with sanctions for failing schools. Public reporting is necessary for the implementation of these other policies, but on its own it had no discernible effect on student achievement.

When school stakes and EOCE policies are not controlled for, states that impose an MCE requirement on their high schools tend to have higher test scores. When, however, other SBR policies are held constant, the positive effects of state-imposed MCEs on achievement in fourth and eighth grade are reduced and become statistically insignificant. State-imposed MCEs had no significant effects on overall test score gains during high school of students with average grades.

The policy having the smallest effects was state-imposed course graduation requirements. They had no impacts on test score gains.

IMPACTS OF GRADUATION REQUIREMENTS ON SCHOOL ENROLLMENT AND GRADUATION RATES. Higher state-mandated minimum course graduation requirements were associated with higher dropout rates and higher probabilities of getting a GED. They were not, however, associated with fewer students getting some kind of diploma—either a regular diploma or a GED. The state cross-section analysis found that state-mandated minimum competency exams had no effects on overall dropout rates or high school completion rates. When, however, we analyzed longitudinal data that controlled for the grades and test scores of students in eighth grade, we found that students at MCE schools with C- grades in eighth grade, while not more likely to drop out, were 7.1 percentage points less likely to get a high school diploma or a GED within six years and 11 percentage points more likely to get their diploma late. MCEs had no significant effect on graduation rates of students with average or above average grades. Students with average grades, however, were more likely to experience delays in getting their diploma.[60] In the NELS-88 analysis New York students were significantly more likely to drop out, to be delayed in getting their diploma, and to get a GED instead of a high school diploma. These effects were larger for students with low GPAs in eighth grade. Despite this, probabilities of getting a diploma or GED before 1994 were no different in New York than other states in the Northeast.

EFFECTS OF GRADUATION REQUIREMENTS ON COLLEGE ATTENDANCE. Two years after the scheduled date of their high school graduation, students from states with an MCE were significantly more likely to be attending college. Students from states with high Carnegie unit graduation requirements, by contrast, were significantly less likely to be attending college.

EFFECTS OF GRADUATION REQUIREMENTS ON LABOR MARKET OUTCOMES. State-imposed course graduation requirements had no significant relationship with employment and earnings but were negatively associated with wage rates. In contrast, students who attended school in states with MCEs earned significantly more in the years immediately after graduating. Students with average grades who lived in states with MCE graduation requirements earned about 7 percent more per month and 9 percent more per year than students in states without MCEs.

Because Regents exam scores are part of student grades and appear on high school transcripts (thus signaling who is taking a more rigorous curriculum), we hypothesized the rewards for academic achievement would be greater in New York state than elsewhere in the nation. This hypothesis was confirmed. However, the existence of the Regents exam system did not improve the labor market success of all students equally the way MCEs appear to have. Recent graduates from New York were not better paid than graduates from other Northeastern states, and those with low GPAs were paid less.

POLICY IMPLICATIONS. When one looks at the totality of the evidence, what can be said about the efficacy of the four state policies—course graduation requirements, stakes for schools, MCEs, and end-of-course exams—that we have been studying?

The policy initiative with the least to recommend it is increases in state-set Carnegie unit minimums for graduating from high school. Test score gains were not larger in these states, but dropout rates were higher and college attendance rates were lower.

Stakes for schools appear to increase student achievement. States that identify and sanction failing schools or reward schools that improve student achievement had higher fourth- and eighth-grade NAEP test scores in 1996 and 1998. We did not investigate whether these policies influence dropout rates or college attendance.

State-imposed MCEs generate important benefits. They induced employers to offer recent high school graduates better jobs, and eighth graders living in MCE states were more likely to be attending college six years later. When we control for other SBR policies, MCEs have positive effects on test scores, but the effects are small and often not statistically significant. These benefits were not costless, however. Students with low GPAs in eighth grade who attended high schools with MCEs were more likely to have their diploma delayed or denied. Nevertheless their earnings and college attendance rates were significantly higher, so low GPA students were probably better off when they lived in an MCE state. Students with average or above average grades in eighth grade were not less likely to graduate or get a GED when they lived in an MCE state, so for them all of the effects of the MCE policy were either neutral or positive.

The hybrid end-of-course exam/minimum competency exam system of New York and North Carolina had by far the largest impacts on achievement in eighth grade and test score gains during high school. By the end of high school, achievement was nearly one grade level equivalent ahead of other comparable states. Low GPA students were more likely to go to college when they lived in New York. On the negative side, New York eighth graders were more likely to drop out in the next four years, more likely to get GEDs instead of regular diplomas, and tended to take longer to get their diploma. They were not, however, less likely to get a diploma or GED. Rewards for academic achievement were greater in New York state, but recent graduates were not better paid than graduates from other states. Students with low GPAs were paid less.

Should more states introduce state-sponsored end-of-course exams? Our answer to that question is yes. The achievement gains generated by adding end-of-course exams to a conventional MCE system are so large that college completion rates and the quality of the jobs obtained by thirty-year-olds are likely to be substantially higher. These benefits, in our view, outweigh the higher dropout rates, delayed graduation rates, and lower starting wage rates that appear to be associated with the New York state policy mix.

---

# Appendix A

*Data for State Cross-Section Analysis of Dropout Rates and Graduation Rates*

State-level data on enrollment rates and high school graduation rates for the early 1990s were analyzed. The dependent variables were the 1990 enrollment rate of seventeen-year-olds (measured in percent) and the high school graduation ratio (the ratio of the number of high school diplomas awarded in the state to the number of seventeen-year-olds).[61] The population of seventeen-year-olds was used as the base instead of eighteen-year-olds because the number of eighteen-year-olds may be inflated by in-migration of college students and military personnel. The sample included forty-nine states plus the District of Columbia. Hawaii was not included because we could not control for the effects of Pacific Islander ethnicity. A large proportion of students are of Pacific Islander ethnicity, and these students have lower test scores and are more likely to drop out than local whites and Asians.

Information on each state's compulsory education laws and high school graduation requirements—minimum competency exams (MCEs) and the number of Carnegie units required to graduate—were obtained from the 1993 issue of the *Digest of Educational Statistics* and by contacting accountability staff in states with ambiguous data. The control variables characterizing the demographic background of the state's high school age youth were as follows:

—A parents' education index equal to the average of the percent of parents with a high school diploma and the percent of parents with a university degree in 1990.

—Incidence of poverty for children under eighteen in 1989.

—Percent of the state's population foreign born.

—Percent of public school students African American.

—Percent of public school students of Hispanic origin.

The policy variables included:

—The state-mandated minimum number of full-year courses required to graduate from public high schools in the state.

—A dummy variable that is equal to one if the state has not set a minimum number of full-year courses that all students must complete to graduate from high school.

—A dummy variable for New York state (testing whether the combination of voluntary Regents exams and an MCE affect dropout rates).

—A dummy variable for the other states with minimum competency examinations that students must pass to graduate from public high school. The states, other than New York, classified as having an MCE applying to 1992 graduates were Alabama, Florida, Georgia, Hawaii, Louisiana, Maryland, Mississippi, Nevada, New Mexico, New Jersey, North Carolina, South Carolina, Tennessee, and Texas.

—A dummy variable for whether seventeen-year-olds are required to be in school by the state's compulsory attendance law.

The results of the regression analysis are presented in table A-1.

## State Cross-Section Analysis of NAEP Test Scores

The analysis of state cross-section data provides estimates of the effects on statewide student achievement of six different but complementary standards-based reform (SBR) strategies:

1. Minimum competency exams.

2. Voluntary end-of-course exams (EOCEs) combined with minimum competency exams; that is, the New York/North Carolina policy mix during the middle of the 1990s.[62]

3. School-by-school reporting of the results of statewide testing.

4. Rewards for schools that improve on statewide tests or exceed targets set for them.

5. Sanctions for failing schools—threats of closure, reconstitution, loss of accreditation, and so on.

6. Assistance programs for low-performing schools.

The dependent variables are state-level means for fourth- and eighth-grade National Assessment of Educational Progress (NAEP) tests in 1992, 1994, 1996, and 1998 in reading, mathematics, and science. For regressions pre-

**Table A-1. Determinants of School Enrollment and High School Graduation Rates**

| | Percent of seventeen-year-olds enrolled in high school | | High school diplomas per one hundred seventeen-year-olds | Fourth-grade reading | Fourth-grade mathematics |
|---|---|---|---|---|---|
| | *1990 census* | *1991 NCES* | *1991 NCES* | *1994 NAEP* | *1992 NAEP* |
| State minimum competency exam[a] | .11 (.81) | .47 (.53) | -.50 (2.27) | 5.37** (2.41) | 2.62* (1.42) |
| New York state | 2.08 (1.90) | .60 (1.24) | .28 (5.35) | 8.6* (4.91) | 5.93+ (3.92) |
| Number of Carnegie units required to graduate | -.30*** (.11) | -.183** (.069) | -.179 (.297) | — | — |
| No Carnegie unit graduation requirement | -5.13** (2.14) | -3.46** (1.40) | .70 (6.02) | — | — |
| Attendance required at age seventeen | .92 (.52) | .36 (.34) | .62 (1.46) | | |
| Parents' education index[b] | .33*** (.105) | .128* (.069) | .759 (.294) | .12 (.28) | .68*** (.22) |
| Percent in poverty (people eighteen years or less)[c] | .052 (.076) | -.022 (.049) | -.027 (.212) | -.38* (.21) | -.35* (.18) |
| Percent foreign born[d] | -.192** (.081) | -.207*** (.053) | -.463** (.228) | -.18 (.23) | -.24 (.19) |
| Percent of public school students black[e] | -.052* (.028) | -.052*** (.019) | -.158* (.079) | -.46*** (.09) | -.32*** (.05) |
| Percent of public school students Hispanic[e] | -.044 (.037) | -.012 (.024) | -.071 (.103) | -.34*** (.11) | -.17* (.09) |
| Adjusted R squared | .5047 | .5528 | .5322 | .7262 | .8414 |
| RMSE | 1.636 | 1.072 | 4.59 | 4.11 | 3.42 |
| Number of observations | 50 | 50 | 50 | 38 | 41 |
| Mean of dependent variable | 88.9 | 84.2 | 76.0 | 213.9 | 217.3 |

Note: NAEP = National Assessment of Educational Progress. RMSE stands for root mean square error or alternatively the standard error of the estimate.
a. Columns 1, 2, and 3 regressions use a minimum competency exam (MCE) variable for 1991 in which Virginia = 0. The MCE for 1996 variable used in columns 4 and 5 adds Ohio and Virginia to the MCE category.
b. Average of the percent of parents obtaining a secondary high school diploma and the percent of parents obtaining a university degree. National Center for Education Statistics (NCES), *Education in States and Nations* (Department of Education, 1991), p. 139.
c. National Center for Education Statistics, *Education in States and Nations*, pp. 49, 129, 119.
d. Bureau of the Census, *1990 Census of Population: Social and Economic Characteristics U.S.* (Government Printing Office), pp. 174–79.
e. National Center for Education Statistics, *Digest of Education Statistics* (Department of Education, 1993), pp. 61, 76.
+ Statistically significant at 10 percent level on a one tail test.
* Statistically significant at 5 percent level on a one tail test.
** Statistically significant at 5 percent level on a two tail test.
*** Statistically significant at 1 percent level on a two tail test.

**Table A-2. Effects of Minimum Competency Exams and New York State Regents Exams on Reading and Mathematics Achievement in Fourth and Eighth Grade**

| | Minimum competency exam | | EOCE/MCE, New York and North Carolina | | Poverty and parent education | African American, Hispanic, foreign born | Adjusted R square | RMSE | Number of observations |
|---|---|---|---|---|---|---|---|---|---|
| | Coefficient | Standard error | Coefficient | Standard error | | | | | |
| *Reading, 1998, eighth grade* | | | | | | | | | |
| Overall average | 1.39 | 1.76 | 7.74*** | 2.46 | x | x | .731 | 2.98 | 35 |
| High school dropout (parents) | 5.66* | 3.07 | 8.83*** | 4.3 | x | x | .217 | 5.21 | 35 |
| High school graduate (parents) | -.47 | 1.97 | 3.6 | 2.76 | x | x | .586 | 3.34 | 35 |
| Some college (parents) | 1.45 | 1.93 | 5.71** | 2.7 | x | x | .425 | 3.27 | 35 |
| College graduate (parents) | 1.61 | 2.22 | 8.07** | 3.11 | x | x | .601 | 3.77 | 35 |
| *Reading, fourth grade* | | | | | | | | | |
| Overall average in 1998 | 3.35+ | 2.24 | 9.9* | 5.7 | x | x | .686 | 4.91 | 39 |
| Overall average in 1994 | 4.64* | 2.35 | 7.35** | 3.17 | x | x | .761 | 3.83 | 38 |
| Overall average in 1992 | 3.64** | 1.43 | 4.53* | 2.37 | x | x | .874 | 3.04 | 34 |

*Math, 1996, eighth grade*

| | | | | | | | | |
|---|---|---|---|---|---|---|---|---|
| Overall average | 2.71+ | 1.78 | 5.56* | 2.93 | x | .879 | 3.77 | 40 |
| High school dropout (parents) | 2.55 | 2.13 | 5.81+ | 3.5 | x | .659 | 4.50 | 39 |
| High school graduate (parents) | 1.09 | 2.19 | 5.61+ | 3.59 | x | .816 | 4.62 | 40 |
| Some college (parents) | 2.89+ | 1.96 | 3.37 | 3.22 | x | .796 | 4.14 | 40 |
| College graduate (parents) | 2.76+ | 1.74 | 5.16* | 2.86 | x | .876 | 3.68 | 40 |
| Math, 1996, fourth grade | 4.18** | 1.88 | 9.7* | 5.10 | x | .728 | 4.45 | 43 |
| Math, 1992, eighth grade | 2.94* | 1.53 | 2.67 | 2.83 | x | .875 | 3.65 | 41 |
| Math, 1992, fourth grade | 3.24** | 1.43 | 2.54 | 2.65 | x | .842 | 3.42 | 41 |
| Science, 1996, eighth grade | 2.51+ | 1.50 | 5.7+ | 3.9 | x | .893 | 3.24 | 39 |

Source: Authors' analysis of National Center for Education Statistics data from state National Assessment of Educational Progress (NAEP) studies in 1998, 1996, 1994, and 1992, the reading report card, and the mathematics report card.

Note: A one grade level equivalent test score differential is about 11.5 points on both the reading and mathematics tests. In all models New York state and North Carolina were coded as EOCE/MCE (end-of-course exam/minimum competency exam), and Alabama, Florida, Georgia, Louisiana, Maryland, Nevada, New Jersey, New Mexico, North Carolina, South Carolina, Tennessee, Texas, and Virginia were coded as a one on the MCE variable. Ohio was introducing an MCE during this period so it was coded as a zero when 1992 test scores were predicted and as a one when 1996 and 1998 test scores were predicted. All of the regressions controlled for the following demographic characteristics of the state's students: the incidence of poverty for children under eighteen (averaged from 1990 to the date of the dependent variable), the percent of population foreign born, the percent of public school students African American, the percent of public school students Hispanic, the percent of public school students Asian, and a parents' education index. The education index was defined as the average of the percent of parents with a secondary high school diploma and the percent of parents with a four-year college degree. Hawaii was not included in the analysis because we could not control for the effects of Pacific Islander ethnicity. The majority of Hawaiian students are Pacific Islanders, and these students do significantly less well on NAEP tests than local whites and Asians. RMSE stands for root mean square error or alternatively the standard error of the estimate.

x = variable controlled for in the model.

+ Statistically significant at 10 percent level on a one tail test.

* Statistically significant at 5 percent level on a one tail test.

** Statistically significant at 5 percent level on a two tail test.

*** Statistically significant at 1 percent level on a two tail test.

dicting 1996 and 1998 NAEP test scores, the MCE variable was set equal to one for Alabama, Florida, Georgia, Louisiana, Maryland, Nevada, New Jersey, New Mexico, Ohio, South Carolina, Tennessee, Texas, and Virginia. Note that New York and North Carolina are coded as zero on the MCE variable, so the coefficient on the EOCE variable measures the combined effects of an EOCE and an MCE.

The models estimated have updated versions of the following demographic controls—the parental education index, poverty rate for children, percent of public school students who are African American, percent of students who are Hispanic, and percent of students who are Asian. For models predicting 1996 NAEP scores, the poverty rate was an average of the 1990 census figure for children under eighteen years old, an overall poverty rate for 1991 to 1993, and an overall poverty rate for 1994 to 1996. For models predicting 1998 NAEP scores, the poverty rate was an average of the 1990 census figure for children under eighteen years old, an overall poverty rate for 1992 to 1994, and an overall poverty rate for 1995 to 1997. The parental education index was based solely on the 1990 census. We did not update the family education index because the small number of Current Population Survey (CPS) respondents in many states made the CPS estimates of state-specific 1990 to 1997 changes in years of schooling of adults unreliable.

The results are presented in table A-2.

The strongest results are for the New York/North Carolina policy mix, a hybrid MCE/end-of-course exam system. The coefficient on the EOCE indicator variable is positive, large, and statistically significant in the models predicting reading, mathematics, and science achievement in 1994, 1996, and 1998. On the NAEP reading and math tests a grade level equivalent (GLE) is about 11.5 points. Thus going to school in New York or North Carolina is estimated to raise fourth-grade math achievement by three quarters of a grade level equivalent and fourth- and eighth-grade reading achievement by roughly two-thirds of a GLE. Science and mathematics achievement of eighth graders is roughly half a grade level equivalent higher.

Do scaled measures of SBR initiatives improve our ability to predict student achievement? The rewards programs, assistance programs, and sanctions programs implemented by various states differ dramatically. Some target many schools, others just a few. Some are well funded, others are not. Some are effective, others are probably ineffective. Why not construct policy intensity scales that distinguish effective SBR programs from ineffective SBR programs and then enter the intensity variables into our cross-state regressions? The problem with this research strategy is that all of the people who know enough about state SBR initiatives to construct such scales also know which states have had the most success in improving student achievement. Inevitably the numeric values they would assign to a state's SBR initiative would be influenced by that knowledge. The scales would not have been defined on an a priori basis and, as a result, tests of the effect of the SBR initiative scales would be invalid. Our solution to this problem was (1) to assign the task of developing SBR intensity indexes to a member of our team who was unfamiliar with which states have raised test scores the most and (2) to construct the indexes by applying a formula to the published indicators of state SBR initiatives published in the January 1999 "Quality Counts" issue of *Education Week*. Four indexes were created: a school report card index, a rewards for improving index, a sanctions for failure index, and an index of assistance for low-performing schools. The results of the analysis are reported in table A-3. Clearly our effort was a failure. None of the SBR indexes we created is a good predictor of student achievement. Why did the simpler dummy variable specifications do so much better? We suspect the reason is that the dummy variables described the policy environment in 1996 and 1997, while the indexes characterized it in 1998–99. Policies have been changing. As a result, the correlation between the 1996–97 dummy variables and the 1999 indexes were only .57 for the rewards indicators, .56 for the sanctions indicators, and .41 for the public reporting index.[63] Because we were predicting 1996 and 1998 test scores, the dummy variables did a better job.

Table A-3. Effects of Stakes for Teachers and Students on Reading and Mathematics Achievement in Fourth and Eighth Grade

| Dependent variable | Stakes for schools and teachers | | Minimum competency exam | | EOCE/MCE, New York and North Carolina | | Adjusted R square | RMSE | Number of observations |
|---|---|---|---|---|---|---|---|---|---|
| | Coefficient | Standard error | Coefficient | Standard error | Coefficient | Standard error | | | |
| *Public reports index* | | | | | | | | | |
| Reading, 1998, fourth grade | .53 | .53 | | | | | .677 | 5.04 | 39 |
| Reading, 1998, eighth grade | .17 | .38 | | | | | .641 | 3.44 | 35 |
| Math, 1996, fourth grade | .38 | .49 | | | | | .694 | 4.72 | 43 |
| Math, 1996, eighth grade | -.25 | .43 | | | | | .859 | 4.08 | 40 |
| Science, 1996, eighth grade | -.36 | .34 | | | | | .894 | 3.21 | 40 |
| *Rewards index* | | | | | | | | | |
| Reading, 1998, fourth grade | -.20 | 1.35 | | | | | .667 | 5.12 | 39 |
| Reading, 1998, eighth grade | .35 | .92 | | | | | .641 | 3.45 | 35 |
| Math, 1996, fourth grade | 1.74+ | 1.12 | | | | | .709 | 4.60 | 43 |
| Math, 1996, eighth grade | .90 | 1.07 | | | | | .860 | 4.06 | 40 |
| Science, 1996, eighth grade | .68 | .85 | | | | | .893 | 3.24 | 40 |
| *Sanctions index* | | | | | | | | | |
| Reading, 1998, fourth grade | .79+ | .50 | | | | | .692 | 4.92 | 39 |
| Reading, 1998, eighth grade | .54+ | .34 | | | | | .670 | 3.30 | 35 |
| Math, 1996, fourth grade | .54 | .44 | | | | | .702 | 4.66 | 43 |
| Math, 1996, eighth grade | .04 | .40 | | | | | .857 | 4.10 | 40 |
| Science, 1996, eighth grade | -.19 | .32 | | | | | .892 | 3.25 | 40 |

| | | | | | | | | | |
|---|---|---|---|---|---|---|---|---|---|
| *Help failing schools index* | | | | | | | | | |
| Reading, 1998, fourth grade | .48 | .41 | | | | | .681 | 5.01 | 39 |
| Reading, 1998, eighth grade | .43+ | .28 | | | | | .668 | 3.31 | 35 |
| Math, 1996, fourth grade | .67 | .79 | | | | | .695 | 4.71 | 43 |
| Math, 1996, eighth grade | .39 | .73 | | | | | .858 | 4.08 | 40 |
| Science, 1996, eighth grade | .00 | .59 | | | | | .891 | 3.27 | 40 |
| | | | | | | | | | |
| *Rewards + sanctions* | | | | | | | | | |
| Reading, 1998, fourth grade | .48 | .41 | | | | | .681 | 5.01 | 39 |
| Reading, 1998, eighth grade | .43 | .28 | | | | | .668 | 3.31 | 35 |
| Math, 1996, fourth grade | .68* | .34 | | | | | .721 | 4.51 | 43 |
| Math, 1996, eighth grade | .19 | .32 | | | | | .858 | 4.08 | 40 |
| Science, 1996, eighth grade | .00 | .26 | | | | | .891 | 3.27 | 40 |
| | | | | | | | | | |
| Reading, 1998, fourth grade | .12 | .44 | 3.51+ | 2.40 | 7.43* | 4.17 | .700 | 4.86 | 39 |
| Reading, 1998, eighth grade | .15 | .29 | 1.06 | 1.92 | 6.93** | 2.88 | .714 | 3.07 | 35 |
| Math, 1996, fourth grade | .32 | .36 | 3.50* | 2.02 | 7.67** | 3.60 | .747 | 4.29 | 43 |
| Math, 1996, eighth grade | -.10 | .34 | 2.95+ | 1.97 | 6.16* | 3.34 | .868 | 3.94 | 40 |
| Science, 1996, eighth grade | -.31 | .26 | 3.31** | 1.49 | 6.34** | 2.52 | .909 | 2.98 | 40 |

Source: Authors' analysis of National Center for Education Statistics data from the National Assessment of Educational Progress reading, mathematics, and science report cards in 1996 and 1998. Indicators of state policy were taken from the January 1999 "Quality Counts" issue of *Education Week*.

Note: The reward + sanctions variable in the bottom two panels is the sanctions index plus two times the reward index. All of the regressions controlled for the following demographic characteristics of the state's students: a parents' education index, updated child poverty, percent African American, percent Hispanic, and percent Asian. EOCE/MCE = end-of-course exam/minimum competency exam. RMSE stands for root mean square error or alternatively the standard error of the estimate. Blank spaces mean the variable was not included in the model.

+ Statistically significant at 10 percent level on a one tail test.

* Statistically significant at 5 percent level on a one tail test.

** Statistically significant at 5 percent level on a two tail test.

*** Statistically significant at 1 percent level on a two tail test.

## Appendix B

Our studies of the dropout behavior, test score gains during high school, college attendance, and post-high school labor market outcomes employ microdata from the National Education Longitudinal Study of 1988 (NELS-88), a longitudinal data set that followed a nationally representative sample of eighth graders in 1988 through the year 1994. All our estimates report Huber-White robust standard errors that account for the clustering of students within schools and states and that deal with the problem of the correlation of errors generated by the cluster-based sampling frame.

Because the outcomes being studied are influenced by a host of other characteristics of the community and the student, we control for as many of them as possible to increase efficiency and reduce omitted variable bias. Our estimations include controls for grade point average (GPA) in eighth grade; an average of eighth-grade test scores in English, mathematics, science, and social studies; whether the student took remedial courses in eighth grade or earlier; whether they took advanced courses; TV and homework hours; reading for pleasure; an indicator for being handicapped; socioeconomic status (SES) of the student's family; logarithm of the number of books in the home; parent involvement index; family size; family structure in eighth grade; locus of control index; self-esteem index; hours working for pay during eighth grade (and its square); an index for smoking in eighth grade; dummies for race, ethnicity, and religion and for rural, suburban, and urban residence; and eight variables describing the quality of the high school. From the principal's questionnaire we took the following indicators of quality of the student's secondary school: dummy variables for Catholic school, for secular private schools, and for schools formed by non-Catholic religious organizations; average teacher salary; the pupil/teacher ratio; percent free lunch; percent students that were white; and average enrollment per high school grade (and its square). Two other measures of the quality of the school attended in tenth grade—the average socioeconomic status and eighth-grade test scores of students at the school—were calculated by averaging student responses for each high school in the NELS-88 data base.[64] In addition, the following characteristics of the state were controlled for: unemployment rate, mean weekly wage in retailing, ratio of the high school graduate earnings to the high school dropout earnings in 1989, ratio of college graduate earnings to high school graduate earnings in 1989, ratio of tuition at four-year public colleges to the weekly earnings in retailing, and dummies for four census regions.

These controls for school characteristics and region may not be sufficient to avoid omitted variable bias. States and school districts with such exams may be different along unmeasured dimensions that have direct effects on graduation rates, college attendance, and wage levels. A positive selection bias is unlikely, however, because most states appear to have adopted minimum competency exams (MCEs) as a response to a perception that the state's schools were failing to teach basic skills. By 1992 MCEs had been adopted by every southern state except Arkansas and Oklahoma. With the exception of New Mexico, none of the Mountain, Plains, or Midwestern states had established an MCE before 1992.[65]

DROPPING OUT AND HIGH SCHOOL COMPLETION. Results of the analysis of dropout rates and high school completion rates are presented in table B-1. The coefficients of the MCE variable and its interaction with GPA are reported in columns 3 and 4. Estimates of impacts on C- and A students are presented in columns 5 and 6. The approximate effect of $X_i$ (at the mean of the dependent variable) on the probability of not completing high school or attending college can be obtained by multiplying $ß_i$ times $P(1 - P)$.

Eighth-grade GPA and eighth-grade test scores have very large effects on the probability of graduating. In non-MCE schools, an increase in the GPA from C+ to B+ together with a one standard deviation increase in test scores lowers the probability of dropping out by 12 percentage points, lowers the probability of not getting a diploma or a general equivalency diploma (GED) by 11 percentage points, lowers the probability of getting a GED by 3 percentage points, and decreases the probability of graduating late by 7 percentage points. Given the low incidence of these outcomes in the data set, these are large effects.

Other traits that increased the risk of not graduating were parents are divorced, living in a single-parent family, smoking in eighth grade, high levels of reading for fun in eighth grade, many siblings, working for pay in eighth grade, and attending a large high school. Traits that significantly lowered the risk of not graduating were socioeconomic status of parents, Asian, Catholic religion, attending a Catholic high school, and attending a high SES high school.

TEST SCORE GAINS. We used the thetas produced by the item response theory (IRT) model because they have the normal distribution called for by the

Table B-1. Effects of Minimum Competency Examinations on High School Completion Outcomes

| High school completion outcome | P bar | State minimum competency exam | State MCE* eighth-grade GPA | State MCE for C- student | State MCE for A student | New York state | New York state* eighth-grade GPA | New York state effect on C- student | New York state effect on A student | State minimum Carnegie units to graduate | Eighth-grade GPA | Eighth-grade average test scores | Pseudo R square/number of observations |
|---|---|---|---|---|---|---|---|---|---|---|---|---|---|
| Ever dropped out | .128 | .049 (.108) | -.016 (.088) | .069 [.59] | .032 [.85] | .472** (.206) | .071 (.199) | .38+ [.19] | .55* [.09] | .030** (.013) | -.62*** (.056) | -.48*** (.046) | .2549 16,153 |
| Dropout in 1990 | .041 | .095 (.174) | .143 (.129) | -.083 [.67] | .251 [.33] | .482 (.32) | .154 (.290) | .29 [.48] | .65+ [.20] | .014 (.022) | -.61*** (.09) | -.71*** (.08) | .2814 16,153 |
| Dropout in 1992 | .074 | .094 (.130) | -.064 (.099) | .174 [.25] | .024 [.90] | .230 (.214) | .075 (.218) | .14 [.66] | .31 [.37] | .019 (.015) | -.59*** (.06) | -.57*** (.06) | .2444 16,116 |
| No diploma or GED | .092 | .074 (.146) | -.225** (.114) | .357*** [.02] | -.17 [.46] | .206 (.229) | .007 (.262) | .20 [.56] | .21 [.61] | .000 (.016) | -.68*** (.07) | -.75*** (.07) | .2902 12,124 |
| Obtained diploma late | .090 | .361** (.151) | -.227* (.117) | .642*** [.00] | .114 [.61] | .94*** (.23) | -.09 (.187) | 1.05*** [.00] | .84*** [.01] | .015 (.018) | -.70*** (.08) | -.14** (.06) | .1685 10,762 |
| Obtained diploma early | .015 | -.168 (.498) | .115 (.204) | -.31 [.57] | -.04 [.94] | 1.06+ (.76) | .43 (.45) | .53 [.61] | 1.52** [.05] | -.018 (.038) | .22* (.13) | -.21** (.10) | .0788 12,119 |
| Obtained GED | .050 | .321* (.179) | .015 (.115) | .30+ [.12] | .34+ [.17] | .84*** (.29) | -.036 (.120) | .88* [.06] | .80*** [.01] | .040* (.021) | -.58*** (.08) | .006 (.068) | .1187 12,124 |

Source: Authors' analysis of National Education Longitudinal Study of 1988 data.

Note: For predicting dropping out, the sample was all eighth graders interviewed in 1994. For high school completion outcomes, the sample was those who were interviewed in 1994. The minimum competency exam (MCE) variable is a one for Alabama, Florida, Georgia, Hawaii, Louisiana, Maryland, Mississippi, Nevada, New Mexico, New Jersey, North Carolina, South Carolina, Tennessee, and Texas. All models contain a full set of student background variables measured in the eighth grade: family socioeconomic status (SES), books in the home, single parent, parents divorced, number of siblings, ethnicity, religion, gender, handicapping condition, test scores, grade point average (GPA) in eighth grade, hours watching TV, hours doing homework, read for fun index, smoking, dummy for taking advanced courses, locus of control index, self-esteem index, and hours working for pay (plus its square). The following characteristics of the school the student attended during tenth grade (or had attended before dropping out) were also controlled: Catholic school, secular private school, private school controlled by a church other than the Catholic church, teacher salary, pupil/teacher ratio, percent student body white, percent free lunch, mean eighth-grade test score, mean family SES, and enrollment per grade (plus its square). The following characteristics of the state were controlled for: unemployment rate, mean weekly wage in retailing, ratio of the high school graduate earnings to the high school graduate earnings in 1989, ratio of college graduate earnings to high school graduate earnings in 1989, ratio of tuition at four-year public colleges to the weekly earnings in retailing, and dummies for four census regions. The GPA variable ranges from .5 to 4. The eighth-grade test scores have been normalized to have a standard deviation of one. Models were run unweighted. Numbers in parentheses below the coefficient are STATA's estimate of Huber-White standard errors that correct for clustering by school. The numbers in brackets in the columns for A students and C- students are the p values for a hypothesis test that MCE's effect on these students is significantly different from zero. The approximate effect of $X_1$ (at the mean of the dependent variable) on the probability of not completing high school or attending college can be obtained by multiplying $\beta_i$ times $P(1 − P)$. Thus, for "no diploma" the multiplier is .0835.

+ Statistically significant at 10 percent level on a one tail test.
* Statistically significant at 5 percent level on a one tail test.
** Statistically significant at 5 percent level on a two tail test.
*** Statistically significant at 1 percent level on a two tail test.

statistical program we are using. Separate models were also estimated for gains from 1988 to 1992 for English, mathematics, science, and social studies. To prevent the measurement error in the test scores from biasing the results, the lagged value of the test whose gain score was being predicted never appeared on the right-hand side of the regression.[66] When the gains on individual tests were being predicted, however, the student's scores on the other three eighth-grade tests were included as control variables. The student's GPA in eighth grade was also one of the control variables in all models.

The effect of minimum competency exams was captured by two variables: a zero-one dummy variable for states (other than New York) with an MCE graduation requirement and an interaction between the MCE dummy variable and the student's eighth-grade GPA (deviated from its mean). The coefficients on the MCE dummy variable (column 3 of table B-2) are estimates of the impact of MCEs on students with average grades.

Test score gains in MCE states were very similar to test score gains in non-MCE states even for the low GPA students who are presumed to be most affected by MCEs. From eighth to twelfth grade, C- students who lived in MCE states gained an extra 16 percent of a grade level equivalent (GLE) on the test score composite, an extra 26 percent of a GLE in science, an extra 30 percent of a GLE in mathematics, and an extra 18 percent of a GLE in social studies. Only the math differential was statistically significant.

We next examine the effect of combining end-of-course exams with MCEs, the policy mix that characterizes New York state at the beginning of the 1990s. The regression included an indicator variable for residence in New York state and an interaction of GPA (deviated from its mean of 2.91) with the New York state dummy variable. Our estimates of the impact of these variables are presented in columns 7, 8, 9, and 10 of table B-2 and graphed in figure 8.[67]

What were the other statistically significant determinants of eighth- to twelfth-grade learning as measured by the four-subject composite? During the four-year interval, males learned .42 of a grade level equivalent more than females, Asians learned .28 GLEs more than whites, African Americans learned .60 GLEs less than whites, and students living in the West learned .29 GLEs more than students in the Northeast. Learning gains were also greater for students from high SES families, for students high on the read for fun index and high on the internal locus of control index, and for students who watched a great deal of TV in eighth grade. Learning gains were greater when pupil/teacher ratios were low, at schools serving high SES students, and at schools in which entering students had low eighth-grade test scores.

# Table B-2. Effect of Minimum Competency Examinations on Test Score Gains by Eighth-Grade GPA

| Gain score | Grade span | State minimum competency exam | State MCE* eighth-grade GPA | State MCE effect on C- student | State MCE effect on A student | New York state | New York state* eighth-grade GPA | New York state effect on C- student | New York state effect on A student | State minimum units to graduate | Pupil/ teacher ratio | Teacher salary | Enrollment per grade | Mean SES | R square/ number of observations | Mean of dependent variable |
|---|---|---|---|---|---|---|---|---|---|---|---|---|---|---|---|---|
| Test average | 8–12 | .215 (.214) | -.059 (.148) | .29 [.34] | .15 [.55] | .72** (.36) | .170 (.256) | .51 [.34] | .91** [1.02] | .003 (.022) | -.060*** (.019) | .017 (.022) | .121+ (.089) | 1.31*** (.23) | .0992 11,566 | 7.43 |
| Test average | 10–12 | .079 (.187) | -.133 (.120) | .24 [.35] | -.06 [.75] | .41+ (.36) | .112 (.266) | .27 [.55] | .53+ [.18] | -.032+ (.020) | -.054*** (.016) | .042** (.021) | .048 (.072) | .21 (.18) | .0256 11,184 | 3.53 |
| Test average | 8–10 | .071 (.175) | .055 (.106) | .00 [.99] | .13 [.51] | .17 (.31) | -.29 (.25) | .53 [.29] | .15 [.68] | .023 (.019) | -.011 (.016) | -.049*** (.019) | .054 (.073) | 1.05*** (.19) | .0801 14,474 | 4.15 |
| Science | 8–12 | .106 (.315) | -.295+ (.216) | .47 [.29] | -.22 [.55] | 1.11* (.58) | .62+ (.42) | .34 [.70] | 1.79*** [1.01] | .008 (.033) | -.071** (.029) | .013 (.033) | .160 (.127) | 1.64*** (.33) | .0748 11,432 | 7.20 |
| Math | 8–12 | .393+ (.244) | -.202 (.167) | .64* [.05] | .17 [.56] | .65+ (.45) | .097 (.294) | .53 [.42] | .76+ [1.11] | -.021 (.026) | -.086*** (.022) | .024 (.025) | .124 (.097) | .99*** (.26) | .1019 11,514 | 8.49 |
| Social studies | 8–12 | .538+ (.350) | .098 (.226) | .42 [.36] | .64+ [.12] | .77 (.51) | .36 (.47) | .32 [.69] | 1.16* [.08] | .005 (.034) | -.013 (.035) | .041 (.038) | -.065 (.146) | 1.96*** (.37) | .0394 11,349 | 9.38 |
| English | 8–12 | -.128 (.276) | .129 (.196) | -.29 [.45] | .01 [.97] | .48 (.46) | -.35 (.44) | .91 [.29] | .10 [.22] | .019 (.033) | -.068** (.028) | -.003 (.032) | .274** (.124) | .78** (.30) | .0513 11,520 | 5.94 |

Source: Authors' analysis of National Education Longitudinal Study of 1988, New York state part of interaction.

Note: Sample is the eighth graders interviewed in 1988 who were also interviewed in 1994. The dependent variables are the difference between a student's thetas (derived from the item response theory scaling model) for grade $t$ and his or her theta for grade $t-2$ or $t-4$, for all four of the tests. In eighth-grade cross-section data, the standard deviation of the thetas is approximately 8.5 for all four of the tests. The minimum competency exam (MCE) variable is a one for Alabama, Florida, Georgia, Hawaii, Maryland, Mississippi, Nevada, New Mexico, New Jersey, North Carolina, South Carolina, Tennessee, and Texas. All models contain a full set of student background variables measured in the eighth grade: family socioeconomic status (SES), books in the home, single parent, parents divorced, number of siblings, ethnicity, religion, gender, handicapping condition, test scores in the three other subjects (not the one for which the gain score is calculated), grade point average (GPA) in eighth grade, hours watching TV, hours doing homework, read for fun index, smoking, dummy for taking advanced courses, dummy for taking remedial courses, locus of control index, self-esteem index, and hours working for pay (plus its square). There are no controls for eighth-grade test scores in the model predicting average test score gains. The following characteristics of the school the student attended during tenth grade were also controlled: Catholic school, other private school, teacher salary, pupil/teacher ratio, percent high school student body non-Hispanic white, percent free lunch, mean eighth-grade test score of the students in the respondent's high school, mean family SES, and enrollment per grade (plus its square). The following characteristics of the state were controlled for: the mean weekly wage in retailing and dummies for four census regions. Models were run unweighted. Numbers in parentheses below the coefficient are Huber-White standard errors that correct for clustering by school. The numbers in brackets in the columns for A students and C- students are the $p$ values for a hypothesis test that the effect of MCEs on these students is significantly different from zero.

+ Statistically significant at 10 percent level on a one tail test.

\* Statistically significant at 5 percent level on a one tail test.

** Statistically significant at 5 percent level on a two tail test.

*** Statistically significant at 1 percent level on a two tail test.

COLLEGE ATTENDANCE. Students with the highest college enrollment rates attended schools serving high SES communities, went to schools that paid their teachers more than average, attended small high schools and Catholic high schools, and lived in communities with high unemployment rates. The school and state characteristics that did not have significant effects on enrollment rates were pupil/teacher ratio, the college/high school wage ratio, weekly earnings in retailing, and the cost of tuition at public four-year colleges.

With respect to the individual control variables, few of the findings are surprising. Holding other characteristics constant, those who attended college tended to come from small, intact, high SES families; to be Asians or African American rather than white; to have a Catholic or Jewish religion rather than Protestant, no religion, or no response; to be high on the internal locus of control index; and to be nonsmokers who did not read for fun much but spent many hours doing homework in eighth grade.

The probability of eighth graders with average grades entering college five years later (the fall after high school graduation if it is not delayed) was not affected by residence in a state with an MCE. However, the variable interacting state MCE and eighth-grade GPA in the model predicting fall 1992 attendance was positive and significant. This means that high GPA students were more likely to enter college in MCE states. Low GPA students in MCE states were less likely to enter college in fall 1992. In fall 1993, however, students from all parts of the GPA distribution were more likely to be enrolled in college when they lived in MCE states (see table B-3).

POST-HIGH SCHOOL LABOR MARKET OUTCOMES. The models predicting these labor market outcomes were generally the same as those used to predict high school completion and college attendance. The first exception to that generalization was the inclusion of controls for high school completion: dummies for "ever dropped out," "obtained a GED," "failed to get either a diploma or a GED," "graduated early," and, for late graduates, "the length of the delay in graduation." The second exception was the inclusion of controls for current and past college attendance: a dummy variable for full-time college attendance during the period for which earnings are measured, a dummy for part-time attendance during that period, and the number of semesters of college attendance before the earnings measurement period.

Table B-4 presents a test of hypothesis 4A that rewards for achievement will be greater in New York state than in other states. It receives considerable support. All four coefficients on the GPA*NYS interaction in the earnings and wage regressions are positive and two are significantly positive at the 10 per-

Table B-3. Effects of High School Graduation Requirements on College Attendance

| Term | P bar | State has MCE | State MCE* eighth-grade GPA | State MCE for C-student | State MCE for A student | New York state | New York state* eighth-grade GPA | New York state effect on C-student | New York state effect on A student | State minimum Carnegie units to graduate | Eighth-grade GPA | Average test score | Pseudo R square/ number of observations |
|---|---|---|---|---|---|---|---|---|---|---|---|---|---|
| Fall 1992 | .53 | .027 | .154* | -.17 | .19+ | .033 | -.178 | .27 | -.16 | -.021** | .70*** | .53*** | .2682 |
| 7 | | (.090) | (.080) | [.22] | [.12] | (.138) | (.141) | [.25] | [.44] | (.010) | (.049) | (.034) | 12,026 |
| Spring 1993 | .54 | -.001 | .149* | -.19+ | .16+ | -.000 | -.156 | .20 | -.17 | -.014+ | .69*** | .50*** | .2589 |
| 0 | | (.088) | (.076) | [.15] | [.19] | (.142) | (.137) | [.38] | [.42] | (.010) | (.05) | (.034) | 12,026 |
| Fall 1993 | .52 | .177** | .037 | .13 | .22* | .119 | -.167 | .33+ | -.06 | -.020** | .70*** | .51*** | .2728 |
| 5 | | (.086) | (.076) | [.31] | [.06] | (.131) | (.156) | [.16] | [.77] | (.010) | (.05) | (.035) | 12,033 |
| Spring 1994 | .50 | .140* | .030 | .10 | .17+ | .135 | -.123 | .29 | .00 | -.027*** | .67*** | .50*** | .2712 |
| 8 | | (.086) | (.076) | [.43] | [.14] | (.132) | (.152) | [.22] | [.99] | (.010) | (.05) | (.035) | 12,027 |

Source: Authors' analysis of National Education Longitudinal Study of 1988.

Note: Sample is the eighth graders interviewed in 1988 who were also interviewed in 1994. The minimum competency exam (MCE) variable is a one for Alabama, Florida, Georgia, Hawaii, Louisiana, Maryland, Mississippi, Nevada, New Mexico, New Jersey, North Carolina, South Carolina, Tennessee, and Texas. All models contain a full set of student background variables measured in the eighth grade: family socioeconomic status (SES), books in the home, single parent, parents divorced, number of siblings, ethnicity, religion, gender, handicapping condition, test scores, grade point average (GPA) in eighth grade, hours watching TV, hours doing homework, read for fun index, smoking, dummy for taking advanced courses, dummy for taking remedial courses, locus of control index, self-esteem index, and hours working for pay (plus its square). The following characteristics of the school the student attended during tenth grade (or had attended before dropping out) were also controlled: Catholic school, secular private school, private school controlled by a church other than the Catholic church, teacher salary, percent student body white, percent free lunch, mean eighth-grade test score, mean family SES, and enrollment per grade (plus its square). The following characteristics of the state were controlled: unemployment rate, mean weekly wage in retailing, ratio of college graduate earnings to high school graduate earnings in 1989, ratio of tuition at four-year public colleges to the weekly earnings in retailing, and dummies for four census regions. Numbers in parentheses below the coefficient are Huber-White standard errors that correct for clustering by school. The approximate effect of $X_i$ (at the mean of the dependent variable) on the probability of not completing high school or attending college can be obtained by multiplying $\beta_i$ times $P(1 - P)$. Thus, for "attending college in fall 1993 semester" the multiplier is .25.

+ Statistically significant at 10 percent level on a one tail test.

* Statistically significant at 5 percent level on a one tail test.

** Statistically significant at 5 percent level on a two tail test.

*** Statistically significant at 1 percent level on a two tail test.

# Table B-4. Effect of Minimum Competency Exams on Employment Outcomes after High School

| | Mean (standard deviation) | State minimum competency exam | State MCE* eighth-grade GPA | State MCE effect on A student | State MCE effect on C- student | New York state | NY state* eighth-grade GPA | New York state effect on C- student | New York state effect on A student | State minimum Carnegie units to graduate | No diploma | Obtain GED | Eighth grade GPA | Average test score | R squared/ number of observations |
|---|---|---|---|---|---|---|---|---|---|---|---|---|---|---|---|
| 1993 annual earnings | $5317 (5694) | 495*** (179) | -103 (171) | 383* [.095] | 623** [.041] | -192 (263) | 321 (319) | -590 [.25] | 158 [.69] | -14 (24) | -2257*** (326) | 178 (440) | -179+ (114) | 111+ (79) | .2374 10,050 |
| Total months worked | 13.42 (7.72) | .076 (.256) | -.667 (.206) | -.65 [.05] | .90 [.01] | .01 (.44) | -.47 (.46) | .59 [.40] | -.50 [.47] | -.001 (.028) | -2.84*** (.37) | -.35 (.43) | .23* (.14) | .05 (.10) | .1479 11,849 |
| Total months unemployed | 1.78 (4.49) | -.117 (.135) | .014 (.121) | -.10 [.55] | -.13 [.54] | -.100 (.22) | .036 (.23) | -.14 [.71] | -.06 [.84] | .000 (.015) | 1.19*** (.25) | .64** (.32) | -.04 (.08) | -.14** (.06) | .0541 11,849 |
| Average earnings per month | $524 ($526) | 37.4** (16.3) | -7.4 (13.8) | 29.4 [.44] | 46.5* [.07] | -19 (25) | 40.7+ (26) | -69+ [.12] | 26 [.44] | -.8 (1.7) | -116*** (27) | 71* (39) | 0.9 (10.0) | -1.0 (6.6) | .1995 11,667 |
| Spring 1994 earnings per month | $495 ($670) | 25.7 (21.6) | -3.9 (17.0) | 22 [.36] | 30.5 [.40] | -48* (28.9) | 69*** (28) | -134 [.01] | 28 [.46] | -1.4 (2.6) | -114*** (42) | 61 (51) | 2.2 (12.7) | -4.6 (8.4) | .1876 11,424 |
| Log hourly wage rate | 1.274 (.569) | .004 (.018) | -.011 (.016) | -.007 [.75] | .018 [.54] | -.025 (.031) | .030 (.030) | -.062 [.22] | .008 [.85] | -.004** (.002) | -.085*** (.030) | .037 (.038) | .002 (.011) | .010 (.008) | .0908 11,790 |

Source: Authors' analysis of National Education Longitudinal Study of 1988, New York state separate interaction.

Note: Sample is the eighth graders interviewed in 1988 who were also interviewed in 1994. The minimum competency exam (MCE) variable is a one for Alabama, Florida, Georgia, Hawaii, Louisiana, Maryland, Mississippi, Nevada, New Mexico, New Jersey, North Carolina, South Carolina, Tennessee, and Texas. Models reported in this table contain controls for whether the respondent graduated from high school or got a general equivalency diploma (GED), when he or she got a high school diploma, whether the respondent was in college full time during spring 1994, whether he or she was a part-time student in spring 1994, and the number of months spent attending college full time and months spent attending part time. Models also contain a full set of student background variables measured in the eighth grade: family socioeconomic status (SES), books in the home, single parent, parents divorced, number of siblings, ethnicity, religion, gender, handicapping condition, test scores, grade point average (GPA) in eighth grade, hours doing homework, read for fun index, smoking, dummy for taking advanced courses, dummy for taking remedial courses, dummies for central city and rural, locus of control index, self-esteem index, and hours working for pay (plus its square). The following characteristics of the school the student attended during tenth grade (or had attended before dropping out) were also controlled: Catholic school, secular private school, private school controlled by a church other than the Catholic church, teacher salary, percent student body white, percent free lunch, mean eighth-grade test score, mean family SES, and enrollment per grade (plus its square). The following characteristics of the state were controlled for: mean unemployment rate, mean weekly wages in retailing and in manufacturing, and dummies for four census regions .The GPA variable ranges from .5 to 4. The eighth-grade test scores have been normalized to have a standard deviation of one. Models were run unweighted. Numbers in parentheses below the coefficient are Huber-White standard errors that correct for clustering by school. The numbers in brackets in the columns for A students and C- students are the p values for a hypothesis test that the state MCE's effects on these students are significantly different from zero.

+ Statistically significant at 10 percent level on a one tail test.

* Statistically significant at 5 percent level on a one tail test.

** Statistically significant at 5 percent level on a two tail test.

*** Statistically significant at 1 percent level on a two tail test.

cent level on a one tail test or better. The model's estimate of the impact of MCEs on A students and on C- students are included in the table. For students with A averages in eighth grade, those who attended a high school with an MCE graduation requirement were paid 4.7 percent extra per hour, earned $37.90 (about 7.3 percent) more per month, and made about 12.6 percent more during 1993. All of these estimates are significantly greater than zero.

Turning briefly to the effects of other variables, not getting a high school diploma or a GED lowered hourly earnings by 7.2 percent and monthly earnings by 21 percent. If the GED was obtained on the same date, unemployment rates are higher but so are monthly earnings. Those with neither a diploma nor a GED earned 42 percent less. Other student characteristics that were associated with significantly lower monthly earnings or lower wage rates were: current attendance at college, female, African American, Asian, handicapped, rural location, Northeastern location, many siblings, and attending a school with a high incidence of free lunch. Monthly earnings were higher for students who had worked for pay in eighth grade, who had an internal locus of control and high self-esteem, and who had parents who set tighter limits on behavior in eighth grade.

---

# Comment by Richard Murnane

John H. Bishop continues to persuasively make the case that the United States must increase incentives for students to focus time and energy on school work. The instrument he sees as powerful is a system of external examinations students must pass to obtain a high school diploma. This paper, which Bishop has written with Ferran Mane, Michael Bishop, and Joan Moriarty, examines the impacts of several types of external examination requirements on a variety of student outcomes.

I applaud the Bishop team for its attempts to inform the debate about the consequences of standards-based reforms—a debate that has been characterized by more heat than light. The use of test score evidence from the National Assessment of Educational Progress (NAEP) and the National Education Longitudinal Survey (NELS), tests that do not involve stakes for students, is particularly valuable. Critics of studies showing improvements in scores on state-mandated tests argue that the gains do not show up in NAEP scores. The Bishop, Mane, Bishop, and Moriarty study does not have this limitation.

Overall, I find persuasive the argument Bishop and his colleagues make. This should not be surprising because, like Bishop, I have been trained as an economist and the idea that incentives matter lies at the core of economics. Students will not learn more unless they devote more time and energy to improving their skills. Teachers' efforts to improve student skills are often watered down by multiple demands. External exams can focus the efforts of both students and teachers.

I can quibble with details of the analyses presented in the paper. First, one of the analyses examines the effect of minimum competency exams on the probability that students obtain a general equivalency diploma (GED). For this analysis the authors grouped into the non-GED category both students who obtained a conventional high school diploma and students who dropped out of school and did not obtain a GED. Because a variety of studies show that GED recipients fare better in the labor market than dropouts without this credential, but they do not fare as well as conventional high school graduates, I do not know how to interpret the results of the analysis.[68]

Second, as the authors point out, the evidence on the effects of end-of-course exams comes from comparing outcomes for students who went to high school in New York state or North Carolina, which had end-of-course exams in the relevant year, with outcomes for students who attended high school in other states. It is not clear the extent to which differences in student outcomes stem from the end-of-course exams or from other respects in which North Carolina and New York differ from other states.

Besides these quibbles, I have two substantive issues to comment upon. First, are increased incentives for students and those who teach them a sufficient policy instrument for improving student outcomes? Incentives by themselves will solve problems that can be defined as individuals not doing things that they know how to do but are not motivated to do. When the external exams assess only low-level skills that can be mastered by more drill, then incentives for teachers and students to drill on basics will improve test scores. However, as states move toward examinations that assess higher-order skills and communication skills—skills that are increasingly important in an economy in which computers do a growing proportion of routine work—then drill alone will not do the job. Students need good instruction to learn to write well and to define and solve complex problems. Many teachers do not know how to help all students to master these skills. A small but growing body of research shows that professional development focused on helping teachers to teach more effectively the skills measured on demanding external assessments results in improved student test scores. In my view these focused professional development efforts are a necessary complement to demanding external assessments. They are especially important for teachers of students whose parents lack college educations and, consequently, are unlikely to be able to help their children learn at home what they do not learn in school.

Second, incentives for what? Bishop and his colleagues present evidence that the long-term labor market payoff to cognitive skills has increased over the last twenty-five years. My research group has also found substantial payoffs to the types of skills that are measured on the exams many states now require students to pass to obtain a high school diploma. For example, my group finds that an educational reform program that increased a student's math skills by a quarter of a standard deviation (the amount economist Henry Levin sees as the upper limit of what reform programs have accomplished) would result in earnings increases with a present discounted value of $22,000, if sustained over a worker's career.[69] This is only one of several ways of illustrating the importance of cognitive skills in today's labor market and, consequently, the importance of creating incentives for students to increase their cognitive skills and for teachers to emphasize the development of these skills.

The variation in labor market earnings among people with the same measured cognitive skills is enormous. If an educational reform program did increase the skills of participating male high school seniors by one quarter of a standard deviation and did produce an increase in their subsequent predicted mean earnings of 3.7 percent (which translates into a present discounted value of $22,000), 47 percent of the participants still would have earnings below the average earnings of nonparticipants.[70] Why make this point? There are two reasons.

First, external exams are powerful instruments. When stakes are attached, they create strong incentives for teachers to focus instruction on the skills measured on the exams. The exams thus should measure skills and knowledge that are worthy of a great deal of instructional time. As the paper by Chester E. Finn Jr. and Marci Kanstoroom argues, most state standards and external exams need improvement. For example, the Massachusetts exams cover too much material, pushing teachers toward superficial treatment of too many topics. The solution is not to scrap standards-based reforms. Instead, the solution is to learn from the responses to the initial exams and make the appropriate adjustments in the content of the exams and in testing procedures.

Second, children learn in different ways. Some thrive with traditional curricula, others with very different curricula emphasizing, for example, the arts or computers. Many effective educators, such as Deborah Meier and Ted Sizer, argue that state-mandated exams inhibit their ability to design schools that are effective with students who do not thrive in traditional school settings. The standards-based reforms should make public education more attractive to innovators such as Meier and Sizer rather than drive them away. A solution that New York state crafted under Education Commissioner Thomas Sobol is to let networks of innovative schools develop alternative ways of assessing whether students have mastered the skills tested on the state-mandated assessments. If the network can make the case that their students must meet standards at least as high as those met by students taking the state-mandated exams, then the schools in the network are allowed to administer their own assessments instead of the state-mandated assessments. I do not see this as backing off standards, but as making standards work for all students and in a way that attracts talent to the teaching profession.

I conclude by summarizing lessons I took away from the paper by Bishop and his colleagues and from the other papers in this volume.

1. Incentives matter. External assessments tightly aligned with curriculum standards make sense.

2. Because external exams with stakes are such a powerful instrument for changing the allocation of instructional time, it is extremely important that the assessments measure critical student skills and knowledge. When stakes are attached to the results of student assessments, what is not tested is unlikely to be taught. Examinations should be done of the extent to which external assessments measure things such as communication skills that are extremely important in workplaces as well as more traditional skills.

3. Consistently high-quality instruction for all students must be an essential component of standards-based educational reform programs. No state in this country has achieved this goal.

4. In assessing the consequences of standards-based educational reform efforts, students who drop out and then obtain "high school graduate status" with a GED need to be distinguished from students who earn a conventional high school diploma. The labor market treats the two credentials differently.

5. Allowing innovative educators to develop alternative ways of demonstrating that students meet high standards makes sense. This is consistent with a policy of requiring that all students meet high standards. And it promotes this goal by helping states to attract talented creative teachers.

## Comment by Laurence Steinberg

John H. Bishop, Ferran Mane, Michael Bishop, and Joan Moriarty are to be commended for bringing sophisticated empirical analysis to an issue that generates considerable ill-informed debate: whether standards-based testing with genuine stakes helps or harms students. More specifically, they have provided an array of carefully conducted analyses designed to examine the impact of two types of standards-based testing (end-of-course exams and minimum competency exams) on several widely watched indicators of student achievement: high school graduation, college enrollment, achievement test scores, and earnings. They have tested a series of well-developed hypotheses using both cross-sectional and longitudinal data and with different data sets. By and large the results are encouraging to those who support standards-based reforms and problematic for those who oppose them. Students, for the most part, do not drop out in large numbers when they are required to pass exams to graduate or receive course credit, and some evidence exists that standards-based testing may increase college attendance and post-high school earnings. On the bases of their analyses, the authors conclude that the most effective type of standards-based reform is one that combines the use of end-of-course exams with the implementation of minimum competency exams.

Is standards-based reform working? As answered in this paper, it depends, in at least three ways. First, standards-based reform has many meanings and many components, and the impact of standards-based reform depends on which component is being examined. Some (such as the use of end-of-course examinations) have stronger effects than others, and others (such as the use of published report cards on schools) apparently have no effects at all. Without clear guidance about which elements of standards-based reform a state or school district ought to implement, a state or district could come away empty-handed and discouraged after attempting to implement a standards-based policy that has good intentions but few discernible consequences.

Second, the impact of standards-based reform depends on which outcome is being assessed. The same reform may have positive effects on one outcome, negative effects on another, and no effects on a third. For instance, in the analyses presented by Bishop and his colleagues, the use of minimum competency testing has a negligible effect on high school enrollment or graduation, once general equivalency diplomas (GEDs) are taken into account; a small positive effect on the achievement of poor students (those with a grade point average [GPA] of C- or below) but a small, negative effect on the achievement of good ones (those with a GPA of A); a positive effect on college enrollment, especially among poor and average students; and a surprisingly significant impact on post-high school employment and earnings, especially among good students. A state or district that failed to evaluate standards-based reform with multiple indicators might come away with a conclusion that was excessively optimistic or excessively pessimistic. Surely the fact that minimum competency testing has stronger effects on college attendance and earning than on achievement is a mixed blessing.

Third, the impact of standards-based reform depends on which students are the focus of the analysis. The same reform may affect a specific outcome differentially among poor students than among affluent ones, among minority students differentially than among white ones, and among poor achievers differentially than among high achievers. Some evidence indicates that the implementation of minimum competency testing may provoke schools to focus more energy on poor-achieving students, but that this laudable response may be accompanied by a troublesome decline in achievement among students with relatively higher grades. Raising the achievement of students at the bottom of the distribution is important, but schools need to find a way to do this without compromising the already mediocre test performance of the best students.

The paper does not say much about the differential impact of various reforms as a function of student race, which is a shame because racial disparity in student achievement continues to be one of the most vexing, if not the single most vexing, problems in American education. From a policy perspective, an important question is whether and by what specific practices standards-based reform can help close the race gap in achievement. Nevertheless, Bishop and his coauthors do admirable work in demonstrating that the impact of different types of reform varies as a function of students' place in the achievement distribution, with some reforms having stronger effects on relatively low-achieving students and weaker, or even opposite, effects on their high-achieving counterparts. The impact of minimum competency exams on changes in high school test scores is a remarkable example of this. Among students whose eighth-grade GPA is poor, minimum competency testing is associated with nearly a 25 percent of a grade level equivalent gain in math test scores and with a 6 percent of a grade level equivalent gain in English scores. However, this same reform is associated with a 16 percent of a grade level equivalent decline in math scores and a 15 percent of a grade level equivalent decline in English scores among students who were achieving at high levels in eighth grade. When it comes to earnings, this pattern is reversed. The use of minimum competency examinations appears to be far more beneficial for high-achieving students than for poor-achieving ones. The reasons for this discrepancy are not clear.

In essence, answering questions about the impact of standards-based testing reforms on student performance requires the data, diligence, and patience to sort through dozens of three-way statistical interactions—interactions among the type of reform, the performance outcome, and the type of student being tested. And this is only scratching the surface, because the paper's data seem to indicate that these three-way interactions also may vary as a function of the historical period during which the data were gathered as well as a host of other contextual and systemic variables that often accompany the implementation of standards-based testing, such as changes in the political, economic, and administrative climates within which schools function. I support the intent of Bishop and his colleagues to search out data that can help fill in some of the empty cells in the matrices presented, but I am less optimistic than the authors that this exercise will reveal an easily interpretable pattern of findings.

The one outcome measure that I would like to see in the analysis, though, is college performance, not simply attendance, including the need for remedial education at the postsecondary level. The problem with high school graduation and college enrollment as outcome variables on which to judge educational policy, as I and others have argued, is that they are more or less meaningless indicators within an educational system that has set the bar so low for either accomplishment that it is barely off the pavement. With the exception of the relatively small group of highly selective colleges attended mainly by upper-middle-class students, enrollment in college is achievable by anyone who can breathe—with or without chewing gum simultaneously.

Although one might be tempted to judge the success of educational reform on the basis of its impact on college enrollment, this temptation should be resisted. On this point the authors and I clearly disagree. In my view, increasing college enrollment in and of itself is a goal of questionable value. Thus, even if standards-based reform were to increase college enrollment, this would not necessarily be something to cheer about, especially because, as the analyses indicate, this effect is primarily felt among low-achieving students whose level of competence (as assessed by achievement tests) has not been appreciably improved as a result of the testing reform. Can American colleges and universities accommodate more poorly prepared entrants, even if they have been certified as minimally competent? One could easily envision a world, for example, in which a given tier of public colleges was required to accept any student who passed a state's minimum competency examinations but where the competencies required to pass such tests were so elementary that they did not indicate any ability to do college-level work. This system would not be an improvement over current practice and might cause more harm than having no standards. The problem with analyses of standards-based testing reforms is that the impact of these tests cannot be assessed without knowing what the tests measure and what it means to be minimally competent.

Of note is that when they are examined head to head, the findings concerning the effects of end-of-course examinations, such as the New York state Regents exams, are, by and large, more consistently positive than the impact of minimum competency tests. Unfortunately, owing to limitations in the data available to Bishop and his colleagues, these two interventions could be compared only with respect to a limited number of outcome variables. Given my concerns about inconsistencies in findings across different sorts of outcomes, one must be cautious about drawing conclusions from this. For this reason, I would like to see Bishop and his colleagues conduct more comparative analyses of the two types of tests with a wider array of outcomes, including high school achievement, college attendance, college graduation, and labor force success. My suspicion is that end-of-course examinations will have a much more consistently positive set of outcomes than minimum competency testing will. But, like minimum competency exams, the impact of end-of-course examinations will depend on their content and scoring. Given this, I wonder what the value is of analyses that simply ask whether a given type of test is present or absent in a state or local system, instead of asking what the content of the test is. The fact that the dichotomous variable of whether a test is present or absent predicts anything makes me suspicious about the mediating processes that link testing with outcomes.

Consider the observation that post-high school earnings are higher when minimum competency testing is in place, especially among high-achieving students. Why is this so? Has the testing improved the competencies of students, or has it merely permitted schools to increase their credibility with local employers? And if the latter is true but the former is not—that is, if the testing increases the value of a high school's diploma but not the skills of its graduates—is this something to strive for? If the goal is increasing post-high school earnings, this can be accomplished through many means (raising the minimum wage, for example) that are not attempts to masquerade as genuine educational reform.

Similarly, the fact that minimum competency testing boosts college attendance but has a negligible impact on high school achievement ought to raise serious questions about the reasons that standards-based testing has positive effects on post-high school outcomes. My worry is that the implementation of minimum competency tests may do little other than foster the illusion that student achievement is improving when the same old worrisome system of social promotion that has persisted for so many years is just being certified. Ultimately, answering the question of whether standards-based reforms are working requires careful thought about what the indicators of successful reform are. Is the goal increasing rates of high school graduation? College attendance? Earnings and employment? Students' performance on tests of knowledge? I vote for the last option.

The problem with analyses such as this one by Bishop and his colleagues and those of other economists is that the question of whether and how standards-based reform is working is probably not easily answerable without companion information on how the reform is affecting the behavior of students, parents, educators, and employers. I am reminded of a joke about two hot-air balloonists, whose balloon crashes in the middle of an expansive desert, with no landmarks in sight. Much to their relief, a man comes walking by. "Do you know where we are?" asks one of the balloonists. The man replies, "Yes, you're in the desert," and keeps walking. "Just our luck," the first balloonist says to his companion. "Of all the people to come walking by, wouldn't you know it would have to be an economist." "How do you know he's an economist?" the companion asks. "Because what he said was absolutely correct but of no help whatsoever."

The paper by Bishop, Mane, Bishop, and Moriarty is a far cry from "no help whatsoever." In some respects, it is enormously helpful. It shows, for example, that some reforms (and exams) are more likely to pay off than others (such as sanctioning schools for poor student achievement), that high- and low-achieving students are differentially affected by the same reforms, and that the impact of any given reform may be a mixed blessing (for example, lowered achievement but increased college enrollment). In so doing, this paper suggests where to focus reform resources and research efforts. But I believe that questions about the relative effectiveness of any type or set of standards-based reforms cannot be answered without more fine-grained analyses of how the attitudes, values, and beliefs of students, parents, educators, and employers change in response to different sorts of interventions. This is, to be sure, my personal bias as a psychologist, but it seems that this sort of analysis, whether through survey data, interview, or ethnography, is needed to describe the mediating mechanisms that link changes in educational policy to changes in student outcomes. The sorts of inconsistencies contained in the paper cry out for some empirically informed interpretation—interpretation that necessitates a different level of data collection and analysis.

## Notes

1. James A. Kulik and Chen-Lin Kulik, "Effects of Accelerated Instruction on Students," *Review of Educational Research*, vol. 54, no. 3 (Fall 1984), pp. 409–25; David Monk, "Subject Area Preparation of Secondary Mathematics and Science Teachers and Student Achievement," *Economics of Education Review*, vol. 13, no. 2 (1994), pp. 125–45; and John H. Bishop, "Incentives to Study and the Organization of Secondary Instruction," in William Baumol and William Becker, eds., *Assessing Educational Practices* (MIT Press, 1996), pp. 99–160.

2. Pam Belluck, "Reason Is Sought for Lag by Blacks in School Effort," *New York Times*, July 4, 1999, p. 15.

3. Longitudinal Survey of American Youth, *Data File User's Manual* (De Kalb, Ill.: Public Opinion Laboratory, 1988), Q. AA17A, AA17B, and AA26A.

4. Longitudinal Survey of American Youth, *Data File User's Manual*, Q. AA37N.

5. William Miles interview with counselor at a wealthy suburban school, August 1997.

6. Ward, "A Day in the Life," *N.Y. Teacher* (January 1994).

7. Jerry Jesness, "Why Johnny Can't Fail?" *Reason* (July 1999), reprinted in *Selected Readings on School Reform* (Washington: Thomas B. Fordham Foundation, Fall 1999), p. 87.

8. Peter D. Hart Research Associates, *Valuable Views: A Public Opinion Research Report on the Views of AFT Teachers on Professional Issues* (Washington: American Federation of Teachers, 1995), pp. 1–24.

9. Laurence Steinberg, B. Bradford Brown, and Sanford M. Dornbusch, *Beyond the Classroom* (Simon and Schuster, 1996), pp. 145–46.

10. Robert P. Strauss, "Who Should Teach in New York's Public Schools? Implications of Pennsylvania's Teacher Preparation and Selection Experience," *Economics of Education Review* (Summer 2000).

11. Richard Ingersoll, *Out of Field Teaching and Educational Equity*, NCES 96040 (Department of Education, National Center for Education Statistics, 1996).

12. The survey was of a stratified random sample of the National Federation of Independent Business membership. Larger firms had a significantly higher probability of being selected for the study. The response rate to the mail survey was 20 percent and the number of usable responses was 2,014.

13. Employers appear to believe that school performance is a good predictor of job performance. Studies of how employers rate job applicant résumés that contain information on grades in high school have found that employers give substantially higher ratings to job applicants with high grade point averages. K. Hollenbeck and B. Smith, *The Influence of Applicants' Education and Skills on Employability Assessments by Employers* (Ohio State University, National Center for Research in Vocational Education, 1984).

14. Toby Friedman and E. Belvin Williams, "Current Use of Tests for Employment," in Alexandra K. Wigdor and Wendell R. Gardner, *Ability Testing: Uses, Consequences, and Controversies*, Part II: *Documentation Section* (Washington: National Academy Press, 1982), pp. 99–169.

15. John H. Bishop, "Impact of Academic Competencies on Wages, Unemployment, and Job Performance," *Carnegie-Rochester Conference Series on Public Policy*, vol. 37 (December 1992), pp. 127–94.

16. M. H. Brenner, "The Use of High School Data to Predict Work Performance," *Journal of Applied Psychology*, vol. 52, no. 1 (1968), pp. 29–30; Department of Labor, *General Aptitude Test Battery Manual* (Superintendent of Documents, 1970); John E. Hunter, James J. Crosson, and David H. Friedman, *The Validity of the Armed Services Vocational Aptitude Battery (ASVAB) for Civilian and Military Job Performance* (Department of Defense, August 1985); John Hartigan and Alexandra Wigdor, eds., *Fairness in Employment Testing* (Washington: National Academy Press, 1989); Bishop, "Impact of Academic Competencies," pp. 127–94; J. C. Hauser and Thomas M. Daymont, "Schooling, Ability, and Earnings: Cross-Sectional Evidence 8–14 Years after High School," *Sociology of Education*, vol. 50 (July 1977), pp. 182–206; Paul Taubman and Terence Wales, "Education as an Investment and a Screening Device," in F. T. Juster, ed., *Education, Income and Human Behavior* (McGraw-Hill, 1975), pp. 95–122; and Henry Farber and Robert Gibbons, "Learning and Wage Dynamics," *Quarterly Journal of Economics* (1996), pp. 1007–47.

17. Large as it is, this 16 percent figure substantially understates the total effect of improved K–12 learning on earnings as an adult. First, test scores influence hours of work and the risk of unemployment, not just wage rates. Second, compared with the minimum competency exams (MCEs) of many states, the Armed Forces Qualification Test (AFQT) is an incomplete measure of what students are learning in high school. If reliable measures of other skills learned in school (such as science, social studies, writing, and technical and computer skills) were included in the model, the total effect of test scores would be larger. Third, and most important, bias comes from using a contemporaneous measure of schooling as a control. Much of the benefit of learning in the first twelve years of school comes from the assistance it provides in continuing schooling beyond high school. Yet, this benefit of learning in high school does not get picked up by the AFQT coefficient. It is captured by the contemporaneous measure of schooling. If a prospective measure of schooling (completed schooling at the time of the AFQT test) were substituted for the contemporaneous measure, the coefficient on the AFQT would have been much larger. Joseph Altonji and Charles Pierret, "Employer Learning and Statistical Discrimination," *Quarterly Journal of Economics* (forthcoming).

18. Admission to a nonselective college is feasible without working in high school, but graduation may not be. Many high school students who avoid tough academic courses or put only the minimum of effort into their academic courses later find that even nonselective colleges are too difficult for them and they drop out. James Rosenbaum, "High Schools' Role in College and Workforce Preparation: Do College-for-All Policies Make High School Irrelevant?" Working Paper (Northwestern University, 1998), pp. 1–35; and Clifford Adelman, *Answers in the Tool Box: Academic Intensity, Attendance Patterns, and Bachelor's Degree Attainment* (Department of Education, Office of Educational Research and Improvement, 1999), pp. 1–87.

19. Ward, "A Day in the Life."

20. "Quality Counts," *Education Week*, January 11, 1999, p. 87.

21. "Quality Counts," p. 93.

22. Many of these schools were located in California. The effects of MCEs established by school districts are not assessed in this paper. Local option MCEs are being examined in another paper.

23. Minimum competency exams are additions to, not a replacement for, teacher-imposed standards. In an MCE regime, teachers continue to control the standards and assign grades in their own courses. Students must still get passing grades from their teachers to graduate. The MCE regime imposes an additional graduation requirement and thus cannot lower standards. See Robert M. Costrell, "Can Centralized Educational Standards Raise Welfare?" *Journal of Public Economics* (1998). The general equivalency diploma (GED), by contrast, offers students the opportunity to shop around for an easier (for them) way to a high school graduation certificate. As a result, the GED option lowers overall standards. This is reflected in the lower wages that GED recipients command. Stephen V. Cameron and James J. Heckman, "The Nonequivalence of High School Equivalents," Working Paper 3804 (Boston, Mass.: National Bureau of Economic Research, 1991).

24. American Federation of Teachers, *Making Standards Matter: 1996* (Washington, 1996), p. 30.

25. End-of-course examinations (EOCEs) are similar to MCEs in the following ways. Both are set by and graded to rubrics devised by a state government or a national organization (for example, the College Board), and both carry consequences for students, the teachers, and school administrators.

26. Costrell, "Can Centralized Educational Standards Raise Welfare?"

27. College Board, *More Schools, Teachers, and Students Accept the AP Challenge in 1998–99* (New York, August 31, 1999), pp. 1–8.

28. Participation rates are calculated by dividing the number of exams taken by the average enrollment per grade in high school. Participation rates have been rising and in 1999 were 52 percent for algebra; about 33 percent for geometry and biology; about 28 percent for U.S. history, Spanish, and written composition; and about 22 percent for economics and chemistry. California Department of Education, "Communications Assistance Packet: Golden State Examinations" (November 1999).

29. Sherman N. Tinkelman, *Regents Examinations in New York State after 100 Years* (Albany, N.Y.: University of the State of New York, New York Education Department, 1966), p. 12.

30. Tinkelman, *Regents Examinations in New York State after 100 Years*, p. 12.

31. John H. Bishop, "Nerd Harassment and Grade Inflation: Are College Admissions Policies Partly Responsible?" Center for Advanced Human Resources Discussion Paper 99–14 (1999).

32. Participation rates are calculated by dividing the number of exams taken by the average enrollment per grade in high school. New York State Education Department, *New York: The State of Learning—Statistical Profile of Public School Districts* (Albany, N.Y., February 1997).

33. Charisse Jones, "New York City to Stiffen Rules for Graduating," *New York Times*, May 2, 1994, p. 1

34. For example, in the new Regents English exam, four essays written under timed conditions responding to source material or literature account for more than half of the points in the exam. A sample writing prompt is: "Write a critical essay in which you discuss two pieces of literature you have read from the perspective of the statement that is provided to you in the 'critical lens.' In your essay, provide a valid interpretation of the statement as you have interpreted it, and support your opinion using specific references to appropriate literary elements from the two works." (Critical lens: "The test of a courageous person is the ability to bear defeat without losing heart.") Another sample prompt is: "Write an article for the community health newsletter. Using relevant information from text and graphs, discuss the factors that influence teenage smoking and the implications of those factors for reducing teenage smoking." Once schools have adjusted to the revised exams and the requirement that all students take them, the

Regents intend to raise the scores necessary to pass from the 55 percent level to 60 percent and then to 65 percent. See www.nysed.gov/rscs/test123.html for copies of the new Regents exams, scoring rubrics, and a complete description of the testing program.

35. John H. Bishop, *Do Curriculum-Based External Exit Exam Systems Enhance Student Achievement?* CPRE Research Report RR–40 (University of Pennsylvania, Consortium for Policy Research in Education, 1998), pp. 1–32; John H. Bishop, "Nerd Harassment, Incentives, School Priorities, and Learning," in Susan Mayer and Paul Peterson, eds., *Earning and Learning* (Brookings, 1999); and John H. Bishop, "Are National Exit Examinations Important for Educational Efficiency?" *Swedish Economic Policy Review* (1999).

36. In models developed by Suk Kang and Robert M. Costrell, some students faced with higher graduation standards conclude that the effort necessary to get a diploma is too great and so give up on the idea of getting a diploma. While these theoretical models associate "giving up" with dropping out of school, this is not necessarily the case. Students who believe they cannot graduate might nevertheless continue to attend high school because they enjoy socializing and playing sports or because they are learning a trade. Suk Kang, "A Formal Model of School Reward Systems," in John H. Bishop, ed., *Incentives, Learning, and Employability* (Ohio State University, National Center for Research in Vocational Education, 1985); and Robert M. Costrell, "A Simple Model of Educational Standards," *American Economic Review*, vol. 84, no. 4 (1994), pp. 956–71.

37. D. T. Miller and M. Ross, "Self-Serving Biases in Attribution of Causality: Fact or Fiction?" *Psychological Bulletin* (1975), pp. 82, 213–25; M. Zukerman, "Attribution of Success and Failure Revisited: Or The Motivational Bias Is Alive and Well in Attributional Theory," *Journal of Personality* (1979), pp. 47, 245–87; and R. Buehler, D. Griffin, and M. Ross, "Exploring the 'Planning Fallacy': Why People Underestimate Their Task Completion Times," *Journal of Personality and Social Psychology* (1994), pp. 67, 366–81.

38. Tabulation of Educational Excellence Alliance survey data collected from 3,949 tenth-grade students in New Jersey, New York, and Ohio who had failed one or more state graduation exams.

39. Dean Lillard and Phillip DeCicca, "Higher Standards, More Dropouts? Evidence within and across Time," *Economics of Education Review* (forthcoming); Dean Lillard and Phillip DeCicca, "The Effects of State Graduation Requirements on High School Dropout Decisions," Cornell University, College of Human Ecology, 1997, pp. 1–27; and Dean Lillard and Phillip DeCicca, "State Education Policy and Dropout Behavior: An Empirical Investigation," Cornell University, College of Human Ecology, 1997, pp. 1–23.

40. When a student moved to another state between tenth and twelfth grade, an average of the MCESTATE variables for tenth and twelfth grade was used. When information on state residence was not available for tenth grade, residence in twelfth grade was used and, if that was missing as well, eighth-grade residence was used. No state changed its policies during the 1990 to 1992 time period. Some school districts in non-MCE states established their own graduation tests. We have examined the effect of local MCEs in other papers, and including a variable for local MCE does not materially change the conclusions regarding the effect of state mandated MCEs presented here.

41. If an unobserved school effect is correlated with the MCE variable, the MCE coefficient will be biased. If unobserved school effects are correlated with the presence of MCEs, the coefficient on the interaction variable may be a better test of the basic hypothesis. As long as the unobserved school effect influences high-ability students as much as low-ability students, the coefficient on the interaction will be unbiased. The GPA*MCE interaction is significantly different from zero for only one—not getting a diploma or GED—indicator.

42. This result is consistent with the state cross-section analysis.

43. Jessica Sandham, "Florida Driver's License Revocations Improve Attendance," *Education Week*, April 26, 2000, p. 28. When, for example, West Virginia established effective enforcement mechanisms for their "no attend, no drive" policy, annual dropout rates dropped from 3.93 percent on average between 1991 and 1996 to 2.87 percent between 1996 and 1999. Event dropout data come from National Center for Education Statistics, *Dropout Rates in the United States in 1996* (Department of Education, 1998); various issues of the *Digest of Educational Statistics*; and the West Virginia Department of Education.

44. The discrepancy is caused in part by the exclusion of incarcerated youth from the Current Population Survey household interview data from which event and status dropout rates are calculated. By contrast, the denominator of the high school graduation ratio includes all seventeen-year-olds whether incarcerated or not. Incarceration rates have been rising, but even if one adds incarcerated youth to the numerator and denominator of the status dropout rates for eighteen- to twenty-four-year-olds, the new ratio would still have fallen substantially during the past thirty years.

45. Barbara Lerner, "Good News about American Education," *Commentary*, vol. 91, no. 3, (March 1990), pp. 19–25.

46. E. Mangino and M. A. Babcock, "Minimum Competency Testing: Helpful or Harmful for High Level Skills," paper presented at the annual meeting of the American Educational Research Association, San Francisco, 1986.

47. Norman Fredericksen, *The Influence of Minimum Competency Tests on Teaching and Learning* (Princeton, N.J.: Educational Testing Service, 1994), p. 8.

48. California is not counted as an EOCE/MCE state because (1) the state did not have an MCE graduation requirement, (2) teachers could not use Golden State exam scores in their own grading, (3) other rewards for doing well on the exams were weak, and (4) the program was being phased in slowly, so by the middle of the 1990s most students and schools were not participating and most participating teachers had not been teaching in the new environment long enough to change their expectations of what students were to achieve.

49. We also estimated models to test for (1) diminishing (or increasing) returns to additional ways of creating stakes for schools and students and (2) an interaction between MCEs and stakes for schools. The coefficients on the square of the number of different standards-based reform programs were negative, small, and far from statistical significance. The coefficients on the interaction between MCEs and (rewards + consequences) tended to be negative but were never significantly different from zero.

50. We present here a summary of empirical work described more fully in John H. Bishop and Ferran Mane, "Signaling and the Returns to High School Achievement," Center for Advanced Human Resources Working Paper 2001–10, pp. 1–45.

51. The generalization of identical sets of control variables has two exceptions. The state unemployment rates and weekly earnings in retailing were updated to 1992 and 1993. The payoff to completing high school was not included in the model.

52. Brenner, "The Use of High School Data to Predict Work Performance," pp. 29–30; Department of Labor, *General Aptitude Test Battery Manual*; Hunter, Crosson, and Friedman, *The Validity of the Armed Services Vocational Aptitude Battery (ASVAB) for Civilian and Military Job Performance*; Hartigan and Wigdor, *Fairness in Employment Testing;* and Bishop, "Impact of Academic Competencies," pp. 127–94.

53. Taubman and Wales, "Education as an Investment and a Screening Device," pp. 95–122; Bishop, "Impact of Academic Competencies," pp. 127–94; Farber and Gibbons, "Learning and Wage Dynamics," pp. 1007–47; and Altonji and Pierret, "Employer Learning and Statistical Discrimination," pp. 1–55.

54. CBS-TV, "America's Toughest Assignments: Solving the Education Crisis," New York, September 6, 1990.

55. Richard Murnane, John Willett, and Frank Levy. "The Growing Importance of Cognitive Skills in Wage Determination," *Review of Economics and Statistics*, vol. 77, no. 2 (May 1995), pp. 251–66.

56. The Commission on Workforce Quality and Labor Market Efficiency, appointed by the secretary of labor, concluded: "The business community should . . . show through their hiring and promotion decisions that academic achievements will be rewarded" (p. 9) and that "national educational and employer associations should work together to develop easily understood transcripts, based on voluntary achievement testing programs, that assess student proficiency in a wide variety of academic and vocational areas." Commission on Workforce Quality and Labor Market Efficiency, *Investing in People: A Strategy to Address America's Workforce Crisis* (Department of Labor, 1989), p. 12. The Competitiveness Policy Council advocated that "external assessments be given to individual students at the secondary level and that the results should be a major but not exclusive factor qualifying for college and better jobs at better wages." Competitiveness Policy Council, *Reports of the Subcouncils* (Washington, March 1993), p. 30.

57. Data on state mean National Assessment of Educational Progress (NAEP) test scores are available for many states as far back as 1990 and 1992. Standards-based reform policies have changed in many states, and the effects of these policy changes may soon show up in state-specific trends on the state NAEP. This is a promising line of future research.

58. John H. Bishop, Joan Moriarty, and Ferran Mane, "Diplomas for Learning: Not Seat Time," *Economics of Education Review* (Summer 2000).

59. Bishop, *Do Curriculum-Based External Exit Exam Systems Enhance Student Achievement?*, pp. 1–32; Bishop, "Nerd Harassment"; and Bishop, "Are National Exit Examinations Important for Educational Efficiency?"

60. It is not clear why the National Education Longitudinal Survey of 1988 (NELS-88) analysis gets larger estimates of the negative effect of MCEs on graduation rates than the state cross-section analysis. One possibility is the inclusion in the model of student background characteristics (for example, eighth-grade test scores, GPA, and attitudes) and school characteristics (for example, pupil/teacher ratios) that may have been influenced by the MCE policy. For example, the state cross-section analysis found that eighth-grade NAEP scores were higher in MCE states. Because students with higher eighth-grade test scores are more likely to complete high school, controlling for eighth-grade test scores results in MCEs not being given credit for the positive effects it has had on graduation probabilities that operate through enhanced eighth-grade achievement.

61. National Center for Education Statistics, *Education in States and Nations* (Department of Education, 1991).

62. See note 48.

63. Education Commission of the States, *Bending without Breaking: Improving Education through Flexibility and Choice* (1996) was the original source of the 1996–97 indicator variables. A survey conducted by *Education Week*, published in the January 1999 "Quality Counts" issue, provided information for 1998. The varying methods of data collection may be an additional reason for some of the differences. Correlations between the two measures of policy were .57 for the rewards indicators, .56 for the sanctions indicators, and .41 for the public reporting index.

64. The survey contractor for NELS-88 was successful in finding and interviewing dropouts. The identity of their most recent school was obtained in most interviews, allowing us to merge high school characteristics into their record. School identifications were available for all eighth graders but, because of attrition, not for all tenth and twelfth graders. When the identification

number for a student's tenth- and twelfth-grade high school was not on his or her record, the high school characteristics faced by that student were assumed to be the mean characteristics of the high schools attended by the other students in his or her eighth-grade school. This last step increased the number of observations in regressions predicting noncompletion of high school by 1,134 students, many of whom were dropouts.

65. National Center for Education Statistics, *The Digest of Education Statistics: 1993* (Department of Education, 1993), p. 149.

66. Robert Meyer, "Applied versus Traditional Mathematics: New Evidence on the Production of High School Mathematics Skills," Institute for Research on Poverty Discussion Paper 966–92 (1994), pp. 1–62.

67. The effect of MCE on a C- student is $\Delta T_{Cstudent} = \beta_{MCE} + (-1.24)*\beta_{MCE*GPA}$. The effect on a B/B- student is $\Delta T_{Bstudent} = \beta_{MCE}$. The effect on an A student is $\Delta T_{Astudent} = \beta_{MCE} + (1.09)*\beta_{MCE*GPA}$. To put the figure into a grade level equivalent metric, the increase in the test score is divided by .25*(the mean gain in test scores from eighth to twelfth grade).

68. Stephen V. Cameron and James J. Heckman, "The Nonequivalence of High School Equivalents," *Journal of Labor Economics,* vol. 11, no. 1 (1993), pp. 1–47; Richard J. Murnane, John B. Willett, and John H. Tyler, "Who Benefits from Obtaining a GED? Evidence from High School and Beyond," *Review of Economics and Statistics* (February 2000); and John H. Tyler, Richard J. Murnane, and John B. Willett, "Estimating the Labor Market Signaling Value of the GED," *Quarterly Journal of Economics* (May 2000).

69. Richard J. Murnane, John B. Willett, Yves Duhaldeborde, and John H. Tyler, "How Important Are the Cognitive Skills of Teenagers in Predicting Subsequent Earnings?" *Journal of Policy Analysis and Management,* vol. 19, no. 4 (Fall 2000), pp. 547–68.

70. Murnane and others, "How Important Are the Cognitive Skills of Teenagers in Predicting Subsequent Earnings?"

# A Diagnostic Analysis of Black-White GPA Disparities in Shaker Heights, Ohio

RONALD F. FERGUSON

T HIS QUANTITATIVE case study explores how race, family background, attitudes, and behaviors are related to achievement disparities among middle school and high school students in Shaker Heights,
Ohio.[1] The purpose is to inform the search for ways of raising achievement
and reducing disparities. Until recently, well-to-do suburbs have escaped the
spotlight of research and journalism about disparities in achievement among
racial groups. Now, however, high-stakes testing and the standards movement
are forcing school leaders to acknowledge that, even in the suburbs, students
of color are underrepresented among high achievers and overrepresented
among students who get low grades and score poorly on standardized exams.

Shaker Heights is an inner-ring suburb on the east side of Cleveland and
widely regarded as a model community. Residents have worked over several
decades to maintain a relatively stable mix of whites and African Americans
as well as a school system that is reputedly among the best in the nation. Graduates go to college in large numbers, many to elite institutions. Even so, as
the national movement to raise standards has gained momentum, Shaker
Heights, like other districts, is confronting achievement gaps. At one extreme,
black and white students in Shaker Heights achieve top scores on college
entrance exams. At the other extreme, students are at risk of failing the exam
that Ohio now requires for high school graduation. The latter group is disproportionately black.

347

The focal measure of achievement in this study is the student's grade point average (GPA) from the most recently completed semester.[2] Black and white students have both high and low GPAs. Nonetheless, the black-white GPA gap equals roughly one letter grade. The mean GPA is in the neighborhood of C+ for blacks and B+ for whites.

## Overview

The data for the study come from a survey developed by John H. Bishop at Cornell University, called the Cornell Assessment of Secondary School Student Culture. Virtually all seventh through eleventh graders in Shaker Heights completed the survey at the end of the spring semester in 1999 and are represented in the data for this study. Often, quantitative studies in education use very small data sets constructed for very narrow purposes. Other times, they use large national data sets that include only a small sample from any particular school, and the contextual differences between-schools can make it difficult to interpret findings about within-school processes. Because Shaker Heights has only one middle school and one high school, all students in each grade attend the same school. Therefore, no between-school effects confound the analysis. The sample is large and complete enough to allow for analyses of subgroups, and the questions in the survey are richly textured enough to capture a variety of important distinctions.

The data have a standard set of limitations. First, they are self-reported by students. Therefore, some measures are less reliable than if the data had come from official records or from observations by trained, objective investigators. Second, methodological requirements (for example, longitudinal data and exogenous sources of variation) necessary to distinguish causal relationships from mere correlation could not be met. Therefore, to be cautious, the text will usually say that the explanatory variables "predict" grade point averages, as opposed to "cause" them. Finally, while some of the issues may deserve separate analyses for different grade levels, the analysis of grade-level differences is beyond the scope of this paper.

Six key findings and interpretations resulted from analysis of the data. First, the characteristics of black and white youth in Shaker Heights that predict black-white GPA differences implicate skills, much more than effort, as the main reasons for the GPA gap.

The analysis of the GPA gap in this paper uses a number of explanatory variables as predictors of GPA in a standard statistical procedure called multiple regression analysis.[3] For an explanatory variable to be an important predictor of the black-white GPA gap, the black-white difference in that variable needs to be nontrivial and a significant predictor of GPA, holding other explanatory variables constant. Many variables meet one or the other of these criteria—that is, a nontrivial black-white difference is found or the variable is a significant predictor of GPA—but only a few meet both. The few that do relate most directly to academic skill and social background advantages, as opposed to effort, interest, or behavior.

Second, compared with white classmates, blacks report spending as much (or more) time doing homework, but a lower rate of homework completion. Note also that the amount of time spent doing homework (a measure of effort) does not help in predicting GPA, once the percentage of homework completed (a measure of effort and proficiency) is taken into account.

Overall, the data indicate that blacks on average spend about twenty minutes less time each night on homework than whites do. However, within a given pattern of course taking (in other words, controlling for the mix of regular, honors, and Advanced Placement [AP] courses) black students report more time on homework than white classmates, but lower rates of homework completion.[4] This finding emerges from simple tabulations and also from statistical estimates that control for family background and many other factors.

Teachers see only the rate of homework completion, not the time devoted to trying. They also see behaviors that are difficult to interpret. For example, blacks in the survey are twice as likely to identify "tough" as a characteristic of popular peers, while whites are more likely to identify "outgoing" and "self-confident." Teachers and administrators in Shaker Heights have told me that black-white differences in tough behavior and rates of homework completion make it appear that blacks exert less effort than whites and have more oppositional attitudes about achievement. The analysis here concurs that black students might behave differently and complete less homework than whites, but not that their effort is less than among white classmates or that their peer culture is more opposed to achievement.[5]

Third, attitudes and behaviors are more important for predicting within-race than between-race GPA disparities.

In contrast to comparisons between blacks and whites, attitudes differ greatly between high and low achievers within each racial group. Together, both skill-related and effort-related attitudes play major roles in predicting

GPAs of B or better for some black students, but C or lower for others. However, how to interpret such results is not clear, because the direction of causation cannot be measured. Over time, attitudes and behaviors can affect achievement, but achievement can also affect attitudes and behaviors, in a process of cumulative causation.[6] Whatever the pattern of causation might be, attitudes and behaviors are an integral part of the story about within-race disparities.

Fourth, to think clearly about achievement gaps, it is important to distinguish: (a) what children know in terms of their stock of academic knowledge, (b) the pace at which they learn new things to add to the stock, (c) their knowledge of techniques and strategies that help them to learn effectively and efficiently and to manage the pace of new learning, (d) the effort that the individual chooses (or is required) to devote to the process, and (e) how individual-level variations in all of the above depend on group-level characteristics, resources, and processes.

Consider, for example, hypothetical runners from two tribes, the Whites and the Blacks, who are competing as individuals in a single long-distance race to acquire academic knowledge. Each step in the race adds to the knowledge that each runner accumulates. Most runners from the White tribe are ahead of most runners from the Black tribe. Variations in effort and natural ability are evident within each tribe, but no systematic differences between the tribes exist on these dimensions. Therefore, neither effort nor natural ability can account for why members of the White tribe tend to be ahead. Instead, the main reasons are that many in the White tribe had head starts at the beginning of the race and many have also received extensive informal coaching from tribal elders on effective running techniques and racing strategies. Superior techniques allow a runner to maintain a given pace with less effort; and knowledge of racing strategies leads to better decisions. Hence, members of the White tribe tend to be ahead not only in terms of academic knowledge accumulated during the race, but they are also more knowledgeable about running techniques and racing strategies.

Individuals in the Black tribe would like to comply with demands that they should run up closer to where most of the Whites are. But this is a tough challenge. There are no shortcuts, so the only way to catch up is to run faster (that is, learn faster) than most of the Whites. But is this possible? Simply exerting greater effort while using old techniques and strategies might do little to close the gap, thereby leading to disappointment and frustration for all but the most talented Black tribal members. The combination of increased effort together with highly effective coaching to refine techniques and strategies might improve prospects considerably. Therefore, expanding the supply of highly effective coaching is a major priority. Another priority is to address social pressures that might discourage some runners from always doing their best.

Fifth, all segments of the school community report negative peer pressures. Black and white students who never take honors or AP courses seem moderately inclined to hold back effort in response to their peers. Conversely, students who take honors or AP courses seem less prone to allow the peer pressures that they experience to hold them back.

As a gauge of holding back, a question in the survey asks whether the respondent agrees, or not, with the statement "I didn't try as hard as I could in school because I worried about what my friends might think." Other things being equal, a student who agrees with the statement has an estimated grade point average that is one-fifth of a letter grade lower, compared with a student who does not agree. By this measure of holding back, 21 percent of black males, 10 percent of black females, 7 percent of white males, and 3 percent of white females report that at least once a week they hold back. These racial differences are associated mostly with whether students take honors and AP courses. By course level, blacks and whites differ hardly at all in their reported propensity to hold back.

Reports of holding back are highest among students who report negative peer pressure and take no honors or AP classes. For example, among both black and white students, more than four of every ten males who take no honors or AP classes and who agree that "my friends make fun of people who try to do real well in school" also report holding back on their own work effort. If they agree in addition that friends disapprove of grade competition, then the rate of holding back rises to over half.

Students who take any honors or AP courses and who agree with the same statements about peer pressure are much less likely (especially among whites) to say that they ever hold back because of what friends might think. Because the nonhonors and non-AP courses are where black students are concentrated, and also where most of the holding back occurs for both blacks and whites who experience peer pressure, the black-white difference in honors and AP course taking predicts much (though not all) of the black-white difference in reports of holding back. Because only one in five black males and one in ten black females reports holding back, and because some white students hold back, too, holding back predicts only a small fraction of black-white GPA gaps. Still, the issue is important to consider because it could be a drag on improvement as Shaker Heights strives to raise achievement levels among the students who are furthest behind. Also, holding back may be more common than the survey responses imply, if not everyone affected by such impulses reports them.

Sixth, honors and AP courses may be socially isolating for black students, which may diminish the degree to which black students aspire to take such courses.

Avoidance of honors and AP courses can be another form of holding back but may not be reported as such in the survey responses. Black students are far less likely to take honors and AP courses, even controlling for attitudes, behaviors, and family background. This black-white difference cannot be explained with any certainty. Because few black students (aside from those already in honors classes) have GPAs of 3.0 or better, many may not be prepared to enter more advanced courses.[7] Nonetheless, some black students could engage their studies differently, perhaps seeking more help from teachers, if they earnestly aspired to take advanced courses.[8]

Concerns about social isolation might deter aspirations to qualify for honors and Advanced Placement courses, even if values among blacks are no more oppositional to hard work and achievement, per se, than among whites. Recall the racing metaphor. Talented runners in the Black tribe might find it easier and socially more satisfying simply to accommodate the slower pace of their friends, instead of breaking away. Breaking away academically while remaining connected socially may require code switching (for example, to speak black slang at the appropriate times) and navigating back and forth between black and white social groups. Inability or unwillingness to do these things to signal his or her identification with other black students may be the main reason for the occasions when black high achievers get accused of "acting white."

In the end, the black-white GPA gap in Shaker Heights seems to be more a skill gap than an effort gap. However, effort, social pressures, and honors and AP enrollments are certainly part of the achievement story. For black students, their teachers, and their parents, substantial narrowing of the achievement gap may require more effort, a more supportive peer culture, and less ambivalence about honors and AP course taking. However, most important, narrowing the gap will almost certainly require more effective and efficient learning techniques and strategies, so that the pace of new learning can accelerate as the level of effort increases.

## Stigmas, Stereotypes, and Marginality

Prominent ideas about underachievement among African American youth emphasize the importance of stigmas and stereotypes. In her book on black youth culture of achievement, Signithia Fordham writes about the sense that black people feel of being the stigmatized, subdominant minority group opposite the dominant "Other" in the form of mainstream, white society.[9] She reports a common need among black adolescents, especially males, to cultivate a sense of identity that is explicitly distinct from this Other and to signal that identity through an identifiably black persona. Young people have many ways of managing this process. Some methods may detract from school performance while others may promote it. An influential set of ideas about how they might detract concerns oppositional culture.

### Oppositional Culture

Anthropologist John Ogbu is the person most identified with the idea that the historical mistreatment and continuing marginality of blacks in the United States foster "attitudes and skills less favorable to white middle-class type school success."[10] He contends that black people born and raised in the United States compare their condition with that of the white majority and feel a sense of resentment and pessimism that helps to foster a reactive, oppositional culture. In Ogbu's thesis, minorities who migrated freely to the United States are "voluntary" as opposed to "involuntary" minorities. Voluntary minorities have not endured as much oppression in the United States as blacks descendant from American slaves. In addition, voluntary minorities are less resentful of their status because their standard of comparison is usually their country of origin, where conditions were worse. The resentment and marginality that involuntary minorities feel is, according to Ogbu, the basis for resistance or incomplete acceptance of school norms and goals, which helps to explain black underachievement.

In contrast, some economists and sociologists have concluded that Ogbu and the school of thought that he represents are wrong about youth in the United States. Economists Philip J. Cook and Jens Ludwig find in nationally representative data for the period around 1990 that black and white youth had essentially equivalent attitudes and behaviors.[11] They find that this is especially true when family characteristics such as education, income, and household structure are taken into account. The attitudes and behaviors that Cook and Ludwig analyzed included indexes of self-perceived popularity tabulated by student GPA and by membership in the honor society, reported time spent on homework, school attendance, and expected years of schooling.

Cook and Ludwig's work has been important because it effectively calls previous, mostly ethnographic, findings into question. They ask: Do African American adolescents report greater alienation from school than non-Hispanic whites? Does academic success lead to social ostracism among black adolescents? Do the social costs or benefits of academic success differ by race? For each question, their answer based on analysis of nationally representative data is, "Apparently not." Further, sociologists James Ainsworth-Darnell and Douglas B. Downey analyzed the same national data and came to essentially similar conclusions, though they found some behavioral differences that Cook and Ludwig did not address.[12] Their findings support the hypothesis that blacks have more problems than whites in a category they call "skills, habits and styles." They find that variables in this category, as distinct from oppositional attitudes about achievement, help in a small way to explain the achievement gap in the data that they analyzed.

### Stereotype Threat and Disidentification

Even if research findings accumulate showing that black students seem no more oppositional to schooling than whites, or perhaps even less so, stigmas and stereotypes could still affect achievement. Some black youth are motivated to prove stereotypes wrong or to defy them.[13] However, research in psychology cautions that setting out to challenge a stigma or to prove a stereotype wrong is not easy. Claude Steele and Joshua Aronson have produced laboratory evidence of "stereotype anxiety," which is induced by "stereotype threat."[14] In the context of race, the anxiety is a nervous anticipation induced by the threat that one's performance might confirm a negative racial generalization. Such anxiety can depress performance even among students who value achievement, know that they have the skills to do very well, and are trying to do their best.

Stereotype anxiety may depress performance most when students both fear and expect that their performance might confirm the stereotype. This can produce disidentification, because it may feel better emotionally to fail because of not trying than because of low ability. To fail after an earnest effort would seem to be confirmation of low ability. In extreme cases, disidentification resulting from discouragement is associated with learned helplessness.[15] In learned helplessness, a person stops trying because he or she believes that even his or her best effort will not be enough. In school situations that are ambiguous in this regard, determination to excel might alternate with feelings of helplessness, such that students sabotage their success with fleeting resolves that move them back and forth between working hard and hardly working.

Among males and females, blacks and whites, Shaker Heights has students who consider schoolwork interesting, pay close attention in class, spend a few hours each night on homework, and try to do their best. At the other extreme, students have experienced academic difficulty and lean toward disidentification as a way of coping.

## The Data

Data for this paper come from a survey developed by John Bishop that was administered in Shaker Heights at the end of the spring semester in 1999.[16] Shaker Heights has one high school with grades nine through twelve and one middle school attended by seventh and eighth graders. All seventh through eleventh graders in attendance were given the survey to complete during a regular class period. A total of 1,699 students responded to the survey, providing, aside from a few who were absent, virtually complete coverage for the five grade levels. Eighty-three percent of respondents were black or white, which are the two groups in the present analysis.[17] All of the data are self-reports. Hence, the usual cautions are in order regarding possible inaccuracies and biases. At the same time, I know of no reason to expect that more accurate data would invalidate my basic findings.

A number of variables were used in the study. Some describe the child and others the family. Parents' average years of schooling and household composition variables aim to capture systematic differences among households in the supports that they are able to provide for achievement. For example, parents' years of schooling may indicate income differences that affect resources in the home, as well as parents' academic orientations and aptitudes passed on from parent to child. Similarly, household composition may reflect differences in financial resources per child, parental supervision, and teen's responsibilities for helping to maintain the household. Variables in other categories measure social perceptions, attitudes, and behaviors that I hypothesize affect, and reflect, school engagement. Means and standard deviations for all variables appear in table A-1. Most variables are coded as yes = 1 and no = 0, or they have been standardized to have a mean of zero and standard deviation of one across all students in the sample.[18] A few variables are measured in other conventional units such as GPA points (on a four-point scale), hours, or proportions.

### Race and Family Background

The race and gender variables in the analysis are indicator variables that identify the race or gender group (that is, black male, black female, white male, or white female) to which each student belongs. The analysis also includes both mother's and father's years of schooling.[19] Preliminary estimates showed no clear evidence that mother's or father's education was a stronger predictor than the other, so the two were combined to form variables for average parental years of schooling: twelve years or fewer, thirteen to fifteen years, sixteen years, and graduate degree.[20] Surprisingly large differences in parental schooling were found between Shaker Heights's black and white students. Mothers and fathers together average at least four years of college in roughly 90 percent of white households, compared with about 45 percent of black households. Parents in one quarter of black households have only twelve or fewer years of schooling. The same is true for less than 5 percent of white households. A larger percentage of parents have postgraduate degrees among whites than have four-year college degrees among blacks.

Household composition is measured by indicator variables for "two parents," "one parent and one stepparent," and "one parent or neither." An unknown number of the "one parent or neither" cases is foster families and children living with relatives. Just as racial differences in parental education are large, so are differences in household composition. The percentage living with "one parent or neither" is 52 percent for black males, 53 percent for black females, 8.6 percent for white males, and 14.6 percent for white females. Black students average between two and three siblings, whites between one and two.

### Reasons for Failing to Study or Complete Homework

Items in this category are reasons that students agree are important for why they sometimes do not study or finish their homework:

—Competing time commitments ("Not enough time [to study or finish homework] because of work and/or school activities").

—Could get a good grade without studying.

—Simply decided not to bother.

    I preferred to party or hang out with friends.

    The assignment was boring or pointless.

    I didn't care about the grade in that course.

    Friends wanted to do something else.

    Didn't work hard is usually a reason when I get a bad grade.

—Carelessness and poor planning.

    Started too late, poor planning.

    I got distracted at home.

    I forgot the assignment.

—The work was too difficult.

    The assignment was too long and difficult.

    No one to help me at home.

    I didn't understand the material.

    The class was hard is usually a reason when I get a bad grade.

The first two items are yes/no variables. Each of the others is a composite of the yes/no values of the individual components. Each composite is scaled to have a mean of zero and is measured in standardized (that is, standard deviation) units.[21]

## Classroom Attitudes and Behaviors

The category of classroom attitudes and behaviors covers what students think and do while in class. Five items gauge the frequency of particular thoughts and behaviors. The question in the survey asks, "How often?" and the respondent can indicate never, seldom, fairly often, often, usually, or always. The five items are: find studies intrinsically interesting, contribute to class discussion, do homework in one class for another, joke around in class, and really pay attention in class. For this study, each measure is transformed to standard deviation units by setting its mean equal to zero and its standard deviation equal to one. The sixth variable in this category is a yes/no question pertaining to the following statement: "I didn't try as hard as I could at school because I worried about what my friends might think." Below, this variable is called "hold back or hide work effort."

## Other Attitudes and Behaviors

Other attitudes and behaviors is a residual category for indexes that do not fit neatly in the categories above. It includes hours of watching television on typical school days, a variable called "aspiration for years of college" measuring the highest level of schooling the student hopes to attain, whether the student copies homework from friends roughly once a week or more, whether the student studies with friends roughly once a week or more, and whether they agree that teachers maintain good discipline in the classroom.[22] It also includes a composite variable called "friends think academic zeal isn't cool." This variable is constructed from indicators of student agreement or disagreement with the following statements. Values are highest for students who agree with the first four and disagree with the last two.

—It's not cool to be competitive about grades.

—It's not cool to frequently volunteer answers or comments in class.

—It's not cool to study real hard for tests and quizzes.

—It's not cool to be enthusiastic about what you are learning in school.

—It's annoying when other students talk or joke around in class.

—It's annoying when students try to get teachers off track.

As a composite of the six items, "friends think academic zeal isn't cool" is a fairly direct measure of peer opposition to expressions of school engagement.[23]

Another variable, "work hard to please adults," measures the degree to which pleasing teachers and parents is among the motivations when the student works hard. Students were asked the following question, "When you work real hard in school, which are important reasons?" Response options included the following:[24]

—I don't want to embarrass my family.

—To please or impress my parents.

—To please or impress my teacher.

—My teachers encourage me to work hard.

Students who score higher on this index care more about pleasing adults.

### Perceptions Regarding Popularity

The data also include measures of what students perceive are the determinants, or at least the correlates, of popularity. A central proposition in conventional wisdom about achievement disparities is that peer effects are important determinants.[25] If black and white students differ systematically in what they report are the styles and routines that most characterize popular peers, then it can be inferred that they probably differ also in the styles and routines to which they are trying to conform to be popular.

**Table 1. Characteristics of Members of the Most Popular Crowd in the First Year of Middle or Junior High School, according to Groups by Gender and Race**

Percent

| | Males | | Females | |
|---|---|---|---|---|
| *Characteristic* | *Black* | *White* | *Black* | *White* |
| Cool clothes | **77** | **61** | 82 | 81 |
| Funny | 73 | 70 | **58** | **46** |
| Good at sports | 72 | 70 | 35 | 55 |
| Tough | **53** | **27** | 38 | 10 |
| Self-confident | **47** | **65** | 57 | 62 |
| Outgoing | **44** | **62** | 58 | 64 |
| Not attentive in class | 26 | 24 | 28 | 22 |
| Attentive in class | 25 | 22 | 31 | 28 |
| Worked hard to get good grades | 23 | 19 | 31 | 27 |
| Made fun of kids who studied a lot | 16 | 18 | 19 | 17 |
| Smart | **14** | **20** | **19** | **29** |
| Number of respondents | 307 | 357 | 322 | 356 |

Note: Boldfaced numbers indicate a statistically significant racial difference at the 0.05 level, by gender.

A question in the survey asked students to complete the following sentence: "During the first year of middle or junior high school, the members of the most popular crowd (my gender) were _____." Respondents could check any characteristic that applied from a list that the survey supplied. Consistent with at least some degree of racial segmentation, both similarities and statistically significant differences, by both race and gender, turned up in their responses.[26]

The correlates of popularity warrant examination. The data in table 1 show that "smart" ranks at the bottom for all but white females and that "cool clothes" ranks at the top for all but white males. "Being funny" ranks second for all but white females. Things that relate most to academic life, from "not attentive in class" to "smart," all rate near the bottom of the ranking. Hence, regarding criteria for popularity, both blacks and whites focus mostly outside the classroom.

Alongside the racial similarities are some differences. Numbers in boldface in table 1 indicate when the black-white difference, within gender, is statistically distinguishable from zero at the 0.05 level. Considering only the statistically significant differences, black males are more likely than white males to cite "cool clothes" and "tough" as characteristics of the most popular crowd. White males are more likely than black males to cite "self-confident," "outgoing.," and "smart" (although, even among white males, only 20 percent cite "smart"). Black females are more likely than white females to cite "funny" and "tough"; white females more frequently cite "good at sports" and "smart."

Students who appear to be outgoing, self-confident, and not especially tough probably fit better with teachers' own personal styles. Differences in how black and white students carry themselves may foster subtle differences in student-teacher relations for black and white students. Informal discussions with teachers in Shaker Heights and other places tend to support this conjecture.

The characteristics that a student identifies as describing the most popular crowd do not necessarily describe that student. They probably do, however, reveal something about the student's sense of identity and tendencies to affiliate with (or aspire to) particular crowds. The list in table 1 is too long to use for the entire analysis. Therefore, the analysis includes only the four categories for which black-white differences are statistically significant: "tough," "outgoing," "self-confident," and "smart." They are included with other variables introduced above, under the broad heading of "attitudes and behaviors."

## Predicting Attitudes and Behaviors

In exploring the relationship of race and other background measures to attitudes and behaviors, questions arise about parental education and household structure, oppositional peer culture, holding back in response to peer pressure, and time-use patterns for homework and television watching. The statistical basis of the analysis is a set of multiple regression equations in which the explanatory variables are race and gender, parental education, number of parents in the household, and number of siblings. In all, thirty-eight equations were estimated, two for each attitude or behavior as the dependent variable. This produced too many numbers to report here, so table 2 provides a qualitative summary. All entries in the table (other than "—") represent statistically significant differences at the 0.05 level or better.

Each line of table 2 pertains to a particular attitude or behavior as the dependent variable and summarizes partial results for two estimated equations. For each line, results from a first equation appear in columns 1a and 1b; results for the second appear in columns 2a through 2d.[27] The equation for columns 1a and 1b includes only the race and gender variables as predictors. Hence, the word *black* or *white* simply indicates whether blacks or whites have the higher value (though not necessarily the best value) for that gender. This is a difference-of-racial-means test, done separately by gender. For comparison,

**Table 2. Statistically Significant Effects of Family Background and Race, within Gender, for School-Related Attitudes and Behaviors**

| School-related attitude or behavior | Specification 1: No background controls | | Specification 2: With background controls | | | |
|---|---|---|---|---|---|---|
| | Males (race with the higher value) (1a) | Females (race with the higher value) (1b) | Males (race with the higher value) (2a) | Females (race with the higher value) (2b) | Parents average twelve years schooling (2c) | Live with one parent or neither (2d) |
| *Important reasons when failing to study or complete homework* | | | | | | |
| Carelessness and poor planning | — | Black | — | — | — | — |
| Competing time commitments | White | White | White | White | Lower | — |
| Could get good grade without it | White | White | White | White | Lower | Lower |
| Simply decided not to bother | White | — | White | White | — | Higher |
| The work was too difficult | White | White | — | — | — | Lower |
| *Classroom behaviors and attitudes* | | | | | | |
| Do homework in one class for another | Black | Black | Black | Black | — | — |
| Hold back or hide work effort | Black | Black | Black | Black | — | — |
| Really pay attention in class | — | — | — | — | Lower | Lower |
| Studies intrinsically interesting | — | White | Black | — | Lower | — |
| Contribute to class discussion | White | White | — | — | Lower | Lower |
| Joke around in class | — | White | White | White | — | — |
| *Life outside the classroom* | | | | | | |
| TV hours per school night | Black | Black | Black | Black | Higher | Higher |
| Aspiration for years of college | White | White | White | Black | Lower | Lower |
| Copy homework from friends | — | — | — | — | — | — |
| Study with friends | — | — | — | — | — | — |
| Friends say academic zeal not cool | White | — | White | White | — | — |
| *What respondent perceives as characteristics of the most popular crowd* | | | | | | |
| Outgoing | White | — | White | — | Lower | — |
| Self-confident | White | — | White | — | Lower | — |
| Smart | White | White | White | White | — | — |
| Tough | Black | Black | Black | Black | — | — |

— = Not significant at the 0.05 level of significance.

the estimation procedure for columns 2a through 2d included (in addition to the race and gender indicators) parental education levels, the number of parents in the household, and the number of siblings. When the entry in column 2a or 2b differs from that in 1a or 1b, it is because of the influence of including the family background variables in the analysis. Some of what appear to be race effects are instead family background effects.

The word *higher* (or *lower*) in column 2c indicates that students whose parents have only twelve or fewer years of schooling report the attitude or behavior more (or less) than those whose parents have postgraduate degrees. I chose to compare "twelve or fewer years" with "graduate degrees" in table 2, because these are the extreme categories and are most likely to capture whether there is any effect of parental education.[28] Similarly, the *higher* (or *lower*) in column 2d indicates that students who live with one or neither of their parents report the behavior more (or less) than students who live with their mother and father. The vast majority of children whose parents have only twelve years of schooling in Shaker Heights, or who live with one or neither parent, are black. However, the fact that some are white allows for distinguishing statistically the degree to which each attitude or behavior is associated with parental education or household structure, as opposed to racial differences that remain to be explained in other ways.

## Parental Education and Household Composition

The estimates summarized in table 2 indicate a clear pattern in the ways that parental education makes a difference. Compared with students whose parents have graduate degrees, those whose parents have only high school degrees report that they pay less attention in class, regard their studies as intrinsically less interesting, and participate less in class discussion. They are also less likely to report that they can get good grades without doing their assignments. Further, they watch more hours of television, have lower college aspirations, and are less likely to say that the most popular crowd is outgoing and self-confident.

Thus, some key advantages of having well-educated parents are that they prepare children to concentrate, to be curious, to enjoy the exchange of ideas, to have high academic aspirations, and to admire people who are outgoing and self-confident. Students most lacking in this type of preparation may be the most prone to disidentify with school, especially when faced with intellectual challenges. These differences probably reflect the child's learning history both at home and at school. In particular, there is residential movement of some households back and forth between Shaker Heights and adjacent neighborhoods in Cleveland, where schools are reputedly not as effective. Children of highly educated parents are more likely to have attended Shaker Heights schools (or similar schools) continuously since kindergarten.

The pattern for students who live with one or neither parent (versus both parents) resembles that for students who live with parents that have only twelve years of schooling (versus graduate degrees), but some differences are related to both interest and effort. First, students from single-parent families appear more often to slack off. They are less likely to say that the work was too difficult and more likely to say that they simply decided not to bother, as explanations for failing to study or complete their homework. This could be face-saving, because it feels better to fail because of not trying than to try and then look or feel stupid. However, if such reports of low effort were face-saving, meant to hide low self-perceived ability, then they would probably appear for children of less educated parents as well, but they do not. Children whose parents have only twelve years of schooling seem the least academically prepared and the most disengaged. Students from single-parent households are just as likely as students from two-parent households to regard their studies as intrinsically interesting. Hence, while the findings for low levels of parental education point to lack of student interest, poor intellectual preparation, and probably some degree of academic disidentification, the findings for single-parent households point to a problem with effort (perhaps because of less supervision or more family responsibilities) among students who nonetheless find their studies interesting.

## No Evidence for Oppositional Culture

A popular proposition in discussions of the black-white achievement gap is that peer culture might be more oppositional to achievement among black students than among whites. The data in table 2 show no support for this (though keep in mind that there may be self-reporting bias). There are a number of attitudes and behaviors for which blacks and whites are not statistically distinguishable, once family background controls are in place (and sometimes even without them). These include "really paying attention in class," "participating in class discussion," "copying homework from friends," and "studying with friends." They also include "carelessness and poor planning" and "the work was too difficult" as reasons for missing homework assignments. Further, compared with white males, black males are more inclined to say that their studies are intrinsically interesting, holding constant family background. Generally, whites express more relaxed, confident, and cavalier attitudes about their studies than blacks express about theirs. Whites are also the most likely to give multiple reasons for failing to study or complete homework. More than blacks, whites report that they have competing time commitments; they some-

Table 3. Peer Pressure, by Race and Gender

Percent agreeing

| School-related attitude or behavior | Black | | White | |
|---|---|---|---|---|
| | Males | Females | Males | Females |
| Friends think it's not cool to | *Panel A* | | | |
| Be competitive about grades* | 33 | 43 | 50 | 58 |
| Frequently volunteer answers or comments in class | 18 | 13 | 19 | 8 |
| Study real hard for tests or quizzes | 12 | 6 | 12 | 5 |
| Be enthusiastic about what you are learning in school | 26 | 14 | 30 | 18 |
| Friends think it's annoying when | | | | |
| Other students talk or joke around in class* | 46 | 56 | 34 | 43 |
| Students try to get teachers off track* | 52 | 63 | 37 | 38 |
| Friends make fun of people who try to do real | *Panel B* | | | |
| well in school | 24 | 10 | 20 | 11 |
| Number of students | (303) | (351) | (328) | (360) |

* Indicates a statistically significant black-white difference at the 0.05 level for both males and females.

times know that they can get a good grade without studying or doing the assignment; and they sometimes simply decide not to bother. Whites also report more than blacks that they joke around in class and that their friends think academic zeal is not cool.

Tabulations for the items that make up the variable named "friends say academic zeal is not cool" are shown in panel A of table 3, under the subheadings "friends think it's not cool to" and "friends think it's annoying when." A larger percentage of whites than blacks report that friends would agree that being competitive about grades is not cool. A larger percentage of blacks report that friends are annoyed when students joke around in class or try to get teachers off track (perhaps because it happens more in their classes). These black-white differences regarding competitiveness and annoyances are statistically significant. Similarly, the survey has a question regarding whether "friends make fun of people who try to do real well in school." Panel B of table 3 tabulates the responses. There are statistically significant differences by gender, but not by race.

Findings here do not support the view that black students' peer culture in Shaker Heights is more oppositional to achievement than whites' (even though behaviors may differ because blacks tend to place a higher value than whites do on appearing tough and so forth).

**Table 4. Peer Pressure and Holding Back, by Race and Gender**

Number of students

| Agreement with statements | Black | | White | | |
|---|---|---|---|---|---|
| | *Male* | *Female* | *Male* | *Female* | *Row total* |

Statement A: Peers make fun of people who try to do real well in school.
Statement B: Peers think it's not cool to be competitive about grades.

*Panel A*

*Students with no honors or Advanced Placement (AP) courses*

| | Black | | White | | |
|---|---|---|---|---|---|
| Neither statement A nor B | 117 | 111 | 22 | 19 | 269 |
| Either statement A or B | 72 | 92 | 14 | 19 | 197 |
| Both statements A and B | 32 | 11 | 8 | 3 | 54 |
| Total | 221 | 214 | 44 | 41 | 520 |

*Students with at least one honors or AP course*

| | Black | | White | | |
|---|---|---|---|---|---|
| Neither statement A nor B | 44 | 71 | 113 | 117 | 345 |
| Either statement A or B | 28 | 59 | 138 | 181 | 406 |
| Both statements A and B | 6 | 7 | 31 | 19 | 63 |
| Total | 78 | 137 | 282 | 317 | 814 |

*Panel B*

*Percent who report that "I didn't try as hard as I could at school because I worried about what my friends might think"*

*Students with no honors or AP courses*

| | Black | | White | | |
|---|---|---|---|---|---|
| Neither statement A nor B | 13 | 12 | 14 | 5 | 12 |
| Either statement A or B | 25 | 8 | 14 | 11 | 15 |
| Both statements A and B | 53 | 36 | 63 | 33 | 50 |
| Total | 23 | 11 | 23 | 10 | 17 |

*Students with at least one honors or AP course*

| | Black | | White | | |
|---|---|---|---|---|---|
| Neither statement A nor B | 5 | 6 | 4 | 1 | 3 |
| Either statement A or B | 14 | 5 | 3 | 3 | 4 |
| Both statements A and B | 17 | 29 | 13 | 0 | 11 |
| Total | 9 | 7 | 4 | 2 | 4 |

## Holding Back as a Response to Peer Pressure

The variable "hold back or hide work effort" comes from the statement "I didn't try as hard as I could at school because I worried about what my friends might think." The answer is coded as a "yes" if the student marked on the survey that he or she does this "about once a week" or more often. Blacks hold back more than whites, and no statistically significant relationship exists of holding back to parental education or the number of parents in the household.[29]

Table 4 focuses on two of the items from table 3 and their relationship to holding back. The panel A of table 4 shows the number of students who agree with neither, one, or both of the following statements from table 3: (A) "Peers make fun of people who try to do real well in school"; and (B) "Peers think it's not cool to be competitive about grades." Just as in table 3, the numbers in table 4 are tabulated by race and gender. However, in table 4, they are also tabulated by whether the student takes any honors or AP classes.

Panel B of table 4 shows that holding back is concentrated among students who report peer pressure and take no honors or AP classes. For example, of the fifty-four students who take no honors or AP courses and who agree with both statements A and B, half report holding back. Conversely, of the sixty-three students who take at least one honors or AP class and who agree with both statements A and B, only 11 percent report that they hold back.

Simple tabulations for the whole sample show that males hold back more than females, and the black/white ratio of holding back for both males and females is 3:1 (see table A-1). However, among students who take no honors or AP classes, the 3:1 ratio goes away and no racial pattern emerges. Multiple regression results (not shown here) demonstrate that racial differences in the propensity to hold back are no longer statistically significant, once honors and AP course taking and peer pressures are taken into account.[30] Other things being equal, the black-white difference in holding back predicts only a very small fraction of the black-white achievement gap, because only a minority of blacks report holding back, and some whites hold back, too. Still, the findings should not be ignored as Shaker Heights and other districts organize to raise achievement levels. The same can be said for time-use and television watching.

*Time-Use, Television, and 'Tribal Differences'*

Black students watch television more than whites. The black/white ratio for the number of hours watched on school nights is almost 2-to-1 for males and almost 2.5-to-1 for females. The time students report watching television plus the time they report doing homework are depicted in figure 1. For all four race and gender groups, graphs are shown for students who take mostly honors or AP courses and for others who take none. Graphs for those who take some, but fewer than half honors and AP courses, are not shown. The largest total is almost six hours per day for black girls in honors courses (these hours may overlap if students do homework and watch TV at the same time). White males and females spend an average of 3.5 to 4 hours, with more of it devoted to homework for those who take mostly honors and AP courses. A statisti-

**Figure 1. Hours of Homework and Television by Race and Gender and Proportion
Honors and Advanced Placement (AP) Courses Taken**

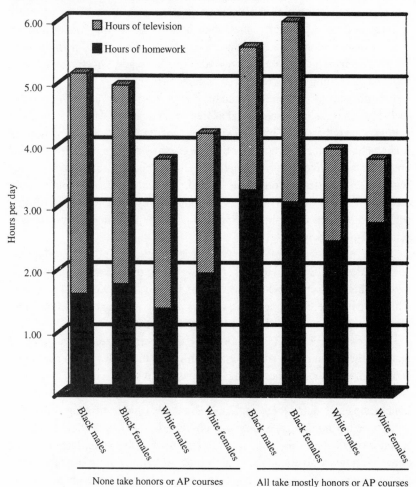

None take honors or AP courses          All take mostly honors or AP courses

cally significant trade-off is evident between watching television and spending time on homework, but it is very small. Specifically, an extra hour watching television predicts only five minutes less on homework.

Watching television could reduce the efficiency of time spent doing homework even though it appears to have very little effect on the amount of time
spent. Black students do report lower homework completion rates than white
students who report the same amount of time doing homework.[31] However,

when a test is conducted to determine whether the lower homework completion rate might be caused by watching television, the result is that the estimated effect of television watching is so small as to be completely
inconsequential. Apparently, the lower homework completion rate is not
because of television. Neither do differences among individuals in time watching television predict differences in grade point averages. Watching television
contributes nothing as a predictor of achievement gaps.

It is difficult to believe that watching television for three or more hours
each day can be as inconsequential as these findings suggest. The only effect
worth noting is that watching television is part of the explanation for why black
students have a greater propensity to do homework for one class in another. I
find that black-white differences in time spent watching television account for
between one quarter and one-third of the black-white difference in the incli-
nation to do homework in one class for another.[32] Even for this effect, further
analysis shows that doing homework for one class in another appears itself to
be a benign practice.[33]

Again, it appears from the analysis of individual-level data that the time
black students in Shaker Heights spend watching television is, for the most
part, not being taken from homework time. Clearly, however, compared with
white students, between one and two hours per day is being taken from something that black youth would otherwise be doing and that white youth might
already be doing. The following thought experiment suggests a way that the
black-white difference in television watching and the achievement gap might
be related, even though the findings do not show it.

Imagine a community with two large tribes. One tribe has a required two-
hour clinic each night where students learn study- and test-taking skills. The
other tribe has no clinic. Assume that children in the tribe without the clinic
spend most of their time watching television while the other tribe is in the
clinic. Children who attend the clinic watch television during their free time,
too, but because of the clinic, they have less of it. In both tribes, family duties
and other miscellaneous factors mean that some children watch television more
than others, and these factors produce variation within each tribe in the amounts
of time that children spend watching television.

In this example, the clinic causes tribal differences in television watching
and achievement. Something analogous could be happening in Shaker Heights.
Not an organized clinic, but nonetheless a system of norms, learning resources
in homes, and enrichment activities take time from watching television and
benefit achievement. However, in this example, the effects on achievement of

tribal-level norms, resources, or activities could not be detected from individual-level data on time watching television.

A final point concerns the social function of television. The data show that no matter whether the student is black or white, those who have more black friends spend more time watching television.[34] During a visit to Shaker Heights's high school, black students were asked why they watched television so much. A high-achieving black male answered, only half jokingly, "You have to watch television to get your material to be funny." He proceeded to explain that much of the social conversation among black youth at the lunch table and after school is about what happens on television. Hence, when young people watch television they are doing their "social homework."[35]

If a student stopped watching television and switched to more high-yield learning activities, the change would have a cost in social terms. That student could not contribute as much to socially important banter about what the group watched or understand shorthand references. Even if friends accepted this, the student would feel more marginal to the group. The social function of television might be why the trade-off between homework time and television time seems so small. If the goal is to have a good day at school, television and homework might be more like complements than substitutes. Both need to get done.

## Predicting Academic Performance

The impact that particular beliefs, attitudes, and behaviors might have on achievement is more difficult to determine than one might initially expect. One category of problems relates to those discussed in the context of television watching. Specifically, the key causal forces might be group- or community-level instead of individual-level phenomena and not detectable using individual-level data. However, another problem is that some attitudes and behaviors are probably causes and effects of achievement. For example, it is easy to think of reasons that high aspirations at the beginning of the school year might cause higher grades during the year and higher grades might reinforce high aspirations. Therefore, it would be wrong to conclude that a positive correlation between grade point average and aspirations is only because high aspirations cause high grades. Causation operates in both directions and is cumulative over time. Unfortunately, for most, if not all, of the attitude and behavior variables in the analysis, the magnitudes of causal effects in each direction are difficult, if not impossible, to sort out. Please keep this caution in mind below and also when citing findings from this study.[36] Findings of no effect are easiest to interpret. However, findings that particular attitudes or behaviors are strong predictors of achievement should be interpreted cautiously as such correlations may not indicate causation.

### The Black-White Gap in GPA

On the survey for this study, students were asked to indicate their GPA for the past semester by marking one letter from among the standard options of A, A-, B+, and so on, down to F. Their responses were later coded in the data as 4.0 for A, 3.67 for A-, and so on, down to 0 for F. In the district's grading scale, grades in Advanced Placement courses receive an extra point, such that an A is worth 5.0 points. Grades in honors courses get an extra half point, making an A worth 4.5. Whether some students inflated the letter grades that they reported, in an effort to reflect the extra points they typically receive for honors or AP grades, could not be determined. If they did, then this is part of what the regression coefficient on the "proportion honors and AP courses" is measuring in the equations predicting GPA.

Measured by grade point averages, an achievement gap exists in Shaker Heights between blacks and whites. On a 4-point scale, the mean GPA in the 1999 data for seventh to eleventh graders is 2.08 for black males, 2.43 for black females, 3.21 for white males, and 3.36 for white females. This amounts to a gap of 1.13 GPA points for males and 0.93 GPA points for females. In attempting to understand the gap, multiple regressions were estimated in which GPA is the dependent variable. I report findings for two specifications. Specification A excludes, but specification B includes, the proportion of courses taken at the honors and AP levels, the rate of homework completion, and the number of hours per day the student typically spends doing homework. Both specifications include the measures of parents' education and household composition and the measures of student attitudes and behaviors.[37] A full set of regression results is reported in the appendix.

For each explanatory variable, multiplying the black-white difference in mean values times the estimated regression weight for that variable produces an estimate of how much the racial gap in that variable contributes to the gap in GPA. This calculation is performed and then the variables are aggregated into six categories for the purpose of summarizing the results. Table 5 has the estimated contribution of each explanatory category to the gap in GPA for

**Table 5. Contribution of Each Explanatory Category to the Black-White Grade Point Average Gap**

| | Males | | Females | |
|---|---|---|---|---|
| Explanatory category | Specification A (1) | Specification B (2) | Specification A (3) | Specification B (4) |
| Parents' education | 0.17 | 0.11 | 0.17 | 0.11 |
| Household composition | 0.10 | 0.05 | 0.09 | 0.05 |
| Attitudes and behaviors | 0.21 | 0.11 | 0.18 | 0.08 |
| Proportion honors and Advanced Placement courses | — | 0.28 | — | 0.26 |
| Homework completion rate | — | 0.11 | — | 0.11 |
| Hours per night on homework | — | 0.00 | — | 0.01 |
| Total predicted difference | 0.47 | 0.66 | 0.43 | 0.61 |
| Total actual difference | 1.12 | 1.12 | 0.93 | 0.93 |
| Predicted/actual | 0.42 | 0.59 | 0.46 | 0.66 |

— = Not included in the estimated regression.

both males and females. No evidence exists in the table that attitudes and behaviors are a major explanation for the black-white GPA gap, though they do predict a small part of it.[38] (The reason that estimated effects for parents' education, household composition, and attitudes and behaviors are smaller in specification B than in specification A is that these same variables in specification B are operating partly through their effects on homework completion, hours on homework, and enrollment in honors courses.)

In specification A, black-white differences in attitudes and behaviors account for 0.21 GPA points of the 1.12 point gap for males and 0.18 GPA points of the 0.93 point gap for females. Inside the attitudes and behaviors category, two variables that contribute most to the 0.21 and the 0.18 are "competing time commitments" and "could get a good grade without studying." Both are reasons students give for failing sometimes to do homework. Both are reported more by whites than blacks and by students whose parents have more schooling. The two variables together account for 0.13 of the 0.18 for girls and 0.09 of the 0.21 for males. An additional 0.08 of the 0.21 for males is associated with differences in college aspirations. Hence for males, three variables account for 0.17 of the 0.21. All seem related to GPA primarily as reflections of academic skill and family background advantages.

Even though they do not help much in predicting the black-white gap, other attitudes and behaviors do help in predicting GPA. An inspection of table

A-2 shows that eleven attitude or behavior variables have statistically significant coefficients at the 0.05 level in specification A, and six in specification
B. The reason for their relatively small role in predicting the black-white GPA
gap is that racial differences in these other attitudes and behaviors are small.
In sum, black-white differences in attitudes and behaviors that help to explain
the GPA gap appear to be mostly related to skill. The attitudes and behaviors
that differ by race and do not seem related to skill, such as believing that "tough"
is popular or watching lots of television, do not help in predicting GPA once
other variables are controlled.

The single largest predictor of the black-white GPA gap is the proportion
of courses taken at the honors and AP levels. The analysis to predict honors
and AP course taking shows that parental education, household composition,
attitudes, and behaviors all play some role in why fewer black than white students take honors and AP courses (see table A-5). Still, half of the racial difference in honors and AP course taking remains unexplained by the variables
in the analysis.

The number of black students who do not enroll in honors or AP courses
but who report grade point averages of B or better is small. So, for the time
being, a strong case cannot be made for pushing students wholesale into honors and AP courses. The biggest single challenge—the core challenge facing
the district—is the low performance level among the large number of black
students, especially males, who take no honors or AP courses. If some black
students are reluctant to move into honors and AP courses and to work at the
level required, addressing this reluctance is a worthwhile component of a more
general strategy for addressing the achievement gap. However, the more general strategy needs to entail a strong focus on the large numbers who take no
honors or AP courses and who will not be candidates for honors in the near-
term future.

### The GPA Gap among Blacks

An appropriate alternative to comparing blacks with whites is using high-
and low-achieving black students as the basis of analysis. Black students for
whom the regressions predict GPAs of C (2.00) or lower are compared with
other black students for whom the regressions predict GPAs of B (3.00) or
higher (see table 6). Because the comparisons of predicted GPA for these groups
are within race and gender, the weights are from regressions on the data for
black males or females, respectively. The numbers reported at the bottom of

**Table 6. Contribution of Each Explanatory Category to the Grade Point Average (GPA) Gap between Black Students with a Predicted GPA of C or Lower versus Those with a Predicted GPA of B or Higher**

| | Males | | Females | |
|---|---|---|---|---|
| Explanatory category | Specification A (1) | Specification B (2) | Specification A (3) | Specification B (4) |
| Parents' education | 0.23 | 0.14 | 0.24 | 0.10 |
| Household composition | 0.15 | 0.09 | 0.26 | 0.12 |
| Attitudes and behaviors | 1.12 | 0.56 | 0.94 | 0.44 |
| Proportion honors and Advanced Placement courses | — | 0.23 | — | 0.32 |
| Homework completion rate | — | 0.59 | — | 0.45 |
| Hours per night on homework | — | 0.13 | — | 0.09 |
| Total predicted difference | 1.50 | 1.74 | 1.44 | 1.52 |
| Mean GPA above 3.00: predicted (actual) | 3.14 (2.93) | 3.35 (3.31) | 3.14 (3.24) | 3.25 (3.31) |
| Predicted number of students in high range | 11 | 19 | 34 | 44 |
| Mean GPA below 2.00: predicted (actual) | 1.64 (1.65) | 1.60 (1.56) | 1.63 (1.77) | 1.72 (1.75) |
| Predicted number of students in low range | 141 | 147 | 64 | 77 |

table 6 show that the means of predicted and actual GPAs among students in these categories are very close.

Similar to the black-white comparisons, parental education, household composition, and the proportion of courses taken at the honors and AP levels are among the predictors of GPA gaps. For both males and females, these three categories account for about half a GPA point, roughly one-third of the gap that is being analyzed. However, in contrast to the story for the black-white gap, a full GPA point of the performance gap is related to homework completion, attitudes, and behaviors. Further, when homework completion is not in the equation, most of its influence on the predicted GPA gap is captured by the attitude and behavior variables.

Table 7 unbundles the attitude and behavior category for males. Table 8 does the same for females. Estimates from specifications A and B appear in both tables. Numbers discussed below are from specification A, unless otherwise indicated. Both tables identify the top five attitudes and behaviors that contribute to the gap because high achievers report them more than low achiev-

**Table 7. Contributions of Attitude and Behavior Variables to Grade Point Average (GPA) Gaps between Black Males with a Predicted GPA of C and Lower versus Those with a Predicted GPA of B and Higher**

| Attitude or behavior variable | Specification A | Specification B |
|---|---|---|
| *High achievers report these more* | | |
| Competing time commitments | 0.22 | 0.12 |
| Could get good grade without study | 0.15 | 0.11 |
| Really pay attention in class | 0.12 | 0.00 |
| Work hard to please adults | 0.10 | 0.05 |
| Schoolwork is intrinsically interesting | 0.04 | 0.00 |
| Subtotal | 0.63 | 0.27 |
| *F*-test probability value for subtotal | 0.000 | 0.000 |
| | | |
| *High achievers report these less* | | |
| Simply decided not to bother | 0.12 | 0.07 |
| Copy homework from friends | 0.08 | 0.03 |
| Carelessness and poor planning | 0.08 | 0.07 |
| Joke around in class | 0.08 | 0.03 |
| Hold back or hide work effort | 0.07 | 0.06 |
| Subtotal | 0.43 | 0.26 |
| *F*-test probability value for subtotal | 0.000 | 0.003 |
| Total | 1.12 | 0.56 |

Note: The small difference between the column total and the sum of the listed numbers is the result of rounding.

ers, and also the top five among negative predictors of GPA that contribute to the gap because high achievers report them less than low achievers do.

As with the black-white gap, some of the most strongly predictive variables in this analysis are probably proxies for accumulated skills and advantages. This seems especially true for "competing time commitments" and "could get a good grade without study." High achievers report both more often than low achievers do as reasons for missing homework. They appear to be proxies for omitted measures of skill and advantage. Together, they account for 0.37 and 0.18 points of the predicted GPA difference for males and females, respectively. Also, by far the most important predictor of the gap among females is the number of years of college that the student hopes to attain.

A number of the other variables measure orientations that affect achievement and do not require skills and family advantages. For example, aside from the variables just mentioned, the third variable that appears in the top five for both males and females is "really pay attention in class." Among things that high achievers do less, two variables appear in the top five for both males and females: "simply decided not to bother" with homework and "holding back

**Table 8. Contributions of Attitude and Behavior Variables to Grade Point Average (GPA) Gaps between Black Females with a Predicted GPA of C and Lower versus Those with a Predicted GPA of B and Higher**

| Attitude or behavior variable | Specification A | Specification B |
|---|---|---|
| *High achievers report these more* | | |
| Number of years of college hope to attain | 0.30 | 0.16 |
| Could get good grade without study | 0.10 | 0.06 |
| Contribute to class discussion | 0.09 | 0.04 |
| Competing time commitments | 0.08 | 0.04 |
| Really pay attention in class | 0.08 | 0.04 |
| Subtotal | 0.65 | 0.34 |
| F-test probability value for subtotal | 0.000 | 0.115 |
| | | |
| *High achievers report these less* | | |
| Simply decided not to bother | 0.08 | 0.01 |
| Hold back or hide work effort | 0.05 | 0.02 |
| Work hard to please adults | 0.04 | 0.03 |
| The work was too difficult | 0.04 | 0.02 |
| The popular crowd is tough | 0.04 | 0.02 |
| Subtotal | 0.25 | 0.10 |
| F-test probability value for subtotal | 0.038 | 0.308 |
| Total | 0.94 | 0.44 |

Note: The small difference between the column total and the sum of the listed numbers is the result of rounding.

or hiding work effort." These things, like paying attention in class, do not require academic skill or family advantages to improve (though they may require social skill). The three—deciding not to bother, holding back, and paying attention—account for about a third of a GPA point among males and a fifth among females. Among males, the other three things high achievers report less are "copying homework from friends," "carelessness and poor planning" (as a reason for missing homework), and "joking around in class." All three connote less seriousness—perhaps more disidentification—among low-achieving than among high-achieving boys.

## Engagement

Generally, black students who are low achievers seem less engaged with schooling than the high achievers. However, they are not anti-achievement or oppositional in the sense that they object to school achievement norms (though acting "tough" may violate some behavior norms). Among black males and females whose predicted GPAs are 2.0 or lower, the mean value of the "friends think academic zeal isn't cool" variable is right around the mean for all students in Shaker Heights. At the same time, 32 percent of these males and 21 percent of the females report that they hold back. The same is true for only one male and one female among blacks with predicted GPAs of 3.0 and higher.

Research emphasizes four categories of factors that affect engagement. The first is purposes or goals. Second, a person needs recipes—or strategies—to apply in pursuing the goals or purposes. Third, they need to have (and believe that they have) sufficient ability, personal resources, and help from others to make at least one strategy feasible. Fourth, rewards need to be sufficient to make the effort worthwhile. If there is no goal or no strategy, if skills and resources are insufficient, or if rewards seem too limited or off target, then engagement is likely to be minimal. Most people, including adolescents, face many competing uses for their time and attention. Choices to pay attention and to engage in one thing instead of another can affect achievement and rewards in each domain toward which attention could potentially be directed. This is not claiming that every action is the result of careful reason. Some actions are habits or impulsive. Nonetheless, implicit purposes, strategies, resources, and rewards (and penalties) can affect even informal behaviors and decisions.[39]

Recall the earlier discussion of holding back and its relationship to peer pressure. Then reflect on the fact that 32 percent of black males and 21 percent of black females with predicted GPAs of 2.0 or lower report holding back. For potential high achievers, there may be a tension between social engagement with low-achieving peers who are seeking ways to cope with their status as low achievers and earnest academic engagement toward high achievement. To the degree that such a tension exists, the challenge for Shaker Heights as a community is to alleviate it. Many low achievers need help with goals, strategies, supports, and rewards to enable and encourage them to overcome any feelings of academic disidentification, to stop holding back, and to begin taking their studies more seriously.

## High Achievers, Black Identity, and Acting White

Anthropologists Ogbu and Fordham offer the oppositional culture explanation as a reason that black students often seem to work below their potential. Economists Cook and Ludwig and sociologists Ainsworth-Darnell and Downey indicate that black students seem no more oppositional than white students to school achievement and associated norms. This paper has similar findings. No evidence exists in this paper's findings that black students are any more opposed than white students to achievement norms in Shaker Heights. Still, according to interviews with black youth in Shaker Heights, they occasionally accuse peers of acting white. What is it that they are objecting to when they make such accusations and should any consequences be expected for achievement?

## Acting White

Adolescents have many ways of classifying one another. Sociologists who catalogue the distinctions cite such catchwords as brains, druggies, jocks, loners, normals, outcasts, populars, toughs, special interest groups (such as band members or student counselors), and others.[40] In addition to these, there is the category of race. Laurence Steinberg, Sanford M. Dornbusch, and B. Bradford Brown studied students at racially integrated high schools in Wisconsin and California. Within racial groups, students could identify one another as members of one of several crowds—jocks, populars, brains, nerds, and so forth. However, "when presented with the name of an African-American classmate, a white student would typically not know the group that this student associated with, or might simply say that the student was a part of the 'black' crowd."[41] Especially for nonwhites in the United States, race is salient in how youth classify themselves socially and is a standard category that others use as well.

The dominant pattern of school achievement across the United States is that black youth tend to earn lower grades and test scores than whites. Explanations are along a continuum from an emphasis on genetics and heredity at one end, to environmental factors at the other, with many blends in the middle.[42] Few, if any, of the explanations are flattering to black people. Especially in racially integrated schools, students see the patterns, hear the explanations, and face decisions about how to respond. The present study and those by Cook and Ludwig and Ainsworth-Darnell and Downey suggest that the response is not typically to question the legitimacy or desirability of school success any more than whites do. In light of this evidence, the idea that black students in the United States are part of an oppositional culture in which the core dynamic is a uniquely high level of resistance to achievement appears to be wrong as a general proposition.

However, there is an oppositional culture that is distinctly African American. Further, it may have an effect on whether achievement aspirations are fully acted upon. Among its essential features is the drive to maintain a shared sense of African American identity that is distinct from—that is, in opposition to—the Other that Signithia Fordham writes about in her book *Blacked Out*. The Other is not white people, especially as individuals. Instead, the Other is the cultural system of white superiority within which negative racial stigma is kept alive and out of which insinuations of black inferiority and marginality emanate.[43] Black racial solidarity serves as a mechanism of mutual validation and a shield against "rumors of inferiority."[44] Any apparent attempt by a black person to escape the stigma of race by joining the Other—by speaking and behaving in ways that appear to seek an exemption from the stigma while leaving it unchallenged—may meet the accusation of acting white. (This is not meant to suggest that people are especially skilled at reading one another's motives when deciding who is trying to escape the stigma and who is not.)[45]

It therefore becomes normal to seek ways as a black teenager (or even as an adult) to signal to others that you "know who you are" and have no intention of "leaving the fold." This is especially so if you are striving toward goals that might seem atypical for blacks. The line between being a source of pride for the community (because your successes represent the community) or a target of resentment (because you appear to be disassociating and distancing your successes from the community) can be thin.

In June 1999 the ABC-TV program *20/20* aired a segment on the topic of acting white as it applies among black high school students.[46] The setting was a racially mixed high school in Wisconsin where reporter Charles Gibson interviewed students who had been accused of acting white and others who had made the accusations. Comments by accusers in the segment were especially telling. When Gibson suggested to one young man that trying to hold others back from reaching their full potential was not a good thing to do, the student's response was, "Yeah, but they were kickin' their old friends to the side for new friends, and that's not right either." A young woman in a similar exchange retorted, "Yeah, I'm gonna call you actin' white if you act like you think you're better than me." Another young man, now a record producer and rap recording artist, had gone away to Exeter, the elite private preparatory school, and come back dressing and speaking differently from when he left. He was accused of acting white. His interpretation of why former friends in the neighborhood were a little "put off" or "taken aback" was not that they resented his success. Instead, his interpretation was sensitive to their concern that he might be trying to escape the stigma. He said they wondered if he had "sold out" to the Other part of society that looked down on people like themselves. He responded by finding ways to share his success and "By letting them know that I'm not ashamed. I can still speak slang. I can still rap, even."

Social cohesion among black students in an integrated school provides a haven. It is a place to "fit."[47] Black students who want to be high achievers and remain socially connected to peers have to invest in their studies and also in signals of racial group fidelity. One form of investing in the signal is keeping up with the popular culture. Watching the right television shows and listening to the right music is doing one's social homework. Because my findings suggest no effect of television watching on grade point averages, no evidence shows that maintaining these routines either helps or detracts from school achievement. However, the need for social cohesion—driven in part by the existence of the Other and by a culture of opposition to it—might affect achievement in more subtle ways.

## Holding Back and Mock Seriousness

Peer pressure may not be the only reason to hold back. Students who have the skills to perform at high levels sometimes hold back because their friends are struggling and they want to fit in. Signithia Fordham provides an illustration:

> Though Sidney and Max scored higher than most of the high-achieving males on the PSAT, nonetheless their response was to avoid learning what their scores were and, once that was no longer possible, to minimize the importance of what they had done. Since their friends are like them—football players and athletes—they do not want to call attention to themselves in areas other than athletics. Max confesses: "I knew what I was capable of doing, but sometimes I held back. I just held myself from doing it, to make somebody else happy. That's all I was doing, really."[48]

Accommodating less skilled members may depress group performance if more skilled members want to fit in and to avoid making others feel inferior. Consider two friends walking on the street, urgently en route to an important destination. The slower walker is not in good physical condition. He does not appear to be able to keep up if the friend who is more fit were to accelerate. A decision by the faster friend to hold back in this situation—to keep walking slowly—would seem completely reasonable based on feelings of empathy and social attachment. Active peer pressure, stigmas, or stereotypes are not required for such voluntary inclinations toward accommodation to operate. The following example, introducing the concept of "mock seriousness," helps to show how the process can operate in the classroom.

In the winter of 1999–2000, anthropologist Sara Stoutland conducted a series of interviews for a project that she and I were doing in the upper-income, racially integrated schools of Brookline, Massachusetts. The two high school teachers that Stoutland interviewed independently identified behaviors among black students that one of the teachers labeled "mock seriousness." An essential feature of their stories is a social tension that seems to develop when a child is about to reach a higher standard. The child breaks the tension with humor involving a small in-group of black classmates—in other words, they "play it off"—and the moment is lost. It is as if the child calls time out and signals, "We all know that this isn't really serious." The following two passages are illustrative. First, the speaker is a dedicated teacher of social studies. He organized a special elective seminar targeted to African American seniors. Most elected to take it for honors, even though many had never had an honors experience. He said:

> They are finding an honors experience a whole other level of hard work. And many are doing well. But there is one kid who is one of the most insightful, perceptive thinkers I've seen in a number of years. And also one of the most courageous in his willingness to take a stand that runs counter to other kids on issues and not having to go along with the crowd. But whenever I congratulate him on what he said, he is so unfamiliar with that experience that he has to showboat or make a joke out of it in some way. And that undermines the seriousness of his accomplishments. And there is a group of guys that he plays off of. And you can tell that they are not used to perceiving themselves as intellectuals. There is a mock seriousness about it, rather than a genuine one. . . . A lot of kids have talked about what it is like to distinguish yourself academically and the potential of isolation. You're not in an environment [that is, the honors classroom] with a lot of other African American kids. And kids do talk about being seen by others as leaving the fold.

Next is a passage from an interview with an experienced teacher of foreign languages. She said:

> In my standard class, there is a group of African American kids and they all want to get good grades. And this is a group of kids that when you call home and their parents get on them, they start to bring in their homework. But then they start to slip. There is the one girl in particular that I think is really, really bright. And she gets it together for awhile and then she just slips. And it's hard for me to push her to the next level. She's in tenth grade. I asked her, "What is going on?" She said, "What I really care about. . . . I just care about my friends. I want to do well and I know that I should, but I'm more interested in my friends. So I don't want to work harder than I have to." So she'll start to be serious and work harder and be right on like my higher achieving kids. But the instant one of the other kids in this group of five African American kids makes some kind of under your breath joke, she is the

**Table 9. Students, by Race and Gender, Taking No Courses at the Honors or Advanced Placement (AP) Level, Taking Less Than Half, or Taking at Least Half**

Percent

| Coursework | Blacks | | Whites | |
|---|---|---|---|---|
| | *Males* | *Females* | *Males* | *Females* |
| No honors or AP courses | 73.7 | 61.9 | 14.3 | 11.6 |
| Some, but less than half | 17.1 | 24.9 | 24.0 | 25.5 |
| Half or more honors and AP courses | 9.2 | 13.2 | 61.7 | 62.9 |
| Number of respondents | (316) | (362) | (334) | (361) |

first one to burst out laughing. . . . She doesn't want to maintain a tone of seriousness for very long. And that is the culture of that group of five or six kids—you don't want to be serious for too long or you're not cool. So they get together and—they are definitely not at-risk kids, I've seen much more at-risk kids. This is a group who could be doing more, but they get it together and get it together and then fall apart. So, they have this dynamic going and they build on it as a group.[49]

Both people quoted are skilled, highly energetic teachers. Both care a great deal about students and have gone far beyond what most teachers do in searching for ways to help black students achieve at high levels. Both believe their students have much potential and both have achieved successes. However, in each of these passages, they identify social processes that interfere with maintaining seriousness at moments when progress seems greatly possible, and they assert that it happens most among black students.

## Honors Courses and the Potential for Social Isolation

Black students who take mostly honors and Advanced Placement courses in Shaker Heights are not the norm. Further, they are socially distinctive in their responses to the questionnaire. Table 9 contains percentages by race and gender for students who take no honors or Advanced Placement classes, those who take some (but less than half), and those who take at least half their courses at the honors or AP levels. The pattern is almost exactly reversed for black and white students. Nonhonors classes primarily serve blacks, while the honors and AP classes serve primarily whites.

Black males who take no honors and those who take mostly honors report essentially the same characteristics of the most popular crowd (see table 10). In contrast, reports from black females are more similar to those from class-

**Table 10. Students Agreeing That 'Tough,' 'Self-Confident,' or 'Outgoing' Described the Most Popular Crowd of Their Gender in the First Year of Middle or Junior High School, by Race, Gender, and Proportion Honors or Advanced Placement (AP) Courses Taken**

Percent

| | Black | | White | |
|---|---|---|---|---|
| *Coursework* | *Male* | *Female* | *Male* | *Female* |
| *Agreed "tough" described the most popular crowd* | | | | |
| No honors or AP courses | 56 | 40 | 34 | 20 |
| | (124 of 222) | (87 of 218) | (15 of 44) | (8 of 41) |
| Some, but less than half | 42 | 42 | 38 | 10 |
| | (22 of 53) | (36 of 86) | (30 of 78) | (9 of 91) |
| Half or more honors and | 56 | 19 | 21 | 8 |
| AP courses | (15 of 27) | (9 of 48) | (42 of 200) | (18 of 223) |
| Total | 53 | 38 | 27 | 10 |
| | (161 of 304) | (135 of 357) | (87 of 322) | (35 of 356) |
| *Agreed "self-confident" described the most popular crowd* | | | | |
| No honors or AP courses | 46 | 51 | 39 | 49 |
| | (102 of 222) | (111 of 218) | (17 of 44) | (20 of 41) |
| Some, but less than half | 55 | 70 | 72 | 58 |
| | (29 of 53) | (60 of 86) | (56 of 78) | (53 of 91) |
| Half or more honors and | 44 | 58 | 68 | 67 |
| AP courses | (12 of 27) | (28 of 48) | (136 of 200) | (149 of 223) |
| Total | 48 | 57 | 65 | 62 |
| | (144 of 304) | (202 of 357) | (209 of 322) | (222 of 356) |
| *Agreed "outgoing" described the most popular crowd* | | | | |
| No honors or AP courses | 41 | 51 | 43 | 51 |
| | (91 of 222) | (112 of 218) | (19 of 44) | (21 of 41) |
| Some, but less than half | 57 | 64 | 64 | 60 |
| | (30 of 53) | (55 of 86) | (50 of 78) | (55 of 91) |
| Half or more honors and | 44 | 75 | 66 | 69 |
| AP courses | (12 of 27) | (36 of 48) | (131 of 200) | (153 of 223) |
| Total | 44 | 58 | 62 | 64 |
| | (135 of 304) | (207 of 357) | (200 of 322) | (229 of 356) |

mates who take the same level courses as they do. Among white students, males who take no honors or Advanced Placement courses appear more similar to other students who take no honors or AP classes. White females have a more mixed profile in which both race and course level seem to be reflected.

The clear impression one gets from the data in table 10 is that at least some black males in honors and Advanced Placement courses are relatively isolated in their classes from their social reference group—other black males. Black

**Table 11. Students Agreeing about Copying Homework, the Link between School Work and Popularity, and Studying with Friends, by Race, Gender, and Proportion Honors or Advanced Placement (AP) Courses Taken**

Percent

| | Black | | White | |
|---|---|---|---|---|
| Coursework | Male | Female | Male | Female |
| *Copy homework from friends weekly* | | | | |
| No honors or AP courses | 44 | 34 | 35 | 34 |
| | (100 of 227) | (75 of 221) | (16 of 46) | (14 of 41) |
| Some, but less than half | 35 | 29 | 40 | 35 |
| | (19 of 54) | (26 of 90) | (32 of 80) | (32 of 91) |
| Half or more honors and AP courses | 21 | 46 | 44 | 33 |
| | (6 of 28) | (22 of 48) | (89 of 204) | (76 of 227) |
| *Agree that studying a lot tends to make you less popular* | | | | |
| No honors or AP courses | 29 | 19 | 24 | 21 |
| | (64 of 224) | (40 of 215) | (11 of 45) | (9 of 42) |
| Some, but less than half | 23 | 9 | 20 | 11 |
| | (12 of 52) | (8 of 90) | (16 of 80) | (10 of 91) |
| Half or more honors and AP courses | 37 | 13 | 24 | 14 |
| | (10 of 27) | (6 of 48) | (49 of 204) | (32 of 224) |
| *Talk with friends about what they learn* | | | | |
| No honors or AP courses | 55 | 59 | 52 | 76 |
| | (124 of 227) | (130 of 222) | (24 of 46) | (31 of 41) |
| Some, but less than half | 55 | 68 | 64 | 78 |
| | (29 of 53) | (61 of 90) | (51 of 80) | (72 of 92) |
| Half or more honors and AP courses | 52 | 77 | 71 | 85 |
| | (14 of 27) | (37 of 48) | (146 of 205) | (194 of 227) |

females appear to be more socially distinct from black students who take no honors or AP courses. The same impression comes from other numbers, shown in table 11. First, black males in mostly honors and AP courses appear to lack friends from whom to copy homework (because they copy less often than any other group). This may be an important disadvantage. For many students copying homework is a normal academic survival strategy. Second, black males in mostly honors and AP courses are the most likely to report that studying makes you less popular (though the difference from white males at the mostly honors level falls short of statistical significance).[50] And third, black males who take mostly honors courses talk to their friends about what they are learning only about as much as students who take no honors courses at all.

These data seem to indicate that concerns about the potential of social isolation is one reason that black students, especially males, might choose to avoid honors and AP courses. Anecdotal evidence is plentiful. For example, at a recent conference of high-achieving minority teenagers from Shaker Heights and a dozen or so similar districts from across the nation, one black male said, "If you're a girl, some guy's always going to talk to you," but if you are a guy, you might end up all by yourself. Hence, when they do enroll in honors and AP classes, black males often take special measures to maintain their standing "within the fold" among other black males. Signithia Fordham writes the following about one of the young men in her ethnographic sample who is bright and whose parents push him to take advanced courses: "He must also repeatedly assure his classmates that though he has to take courses generally identified with the school's brainiacs, he is still very much one of the 'homeboys.' It is not Max's friends who are holding him back. It is, rather, his personal sense of marginality, his desire . . . to maintain his connectedness to the African American community."[51]

Regarding girls, a conversation I had with a young woman at the conference may be instructive. She said, "If you did everything that's required to stay in tight with the other black girls, you couldn't make it in honors or AP courses," because it would be too time-consuming. She indicated that girls like herself, because they are unwilling or unable to comply with some social requirements, are often unwelcome among girls who take no honors or AP classes. Boys, she says, have it easier. However, she echoed the quotation from the young man that "some guy's always going to talk to you" if you are a girl. She said that the main way she and some of her friends stay socially connected with other black students is that the boys bring them in, often to the dismay of the other black girls. She was clear, however, that there is no stigma on high achievement: "The attitude is that if you want to get A's, go on and get 'em." When she gets accused of acting white, it is because of the way she speaks and wears her hair. She lacks the skill to speak slang or to "sound black." However, she has become more socially accepted because now she at least tries (and friends laugh).

To summarize, black students who take mostly honors and Advanced Placement classes risk social isolation. They may find themselves suspended between the black and white communities—feeling fully connected to neither. Rather than be isolated, black high achievers seem to take the necessary measures to feel connected socially. It can be a challenge. However, the answer is only partly to give them more company, by getting larger numbers of black students into higher-level courses. Based on grades, the number currently prepared for such courses appears to be small. The more appropriate response is to improve supports and instruction—ranging from social skills to lessons on learning techniques—at every level of course taking and for all students.[52] As achievement levels rise in the courses where black students are concentrated, more will qualify for higher-level classes and enter them prepared to succeed.

### Conclusion

Over the past decade, ethnographic researchers and news reporters have popularized the idea that alienation and social marginality among black Americans foster an oppositional culture that devalues academic performance and puts down high achievers by accusing them of acting white. The present study of the achievement disparities in Shaker Heights, Ohio, relies on self-reported survey data from seventh-to-eleventh graders collected in the spring of 1999. Upon first inspection, some patterns in the data seem consistent with the oppositional culture perspective. Among both males and females, black teenagers in Shaker Heights complete less homework on average than whites, participate less in class discussions, and are more inclined than white students to act tough and get into fights.[53] Black students also enroll in honors and AP courses at a much lower rate than whites, and it is well known in Shaker Heights that peers sometimes accuse blacks who enroll in such courses of acting white.

While these patterns seem consistent with the oppositional culture explanation for black-white achievement disparities, this paper tells a more complicated story. First, some things that appear to be elements of black youth culture are best understood nonracially, in terms of socioeconomic background. For example, blacks' lower self-reported propensity to participate in class discussion disappears once I control for parental education and other nonracial measures of family background. Holding family background constant, black males report more interest in their studies than white males and there is no black-white difference among females.

Second, black students report spending as much (or more) time doing their homework each day as white students who take the same classes.[54] This and related findings suggest that the reason blacks complete less homework than whites may be that they have fewer skills and get less help at home, not that they care less or exert less effort.

Third, the percentage of youth who report peer pressure against hard work and academic competition is similar among blacks and whites.

Fourth, blacks and whites seem equally happy with their teachers. For example, 77 percent of black males, 81 percent of white males, 82 percent of black females, and 85 percent of white females agree that teachers grade them fairly.[55]

Fifth, 53 percent of black males but only 27 percent of white males, and 38 percent of black females but only 10 percent of white females, believe that being tough contributes to popularity. However, once other variables are controlled, this belief is not a statistically significant predictor of the student's grade point average and does not help in predicting the black-white GPA gap.[56]

Sixth, whether judged by grades, standardized test scores or other criteria, the average black student in Shaker Heights is less well prepared than the average white student to do well in honors and AP courses. For example, on the Ohio Sixth Grade Proficiency Test in 1999, 91 percent of white males and 89 percent of white females passed the reading portion as opposed to 51 percent of black males and 41 percent of black females. Math results were similar. (All of these passing rates were above the statewide averages for the respective groups.) Student-level data for this study do not include test scores. However, given the size of the test score gap that exists at sixth grade, it is plausible that skill differences account for most of the black-white difference in honors and AP enrollment from seventh grade on.[57] Any residual difference would most likely reflect the tendency of both blacks and whites to take classes with friends and avoid classes in which the other racial group is in the vast majority. Students attest that there is such a tendency, but my data do not allow me to estimate its effect on enrollment patterns. In addition, the role of the student advising system may be important as well, if racial biases exist in the advice that students get about which classes to take.[58]

Seventh, black students who take mostly honors and AP level courses face difficult time pressures and emotional stresses when they try to meet both academic and social requirements. Academically, honors and AP homework assignments can take several hours each day. Socially, keeping up with other black students can involve watching television for two to three hours nightly to participate in daily lunch-table discussions, staying current with new music releases, playing sports, and staying on pace with changing fads in clothing and hair styles (hair is a major focus among black girls).

Despite the difficulties, some struggle to meet both academic and social demands. Others, most often girls, decide to minimize time-consuming and academically unproductive social involvement with black peers who take no honors or AP courses, in favor of spending time with honors and AP class-mates (frequently whites) who can also be study partners. A consequence for the latter youth is that black peers may accuse them of acting white. What blacks who make the accusations find offensive, however, is not academically successful students' accomplishments or ambitions, but their apparent rejec-tion of black friends (and sometimes black identity) in favor of white ones. Given both the time pressures and the potential for social isolation from black peers, it is easy to understand why some black students who have the ability to do higher-level work decide to remain instead in nonhonors, non-AP courses.

In conclusion, the present study finds no clear evidence that black students in Shaker Heights are any more opposed to achievement, any less satisfied with school, or any less interested in their studies than their white counter-parts—especially those who have similar family backgrounds.

Even so, the black-white GPA gap among seventh-to-eleventh graders in Shaker Heights is roughly one letter grade and the difference among seniors on the Scholastic Assessment Test (SAT) for college entrance is 200 points.[59] The conclusion most in line with the evidence is that skills and learning tech-niques, not oppositional culture, should be the focus of efforts to close the achievement gap.

Table A-1. Means and Standard Deviations for the Entire Shaker Heights, Ohio, Sample and Means for Black and White Males and Females

| Variable name | Mean for the entire sample[a] | Standard deviation for entire sample[a] | Means for race and gender groups | | | |
|---|---|---|---|---|---|---|
| | | | Black males | Black females | White males | White females |
| | (1) | (2) | (3) | (4) | (5) | (6) |
| Grade point average (as reported) | 2.784 | 0.934 | 2.083 | 2.428 | 3.211 | 3.354 |
| Proportion honors and Advanced Placement courses | 0.324 | 0.331 | 0.110 | 0.160 | 0.510 | 0.527 |
| Homework completion rate (z) | -0.001 | 0.998 | -0.295 | -0.115 | 0.144 | 0.309 |
| Hours per night on homework (hours) | 2.226 | 1.470 | 1.879 | 2.150 | 2.167 | 2.588 |
| *Parents' average years of schooling*[b] | | | | | | |
| Twelve years or fewer (0, 0.5, 1) | 0.152 | 0.298 | 0.250 | 0.255 | 0.043 | 0.047 |
| Thirteen to fifteen years (0, 0.5, 1) | 0.191 | 0.322 | 0.316 | 0.319 | 0.064 | 0.072 |
| Sixteen years (0, 0.5, 1) | 0.325 | 0.372 | 0.261 | 0.263 | 0.389 | 0.388 |
| Graduate degree (0, 0.5, 1) | 0.332 | 0.396 | 0.173 | 0.163 | 0.503 | 0.493 |
| *Household composition* | | | | | | |
| Two parents (0,1) | 0.554 | 0.497 | 0.355 | 0.349 | 0.853 | 0.760 |
| One birth parent and a stepparent (0,1) | 0.102 | 0.303 | 0.119 | 0.134 | 0.060 | 0.096 |
| One parent or neither (0,1) | 0.311 | 0.463 | 0.519 | 0.518 | 0.087 | 0.143 |
| Number of siblings | 2.116 | 1.574 | 2.394 | 2.539 | 1.734 | 1.802 |
| *Important reasons when failing to study or do homework* | | | | | | |
| Competing time commitments (0,1) | 0.479 | 0.497 | 0.380 | 0.388 | 0.538 | 0.656 |
| Could get good grade without study (0,1) | 0.499 | 0.498 | 0.420 | 0.347 | 0.650 | 0.616 |
| Simply decided not to bother (z) | 0.000 | 1.000 | 0.020 | -0.155 | 0.231 | -0.034 |
| Carelessness and poor planning (z) | 0.000 | 1.000 | -0.049 | 0.173 | -0.123 | -0.024 |
| The work was too difficult (z) | 0.000 | 1.000 | -0.294 | 0.096 | -0.108 | 0.252 |

*Other attitudes and behaviors*

| | | | | | |
|---|---|---|---|---|---|
| Work is intrinsically interesting (z) | 0.000 | 1.000 | 0.032 | -0.066 | -0.022 | 0.084 |
| Contribute to class discussion (z) | 0.000 | 1.000 | -0.044 | -0.091 | 0.139 | 0.091 |
| Do homework for one class in another (z) | 0.000 | 1.000 | 0.161 | 0.070 | -0.095 | -0.159 |
| Joke around in class (z) | 0.000 | 1.000 | 0.187 | -0.306 | 0.330 | -0.115 |
| Really pay attention in class (z) | 0.000 | 1.000 | -0.123 | 0.055 | -0.076 | 0.130 |
| Hold back or hide work effort (0,1) | 0.097 | 0.294 | 0.207 | 0.102 | 0.067 | 0.033 |
| Copy homework from friends (0,1) | 0.370 | 0.475 | 0.405 | 0.341 | 0.415 | 0.341 |
| Study with friends (0,1) | 0.349 | 0.467 | 0.279 | 0.393 | 0.311 | 0.419 |
| Agree teachers maintain discipline (0,1) | 0.728 | 0.440 | 0.686 | 0.705 | 0.776 | 0.767 |
| TV hours per school night | 2.311 | 2.162 | 3.234 | 3.061 | 1.744 | 1.273 |
| Number years of college hope to attain (z) | 0.000 | 1.000 | -0.505 | 0.069 | 0.156 | 0.224 |
| Work hard to please adults (z) | 0.000 | 1.000 | 0.157 | 0.062 | -0.226 | 0.013 |
| Friends think academic zeal isn't cool (z) | 0.000 | 1.000 | -0.038 | -0.139 | 0.223 | -0.040 |
| Agree popular crowd is "tough" (0,1) | 0.309 | 0.456 | 0.526 | 0.378 | 0.270 | 0.099 |
| Agree popular crowd is "outgoing" (0,1) | 0.565 | 0.481 | 0.438 | 0.579 | 0.621 | 0.643 |
| Agree popular crowd "self-confident" (0,1) | 0.556 | 0.489 | 0.472 | 0.566 | 0.649 | 0.624 |
| Number of students | (1,699) | | (318) | (367) | (334) | (363) |

a. The means and standard deviations in columns 1 and 2 for the entire sample include all racial groups, not only blacks and whites.

b. 0.5 = one parent in the category; 1 = two parents.

Table A-2. Multiple Regression Results for Grade Point Average

| Explanatory variable | Specification A | | | Specification B | | |
|---|---|---|---|---|---|---|
| | Coefficient (1) | Standard error (2) | Probability value (3) | Coefficient (4) | Standard error (5) | Probability value (6) |
| Proportion honors and Advanced Placement courses | — | — | — | 0.697 | 0.092 | 0.000 |
| Homework completion rate (z) | — | — | — | 0.248 | 0.025 | 0.000 |
| Hours per night on homework (hours) | — | — | — | 0.016 | 0.015 | 0.264 |
| *Race and gender* | | | | | | |
| White female is the base category | — | — | — | — | — | — |
| Black male (0,1) | -0.704 | 0.077 | 0.000 | -0.507 | 0.075 | 0.000 |
| Black female (0,1) | -0.480 | 0.066 | 0.000 | -0.306 | 0.065 | 0.000 |
| White male (0,1) | -0.062 | 0.048 | 0.194 | -0.051 | 0.043 | 0.237 |
| *Parents' average years of schooling*[a] | | | | | | |
| Advanced degree is the base category | — | — | — | — | — | — |
| Twelve years or fewer (0, 0.5, 1) | -0.546 | 0.101 | 0.000 | -0.328 | 0.095 | 0.001 |
| Thirteen to fifteen years (0, 0.5, 1) | -0.281 | 0.083 | 0.001 | -0.180 | 0.076 | 0.018 |
| Sixteen years (0, 0.5, 1) | -0.118 | 0.054 | 0.029 | -0.012 | 0.048 | 0.808 |
| *Household composition* | | | | | | |
| Two parents is the base category | — | — | — | — | — | — |
| One birth parent and a stepparent (0,1) | -0.135 | 0.073 | 0.064 | -0.043 | 0.064 | 0.508 |
| One parent or neither (0,1) | -0.147 | 0.056 | 0.008 | -0.056 | 0.051 | 0.272 |
| Number of siblings | -0.038 | 0.014 | 0.008 | -0.030 | 0.014 | 0.026 |
| *Important reasons when failing to study or complete homework* | | | | | | |
| Competing time commitments (0,1) | 0.262 | 0.040 | 0.000 | 0.179 | 0.036 | 0.000 |

| | Coef. | SE | p | Coef. | SE | p |
|---|---|---|---|---|---|---|
| Could get good grade without study (0,1) | 0.206 | 0.039 | 0.000 | 0.143 | 0.037 | 0.000 |
| Simply decided not to bother (z) | -0.096 | 0.020 | 0.000 | -0.047 | 0.018 | 0.011 |
| Carelessness and poor planning (z) | -0.038 | 0.021 | 0.066 | -0.019 | 0.019 | 0.327 |
| The work was too difficult (z) | -0.047 | 0.021 | 0.025 | -0.042 | 0.019 | 0.029 |
| *Other attitudes and behaviors* | | | | | | |
| Work is intrinsically interesting (z) | 0.021 | 0.024 | 0.374 | -0.007 | 0.022 | 0.746 |
| Contribute to class discussion (z) | 0.056 | 0.024 | 0.019 | 0.030 | 0.022 | 0.173 |
| Do homework for one class in another (z) | 0.037 | 0.023 | 0.112 | 0.043 | 0.022 | 0.055 |
| Joke around in class (z) | -0.068 | 0.024 | 0.005 | -0.056 | 0.022 | 0.011 |
| Really pay attention in class (z) | 0.070 | 0.027 | 0.010 | 0.023 | 0.026 | 0.379 |
| Hold back or hide work effort (0,1) | -0.216 | 0.083 | 0.009 | -0.111 | 0.078 | 0.155 |
| Copy homework from friends (0,1) | -0.090 | 0.045 | 0.045 | -0.069 | 0.041 | 0.094 |
| Study with friends (0,1) | 0.082 | 0.040 | 0.039 | 0.012 | 0.037 | 0.744 |
| Agree teachers maintain discipline (0,1) | 0.081 | 0.047 | 0.085 | 0.064 | 0.043 | 0.138 |
| TV hours per school night | 0.001 | 0.012 | 0.916 | 0.008 | 0.012 | 0.519 |
| Number years of college hope to attain (z) | 0.115 | 0.029 | 0.000 | 0.075 | 0.027 | 0.005 |
| Work hard to please adults (z) | -0.013 | 0.021 | 0.522 | -0.006 | 0.019 | 0.760 |
| Friends think academic zeal isn't cool (z) | 0.029 | 0.021 | 0.167 | 0.030 | 0.020 | 0.139 |
| Agree popular crowd is "tough" (0,1) | -0.081 | 0.048 | 0.093 | -0.034 | 0.044 | 0.449 |
| Agree popular crowd is "outgoing" (0,1) | 0.061 | 0.042 | 0.149 | 0.026 | 0.039 | 0.501 |
| Agree popular crowd is "self-confident" (0,1) | -0.050 | 0.042 | 0.231 | -0.053 | 0.038 | 0.164 |
| Constant | 3.274 | 0.078 | 0.000 | 2.806 | 0.088 | 0.000 |

N = 1,267

R-square = 0.505    R-square = 0.586

— = Not included in the regression.

a. 0.5 = one parent in the category; 1 = two parents.

Table A-3. Multiple Regression Results for Homework Completion Rate

| | Specification A | | | Specification B | | |
|---|---|---|---|---|---|---|
| Explanatory variable | Coefficient (1) | Standard error (2) | Probability value (3) | Coefficient (4) | Standard error (5) | Probability value (6) |
| Proportion honors and Advanced Placement courses | | | | -0.033 | 0.091 | 0.716 |
| Hours per night on homework (hours) | | | | 0.128 | 0.019 | 0.000 |
| *Race and gender* | | | | | | |
| White female is the base category | — | | | — | | |
| Black male (0,1) | -0.162 | 0.084 | 0.055 | -0.178 | 0.081 | 0.028 |
| Black female (0,1) | -0.117 | 0.071 | 0.100 | -0.128 | 0.071 | 0.070 |
| White male (0,1) | 0.014 | 0.060 | 0.816 | 0.031 | 0.060 | 0.604 |
| *Parents' average years of schooling*[a] | | | | | | |
| Advanced degree is the base category | — | | — | — | | — |
| Twelve years or fewer (0, 0.5, 1) | -0.293 | 0.104 | 0.005 | -0.243 | 0.102 | 0.017 |
| Thirteen to fifteen years (0, 0.5, 1) | -0.072 | 0.096 | 0.454 | -0.045 | 0.093 | 0.627 |
| Sixteen years (0, 0.5, 1) | -0.059 | 0.070 | 0.395 | -0.034 | 0.069 | 0.622 |
| *Household composition* | | | | | | |
| Two parents is the base category | — | | — | — | | — |
| One birth parent and a stepparent (0,1) | -0.046 | 0.082 | 0.579 | -0.039 | 0.082 | 0.632 |
| One parent or neither (0,1) | -0.177 | 0.063 | 0.005 | -0.170 | 0.061 | 0.005 |
| Number of siblings | -0.012 | 0.015 | 0.440 | -0.006 | 0.015 | 0.675 |
| *Important reasons when failing to study or complete homework* | | | | | | |
| Competing time commitments (0,1) | 0.182 | 0.046 | 0.000 | 0.148 | 0.045 | 0.001 |
| Could get good grade without study (0,1) | 0.057 | 0.047 | 0.227 | 0.057 | 0.047 | 0.228 |

| | Model 1 | | | Model 2 | | |
|---|---|---|---|---|---|---|
| | Coef. | SE | p | Coef. | SE | p |
| Simply decided not to bother (z) | -0.161 | 0.025 | 0.000 | -0.146 | 0.025 | 0.000 |
| Carelessness and poor planning (z) | -0.093 | 0.024 | 0.000 | -0.098 | 0.023 | 0.000 |
| The work was too difficult (z) | -0.015 | 0.023 | 0.521 | -0.020 | 0.022 | 0.382 |
| *Other attitudes and behaviors* | | | | | | |
| Work is intrinsically interesting (z) | 0.092 | 0.026 | 0.000 | 0.078 | 0.025 | 0.002 |
| Contribute to class discussion (z) | 0.068 | 0.027 | 0.012 | 0.073 | 0.026 | 0.006 |
| Do homework for one class in another (z) | -0.022 | 0.027 | 0.413 | -0.008 | 0.027 | 0.771 |
| Joke around in class (z) | -0.068 | 0.029 | 0.020 | -0.052 | 0.028 | 0.066 |
| Really pay attention in class (z) | 0.209 | 0.032 | 0.000 | 0.191 | 0.031 | 0.000 |
| Hold back or hide work effort (0,1) | -0.230 | 0.083 | 0.006 | -0.205 | 0.083 | 0.013 |
| Copy homework from friends (0,1) | -0.117 | 0.050 | 0.020 | -0.108 | 0.049 | 0.028 |
| Study with friends (0,1) | 0.119 | 0.046 | 0.010 | 0.088 | 0.046 | 0.055 |
| Agree teachers maintain discipline (0,1) | -0.043 | 0.054 | 0.424 | -0.053 | 0.052 | 0.314 |
| TV hours per school night | -0.008 | 0.014 | 0.550 | 0.001 | 0.014 | 0.962 |
| Number years of college hope to attain (z) | 0.049 | 0.029 | 0.097 | 0.024 | 0.029 | 0.401 |
| Work hard to please adults (z) | 0.043 | 0.023 | 0.068 | 0.032 | 0.023 | 0.171 |
| Friends think academic zeal isn't cool (z) | -0.002 | 0.026 | 0.952 | -0.002 | 0.026 | 0.950 |
| Agree popular crowd is "tough" (0,1) | -0.059 | 0.056 | 0.286 | -0.042 | 0.055 | 0.446 |
| Agree popular crowd is "outgoing" (0,1) | 0.027 | 0.049 | 0.575 | 0.032 | 0.048 | 0.501 |
| Agree popular crowd is "self-confident" (0,1) | -0.024 | 0.049 | 0.619 | -0.040 | 0.048 | 0.406 |
| Constant | 0.311 | 0.095 | 0.001 | 0.002 | 0.109 | 0.986 |
| N = 1,377 | R-square = .328 | | | R-square = .355 | | |

— = Not included in the regression.

a. 0.5 = one parent in the category; 1 = two parents.

Table A-4. Multiple Regression Results or Hours per Day Doing Homework

| Explanatory variable | Specification A | | | Specification B | | |
|---|---|---|---|---|---|---|
| | Coefficient (1) | Standard error (2) | Probability value (3) | Coefficient (4) | Standard error (5) | Probability value (6) |
| Proportion honors and Advanced Placement courses | — | — | — | 1.384 | 0.159 | 0.000 |
| *Race and gender* | | | | | | |
| White female is the base category | — | — | — | — | — | — |
| Black male (0,1) | 0.061 | 0.141 | 0.666 | 0.353 | 0.143 | 0.014 |
| Black female (0,1) | 0.027 | 0.131 | 0.834 | 0.299 | 0.134 | 0.026 |
| White male (0,1) | -0.135 | 0.104 | 0.192 | -0.123 | 0.100 | 0.220 |
| *Parents' average years of schooling*[a] | | | | | | |
| Advanced degree is the base category | — | — | — | — | — | — |
| Twelve years or fewer (0, 0.5, 1) | -0.433 | 0.153 | 0.005 | -0.177 | 0.147 | 0.229 |
| Thirteen to fifteen years (0, 0.5, 1) | -0.228 | 0.163 | 0.162 | -0.061 | 0.154 | 0.695 |
| Sixteen years (0, 0.5, 1) | -0.228 | 0.118 | 0.052 | -0.038 | 0.112 | 0.738 |
| *Household composition* | | | | | | |
| Two parents is the base category | — | — | — | — | — | — |
| One birth parent and a stepparent (0,1) | -0.063 | 0.117 | 0.593 | 0.073 | 0.117 | 0.534 |
| One parent or neither (0,1) | -0.066 | 0.096 | 0.496 | 0.018 | 0.093 | 0.846 |
| Number of siblings | -0.045 | 0.022 | 0.046 | -0.038 | 0.022 | 0.081 |
| *Important reasons when failing to study or complete homework* | | | | | | |
| Competing time commitments (0,1) | 0.220 | 0.073 | 0.003 | 0.144 | 0.071 | 0.043 |
| Could get good grade without study (0,1) | 0.017 | 0.073 | 0.815 | -0.084 | 0.072 | 0.244 |
| Simply decided not to bother (z) | -0.126 | 0.037 | 0.001 | -0.114 | 0.036 | 0.001 |

| | (1) | | | (2) | | |
|---|---|---|---|---|---|---|
| Carelessness and poor planning (z) | 0.042 | 0.038 | 0.265 | 0.035 | 0.037 | 0.345 |
| The work was too difficult (z) | 0.037 | 0.034 | 0.285 | 0.038 | 0.033 | 0.252 |
| *Other attitudes and behaviors* | | | | | | |
| Work is intrinsically interesting (z) | 0.110 | 0.043 | 0.010 | 0.102 | 0.041 | 0.013 |
| Contribute to class discussion (z) | -0.031 | 0.042 | 0.472 | -0.040 | 0.042 | 0.331 |
| Do homework for one class in another (z) | -0.116 | 0.039 | 0.003 | -0.116 | 0.038 | 0.003 |
| Joke around in class (z) | -0.117 | 0.043 | 0.007 | -0.133 | 0.041 | 0.001 |
| Really pay attention in class (z) | 0.138 | 0.043 | 0.001 | 0.153 | 0.043 | 0.000 |
| Hold back or hide work effort (0,1) | -0.211 | 0.129 | 0.102 | -0.111 | 0.126 | 0.382 |
| Copy homework from friends (0,1) | -0.055 | 0.077 | 0.477 | -0.075 | 0.075 | 0.313 |
| Study with friends (0,1) | 0.251 | 0.077 | 0.001 | 0.185 | 0.076 | 0.014 |
| Agree teachers maintain discipline (0,1) | 0.076 | 0.084 | 0.365 | 0.033 | 0.080 | 0.683 |
| TV hours per school night | -0.072 | 0.021 | 0.001 | -0.058 | 0.021 | 0.005 |
| Number years of college hope to attain (z) | 0.190 | 0.043 | 0.000 | 0.138 | 0.042 | 0.001 |
| Work hard to please adults (z) | 0.079 | 0.041 | 0.053 | 0.114 | 0.039 | 0.004 |
| Friends think academic zeal isn't cool (z) | 0.003 | 0.038 | 0.935 | 0.008 | 0.036 | 0.836 |
| Agree popular crowd is "tough" (0,1) | -0.153 | 0.084 | 0.069 | -0.083 | 0.080 | 0.303 |
| Agree popular crowd is "outgoing" (0,1) | -0.024 | 0.076 | 0.753 | -0.088 | 0.075 | 0.242 |
| Agree popular crowd is "self-confident" (0,1) | 0.121 | 0.076 | 0.113 | 0.105 | 0.074 | 0.158 |
| Constant | 2.546 | 0.149 | 0.000 | 1.854 | 0.148 | 0.000 |
| N = 1,376 | R-square = .214 | | | R-square = .266 | | |

— = Not included in the regression.
a. 0.5 = one parent in the category; 1 = two parents.

**Table A-5. Multiple Regression Results for Proportion Honors and Advanced Placement Courses**

| Explanatory variable | Coefficient (1) | Standard error (2) | Probability value (3) |
|---|---|---|---|
| *Race and gender* | | | |
| White female is the base category | — | — | — |
| Black male (0,1) | -0.207 | 0.025 | 0.000 |
| Black female (0,1) | -0.197 | 0.023 | 0.000 |
| White male (0,1) | -0.007 | 0.020 | 0.713 |
| *Parents' average years of schooling*[a] | | | |
| Advanced degree is the base category | — | — | — |
| Twelve years or fewer (0, 0.5, 1) | -0.187 | 0.030 | 0.000 |
| Thirteen to fifteen years (0, 0.5, 1) | -0.119 | 0.029 | 0.000 |
| Sixteen years (0, 0.5, 1) | -0.138 | 0.022 | 0.000 |
| *Household composition* | | | |
| Two parents is the base category | — | — | — |
| One birth parent and a stepparent (0,1) | -0.100 | 0.023 | 0.000 |
| One parent or neither (0,1) | -0.059 | 0.018 | 0.001 |
| Number of siblings | -0.005 | 0.004 | 0.276 |
| *Important reasons when failing to complete homework* | | | |
| Competing time commitments (0,1) | 0.057 | 0.014 | 0.000 |
| Could get good grade without study (0,1) | 0.073 | 0.014 | 0.000 |
| Simply decided not to bother ($z$) | -0.008 | 0.007 | 0.234 |
| Carelessness and poor planning ($z$) | 0.005 | 0.007 | 0.486 |
| The work was too difficult ($z$) | -0.002 | 0.007 | 0.823 |
| *Other attitudes and behaviors* | | | |
| Work is intrinsically interesting ($z$) | 0.004 | 0.007 | 0.571 |
| Contribute to class discussion ($z$) | 0.008 | 0.008 | 0.306 |
| Do homework for one class in another ($z$) | 0.000 | 0.007 | 0.980 |
| Joke around in class ($z$) | 0.011 | 0.008 | 0.186 |
| Really pay attention in class ($z$) | -0.009 | 0.008 | 0.255 |
| Hold back or hide work effort (0,1) | -0.078 | 0.023 | 0.001 |
| Copy homework from friends (0,1) | 0.017 | 0.015 | 0.252 |
| Study with friends (0,1) | 0.047 | 0.014 | 0.001 |
| Agree teachers maintain discipline (0,1) | 0.034 | 0.016 | 0.031 |
| TV hours per school night | -0.010 | 0.004 | 0.006 |
| Number years of college hope to attain ($z$) | 0.040 | 0.008 | 0.000 |
| Work hard to please adults ($z$) | -0.025 | 0.007 | 0.000 |
| Friends think academic zeal isn't cool ($z$) | -0.002 | 0.007 | 0.814 |
| Agree popular crowd is "tough" (0,1) | -0.051 | 0.015 | 0.001 |
| Agree popular crowd is "outgoing" (0,1) | 0.048 | 0.015 | 0.001 |
| Agree popular crowd is "self-confident" (0,1) | 0.010 | 0.015 | 0.494 |
| Constant | 0.494 | 0.028 | 0.000 |
| N = 1,373 | | R-square = .494 | |

— = Not included in the regression.
a. 0.5 = one parent in the category; 1 = two parents.

## Comment by Jens Ludwig

Despite considerable progress in improving the educational opportunities for African Americans in the United States, a persistent gap remains between black and white students in average standardized test scores. While many people believe the differences in test scores result from problems with the testing instruments, the test score gap reflects at least in part real differences in what students have learned.[60] What causes these differences, and what might be done to eliminate them?

One explanation for black-white differences in achievement that has gained prominence in recent years is the possibility that peer culture is more anti-academic among black than white students. This explanation has been supported by ethnographic and media interviews with African American teens, who sometimes report that high achievement engenders a negative reaction from their peers. But interviews with selected black students cannot reveal how prevalent these peer pressures are among minority students nationwide, whether the prospect of opprobrium among one's peers significantly affects academic performance, or whether the nature or consequences of peer norms are systematically different for black and white students.

Understanding whether much of the black-white difference in academic outcomes stems from differences in peer norms and student effort is important for education policy for several reasons. First, a widespread belief that black-white differences in achievement are the result of differences in student effort may undermine popular support for programs to improve equality of educational opportunity. Voters may be reluctant to fund improvements to schools if they believe that students are not fulfilling their end of the bargain by exerting themselves to the fullest. Second, income inequality in the United States is explained in part by differences in the educational outcomes of workers.[61] How society feels about the current income distribution thus depends in part on what it believes explains variation in schooling outcomes. Third, many analysts bemoan the lack of effort by American students and argue that most students face limited incentives to work hard in school.[62] If the problem of low student effort is particularly acute among minority students, then specially targeted interventions may be necessary. Finally, questions about peer norms among black and white students are relevant for evaluating policies that affect the racial mix of schools and neighborhoods such as school desegregation plans, school choice, and housing vouchers. For example, systematic differences across race or ethnic groups in peer norms may provide one argument for policies that reduce racial segregation within schools and neighborhoods.

The excellent paper by Ronald F. Ferguson provides important new insight into the issue of peer norms by gathering detailed information about student effort and attitudes for a single high school in Shaker Heights, Ohio. The advantage of Ferguson's case-study approach comes from the richness of the data that can be gathered for a single site. The drawback is that findings from a single school may not generalize to other schools and students, particularly when the school is located in what Ferguson describes as a "model community." In any case, Ferguson's study is useful in helping to resolve some questions about the role of peer norms in explaining the black-white achievement gap, and in the process it raises a number of important new questions.

### Student Effort

One important prediction of the oppositional culture hypothesis is that African American students devote less effort to school than whites. Isolating the independent effects of race and ethnicity on student effort requires some adjustment for family background, given the persistent differences in average socioeconomic status between blacks and whites in the United States and the association between family background with student effort and achievement.[63] The real question of interest is thus whether black students expend less effort on schoolwork than whites with the same family background.

Data from the 1988 National Education Longitudinal Survey (NELS) and other national surveys show that blacks on average complete more years of schooling than whites from similar backgrounds, are less likely to miss school, are more likely to participate in academic activities such as science fairs or the honors society, and do about as much homework per week. While the hardest-working white students seem to spend a bit more time on homework than the hardest-working blacks, this difference is fairly modest.[64]

Ferguson's analysis of data from Shaker Heights produces generally similar findings. Black students are more likely than similarly situated whites to report that they find their studies intrinsically interesting and seem to be less likely to joke around in class. Black and white students are equally likely to say that they "really pay attention in class" and contribute to class discussion. However, African American students spend more time watching television each night and are more likely to report that "I didn't try as hard as I could at school because I worried about what my friends might think."

Taken together these findings suggest that after controlling for family background, black and white students appear to be similar with respect to most major indicators of academic effort, although there may be some differences along more subtle dimensions.

## Oppositional Culture

If subtle differences in school effort do exist between black and white students, why is this so and what might be done about it? For many years, newspaper reporters and scholars alike believed that black teen culture was less supportive than white teen culture of school success and, as a result, that differences in student effort could explain an important share of the black-white gap in achievement. This belief stemmed in large part from the ethnographic fieldwork of anthropologists John Ogbu and Signithia Fordham. Their ethnographic work documented situations in which African American students reported withholding effort in school for fear of being taunted as "acting white" by their friends.

Initial empirical work on this topic relied on nationally representative data from the NELS. As Philip J. Cook and I argued, the similarity in school effort between black and white students from similar backgrounds suggests that the oppositional culture hypothesis is unlikely to explain much of the black-white achievement gap.[65] The NELS data also revealed few differences between black high achievers and other black students in their social standing (the "achievement penalty") or much of a difference in the achievement penalty experienced by black and white students. Findings from the NELS data thus built a strong circumstantial argument against the oppositional culture hypothesis, although, as Ferguson noted, more direct measures of peer attitudes toward academic effort would help seal the case.[66]

Fortunately, Ferguson's Shaker Heights survey includes a number of questions that help to directly capture peer attitudes toward achievement. While the peer measures available in Ferguson's survey represent an improvement over the NELS data, even these new measures are not perfect. The survey attempts to measure whether students' "friends think academic zeal isn't cool" by asking respondents six questions about whether they think different pro- and anti-achievement behaviors are "cool." But some of these questions are not as closely tied to oppositional culture as one would like. For example, students are asked whether they think "it's not cool to be competitive about grades." One need not have an anti-achievement orientation to find potentially cut-throat or "grade-grubbing" behavior unappealing (as even teachers and college professors can attest). Two of the other items used in the construction of Ferguson's peer-attitude index come from student reactions to the statements "It's annoying when other students talk or joke around in class" and "It's annoying when students try to get teachers off track." Sometimes annoying behavior is annoying, regardless of whether it has a pro- or anti-academic orientation.

These measurement issues notwithstanding, Ferguson's study provides the important finding that black students are less likely than whites to report that academic zeal is not cool among their friends. This finding receives further support from evidence that popularity in Shaker Heights appears to be largely defined independently of academic success. The results of Ferguson's analysis lead him to a conclusion similar to the one Cook and I reached in our study: "The idea that black students in the United States are part of an oppositional culture in which the core dynamic is a uniquely high level of resistance to achievement appears to be wrong as a general proposition."

### Peers Do Matter—Somehow

Yet peer groups do seem to matter, as evidenced by Ferguson's finding that black students are more likely than whites to report that "I didn't try as hard as I could at school because I was worried about what my friends might think." Unfortunately, more detailed information is not available about what it means to "not try as hard as I could at school." Agreement with this statement could in principle mean anything from trivial withdrawals of effort up to and including dropping out of high school. Nevertheless, the findings raise the question: Why do peer dynamics cause African American students to hold back more in school than whites, if black peer groups are no more likely to think that doing well in school is uncool?

Ferguson offers one possible explanation: African American students may withhold effort to avoid showing up their friends, who on average may have lower achievement levels than the peer groups of white students. This might be termed a "passive peer effect," because it does not rely on active peer discouragement of academic effort as in the oppositional culture hypothesis.

While a direct test of this hypothesis with the Shaker Heights data is not possible, future research should exploit the fact that similar data have been gathered for other schools by Cornell economist John H. Bishop. Ferguson's hypothesis suggests that after controlling for individual and family characteristics, the academic effort of African American students should be negatively correlated with the average achievement level of the other black students within the school. Ferguson's hypothesis would also seem to suggest that the correlation between an individual's effort in school and the average achievement level of other students in the school of the same race should be stronger for blacks than whites. Evidence to this effect from Bishop's multischool data set would be supporting but not definitive evidence for Ferguson's hypothesis.

If students withhold effort in an attempt to avoid showing up their lower-achieving friends, it may be useful to encourage more group-oriented learning activities in which students teach one another. This type of focus might help recast superior performance as an advantage that generates benefits for the social group, instead of an implicit put-down to one's friends.

### Effort and Achievement

The data from Shaker Heights suggest that some differences may exist in school effort between black and white students along some fairly subtle dimensions and that these differences may be in part related to peer interactions (although the nature of this peer effect remains something of a mystery). Whether any differences in peer influences or student efforts between black and white students reflect an important policy concern depends in large part on whether these differences have any practical importance for student achievement.

Ferguson attempts to identify the net effects of whatever differences in effort exist between black and white students on the black-white achievement gap by estimating regression models that predict student grade point averages (GPAs). One problem with using GPA as a measure of student achievement is that a given grade may correspond to different levels of achievement across academic tracks. For example, a B in an Advanced Placement (AP) or honors class presumably signals a higher level of academic achievement than a B in the college preparatory, vocational, or other tracks. Statistically controlling for AP or honors course work in the multivariate regression is an imperfect fix for this problem. Imagine, for example, that the regression reveals, after controlling for AP and honors course work, no difference in average GPA between black and white students. This finding would not imply equal learning across groups if proportionally fewer African American students are enrolled in AP and honors courses.[67] More generally, variation may exist in the difficulty of course work even across students within the same grade and track. For example, some high school juniors and seniors on the standard academic track may be enrolled in algebra or geometry classes, while others are already taking pre-calculus or even calculus courses.

In any case, Ferguson finds that the effort and attitude variables in his data set explain about 40 to 60 percent of the GPA difference between black and white students in Shaker Heights, although most of this explanatory power appears to come from the measures of family socioeconomic status.[68] Any differences in effort between black and white students that may exist seem to explain only a small share of the difference across groups in GPA.

## *The Efficiency of Effort*

In the end I find Ferguson's argument persuasive that "the characteristics of black and white youth in Shaker Heights that predict black-white GPA differences implicate skills, much more than effort, as the main reasons for the GPA gap." One important way that differences in skills seem to matter is by affecting the efficiency with which educational inputs are translated into outputs for black and white students.

One striking finding in Ferguson's paper is that African American students in Shaker Heights appear to complete less of their homework than whites, even though the two groups reportedly spend similar amounts of time on homework each night. While the data are not definitive, Ferguson's analysis suggests that differences between black and white students in homework completion do not appear to be related to differences in the tendency to do homework in front of the television. Why is homework time less productive for blacks than whites? Are parents less helpful in black than white households? If so, is this because of differences in the educational backgrounds of the parents or differences in parenting styles? Is something else about the home environment less academically productive for one group than another?

The ways in which African American students and teachers interact could account for differences in how effort is translated into achievement. For example, James W. Ainsworth-Darnell and Douglas B. Downey find that African American students are less likely than whites to report that rule-breaking or cheating is acceptable or that other students perceive them as troublemakers and they are more likely to report that they derive satisfaction from doing what they are supposed to be doing in class.[69] At the same time, teachers are more likely to report disruptive behaviors and lack of effort by black students compared with whites.

Ferguson's research offers one possible explanation for the apparent difference between the student and teacher reports in the study by Ainsworth-Darnell and Downey: African American students in Shaker Heights are more likely than whites to report "tough" as one of the attributes that characterizes the popular crowd and thus may reflect a difference in the type of behavior or style to which black and white students aspire. As Ferguson notes, this raises the possibility that "differences in how black and white students carry themselves may foster subtle differences in student-teacher relations for black and white students."

Identifying why time spent on homework and in school seems to be less productive for black than white students thus remains an important goal for future research. Answering this question is likely to require the meticulous collection of the same detailed effort and attitudinal information as used in Ferguson's study, but perhaps for a larger sample of students who are re-interviewed over time.

## Conclusion

Ferguson provides further evidence that African American students do not appear to be more opposed to schooling than whites from similar family backgrounds. The Shaker Heights data do raise the possibility that black students may withdraw effort to some degree in an attempt to avoid showing up their friends. However, whatever differences may exist between black and white students in their academic behaviors appear to have modest effects on achievement once some statistical control is made for family background. Nevertheless, given the modest academic effort of most teens in America, identifying interventions that can improve the academic engagement of all students remains an important goal.[70] More important still is understanding how to increase the learning that results from the time that students, teachers, and parents already devote to the educational process.

---

# Comment by Wilbur Rich

Ronald F. Ferguson has produced an excellent and provocative study of student performance in a suburban school district. Ferguson offers a fascinating analysis of the contradictions and misconceptions of a middle-class adolescent subculture. The standards reformers have argued, explicitly and persuasively, that raising educational standards will benefit all social groups; that is, a rising tide will lift all boats. Standards advocates would agree that many inner-city minority students are in small and often unseaworthy boats. As Ferguson notes, minority students, regardless of socioeconomic status, are fellow passengers in those leaky boats. If higher standards are imposed on black suburban students, many could fall further behind.

Ferguson found that black students were not taking advantage of their middle-class status. Instead, some suburban black students were squandering their opportunity to get a first-rate education. His data show that black students had experienced problems with homework, worked below their ability levels, and avoided enrolling in honors and Advanced Placement (AP) courses. Ferguson also found that black students spent, what he considered, an inordinate amount of time on peer-related activities.

### Cultural Traps and Individual Performance

The overall question is whether these attitudes and behaviors constitute cultural traps. In the United States, black youths are forced into what sociologist Mark Granovetter calls a "tightly coupled" group. Such linkages can inhibit associations with other groups. In the case of black students, a cultural trap may be expressed in an overinvestment in racial identity and loyalty issues and an underinvestment in academic skills that will improve school performance. Free from this cultural trap and armed with a propensity to seek such skills, white cohorts are outperforming blacks. This finding is troubling because it involves blacks in a suburban and middle-class community—Shaker Heights, Ohio. Hence, the alarm sounded by Ferguson.

Shaker Heights has long enjoyed a reputation of being a promised land for progressive and upwardly mobile middle-class Clevelanders. Black acceptance in that community represents an important breakthrough in race relations. The Shaker Heights phenomenon, touted as a model of racial tolerance, does not offset the achievement differences between blacks and whites. Ferguson is not challenging the social and political incorporation of black families into that community, but instead he raises questions about the lack of educational achievement among their children. His data suggest that black and white students are not socially isolated. Nevertheless, better equipment, good teachers, and good learning environment have not equalized the competition for blacks. The search for good schools is one of the principal reasons that inner-city black parents moved to Shaker Heights. Ferguson's findings should come as a shock to them.

Ferguson has identified several perceptions, attitudes, and behaviors that seem to inhibit school engagement. These include not trying to do one's best in school (that is, holding back), limiting friendship clusters to one's racial group, poor study habits, and poor time management outside the classroom.

Ferguson's paper makes one wonder if the nascent sociology literature on the emerging black middle class and fears of class cleavages is wrongheaded. If middle-class black students are not fully engaged in schoolwork, then they are no better off educationally than their inner-city cohorts.

Equally troubling is the notion that black students who attempt to escape these cultural traps are accused of "acting white." It may come as a surprise to whites to learn that for many black people "acting white" is tantamount to being a "sellout." Blacks who are so accused are seen as willing to join with whites in the onslaught against black people. (No functional equivalent exists of race disloyalty for whites.) When an adolescent is tagged as "acting white," he or she may spend an enormous amount of energy refuting the charge, which could take time away from schoolwork. The pernicious accusation of "acting white" is a byproduct of distrust between the races. Without more meaningful social interaction, this distrust will probably continue.

Although Ferguson's study found no data to support the oppositional culture explanation for poor performance among black students, it does not take anthropologist John Ogbu's work off the discussion table. Ogbu's "cultural inversion theory" holds that minority children reject curriculum materials if they contradict the subcultural norms of their communities. Ferguson, not surprisingly, did not encounter openly held anti-achievement views among middle-class blacks. Their inner-city cohorts may share pro-achievement attitudes, but most are realistic about their life chances. Some inner-city children conclude that school learning is not of much use as a coping mechanism in their communities. For them, a difference is drawn between school life and real life. Real life, in part, is about adhering to a code of street conduct, presenting a carefully constructed self or front, demonstrating survival skills, and providing loyalty to their black peers. This is done by wearing the "right" clothes, speaking street language, and being "hip" or, to use the word Ferguson heard repeatedly, "cool." Ferguson hints at these behavioral patterns among black middle-class adolescents in Shaker Heights schools. However, these same students would not say school is useless or that they take pride in poor performance. Middle-class black students see and hear enough stories of discrimination outside the classroom to make them aware of the structural barriers to their ambitions.

Ferguson's finding of a conscious and articulated belief in the saliency of educational achievement among all the students is interesting, but his major contribution is the deconstruction of the Shaker Heights myth. His study suggests that housing and school integration are not silver bullets for ending the school achievement gap between the races. The competitive advantage of whites, which includes academic skills and motivation or what Pierre Boudieu calls "cultural capital," is not offset by housing integration. Despite integrated schools, income parity, and racial proximity, whites were able to maintain their competitive academic advantage. Middle-class black parents have not been able to offset this advantage. This may be reassuring news for white parents, but it is troubling for inner-city black families hoping to escape to the suburbs. Apparently, the long arm of the inner-city subculture reaches into the suburbs, and blacks cannot escape its ensnaring effects.

Overall, I would agree with some of Ferguson's descriptions and the direction of his argument, but not with the subtext. The subtext is that black subculture is suspect and diverts its adherents from preparatory action necessary to be competitive with whites. Combined with peer pressure, the black subculture can neutralize middle-class status and trump mainstream adolescent subculture.

Precious energy and time are being diverted into activities that, at first glance, seem mindless and impulsive. However, most of these subcultural preoccupations are utilized in the service of self-preservation (a point that Ferguson concedes). Black students are attempting to preserve their identity in a society in which their images have been negatively constructed.

Group- and self-images are important to the learning process. Equally important are the messages sent by the political system. To understand the impact of these messages, two assumptions are important to note: (1) adolescence is a critical time for receiving and internalizing societal messages, and (2) black adolescents are especially vulnerable to negative messages.

### Segmented Messages and Images

The United States is replete with continuous race-related messages. These messages attempt to define individuals, their relations to others, and what society expects from them. The channels of these messages are the media, schools, social organizations, and churches. Different racial groups receive different messages. Hence, U.S. society needs to segment messages for a multiple audience. Regarding the educational system, messages are segmented by race, class, and gender. Schools, the second most important socializer outside the family, play an important role in adolescent socialization. As a major transmitter of messages, schools socialize and sort individuals into social roles. Consequently, teachers—the designated agents of socialization—are critical to the sorting process. Accordingly, schools can play a part in the negative construction of out-groups.

Ferguson's paper could be read to suggest that race lessons are not a part of the subtext of the American high school curriculum. History suggests otherwise. Although parents are the first teachers of race, the school plays a critical role in this learning process. Because students come to school with lessons about race, schools can either reinforce or modify those lessons. Most parents might try to send a message of racial equality to their children, but some add a disclaimer: "You are just as good as the white students, but they will treat you unfairly." This disclaimer is designed to alert and protect their children against "rumors of inferiority" and condescending teachers. Negative encounters with whites serve to make black adolescents suspicious of their white teachers and classmates.

Unlike their white cohorts, black students are forced to deal with negative racial messages as well as those ubiquitous disclaimers. Such messages promote a sense of unworthiness, inadequacy, and powerlessness. For example, a teacher's response to a black child's behavior can trigger a variety of interpretations and reactions, some of which may be at variance with the teacher's intent. For example, some black children may interpret a personal slight or a negative remark as an example of teacher racism. Forming a learning relationship with a teacher is difficult if the student believes that he or she is a racist. The student also can more easily make the teacher a scapegoat for his or her own shortcomings. This holds, too, for the well-meaning white teachers from Brookline High School, whom Ferguson quotes. Accordingly, "mock seriousness" may be part of an ongoing peer discourse about whether a teacher is or is not a racist. Many adolescents seem to enjoy occasionally putting their teachers on and off.

The lesson I took from the Ferguson paper was that black parents should invest more time in preparing their children for school. Ferguson's research suggests that the white advantage in school performance can be traced to preparation and motivation. I would add that blocking negative messages is critical to the success of black students. Some black students fight an ongoing battle to block such messages and an even more intense battle to refute them. Some black students do win these battles, but too many of them internalize the negative messages and wind up taking themselves out of the school achievement competition.

Although Ferguson did not discuss individual teachers in the Shaker Heights schools, their role cannot be underestimated. Teachers are not neutral actors. Most are aware of the power imbalance between white and black parents. Accordingly, they relate, consciously and unconsciously, differently to black students. Teachers must appreciate that what they say and do in the classroom will have a profound effect on a child's perception of school. They must be sensitive to the fact that students bring race lessons to schools. Teachers must be careful not to contribute unfairly to the competitive advantage of white students.

## Notes

1. I gratefully acknowledge very helpful comments from William Dickens, Roland Fryer, Derrick James, Christopher Jencks, John Kain, Larry Kilian, Jens Ludwig, Jal Mehta, James Paces, Wilbur Rich, and Sara Stoutland. Thanks also go to John H. Bishop, who developed the survey upon which the paper relies for data; to all of the people in Shaker Heights, Ohio, who assisted in getting the survey administered; and to the Cleveland and Gund Foundations for their support of this and other work to bolster achievement in Shaker Heights.

2. Students had the option to indicate any one of A, A-, B+, and so on, ranging down through F. For the 4-point scale, A = 4 points, A- = 3.67 points, B+ = 3.33 points, and so on ranging down through F = 0 points.

3. In effect, the question regarding each explanatory variable is: "How significant is it as a predictor of GPA [grade point average], considering both the magnitude and statistical uncertainty of the estimated relationship between that explanatory variable and GPA, holding constant the other explanatory variables?"

4. The homework completion question is: "When your teacher assigns homework, how much of the homework do you usually do?" It was asked separately for math, English, social studies, and science, with six forced-choice answers from which students could choose.

5. Perhaps if teachers knew more about the time and effort that students devoted to homework and also kept in mind that even tough students want to learn (and usually respond to respect and caring), they might relate differently to students and engage them more effectively.

6. The most reasonable interpretation of why students who enroll in honors and Advanced Placement (AP) courses achieve at higher levels is that causation runs in both directions: High-achieving students tend to enroll in high-level courses, and high-level courses promote high levels of achievement.

7. Standardized test scores might be a more appropriate basis for this judgment, but the scores are not part of the data.

8. No evidence turned up that peer culture among black students is any more oppositional than among whites regarding hard work, and no important racial differences exist in reports of peer support for (or against) getting high grades. However, among males who take most of their courses at the honors and AP levels, 60 percent of whites, but only 37 percent of blacks, respond that their friends think it important to "be placed in the high achieving class."

9. Signithia Fordham, *Blacked Out: Dilemmas of Race, Identity, and Success at Capital High* (University of Chicago Press, 1996). The role of the "Other" is a theme of the book.

10. John Ogbu, *Minority Education and Caste: The American System in Cross-Cultural Comparison* (New York: Academic Press, 1978), p. 357. See also John Ogbu, "Minority Status and Schooling in Plural Societies," *Comparative Education Review*, vol. 27, no. 2 (1983), pp. 168–203; John Ogbu, "Opportunity Structure, Cultural Boundaries, and Literacy," in Judith Langer, ed., *Language, Literacy, and Culture: Issues of Society and Schooling* (Norwood, N.J.: Ablex Press, 1987); and Signithia Fordham and John Ogbu, "Black Students' School Success: Coping with the 'Burden of "Acting White,"'" *Urban Review*, vol. 18, no. 3 (1986), pp. 176–206.

11. Philip J. Cook and Jens Ludwig, "Weighing the Burden of Acting White: Are There Race Differences in Attitudes toward Education?" *Journal of Policy Analysis and Management*, vol. 16, no. 2 (1997), pp. 656–78; and Philip J. Cook and Jens Ludwig, "The Burden of 'Acting White': Do Black Adolescents Disparage Academic Achievement?" in Christopher Jencks and Meredith Phillips, eds., *The Black-White Test Score Gap* (Brookings, 1998), pp. 375–400. The data that they analyzed were from the National Education Longitudinal Study sponsored by the U.S. Department of Education. Cook and Ludwig use data from the 1990 follow-up when most students were in the tenth grade.

12. James W. Ainsworth-Darnell and Douglas B. Downey, "Assessing the Oppositional Culture Explanation for Racial/Ethnic Differences in School Performance," *American Sociological Review*, 63 (August 1998), pp. 536–53.

13. Examples are provided in Fordham, *Blacked Out*. Fordham also quotes Stephan L. Carter regarding a "burning drive to prove the racists wrong." Quote from Stephan L. Carter, "The Black Table, the Empty Seat, and the Tie," in Gerald Early, ed., *Lure and Loathing: Essays on Race, Identity, and the Ambivalence of Assimilation* (New York: Allen Lane, Penguin Press, 1993), p. 76.

14. See Claude Steele and Joshua Aronson, "Stereotype Threat and the Test Performance of Academically Successful African Americans," in Christopher Jencks and Meredith Phillips, eds., *The Black-White Test Score Gap* (Brookings, 1998). Steele and Aronson point out that their work builds on efforts by Irwin Katz and others during the 1960s, which studied how blacks' performance on IQ (intelligence quotient) tests depended on the conditions of test administration. See, for example, Irwin Katz, "Review of Evidence Relating to Effects of Desegregation on the Intellectual Performance of Negroes," *American Psychologist*, 19 (1964), pp. 381–99; Irwin Katz, E. G. Epps, and L. J. Axelson, "Effect upon Negro Digit Symbol Performance of Comparison with Whites and with Other Negroes," *Journal of Abnormal and Social Psychology*, 69 (1964), pp. 963–70; and Irwin Katz, S. O. Roberts, and J. M. Robinson, "Effects of Task Difficulty, Race of Administrator, and Instructions on Digit Symbol Performance of Negroes," *Journal of Personality and Social Psychology*, 2 (1965), pp. 53–59. Katz's findings were analogous to what Steele and Aronson report. Building on his work with Steele, Aronson has collaborated on a recent work showing that black students' school performance could be improved by affecting their theories of intelligence. See Joshua Aronson and Carrie B. Fried, "Reducing the Effects of Stereotype Threat on African American College Students: The Role of Theories of Intelligence," unpublished manuscript, University of Texas, Austin.

15. See, for example, Christopher Peterson, Steven F. Maier, and Martin E. P. Seligman, *Learned Helplessness: A Theory for the Age of Personal Control* (New York: Oxford University Press, 1993).

16. John H. Bishop developed the survey as part of a project involving many schools across several states to study the effects of high school exit exams.

17. Data not used here include those for the 1 percent of respondents who are Latinos, 0.5 percent who are Native Americans, 3.5 percent who are Asians, 2 percent mixed black and

Latino, 4.5 percent mixed black and white, and 5 percent who left the race variable blank. Preliminary analysis for groups other than blacks and whites was hampered by small sample sizes, and it also reached a level of complexity that was too much to attempt in the space of this paper.

18. This standardization included the whole sample, not just blacks and whites.

19. When a student left one of these variables blank, the average value for the racial group was substituted and a separate indicator variable was included in regression analyses to adjust for any systematic differences between students who left the variable blank and those who did not. Father's education was the variable most frequently missing, with 4 percent of white students and 18 percent black students leaving it blank. Far fewer of the other variables in the analysis were blank. When they were blank, the missing values were predicted using the race and family background variables so that the observations would not have to be dropped from regression equations. When the missing value was for the dependent variable, that observation was dropped from the regression.

20. Versions of these four variables were first formed separately for mothers and for fathers as 0,1 indicator variables. Then, for each level of schooling, the indicators for mothers and fathers were added and divided by 2. Hence, for example, the "twelve years or fewer" variable that is used in the text equals 0 if both parents had more schooling than twelve years; it equals 0.50 if one parent had twelve years or fewer; and it equals 1 if both parents had twelve years or fewer. Analogous statements apply for the other three variables. In practice, these function the same as 0,1 indicator variables, even though each can take on three values. One parental education variable (for example, parents with graduate degrees) has to be omitted from each regression as the base category relative to which the coefficients for the other three are calibrated and can be interpreted. Hence, for example, the coefficient estimated for "parents have sixteen years of schooling" represents the difference in the value of the dependent variable for parents who have sixteen years of schooling versus parents in the base category. Here, parents with graduate degrees are always used as the base category.

21. The scale reliability coefficients are 0.45 for "simply decided not to bother," 0.40 for "carelessness and poor planning," and 0.34 for "the work was too difficult." These reliabilities would be too low for making judgments that have important consequences for individuals, and they are low even for exploratory work with fairly large samples as in this paper. Future work may develop (or locate) more refined measures of these constructs.

22. The question in the survey asked about hours watching television or playing video games, but the text refers only to watching television. This is to save on wording and because, based on conversations with youth in Shaker Heights, television watching is the main activity that this variable is measuring.

23. The scale reliability coefficient is 0.50.

24. The scale reliability coefficient is 0.54.

25. Studies of peer effects in other contexts identify two main mechanisms. First is modeling and imitation. Sometimes on purpose and sometimes less consciously, youth copy or adapt some of the behaviors that they observe and use them in forming their own personal styles. They tend to imitate models that they admire and with whom they identify on race, gender, age, and other bases. There are limits, given that, for modeling to succeed, the behavior has to seem feasible for the person inclined to imitate it. The second mechanism is social reinforcement. See any textbook on adolescent development. For example, Rolf E. Muuss, *Theories of Adolescence* (McGraw-Hill, 1988).

26. About 60 percent of black students in grades seven through eleven report at least one person of a different race among their six closest friends at school. The same is true for about three quarters of whites. Thus, fewer than 25 percent of white students report that none of their

six closest friends is of a different group, but about 40 percent of black students do. A larger segment of the black student body has, for whatever reasons, remained more insular.

27. Ordinary least squares (OLS) are used for the variables that have more than two values and probit for the variables that have 0,1 values. Ordered probit results for the variables that have several values did not differ from the OLS results.

28. "Thirteen to fifteen years" and "sixteen years" of parental education were also included in the estimated equations but are not reported here because of space considerations.

29. The ratio of coefficients to standard errors is 0.71 for parents with twelve years of schooling and 0.39 for living with only one parent. Students with more siblings are slightly more likely to hold back, and the ratio of the coefficient to standard error is 2.74.

30. The same multiple regressions include the desire to please adults as an additional explanatory variable. Students who hold back are more likely to say that pleasing adults is among the reasons that they work hard in school. Black students report this more than white students, which helps in predicting the black-white difference in holding back.

31. The estimate is that, other things being equal, black students' homework completion rate is about 0.15 to 0.20 standard deviations lower than for same-gender white students.

32. The coefficient on time watching television and video games was between 3.5 and 4.0 times its standard error, depending on what else was in the regression equation.

33. It does not significantly affect the homework completion rate, and it has a small positive and statistically significant predicted effect on grade point average, other things being equal. "Other things being equal" means that this result comes from an equation in which many other things were controlled. The result could mean that, among students whose homework is not done, those who keep trying to finish until the last possible minute do slightly better.

34. Whether a student has more black friends is determined from the question about the racial makeup among the student's six closest friends at school. Because 83 percent of all students are either black or white, the assumption is that when a white student says a friend is from a different racial group, that friend is probably black. There is no way of knowing for sure from these data.

35. This racial difference in television watching among teens is not unique to Shaker Heights. It is mirrored in national data and has been true for some time.

36. The data for Shaker Heights are not the kind of longitudinal or experimental data that would allow tracking of how changes in attitudes and behaviors lead to changes in school performance. Perhaps such data can be developed. In the meantime, causation in the models estimated presumably operates only in one direction—from the explanatory to the outcome measures. The greater the extent to which this assumption is wrong, the more the estimates will be biased measures of the chosen relationships.

37. The only variables not included are some of the characteristics that students identified as those of the most popular crowd. The three perceived characteristics of the most popular crowd that are included in the regressions are "tough," "outgoing," and "self-confident."

38. Attitude and behavior effects might operate through the family background variables, but there is no way to calibrate how much. Black-white differences also could exist in the implicit standards relative to which blacks and whites are calibrating their answers. But that, too, is impossible to know and probably should not be assumed.

39. Consistent with these ideas, many things might affect school engagement and thereby the pace of progress toward raising school achievement—for example, personal standards (and, hence, goals) for what constitute acceptable behaviors, grades, and levels of achievement; long-term aspirations and the degree to which children believe that academic success is necessary or sufficient for getting what they want in life; (mis)understanding of effective strategies for

securing supportive responses from helpers; initial skills and knowledge as they arrive at their particular grade levels and that affect their ability to keep up and assimilate new material during the year; self-concept of academic ability and beliefs about the nature of intelligence and personal capacity for intellectual growth; feelings of social fit with the school environment and beliefs about whether people at school have the obligation, will, and capacity to respond effectively in helping the child to learn; habits of mind and behavior related, for example, to attentiveness and communication in the classroom and also to effective time management routines for school-related tasks; psychological vulnerability and responsiveness to given social pressures, pro and con, related to achievement; extracurricular opportunities and experiences after school and during summers, and the degrees to which these experiences reinforce or compete with school; intellectual and social norms among the particular parents, peers, teachers, and others from whom the child receives supports and incentives; beliefs and feelings about the appropriateness of particular behaviors and achievements and the propensity to imagine, accept, and aspire to particular current and future selves and associated social worlds.

40. Muuss, *Theories of Adolescence*, p. 315.

41. Laurence Steinberg, Sanford M. Dornbusch, and B. Bradford Brown, "Ethnic Differences in Adolescent Achievement: An Ecological Perspective," *American Psychologist*, vol. 47, no. 6 (1992), pp. 723–29, quote on p. 727.

42. See Christopher Jencks and Meredith Phillips, eds., *The Black-White Test Score Gap* (Brookings, 1998), for a variety of explanations for the black-white test score gap. See also important new work by William T. Dickens and James R. Flynn, "The Interaction of Environment and Measured Intelligence," draft paper (Brookings, 2000), on the masking of environmental effects as genetic effects, and vice versa.

43. For an excellent piece of writing on racial stigmas, see Glenn C. Loury, "The Economics and Ethics of Racial Classification," paper prepared for the W.E.B. Du Bois Lectures at Harvard University, April 25–27, 2000.

44. See Jeff Howard and Raymond Hammond, "Rumors of Inferiority," *New Republic* (September 1985), pp. 17–21.

45. Among junior high and high school students, many strange interpretations are made of others' styles and behaviors, and even the most racially conscious acts can be misinterpreted as disloyalty. For example, black girls in suburban high schools are accused of acting white sometimes when they wear short afro haircuts and other low-maintenance hairdos. One reason is that they appear to be seeking the same freedom from hair problems that white girls experience after compulsory swimming during the gym period. I have encountered this story in conversations in Shaker Heights and also with regard to a high school in Wisconsin.

46. The segment aired on June 7, 1999.

47. See, for example, Beverly Daniel Tatum, *Why Are All the Black Kids Sitting Together in the Cafeteria?* (Basic Books, 1997).

48. Fordham, *Blacked Out*, p. 291. The PSAT is a practice exam that eleventh graders often take in preparation for the Scholastic Assessment Test (SAT) college entrance exam that they take as twelfth graders.

49. Note that the foreign language department at Brookline High does not use a special term to refer to its nonaccelerated or lowest level of classes. These classes are referred to merely as Spanish 1 or Spanish 2. The two accelerated levels are called honors and Advanced Placement. To avoid confusion in the interview, Sara Stoutland asked this teacher to refer to the nonaccelerated as "standard" classes.

50. The probability value is 0.14 for the null hypothesis that black and white males at the mostly honors and AP level have the same opinion about whether studying a lot makes you less popular.

51. Fordham, *Blacked Out*, p. 306.

52. I have mentioned the importance of learning techniques both here and in the opening overview of the paper. However, developing this point is beyond the scope of the paper. For an introduction, see National Research Council, *Improving Student Learning: A Strategic Plan for Education Research and Its Utilization* (Washington: National Academy Press, 1999).

53. The survey finding is that blacks regard being tough as more important to popularity than whites do. School officials confirm that black students are much more likely to be involved in fights.

54. Blacks take fewer honors and AP courses, where homework assignments are longest, so on average they spend somewhat less time each day on homework than whites. The comparison in the text regarding homework time is between students who take the same classes. Most comparisons show that blacks self-report more time on homework than white classmates.

55. These differences of 4 percent among males and 3 percent among females are not statistically distinguishable from zero.

56. Because this study lacks a question about whether the student personally acts tough, it is not possible to estimate the relationship of tough behavior to measures of academic interest or achievement.

57. It would not be difficult to test whether standardized test scores overpredict or underpredict honors and AP enrollments for blacks versus whites in Shaker, but no such analysis has been done to date.

58. There are conflicting opinions in the district about whether the student advising system leads more or fewer blacks to take honors and AP courses than a race-blind advising system would produce.

59. Black students' SAT scores in Shaker are 100 points above the national average for all black students, but whites' scores are 150 points above the national average for whites.

60. Christopher Jencks, "Racial Bias in Testing," in Christopher Jencks and Meredith Phillips, eds., *The Black-White Test Score Gap* (Brookings, 1998), pp. 55–85.

61. See, for example, Richard J. Murnane, John B. Willett, Yves Duhaldeborde, and John H. Tyler, "How Important Are the Cognitive Skills of Teenagers in Predicting Subsequent Earnings?" *Journal of Policy Analysis and Management*, vol. 19, no. 4 (2000), pp. 547–68.

62. For example, the average high school student in America spends only around one hour per day on homework. See B. Bradford Brown and Laurence Steinberg, "Final Report: Project 2; Noninstructional Influences on Adolescent Engagement and Achievement," paper prepared for the Department of Education, 1991; and James W. Ainsworth-Darnell and Douglas B. Downey, "Assessing the Oppositional Culture Explanation for Racial/Ethnic Differences in School Performance," *American Sociological Review*, vol. 63 (August 1998), pp. 536–53. Around a third skip at least one class per semester, and 10 percent miss more than ten days of school per term. See Cook and Ludwig, "Weighing the Burden of 'Acting White' "; and Cook and Ludwig, "The Burden of 'Acting White.' " See also John H. Bishop, "Signaling, Incentives, and School Organization in France, the Netherlands, Britain, and the United States," in Eric A. Hanushek and Dale W. Jorgenson, eds., *Improving America's Schools: The Role of Incentives* (Washington: National Academy Press, 1996), pp. 111–45; John H. Bishop, "The Effect of National Standards and Curriculum-Based Exams on Achievement," *American Economic Review*, vol. 87, no. 2 (1997), pp. 260–64; and John H. Bishop, "The Effect of Curriculum-Based External Exit Exam Systems on Student Achievement," *Journal of Economic Education*, vol. 29, no. 2 (1998), pp. 171–82.

63. Gerald David Jaynes and Robin M. Williams, *A Common Destiny: Blacks and American Society* (Washington: National Academy Press, 1989); Susan E. Mayer, *What Money Can't Buy* (Harvard University Press, 1997); and Meredith Phillips, Jeanne Brooks-Gunn, Greg J.

Duncan, Pamela Klebanov, and Jonathan Crane, "Family Background, Parenting Practices, and the Black-White Test Score Gap," in Christopher Jencks and Meredith Phillips, eds., *The Black-White Test Score Gap* (Brookings, 1998), pp. 103–48.

64. Cook and Ludwig, "Weighing the Burden of 'Acting White' "; and Cook and Ludwig, "The Burden of 'Acting White.' " My analysis of the National Education Longitudinal Survey data with Philip J. Cook finds that black and white students from similar family backgrounds are equally likely to do two or more hours of homework out of school per week. However, blacks are less likely than whites to do four or more hours of homework (41 versus 37 percent) and are less likely to do ten or more hours per week (13 versus 10 percent). See Cook and Ludwig, "The Burden of 'Acting White.' " The differences at the top of the homework distributions translate into a difference in average homework time between black and white students equal to around fifteen minutes per week.

65. Cook and Ludwig, "Weighing the Burden of 'Acting White' "; and Cook and Ludwig, "The Burden of 'Acting White.' "

66. Ronald F. Ferguson, "Comment on Cook and Ludwig," in Christopher Jencks and Meredith Phillips, eds., *The Black-White Test Score Gap* (Brookings, 1998), pp. 394–97.

67. The survey administered to the Shaker Heights, Ohio, students asks them to report their grade point average on a scale ranging from F to A. However, as Ronald F. Ferguson notes, the Shaker Heights high school assigns grades in Advanced Placement courses additional grade points. Whether students enrolled in AP courses make some adjustment for this fact when reporting their GPAs (for example by counting their C in an AP class as a B on the survey scale) is not clear. Also unclear is whether the Shaker Heights GPA adjustment accurately reflects the true differences in difficulty and achievement level across tracks.

68. For example, Ferguson reports in table 5 that his specification A (which includes family background as well as other attitude and behavior measures) for males explains 0.47 GPA points of the 1.12 point gap between black and white students. Adding behavioral measures together with the student's homework completion rate (specification B) produces a model that explains 0.66 grade points of the gap, although the homework completion rate is arguably in part a measure of the efficiency, not the level, of student effort. In unpublished calculations that he was kind enough to share, Ferguson reports that the family background measures alone explain 0.41 points of the gap.

69. Ainsworth-Darnell and Downey, "Assessing the Oppositional Culture Explanation for Racial/Ethnic Differences in School Performance."

70. Cook and Ludwig, "The Burden of 'Acting White.' "